SECULAR HYMNAL

– 144 Hymn Tunes Made Inclusive For All –

– Secretary Michael

"Secular Hymnal"
by Secretary Michael

ISBN: 978-1-888712-20-9
- 9th Revision -

This book is a compilation of all
Secular Hymnal ("Roadway") volumes 1-12

All 144 Secular Hymns (both unison/guitar and SATB arrangements)
are available for free download: www.secularhymnal.com

Dedicated to my teacher: Mara Hill

All works by Secretary Michael have been placed into the
Public Domain. They may be freely copied and performed.

*All music is for everybody. It is my hope that these peaceful hymns
will forever give voice to that ideal.*
                                                -Secretary Michael

CONTENTS

Index of Secular Hymns 4

Secular Hymn Scores (*hymn numbers used instead of page numbers*) 6

"Traditional Hymn / Secular Hymn" Correlation Table 298

Personal Notes and Explanations:
    Lyrics, Word Division, Sol-Fa Songs, Chord Symbols 306
    Changes to the Music, Sources, Copyright, Typesetting 307

Notes on each of the 144 Hymns (History, Sources, Topics) 308

144 Secular Hymns
(in Alphabetical Order with Key Signatures)

1. A Beauty Hides in Everyone (C)
2. A Long, Long Way We've Come Today (C)
3. A Peaceful Walk (E♭)
4. Accommodating Others (E♭)
5. Achieving Disagreement (E♭)
6. All Need To Feel Significant (E)
7. All Praise to the Troubled (G)
8. All the Seven Deadly Sins (B♭)
9. Assuming There's Peace (G)
10. "Bad" is Not a Name (Dm)
11. Because Violence Can't End Violence (C) SOL-FA
12. Borders, Boundaries, Walls and Fences (C)
13. Building a Door (G)
14. Climbing Up the Ladder (D)
15. Climbing Up the Mountain (F)
16. Come Live With Us (F)
17. Communication is the Answer (G)
18. Crank and Sprocket (C)
19. Disassemble Every Gun (D) SOL-FA
20. Diversity in Thought (F) SOL-FA
21. Don't Choose Sides (B♭)
22. Don't Know How I Got Here (B♭)
23. Each Little Raindrop (E♭) SOL-FA
24. Education Is Our Destination (C) SOL-FA
25. Every Space for Every Face (D)
26. Everybody Has Their Issues (D) SOL-FA
27. Everyone Must Make a Living (F) SOL-FA
28. Everything's Changing (D)
29. For Those Who Have Beliefs Bizarre (Dm) SOL-FA
30. For What I've Done (F) SOL-FA
31. Go Further Farther (E♭)
32. Going Up, Going Up (G)
33. Grief Has Got To Take Its Time (G) SOL-FA
34. Happy Be (G)
35. Harvesting Hunger (F)

36. I am a Terrorist (F)
37. I am the Captain Of My Boat (G)
38. I Declare a Brand-New Me (F) SOL-FA
39. I Have a Garden in the Park (F) SOL-FA
40. I Have a Puzzle of the World (D)
41. I Once Was So Certain (G)
42. I Surrender (C) SOL-FA
43. I Think I Could Work in a Castle (E♭)
44. I Think I'm Right (A) SOL-FA
45. I Will Look and I Will See (G)
46. If We're Not the Ones (C)
47. I'm Marching, Marching (G) SOL-FA
48. In the End (C)
49. Informed People (G) SOL-FA
50. Injustice to You is Injustice to Me (G)
51. Intelligence is a Bouquet (F)
52. It's Great to Know Some Things by Heart (E♭)
53. I've Never Known a Sinner (F) SOL-FA
54. Journey Forward (B♭)
55. Just Because (D) SOL-FA
56. Land of Gray (F) SOL-FA
57. Let's Make a Right (F)
58. Let's Ride In Our Time Machines (G)
59. Let's Start a Big Commotion (C) SOL-FA
60. Let's Stop Making Weapons (B♭)
61. Let's Try Something Different (B♭)
62. Long Road (Am)
63. Make Just One Brand New Friend (G) SOL-FA
64. May We Make Moments of Peace (C)
65. No Cheers For David (D)
66. No Need to Sing the Same Notes (A♭)
67. Nonviolence May Take a Long Time (G) SOL-FA
68. Nonviolence Must Be Taught (E♭)
69. Nothing's Heavy With Lots Of Hands (F) SOL-FA
70. Oh Child Do Not Despair (F) SOL-FA
71. Ojalá (F) SOL-FA
72. Onward, Upward (D)
73. Open, Open Up the Window (D)
74. Our Garden Full of Flowers (Am)
75. Pain Can Cause (D)

76. Parents Gone (D dorian)
77. Past Performance is No Guarantee (E)
78. Peace Is Not What I Looked For (E♭)
79. Peace Like a River (G)
80. People Are More (Dm)
81. People We Need To Meet (D) SOL-FA
82. People Will Change (F)
83. Relieving Suffering (G)
84. Rise and Shine (G) SOL-FA
85. Seen, Heard and Understood (E♭) SOL-FA
86. Skating, Skating (F)
87. So Many Ways (D)
88. Some Are Young, Some Old (F)
89. Someday When Guns Are Gone (E♭)
90. Someone Should (F) SOL-FA
91. Spent Our Treasure (E♭)
92. Standing At Bat (F)
93. Step By Step (C) SOL-FA
94. Storms Will Come (A)
95. Striving To Be (G)
96. Swapping Shoes (G) SOL-FA
97. Tall Oaks From Little Acorns Grow (D) SOL-FA
98. The Greatest Walk (D)
99. The Many Truths (F)
100. The Only Path to Peace is Peace (C)
101. Them Over There (D)
102. There Are Times (C)
103. There is a Game (G)
104. There is a Rule of Thumb (D)
105. There is an Empty Box (D)
106. There is Something Wrong (A♭)
107. There's a Better Way (G) SOL-FA
108. There's a Road Between Our Lands (G)
109. There's Claim Number One (E♭) SOL-FA
110. There's More Than One Way (G)
111. Things Are The Way They Are (D)
112. This Day, This Day (F)
113. Tick-Tock (B♭)
114. Tis a Gift (F) SOL-FA
115. To Find a Place (C)

116. To Live Our Lives Addiction-Free (B♭)
117. To Make the World a Better Place (D)
118. To Soldiers Lost (Gm)
119. To Those Who Came Before (D)
120. Today is My Day (E♭)
121. Today's the Day (C)
122. Together For So Long (G) SOL-FA
123. Towards a World That Has No Guns (F)
124. Trusting You, Trusting Me (C)
125. Ultimately We May Not Have Free Will (Em)
126. Unconscious Bias (Em)
127. Unless There's No-One Watching (F) SOL-FA
128. Wake, Awake (C)
129. Walking in Someone's Shoes (E♭)
130. We Are People, Plastic People (C)
131. We Are Searching (C)
132. We Can Be Tolerant (D) SOL-FA
133. We Can Get Things To Happen (D)
134. We Mean "Will You Love Me?" (E♭) SOL-FA
135. We're Not Alone (D)
136. We're Not At Our Best (F) SOL-FA
137. We're Parents of a Soldier (B♭) SOL-FA
138. What Are We Doing? (D)
139. When Feeling Lost (Em)
140. When I Am Down (A) SOL-FA
141. When Playing Cards (B♭)
142. Who's My Neighbor? (D) SOL-FA
143. Why Does This Phrase Have Five Measures? (D)
144. You Took the One Road (G) SOL-FA

(Hymns with the "SOL-FA" designation are solfege-friendly, being in a major key with no accidentals in any voice. See the "Personal Notes" section in back for more information.)

(Note: chord symbols support the soprano melody, not necessarily the SATB harmony)

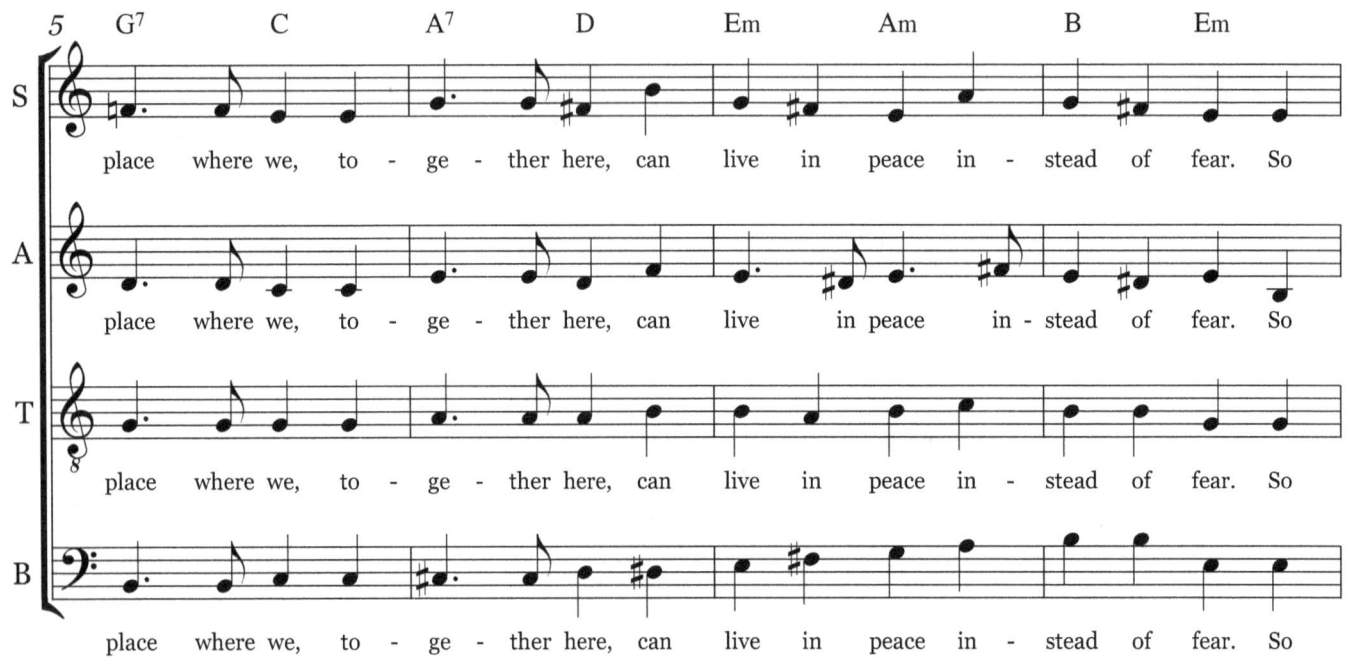

(Note: chord symbols support the soprano melody, not necessarily the SATB harmony)

3. A Peaceful Walk
(From the Secular Hymnal)

Words: Secretary Michael

Tune by Ralph E. Hudson, 1885
(traditional hymn: "At the Cross")

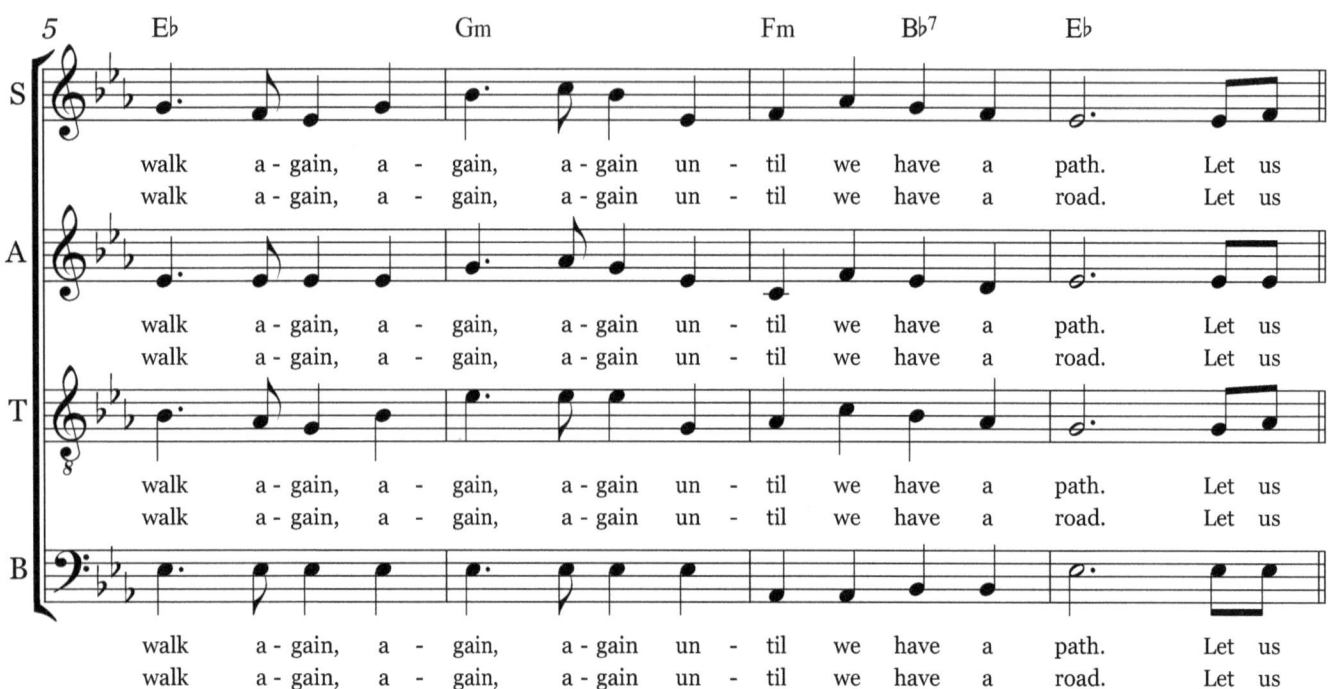

All works by Secretary Michael have been placed in the Public Domain. They may be freely copied and performed.

(Note: chord symbols support the soprano melody, not necessarily the SATB harmony)

4. Accommodating Others

(From the Secular Hymnal)

Words: Secretary Michael

Music: "Penlan" by David Jenkins, 1898
(traditional hymn: "In Heavenly Love Abiding")

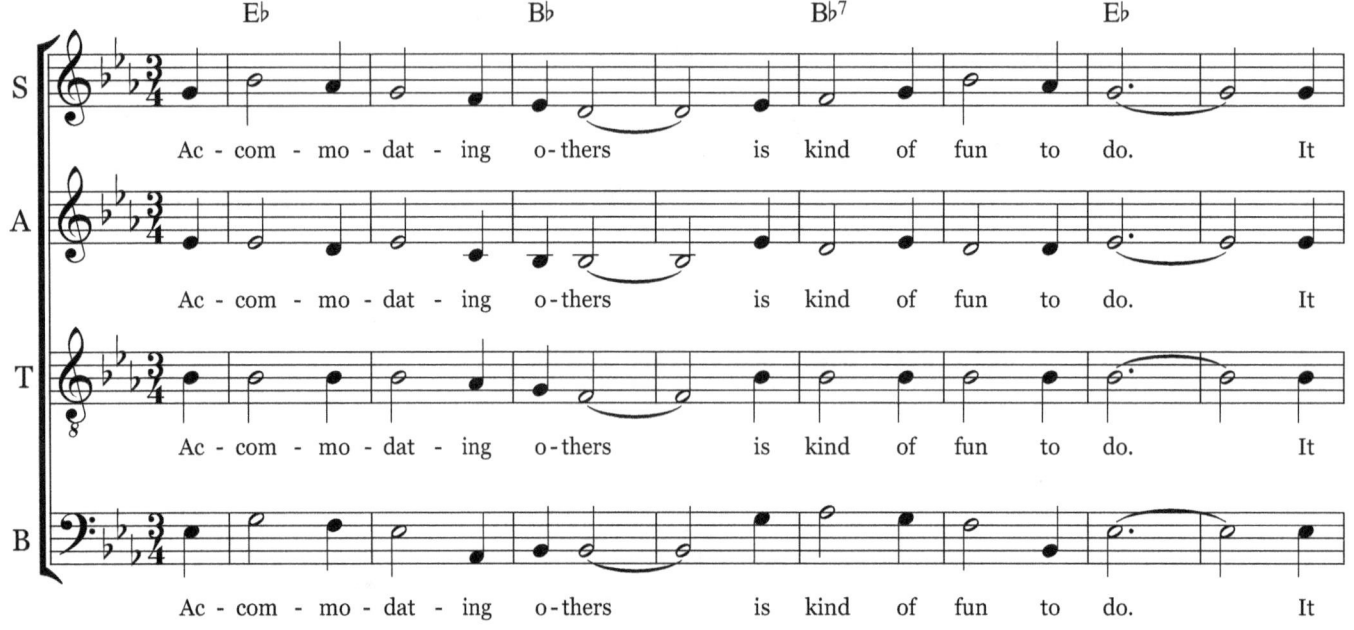

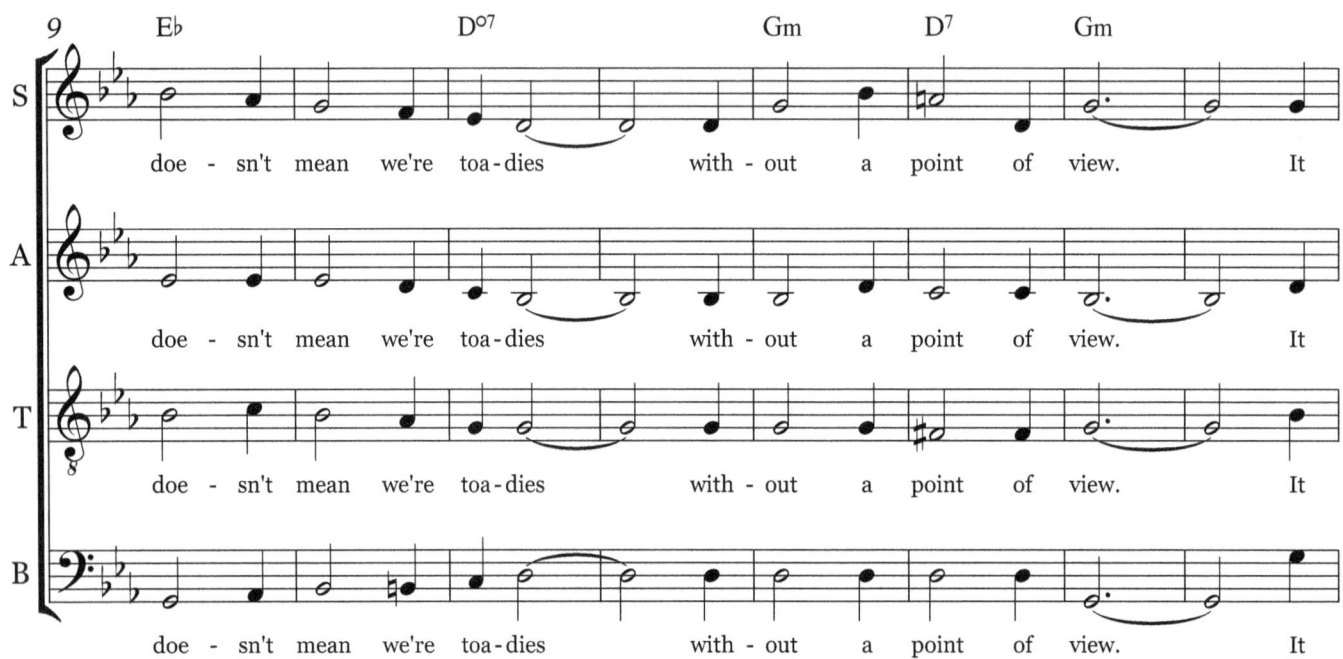

All works by Secretary Michael have been placed in the Public Domain. They may be freely copied and performed.

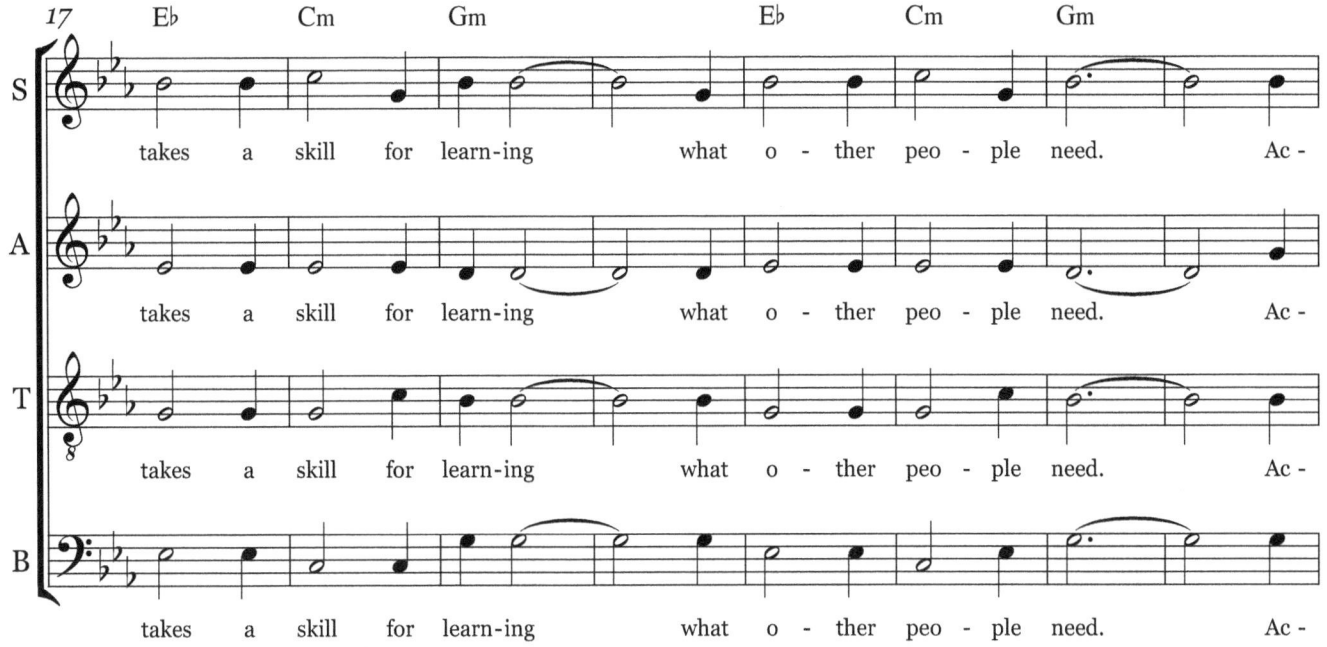

(Note: chord symbols support the soprano melody, not necessarily the SATB harmony)

5. Achieving Disagreement

(From the Secular Hymnal)

Words: Secretary Michael

Music: "Angel's Story" by Arthur Henry Mann, 1881
(traditional hymn: "O Jesus I Have Promised")

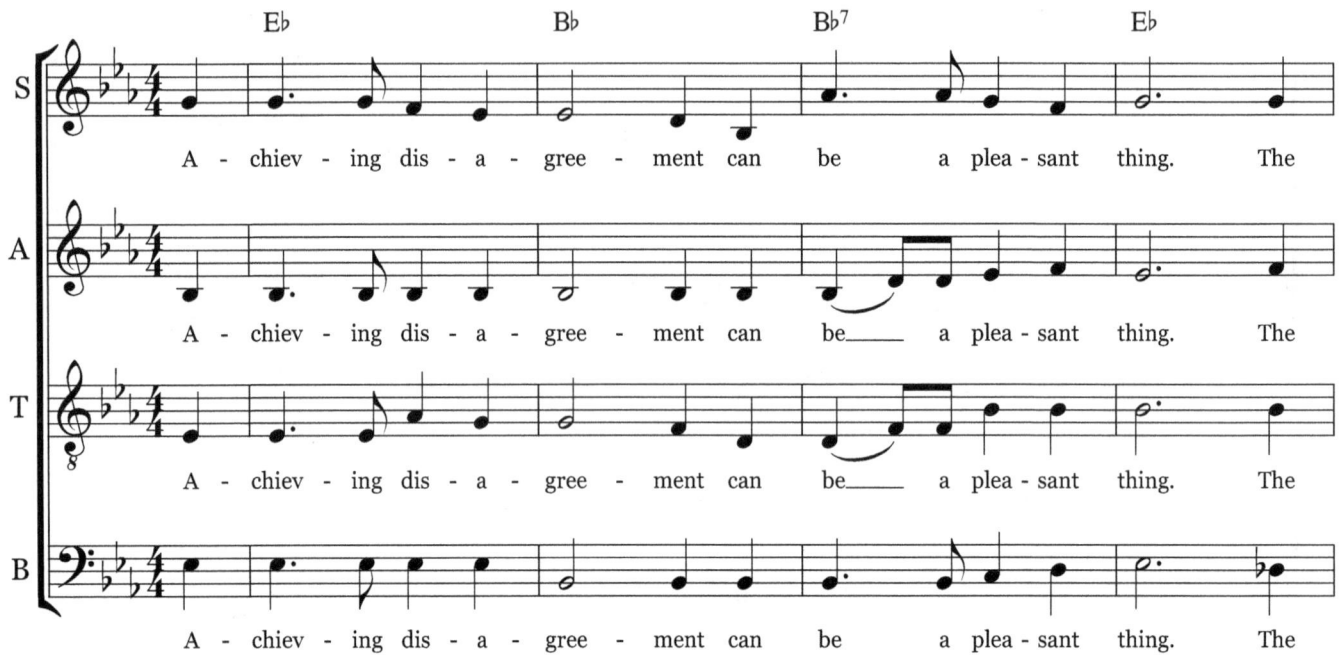

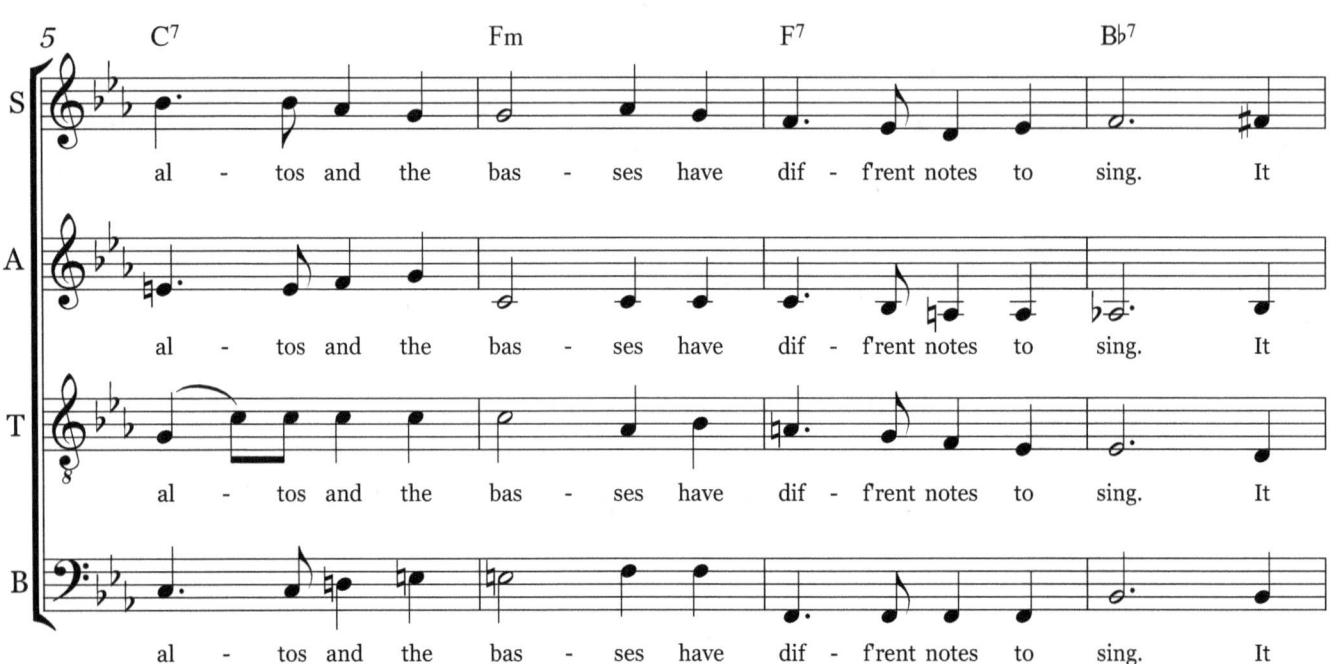

All works by Secretary Michael have been placed in the Public Domain. They may be freely copied and performed.

(Note: chord symbols support the soprano melody, not necessarily the SATB harmony)

(Note: chord symbols support the soprano melody, not necessarily the SATB harmony)

7. All Praise to the Troubled
(From the Secular Hymnal)

Words: Secretary Michael

Music by William Howard Doane, 1875
(traditional hymn: "To God Be the Glory")

All works by Secretary Michael have been placed in the Public Domain. They may be freely copied and performed.

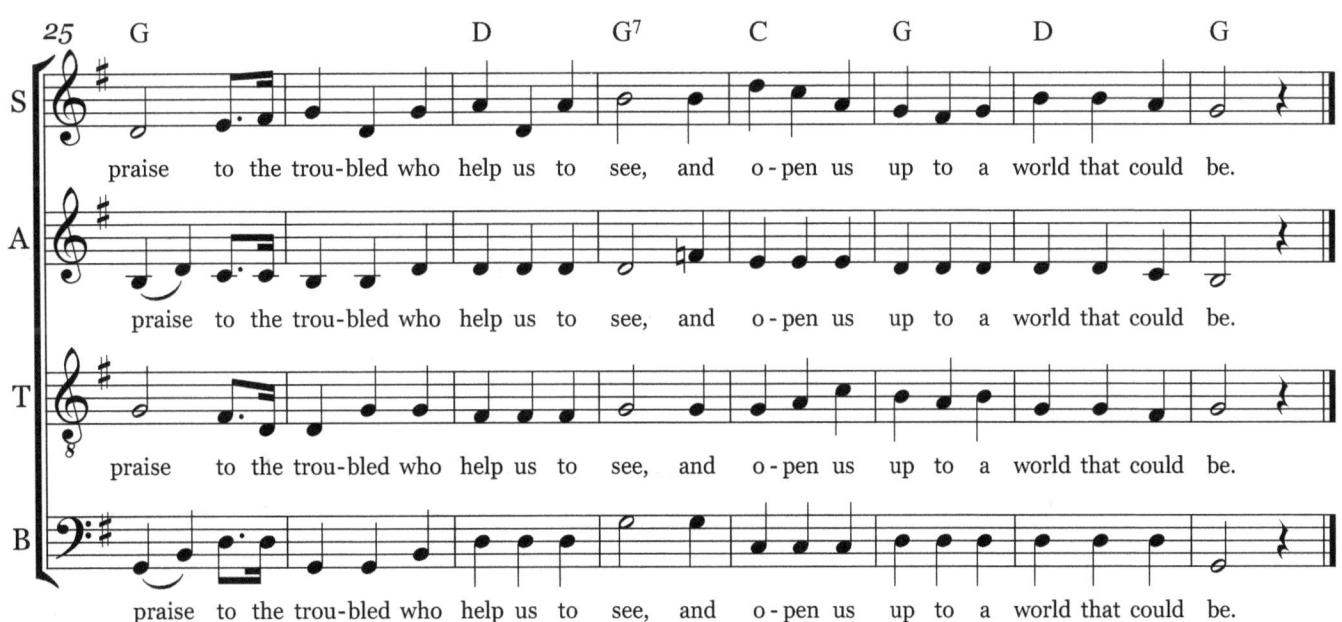

(Note: chord symbols support the soprano melody, not necessarily the SATB harmony)

(Note: chord symbols support the soprano melody, not necessarily the SATB harmony)

9. Assuming There's Peace

(From the Secular Hymnal)

Words: Secretary Michael

Music: "Lyons" by Johann Michael Haydn, 1770
Arranged by William Gardiner, 1815
(traditional hymn: "O Worship the King")

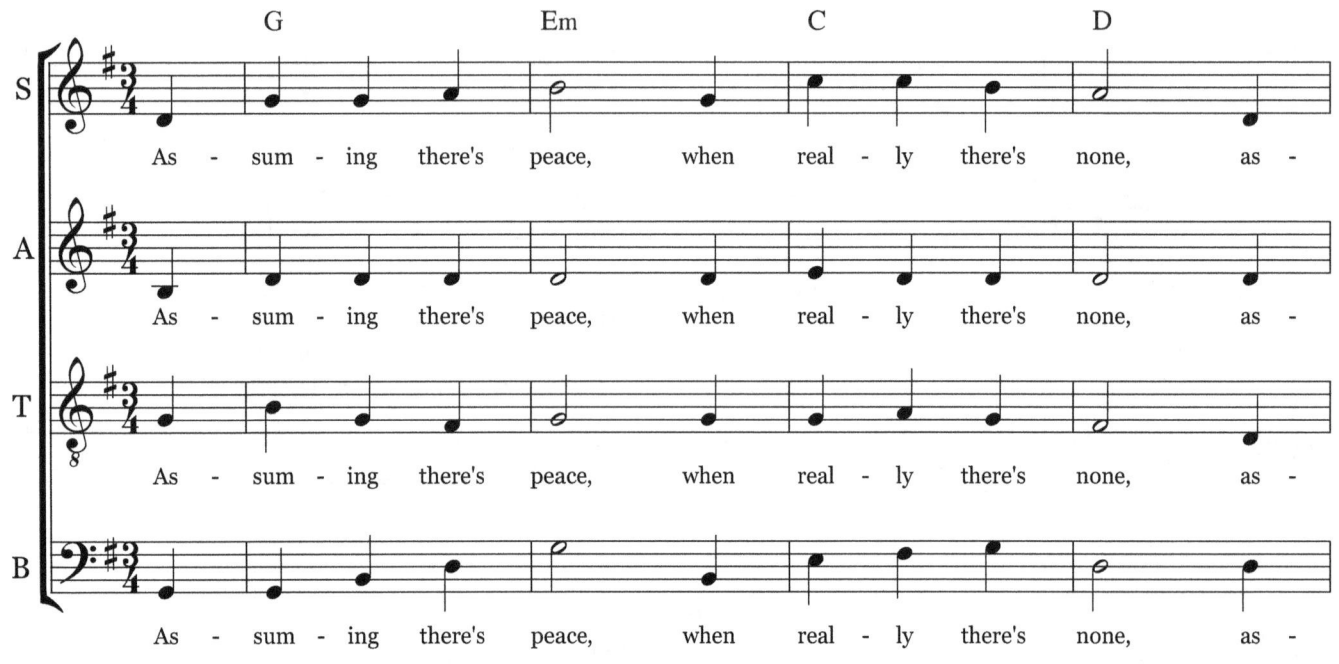

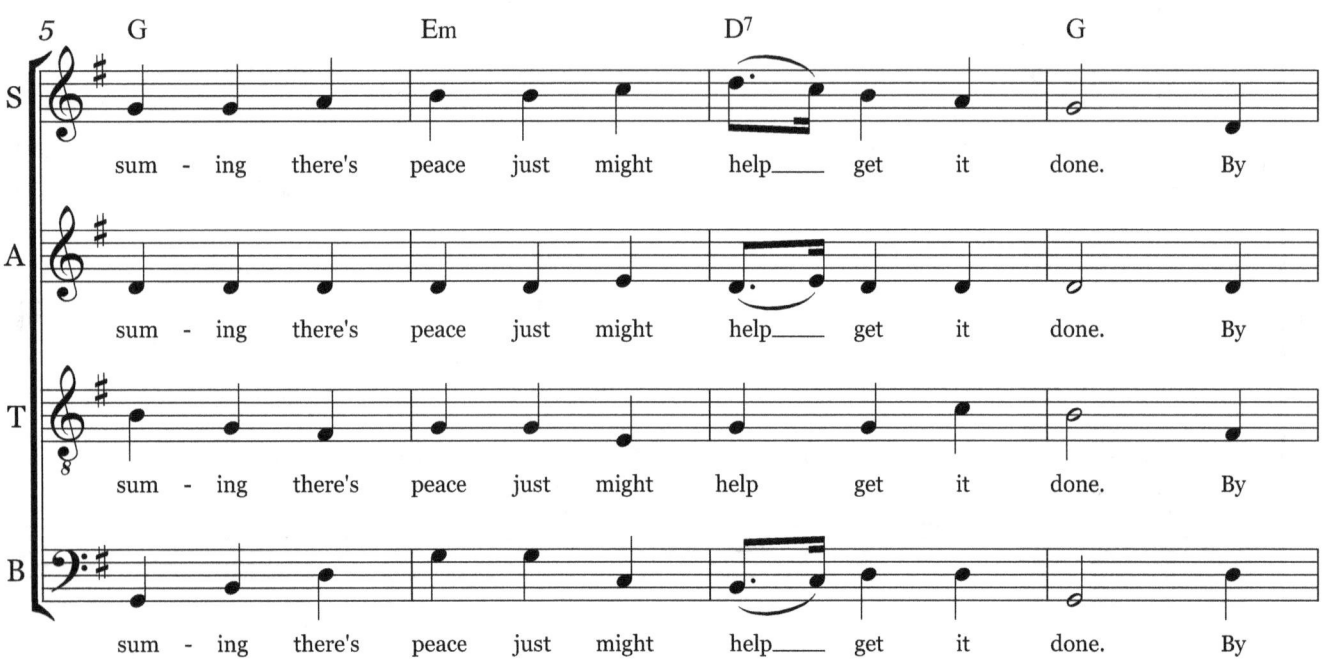

All works by Secretary Michael have been placed in the Public Domain. They may be freely copied and performed.

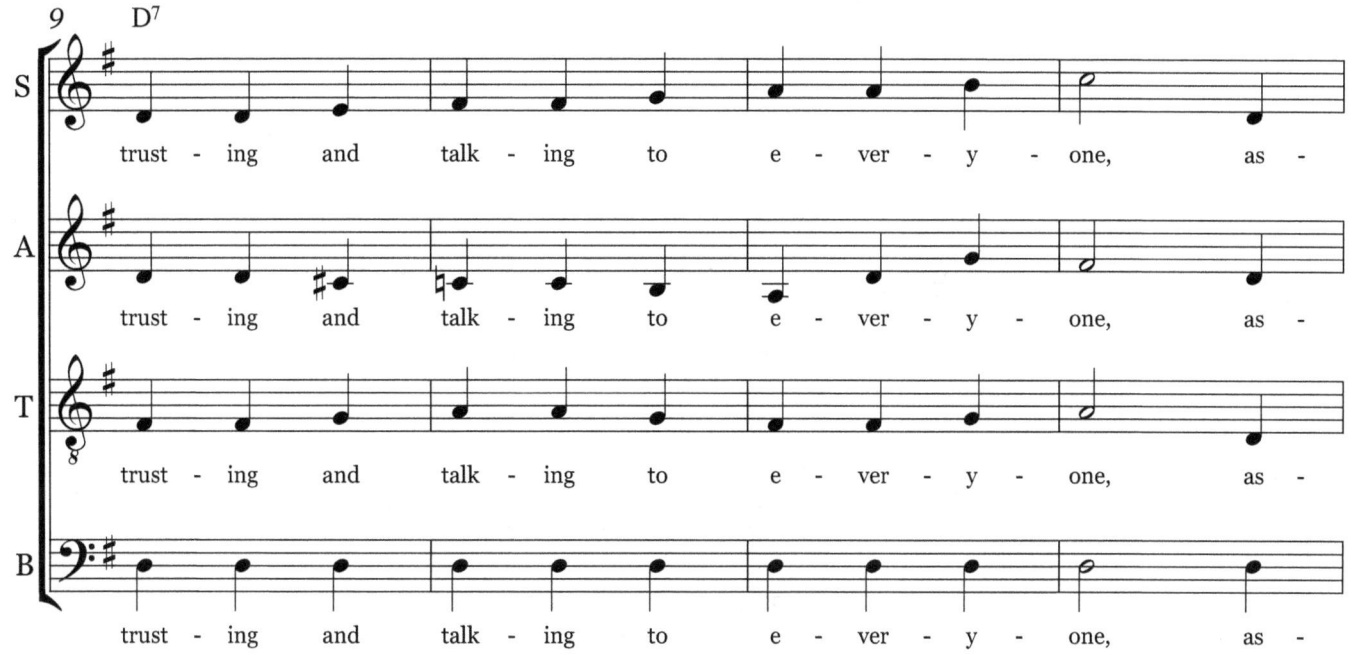

(Note: chord symbols support the soprano melody, not necessarily the SATB harmony)

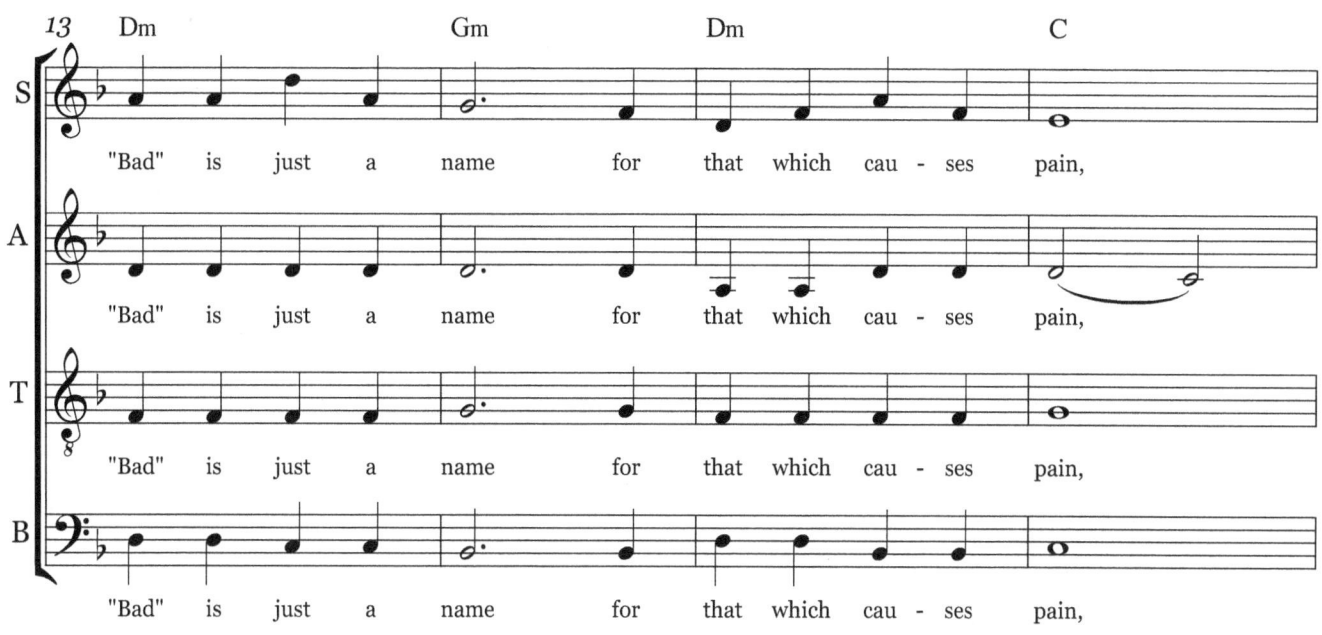
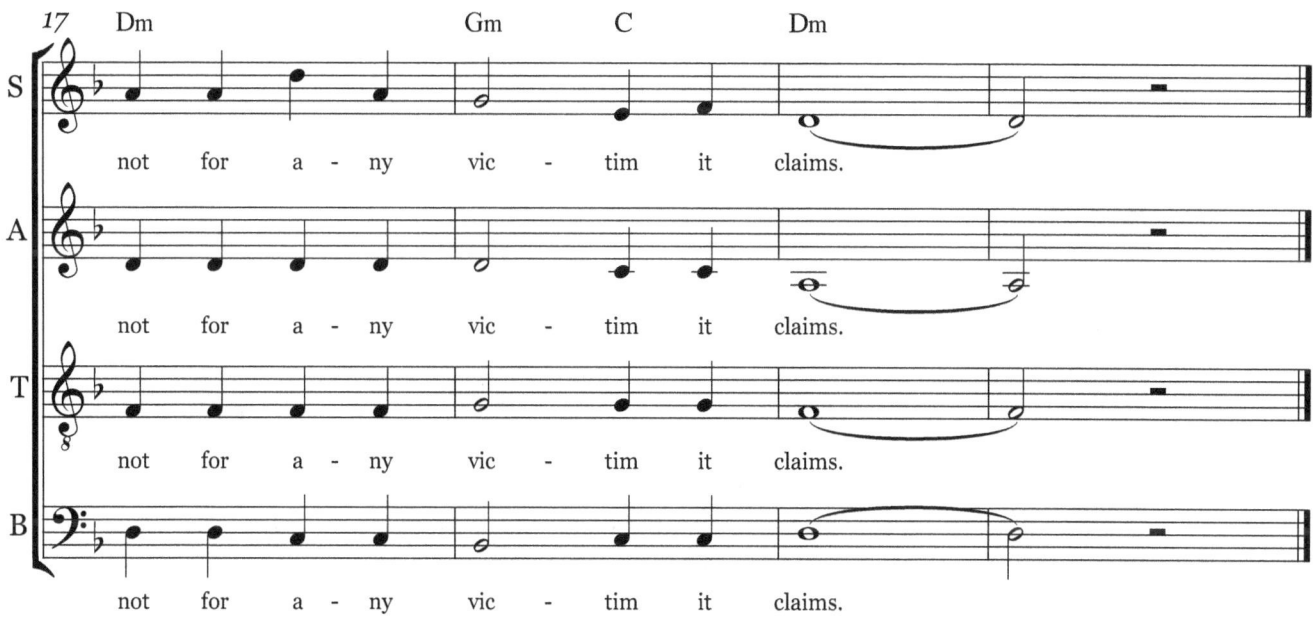

(Note: chord symbols support the soprano melody, not necessarily the SATB harmony)

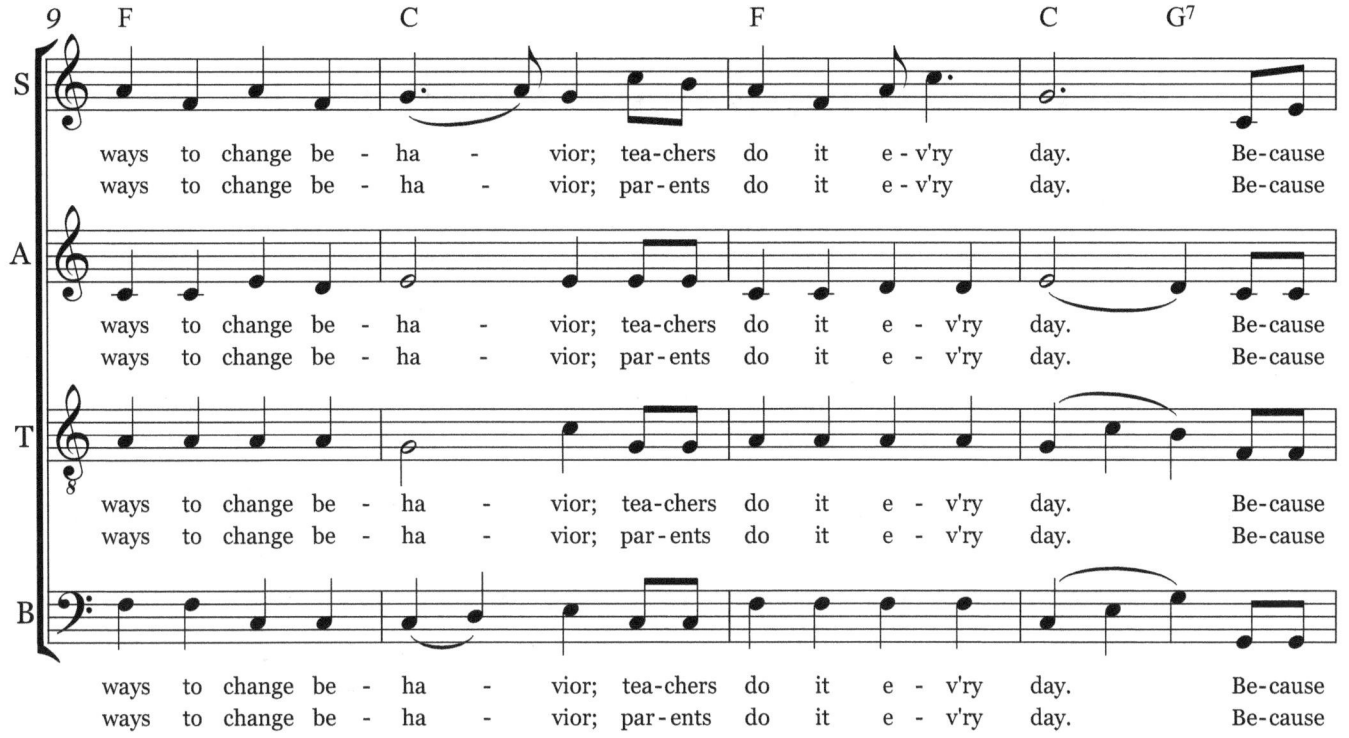
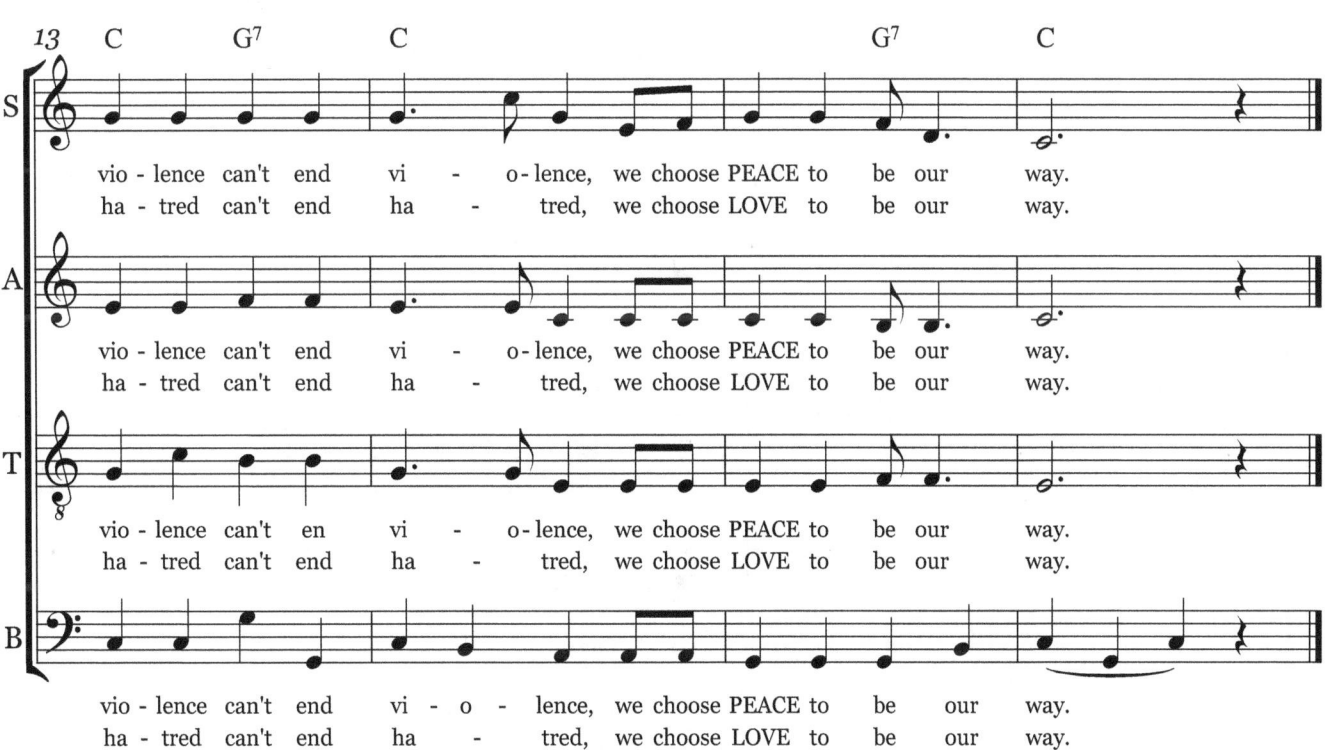

(Note: chord symbols support the soprano melody, not necessarily the SATB harmony)

12. Borders, Boundaries, Walls and Fences

(From the Secular Hymnal)

Words and Music: Secretary Michael

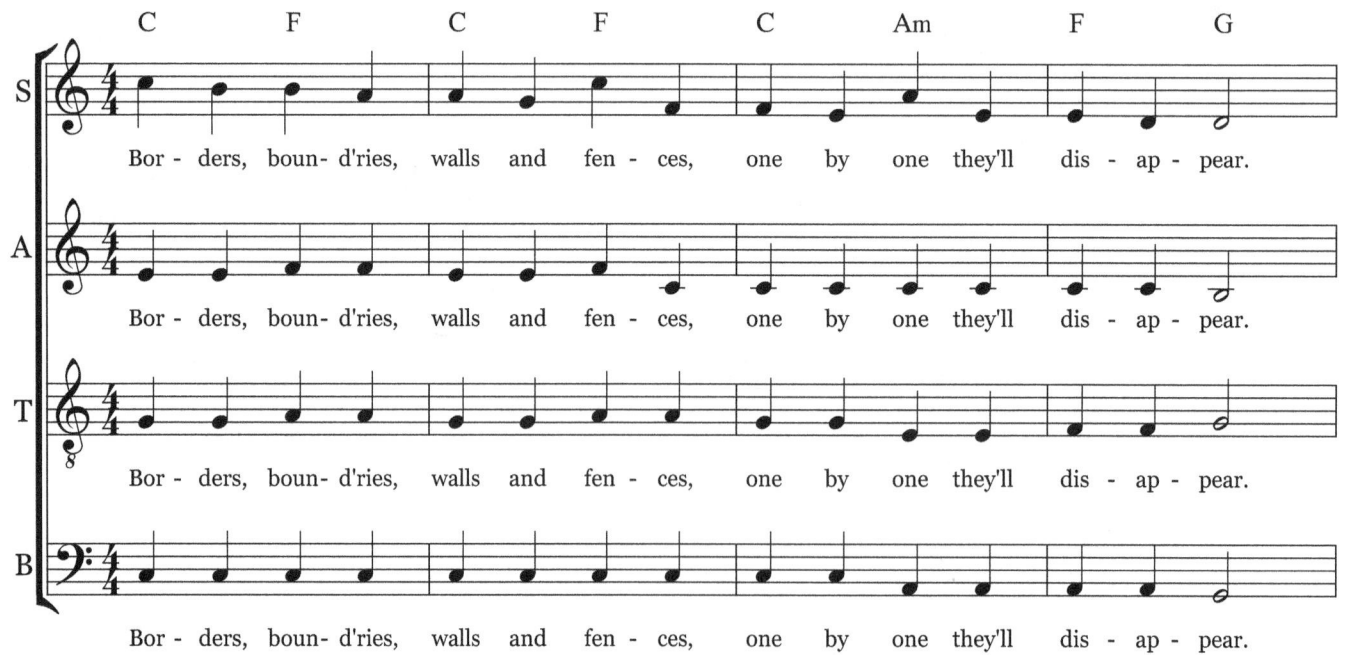

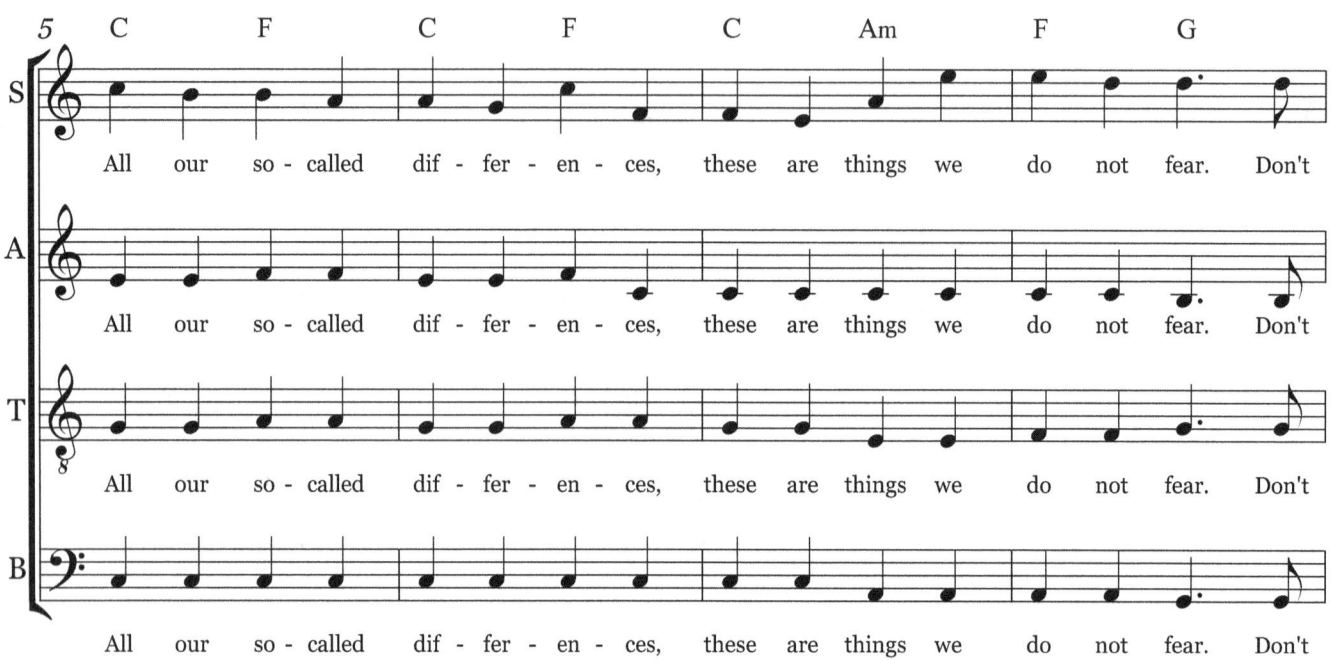

All works by Secretary Michael have been placed in the Public Domain. They may be freely copied and performed.

13. Building a Door
(From the Secular Hymnal)

Words: Secretary Michael

Music: "St. Catherine" by Henri F. Henry, 1864
Arranged by James George Walton, 1864
(traditional hymn: "Faith Of Our Fathers")

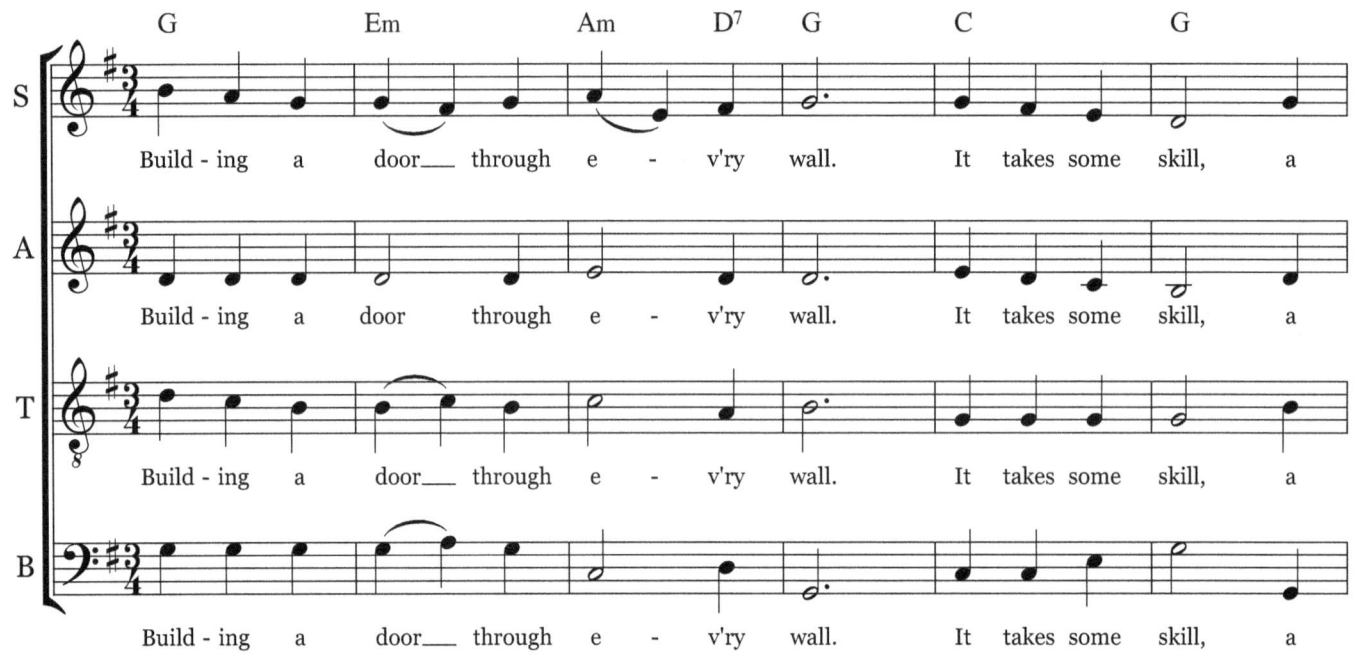

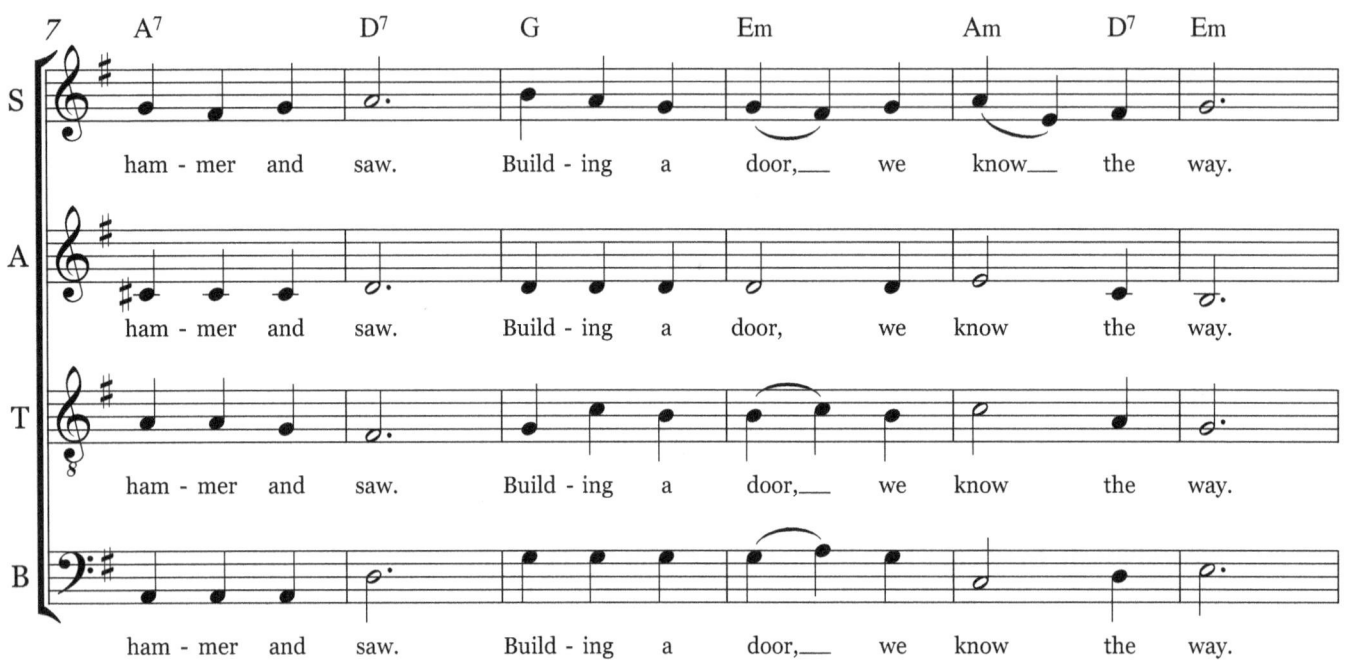

All works by Secretary Michael have been placed in the Public Domain. They may be freely copied and performed.

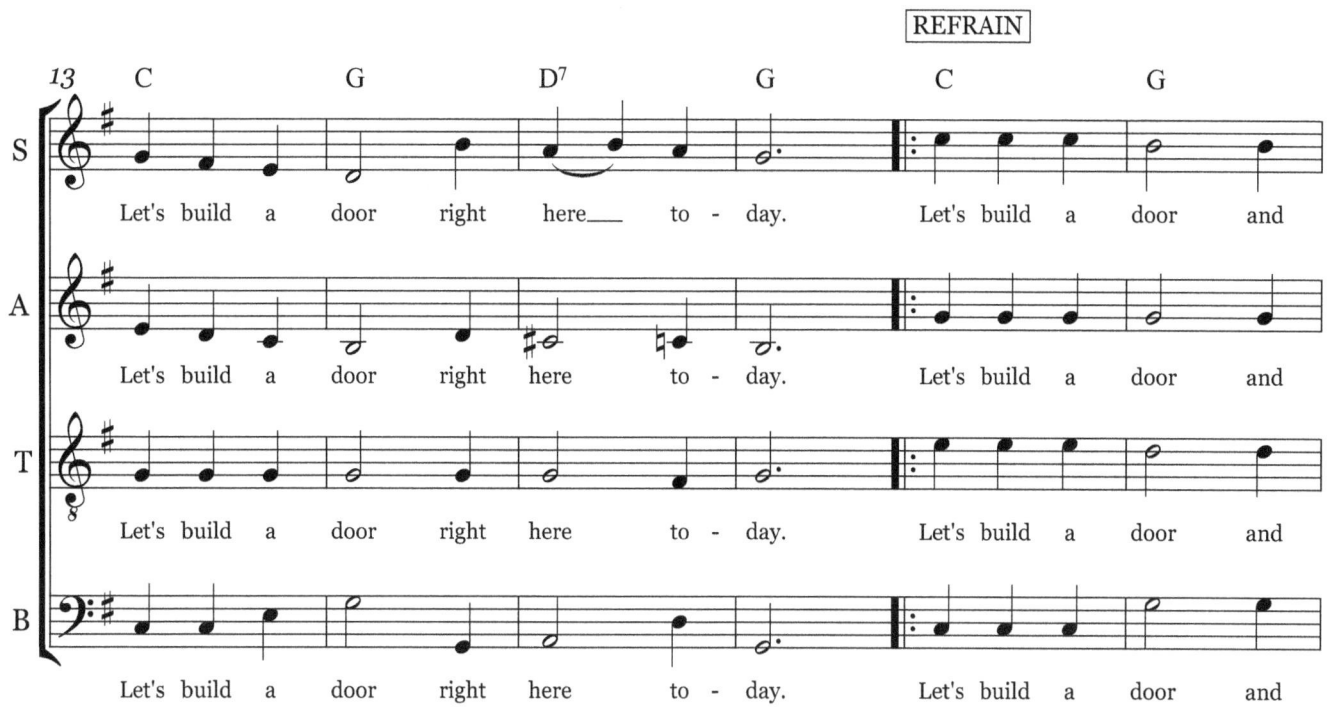
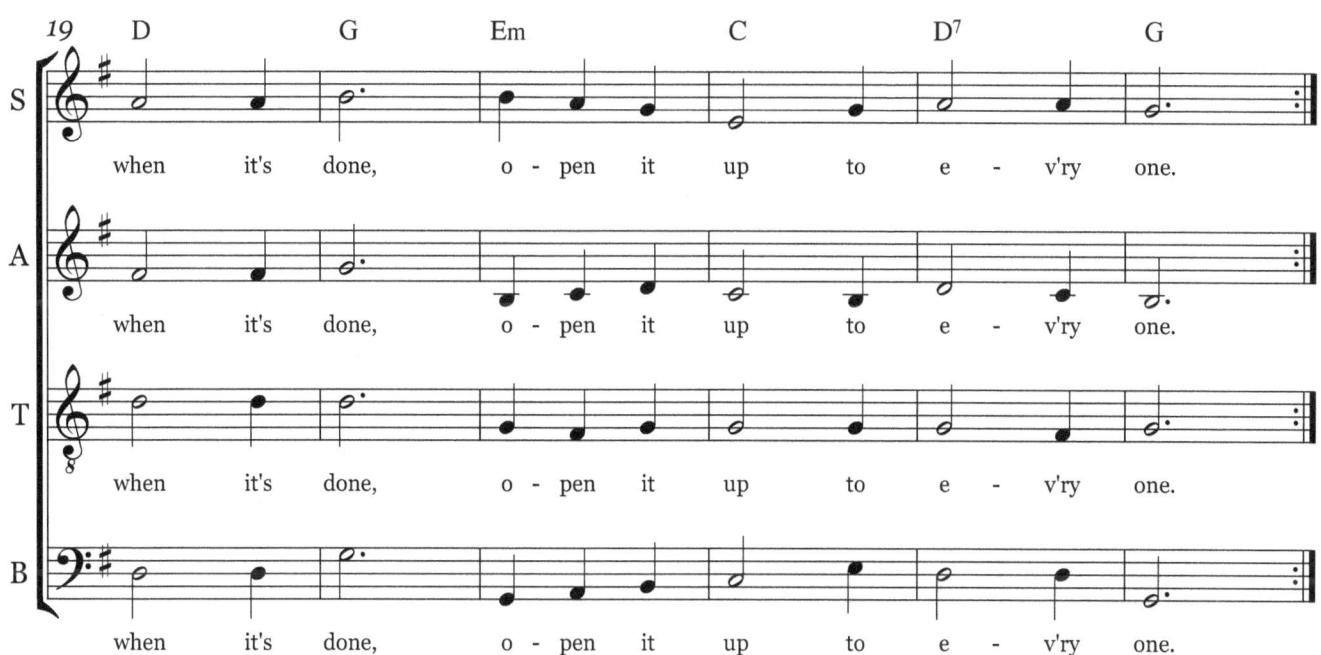

(Note: chord symbols support the soprano melody, not necessarily the SATB harmony)

14. Climbing Up The Ladder

(From the Secular Hymnal)

Words: Secretary Michael

Music: "Nicaea" by John Bacchus Dykes, 1861
(traditional hymn: "Holy, Holy, Holy")

PD   All works by Secretary Michael have been placed in the Public Domain. They may be freely copied and performed.

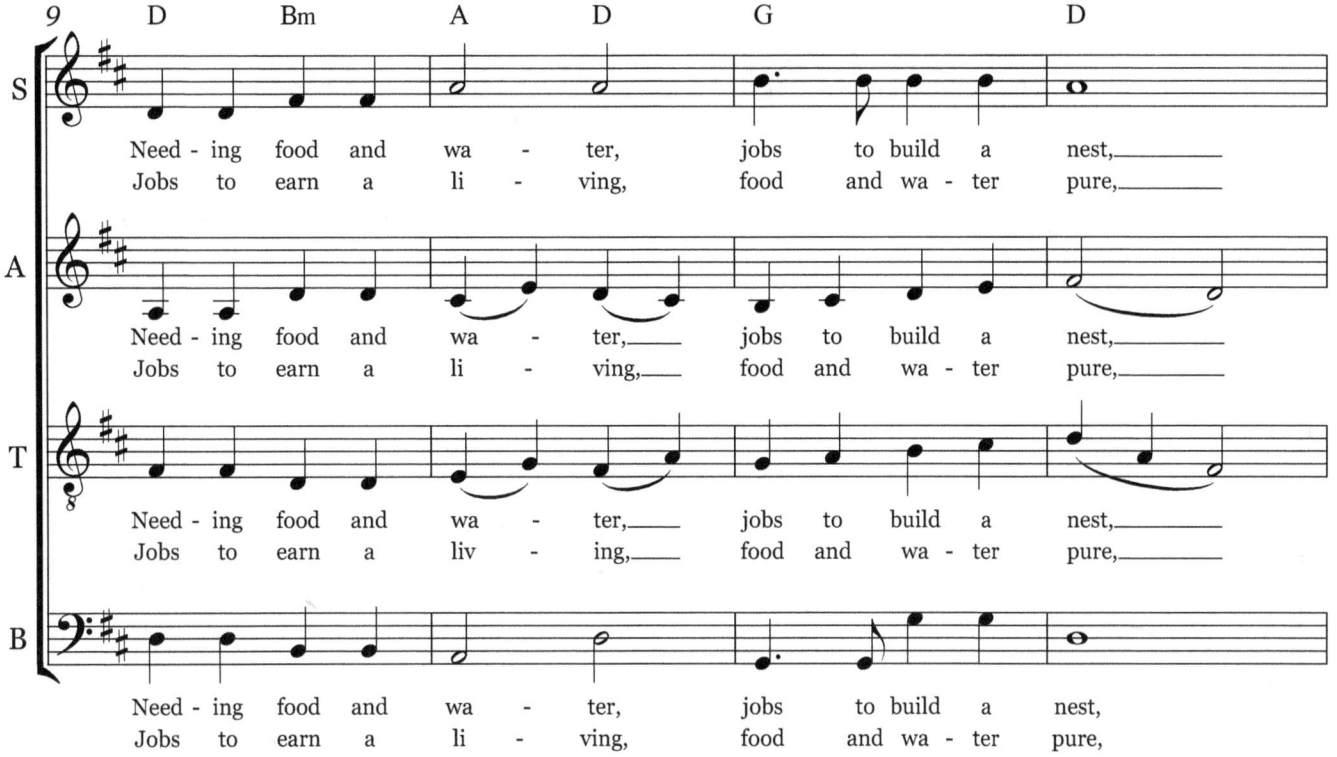
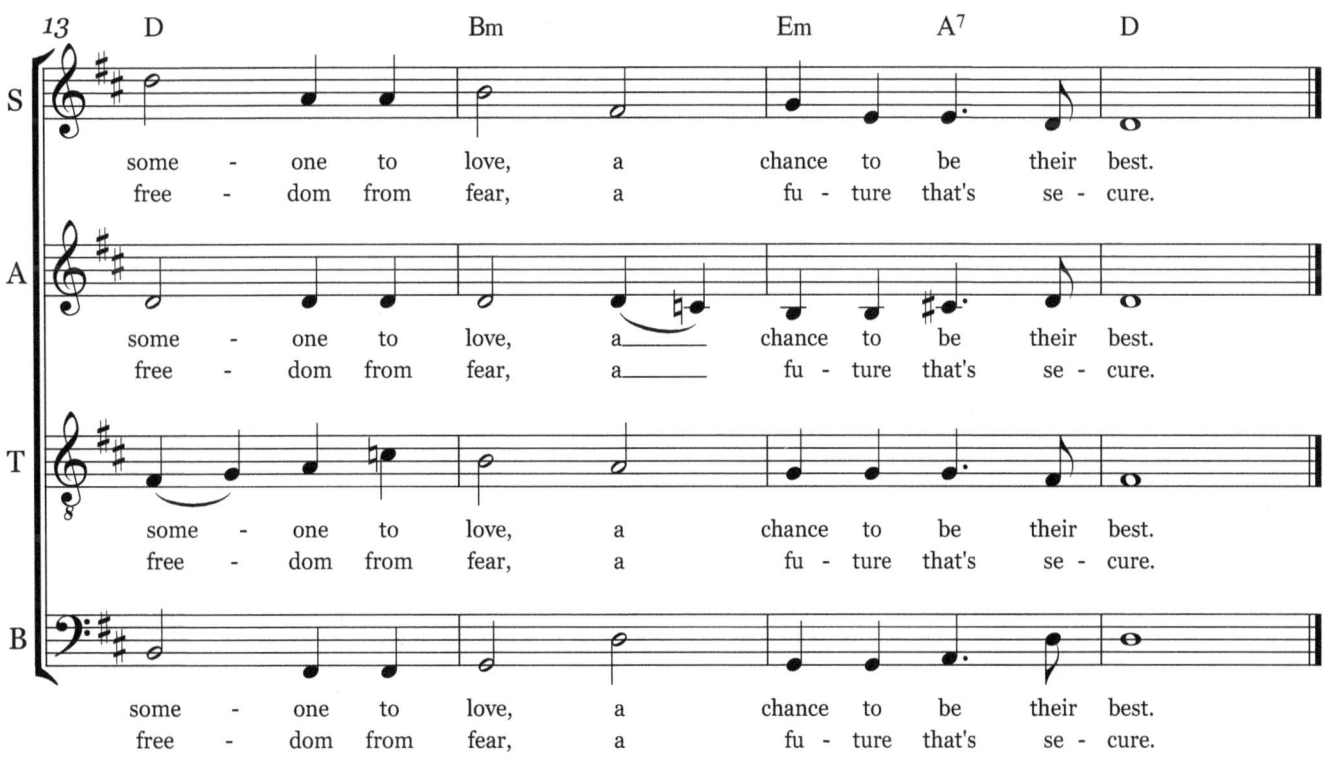

(Note: chord symbols support the soprano melody, not necessarily the SATB harmony)

15. Climbing Up The Mountain

(From the Secular Hymnal)

Words: Secretary Michael

Music: "Wye Valley" by James Mountain, 1876
(traditional hymn: "At the Name of Jesus")

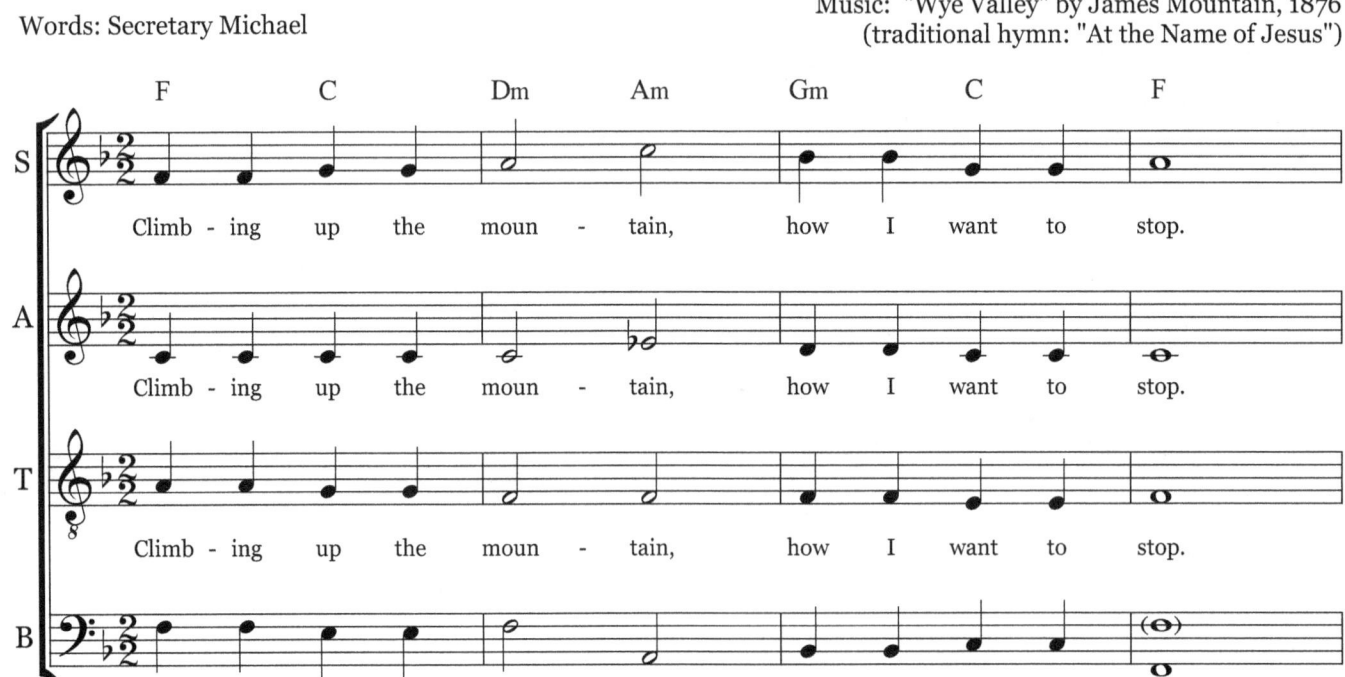

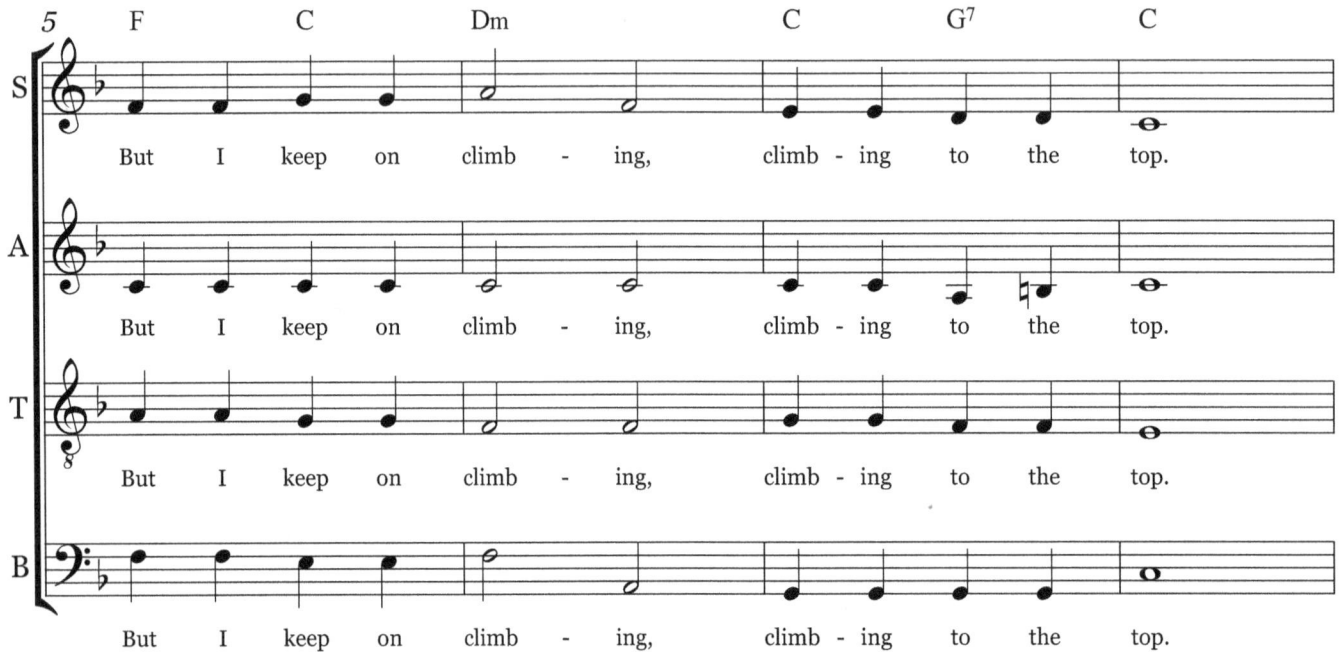

All works by Secretary Michael have been placed in the Public Domain. They may be freely copied and performed.

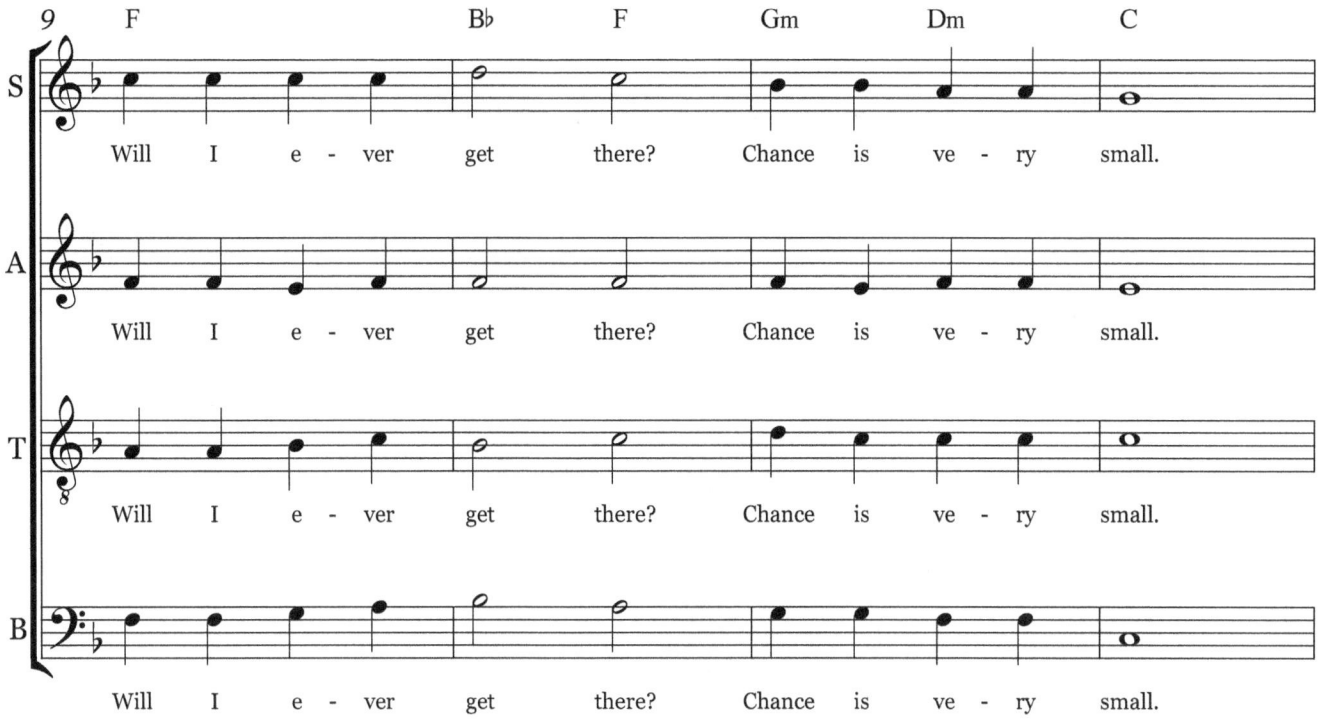

(Note: chord symbols support the soprano melody, not necessarily the SATB harmony)

16. Come Live With Us

(From the Secular Hymnal)

Words and Music: Secretary Michael

All works by Secretary Michael have been placed in the Public Domain. They may be freely copied and performed.

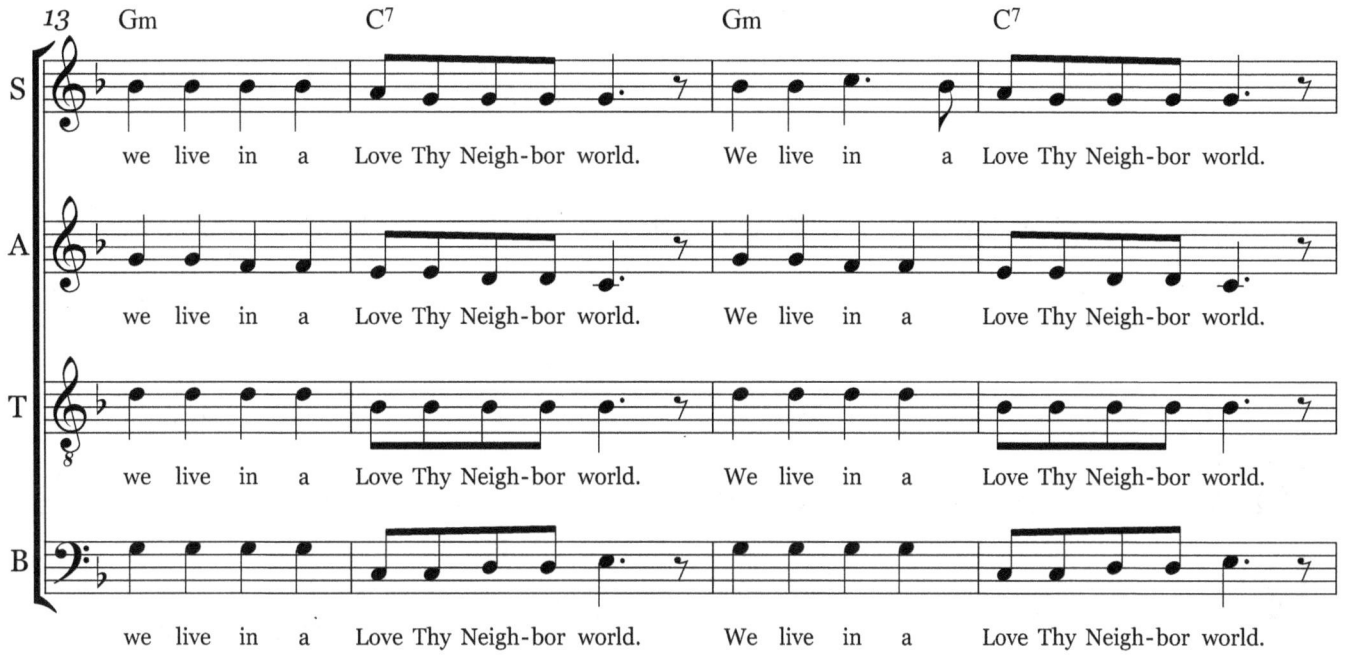

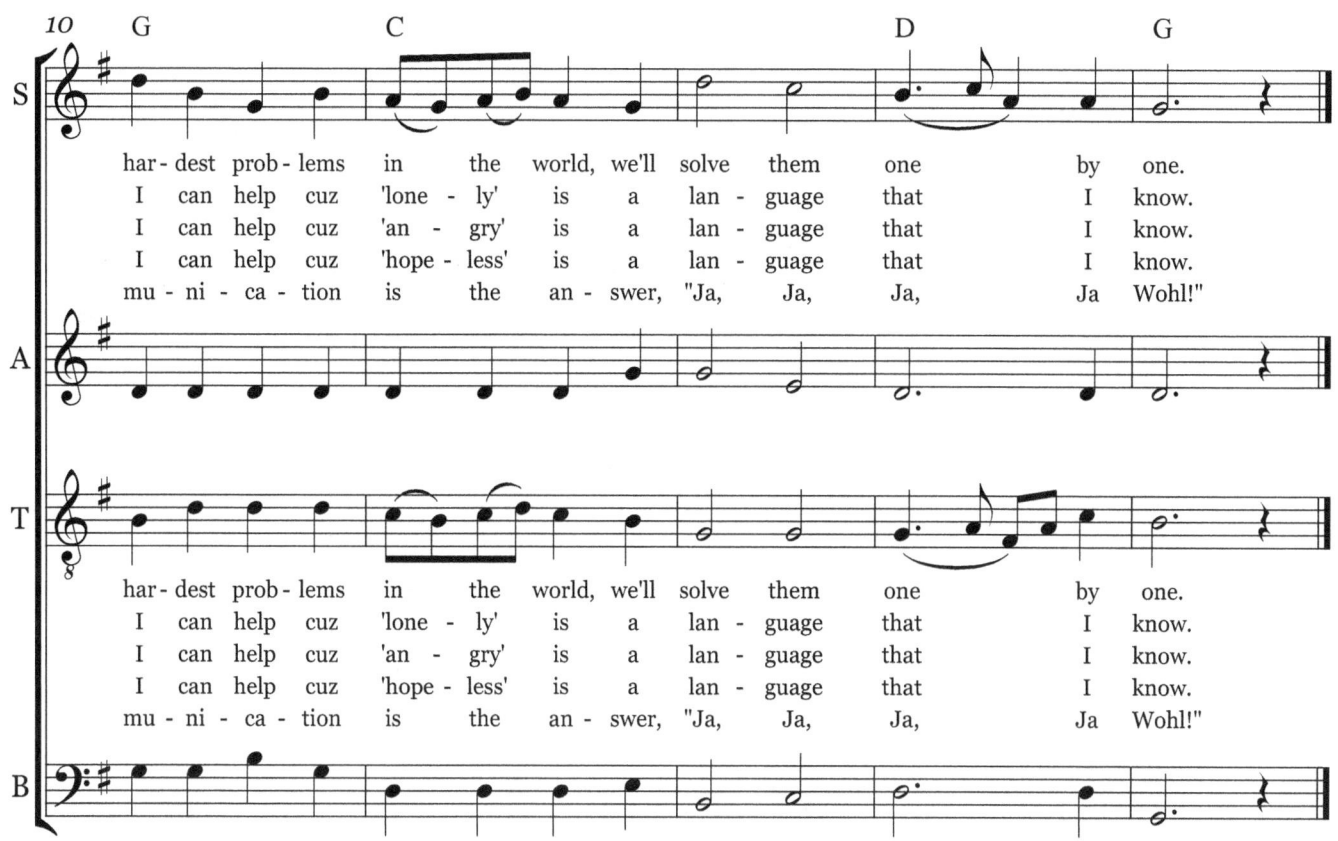

* "Ja Wohl" (pronounced "ya vole") is a German expression meaning "Yes Indeed"

(Note: chord symbols support the soprano melody, not necessarily the SATB harmony)

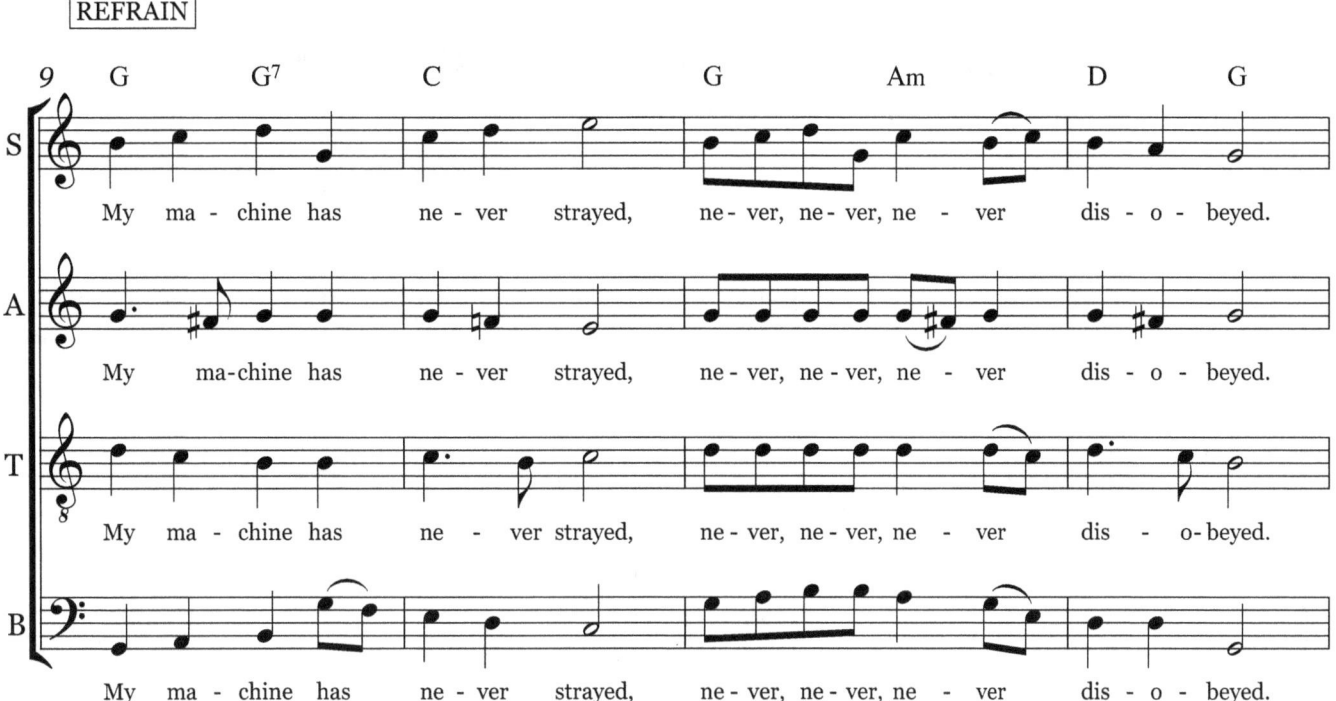

(Note: chord symbols support the soprano melody, not necessarily the SATB harmony)

19. Disassemble Every Gun

(From the Secular Hymnal)

Words: Secretary Michael

Music: "Nettleton", 1813
(traditional hymn: "Come Thou Fount of Every Blessing")

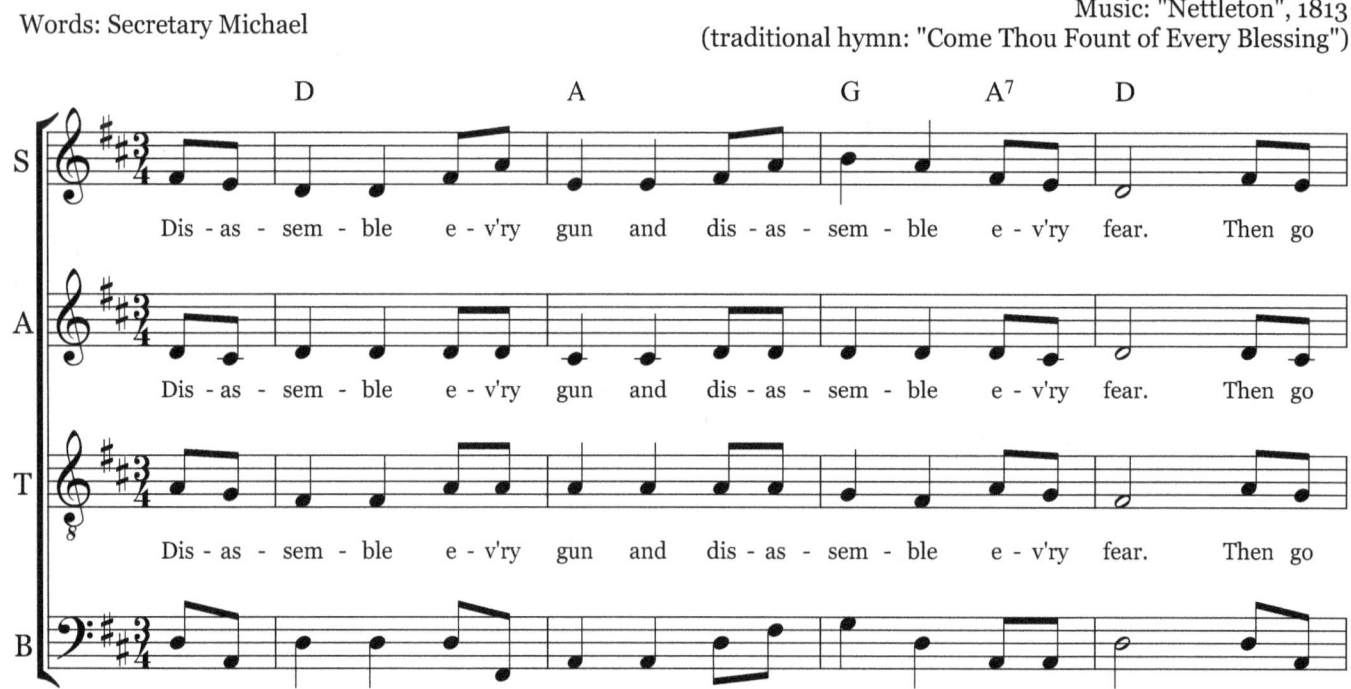

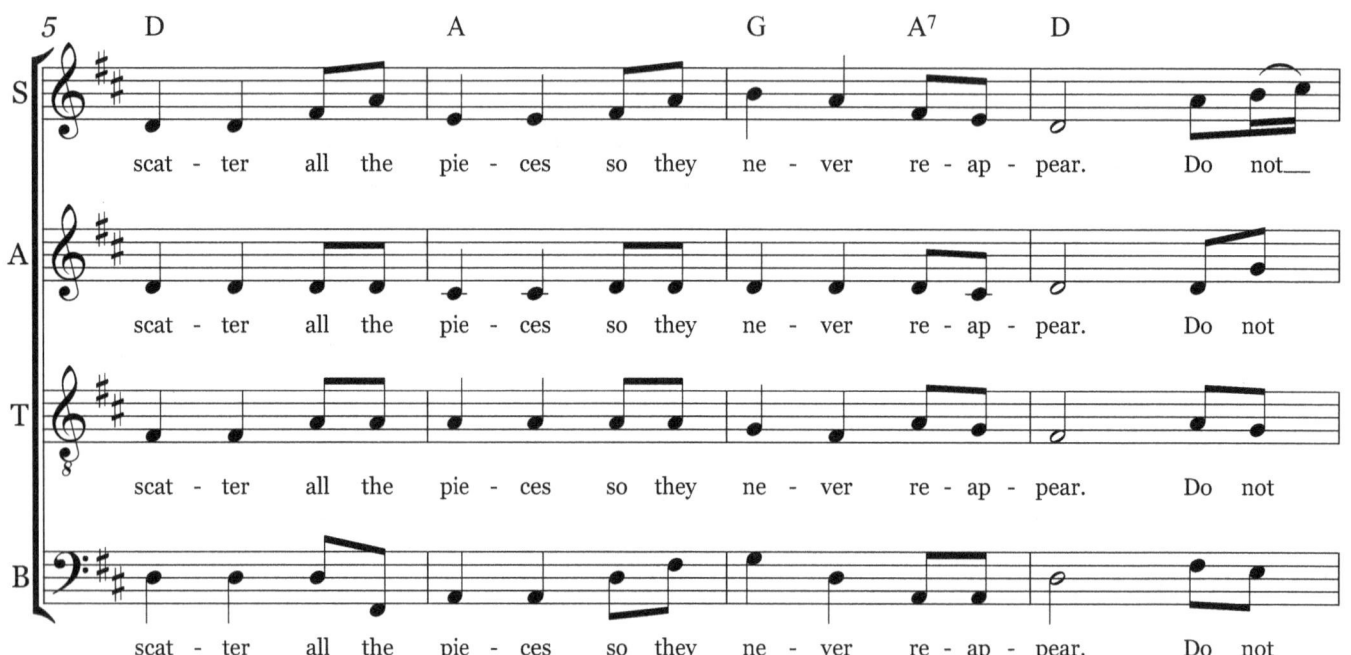

All works by Secretary Michael have been placed in the Public Domain. They may be freely copied and performed.

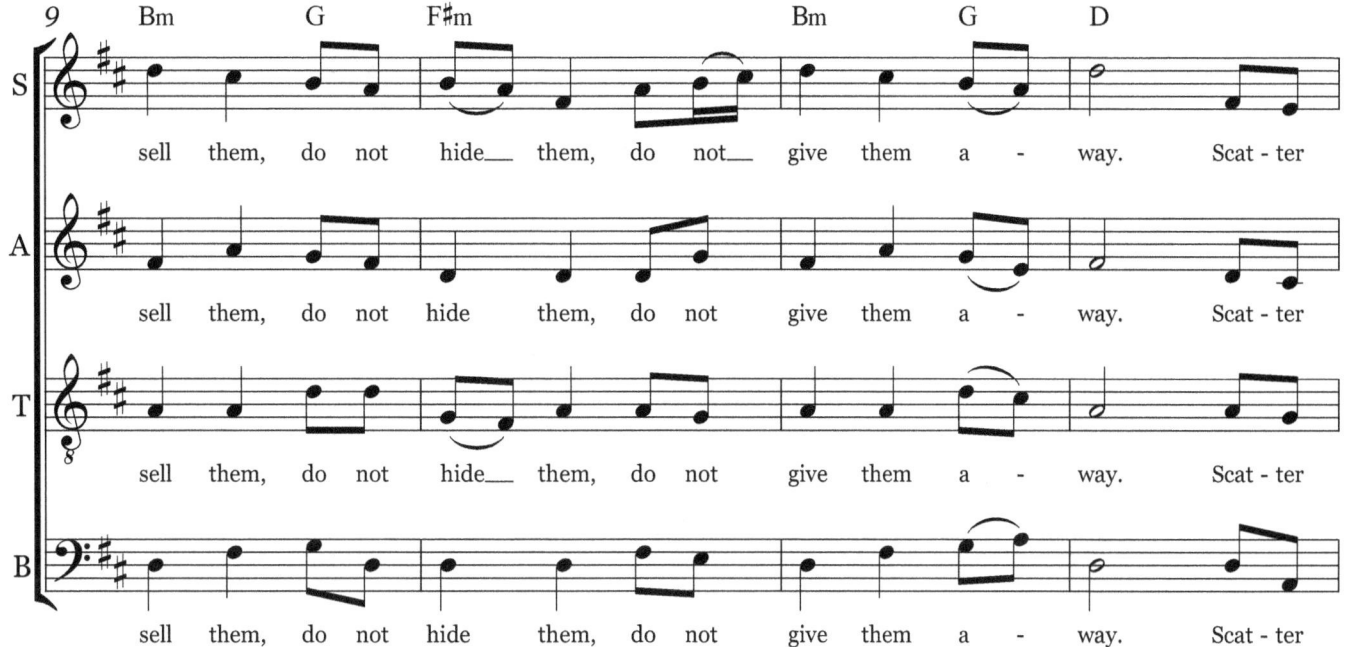
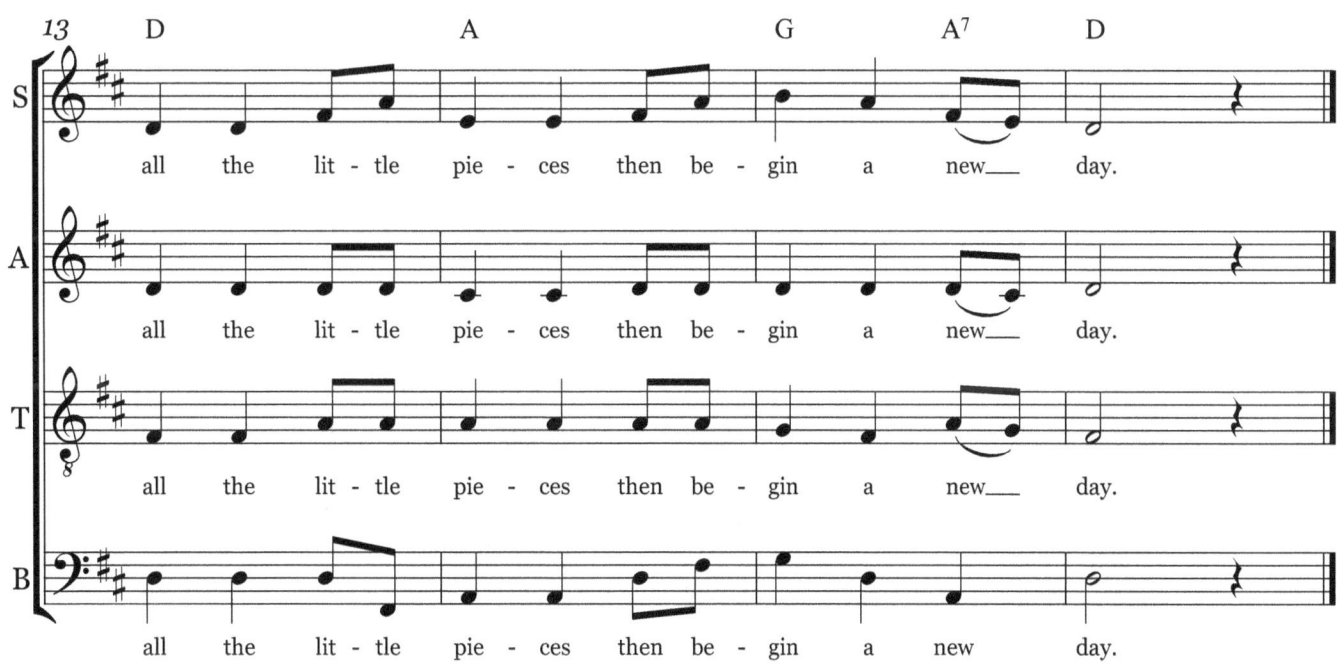

(Note: chord symbols support the soprano melody, not necessarily the SATB harmony)

20. Diversity in Thought

(From the Secular Hymnal)

Words: Secretary Michael

Music: "Rhosymedre" by John Edwards, 1840
(traditional hymn: "My Song Is Love Unknown")

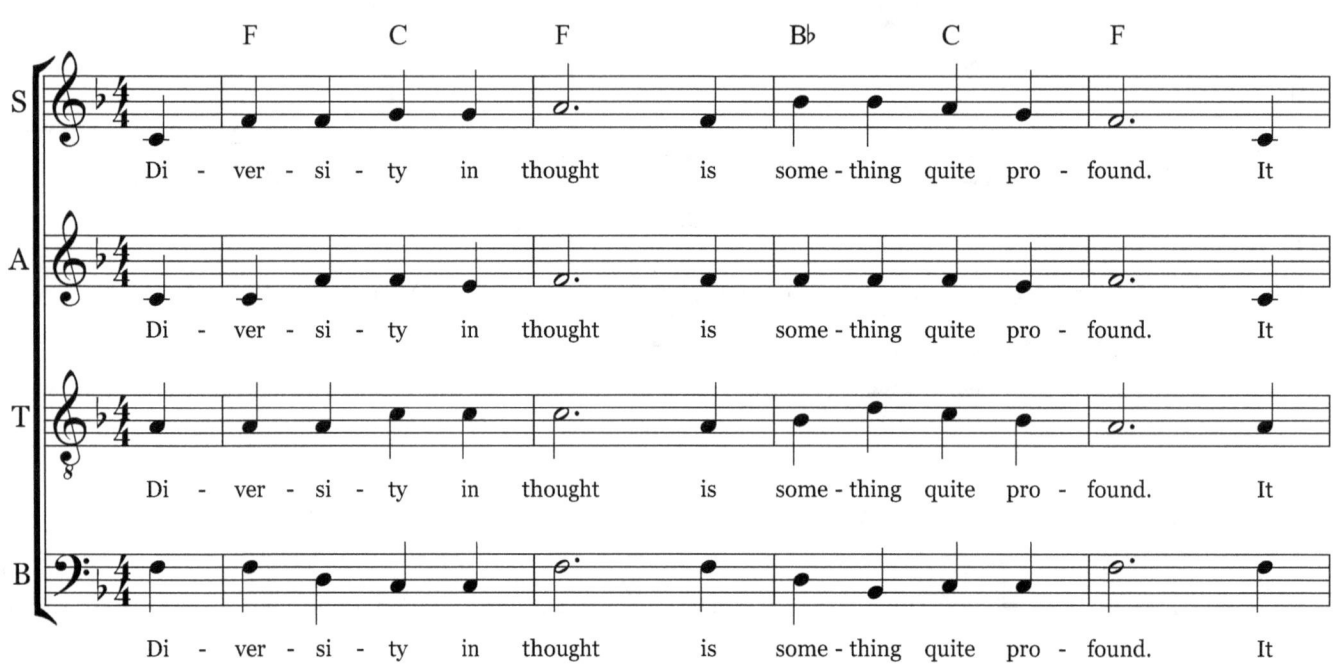

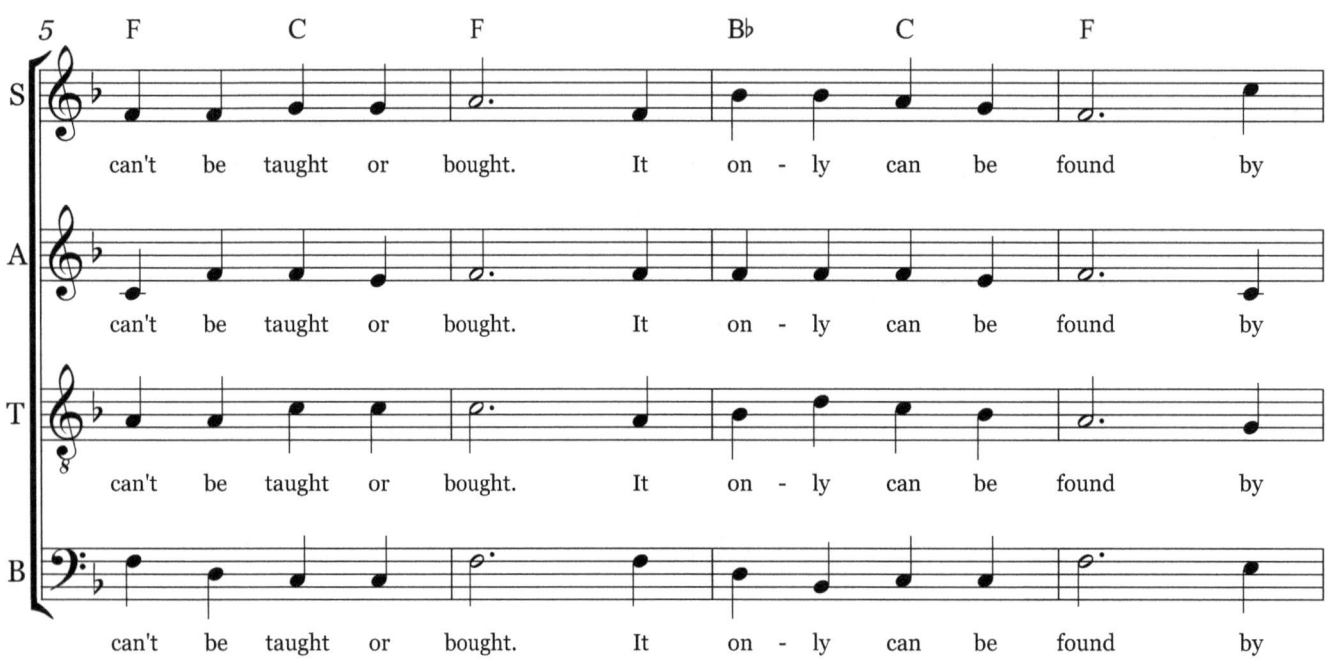

All works by Secretary Michael have been placed in the
Public Domain. They may be freely copied and performed.

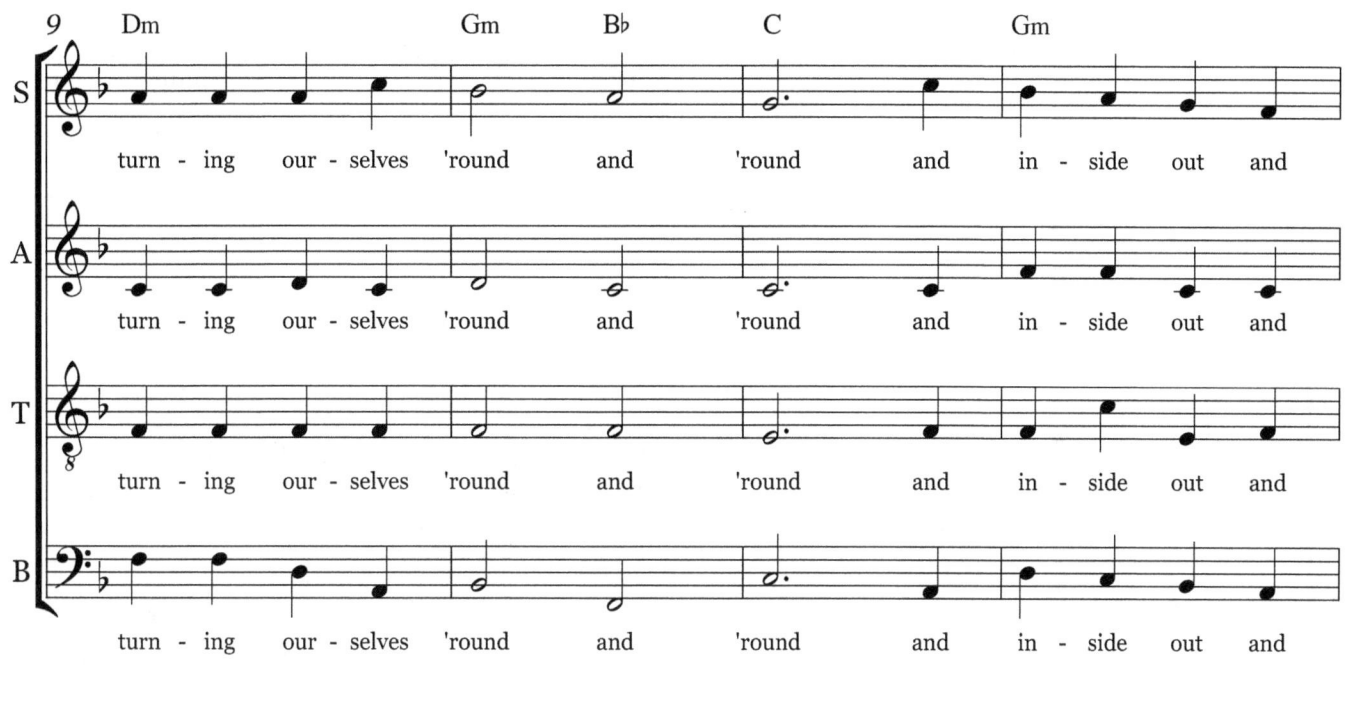
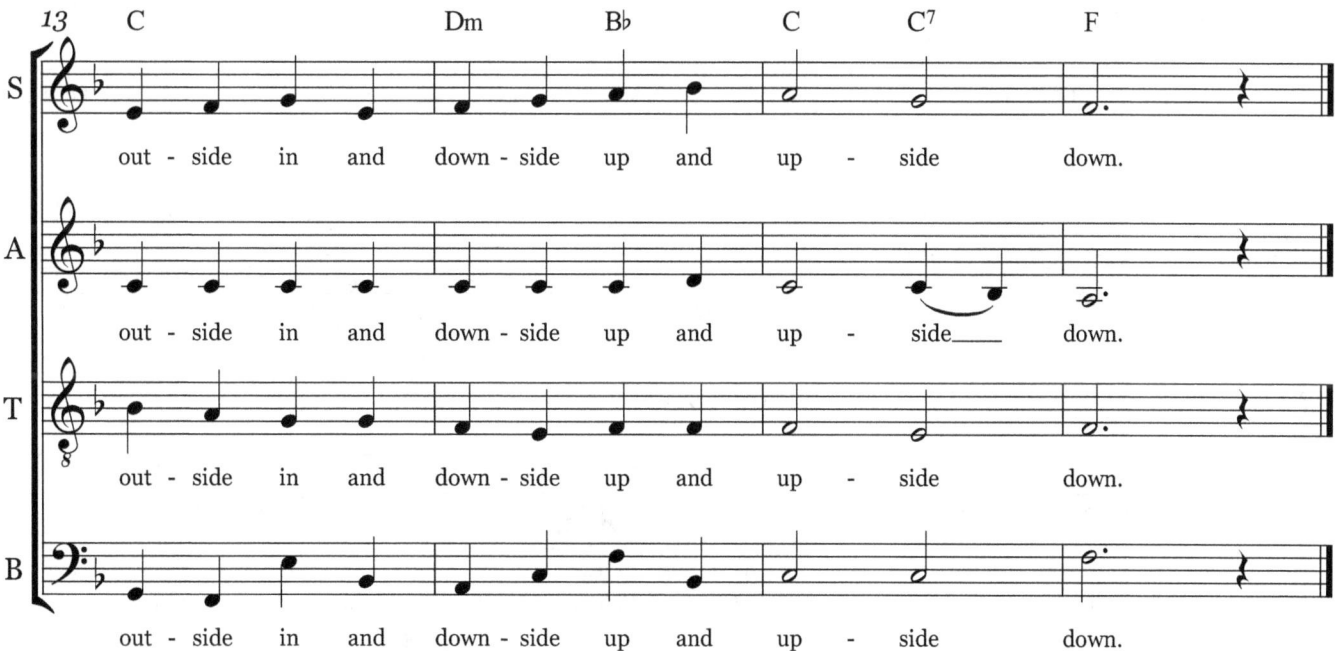

(Note: chord symbols support the soprano melody, not necessarily the SATB harmony)

21. Don't Choose Sides
(From the Secular Hymnal)

Words: Secretary Michael

Music: "Salve Regina" Hermann of Reichenau, c. 1050
(traditional hymn: "Hail Holy Queen Enthroned Above")

All works by Secretary Michael have been placed in the Public Domain. They may be freely copied and performed.

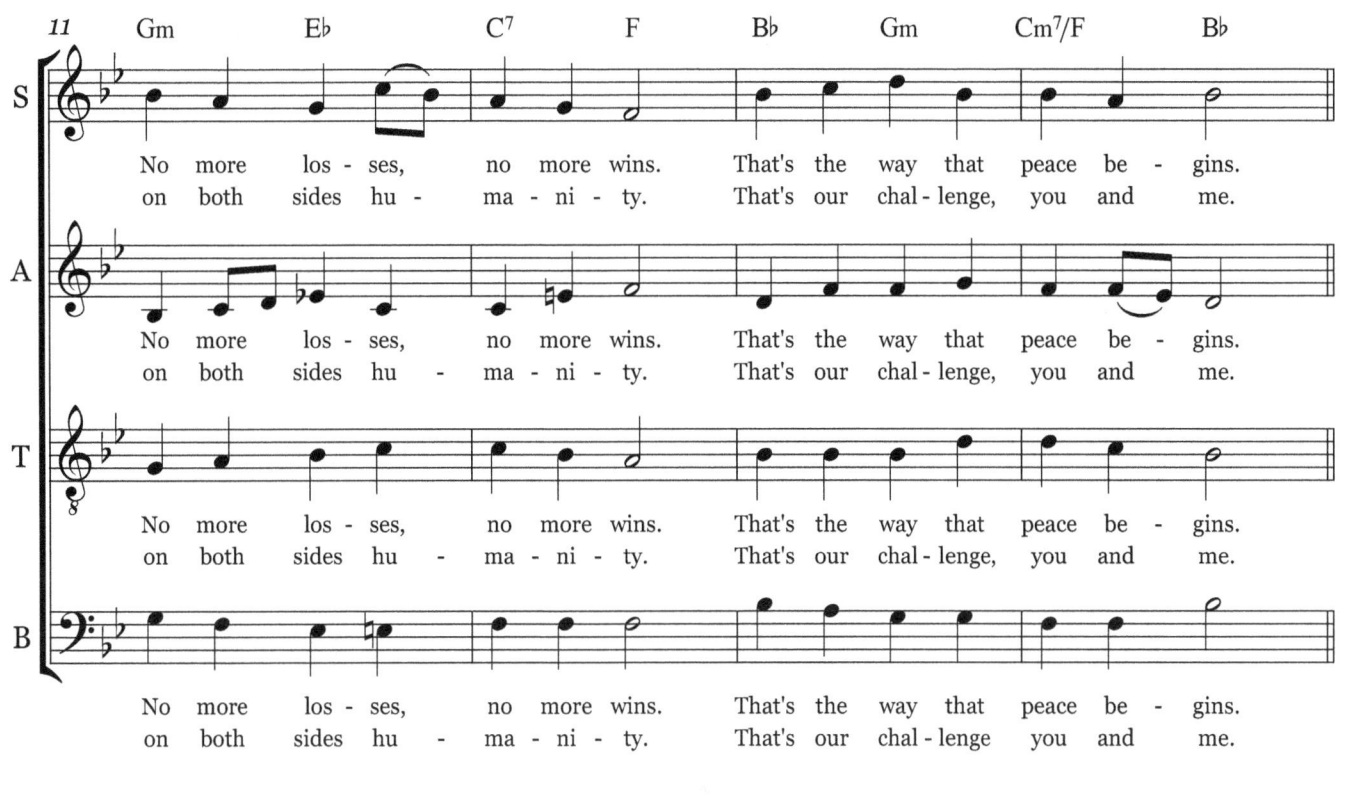

(Note: chord symbols support the soprano melody, not necessarily the SATB harmony)

22. Don't Know How I Got Here

(From the Secular Hymnal)

Words: Secretary Michael

Music: "Ville Du Havre" (Harbor City) by Philip Paul Bliss, 1876
(traditional hymn: "It Is Well With My Soul")

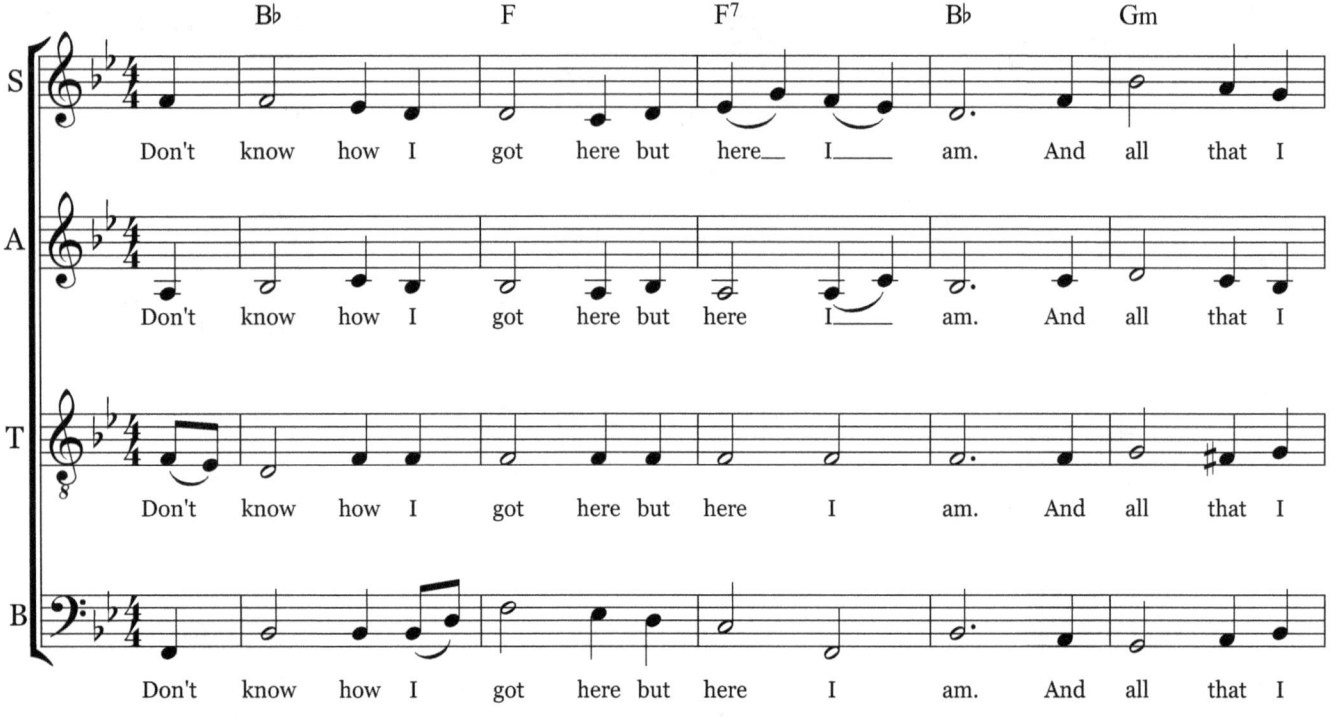

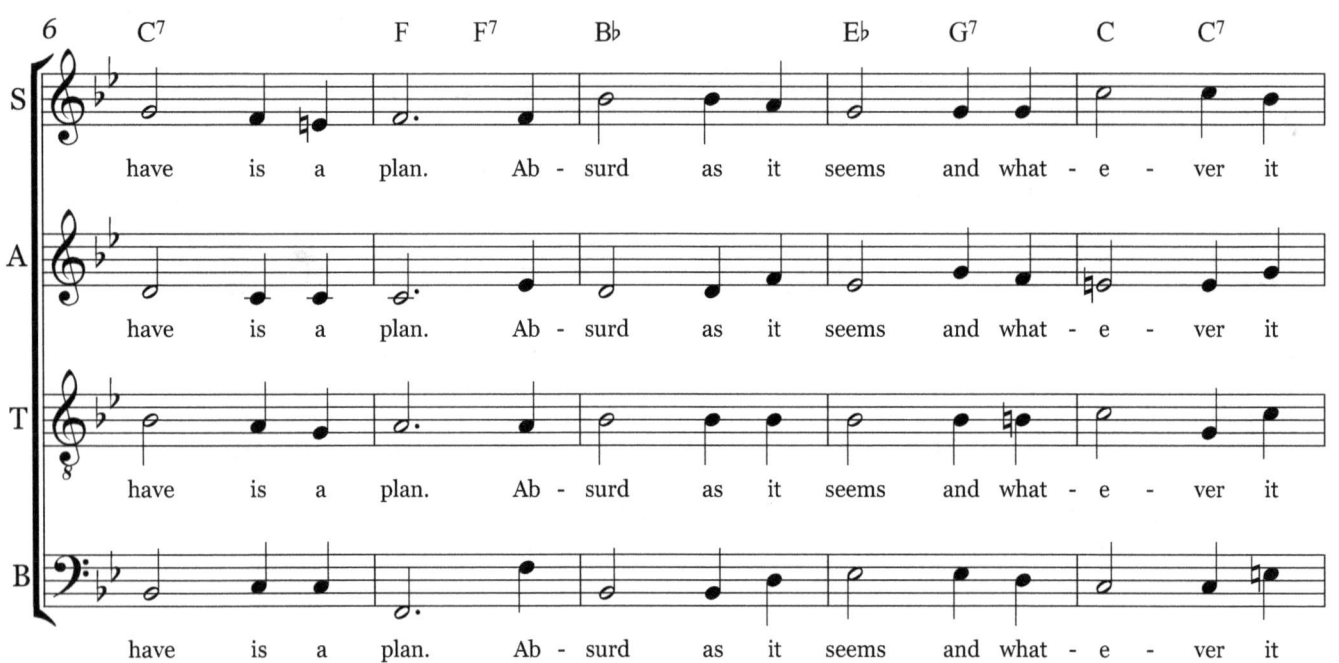

All works by Secretary Michael have been placed in the Public Domain. They may be freely copied and performed.

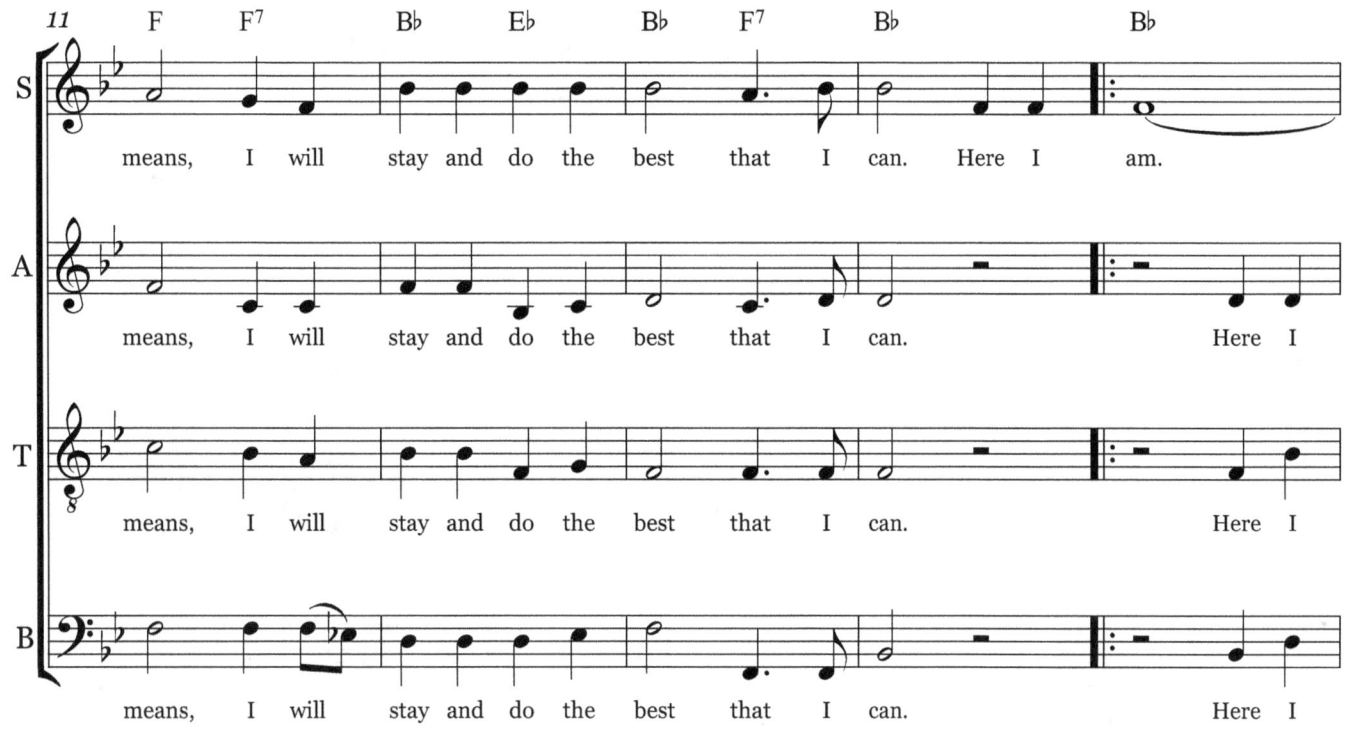

(Note: chord symbols support the soprano melody, not necessarily the SATB harmony)

23. Each Little Raindrop

(From the Secular Hymnal)

Words: Secretary Michael

Music: "Sutra Hymn" by Secretary Michael

All works by Secretary Michael have been placed in the Public Domain. They may be freely copied and performed.

25. Every Space for Every Face

(From the Secular Hymnal)

Words: Secretary Michael

Music: "Salzburg" by Jacob Hintze, 1678
Harmonized by J.S.Bach
(traditional hymn: "At the Lamb's High Feast We Sing")

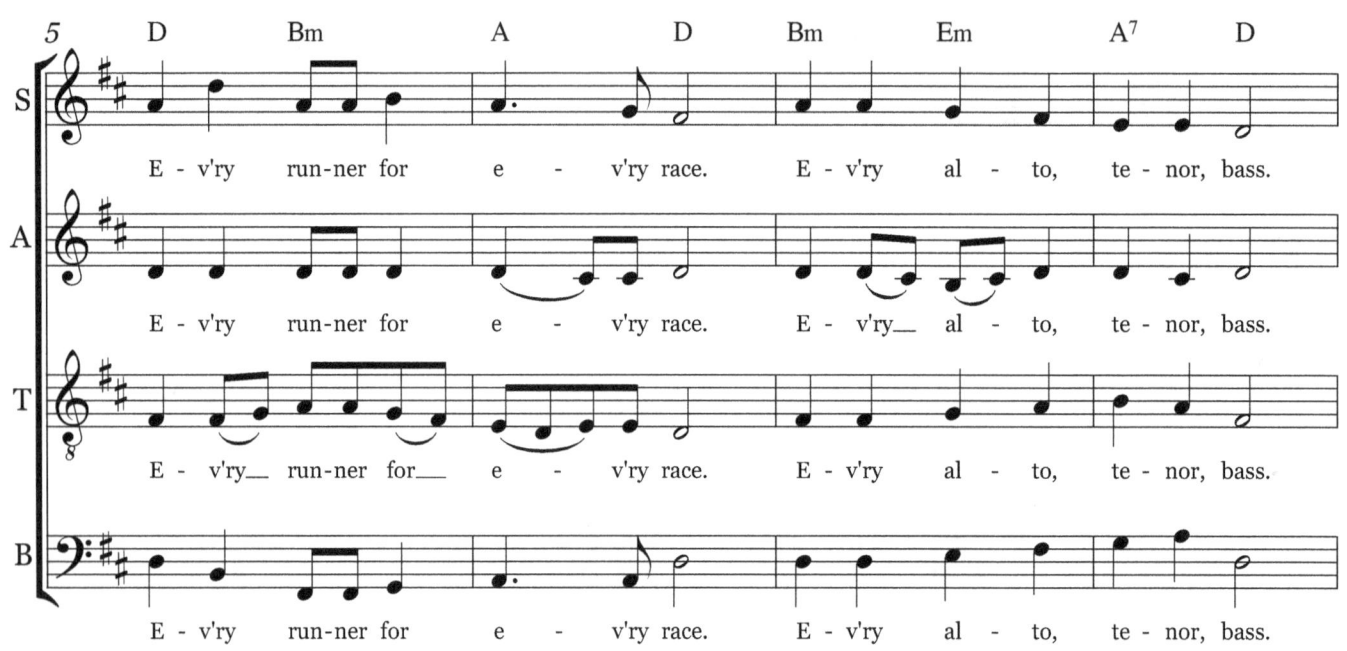

All works by Secretary Michael have been placed in the Public Domain. They may be freely copied and performed.

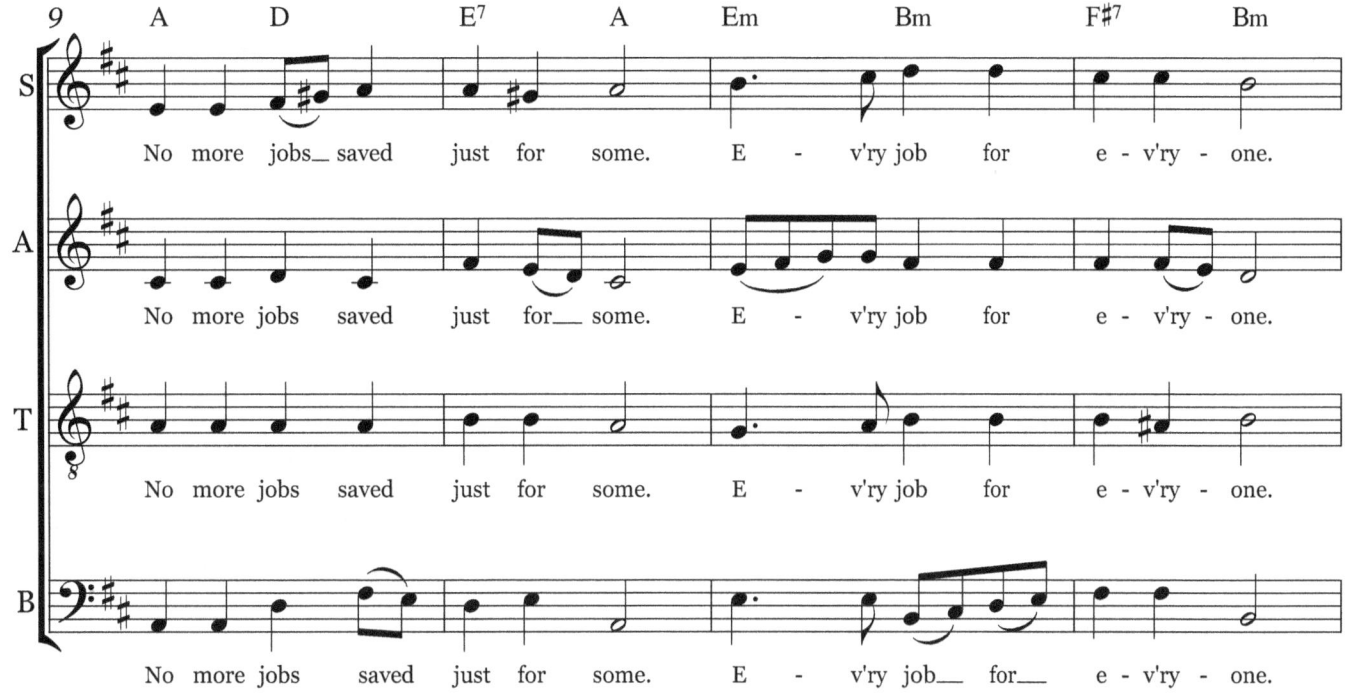

(Note: chord symbols support the soprano melody, not necessarily the SATB harmony)

26. Everybody Has Their Issues

(From the Secular Hymnal)

Words: Secretary Michael

Tune: "There is a Balm in Gilead"
(a traditional African-American spiritual)
SATB Arrangement: Secretary Michael

PD *All works by Secretary Michael have been placed in the Public Domain. They may be freely copied and performed.*

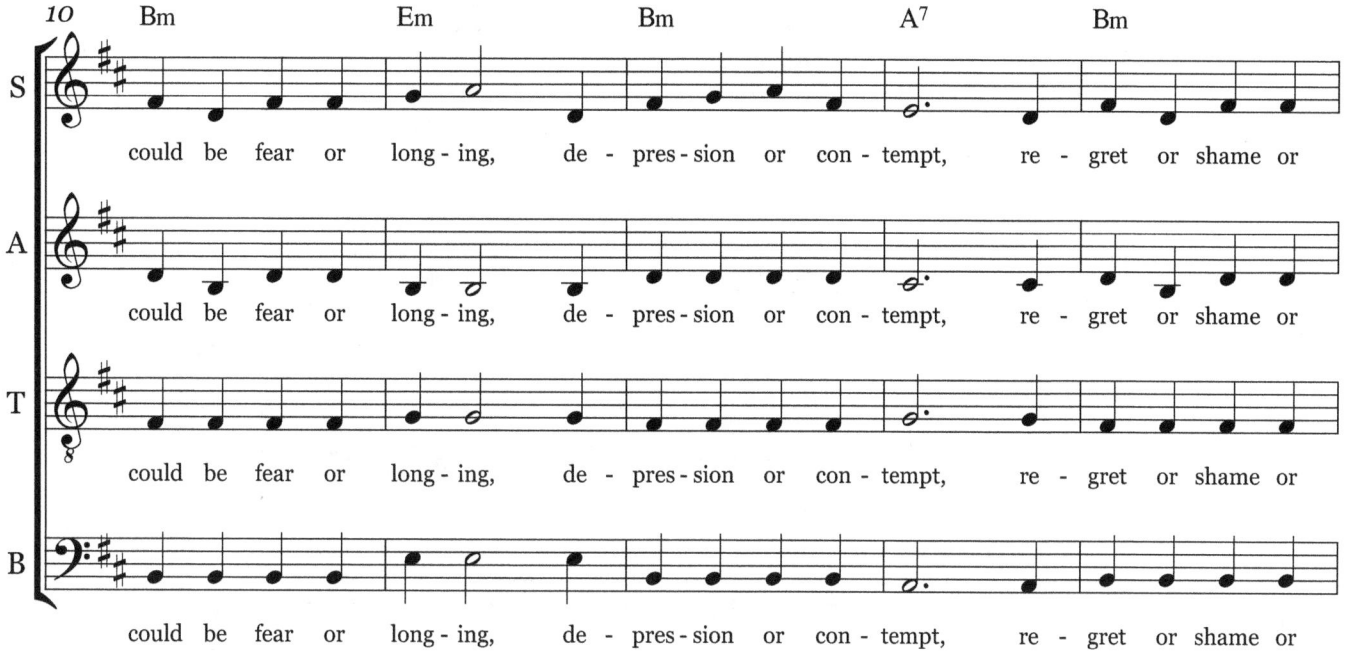
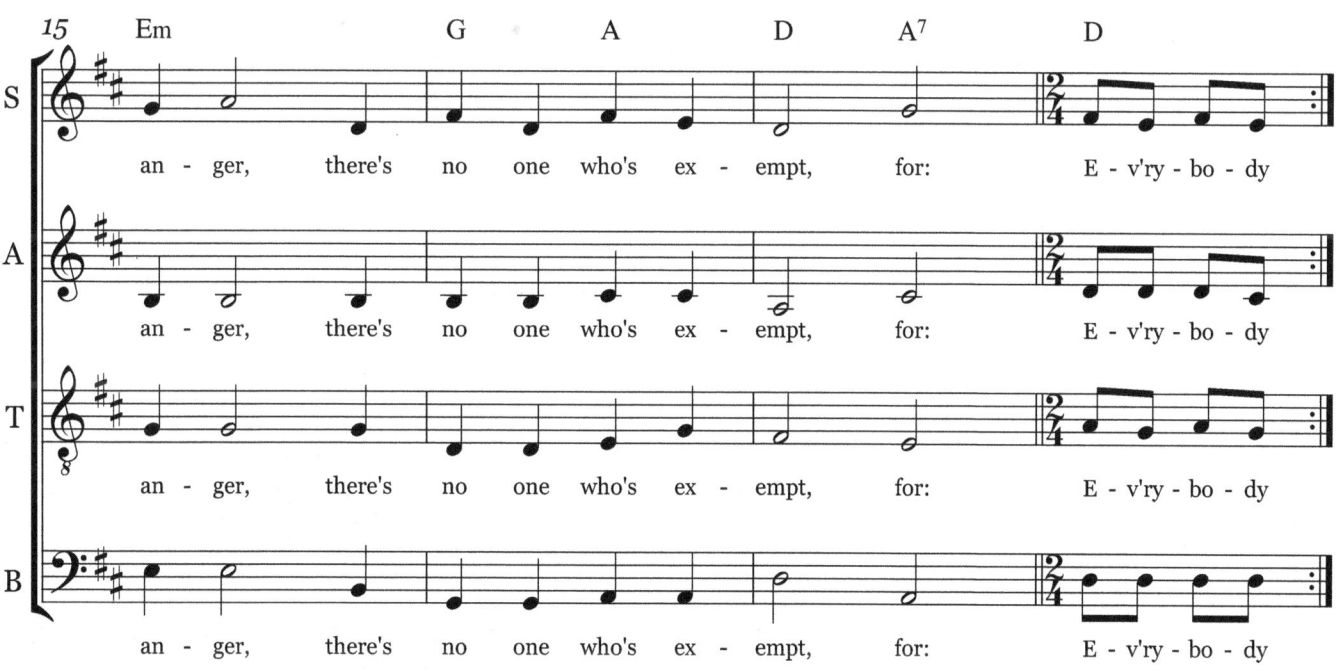

27. Everyone Must Make a Living
(From the Secular Hymnal)

Words: Secretary Michael

Music: "Pleading Savior" by Joshua Leavitt (c. 1830)
(traditional hymn: "Sing of Mary")

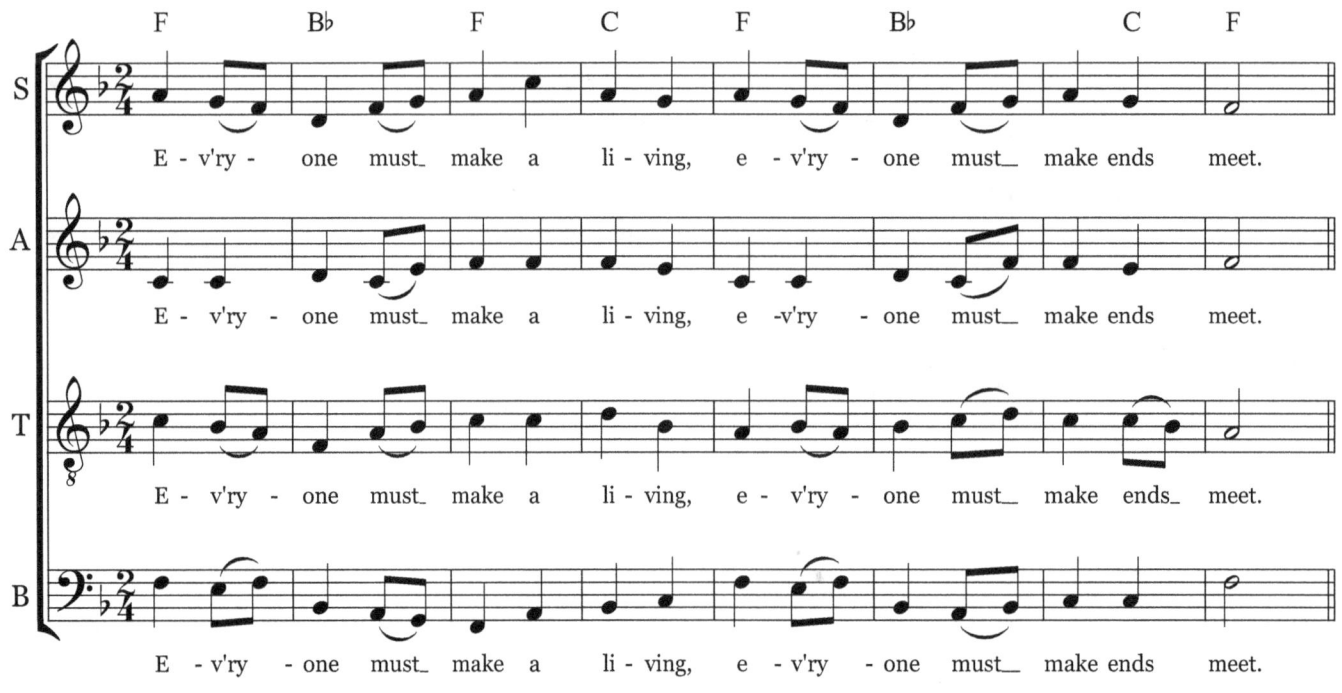

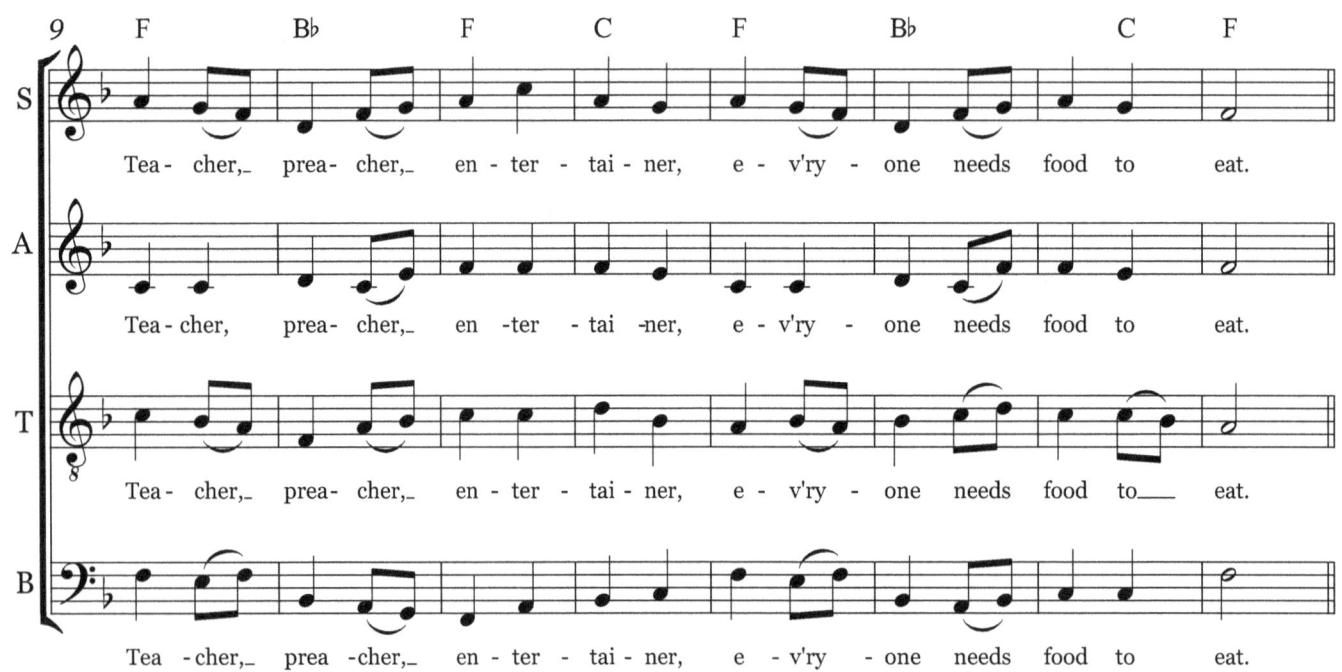

All works by Secretary Michael have been placed in the Public Domain. They may be freely copied and performed.

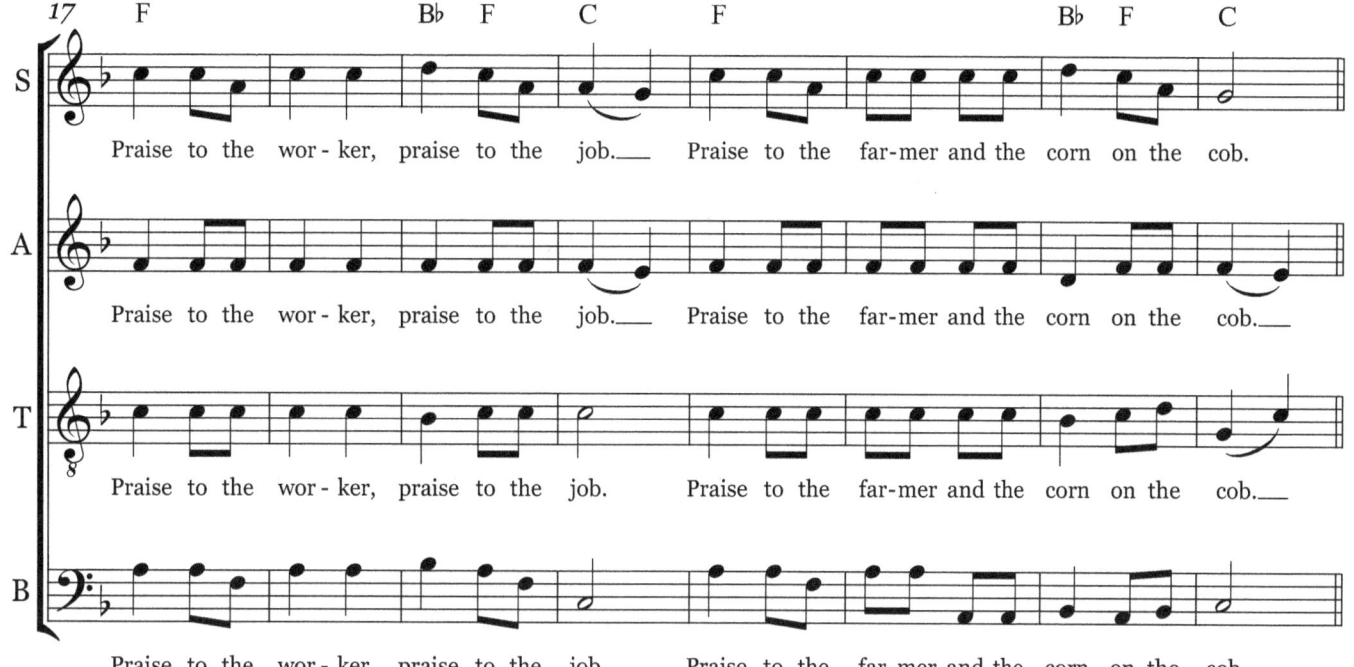
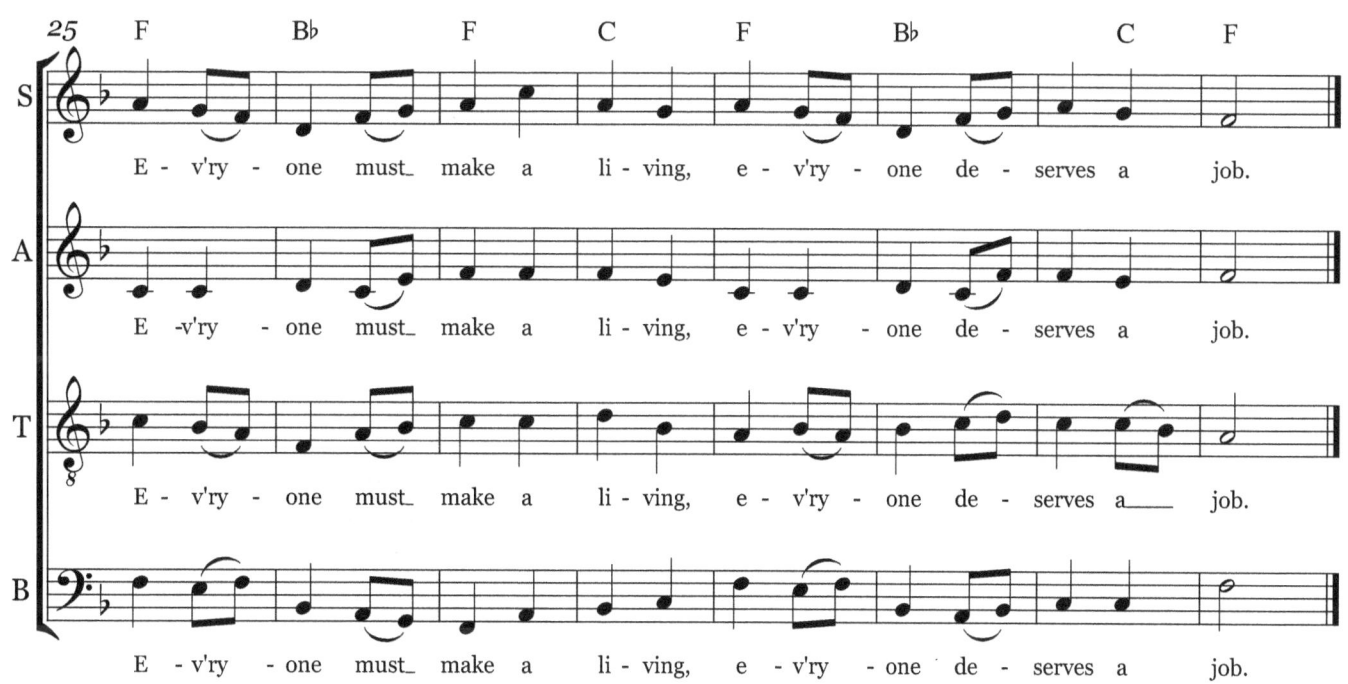

(Note: chord symbols support the soprano melody, not necessarily the SATB harmony)

28. Everything's Changing
(From the Secular Hymnal)

Words: Secretary Michael

Music: "Consolation" by Felix Mendelssohn, 1834
(traditional hymn: "Still, Still With Thee")

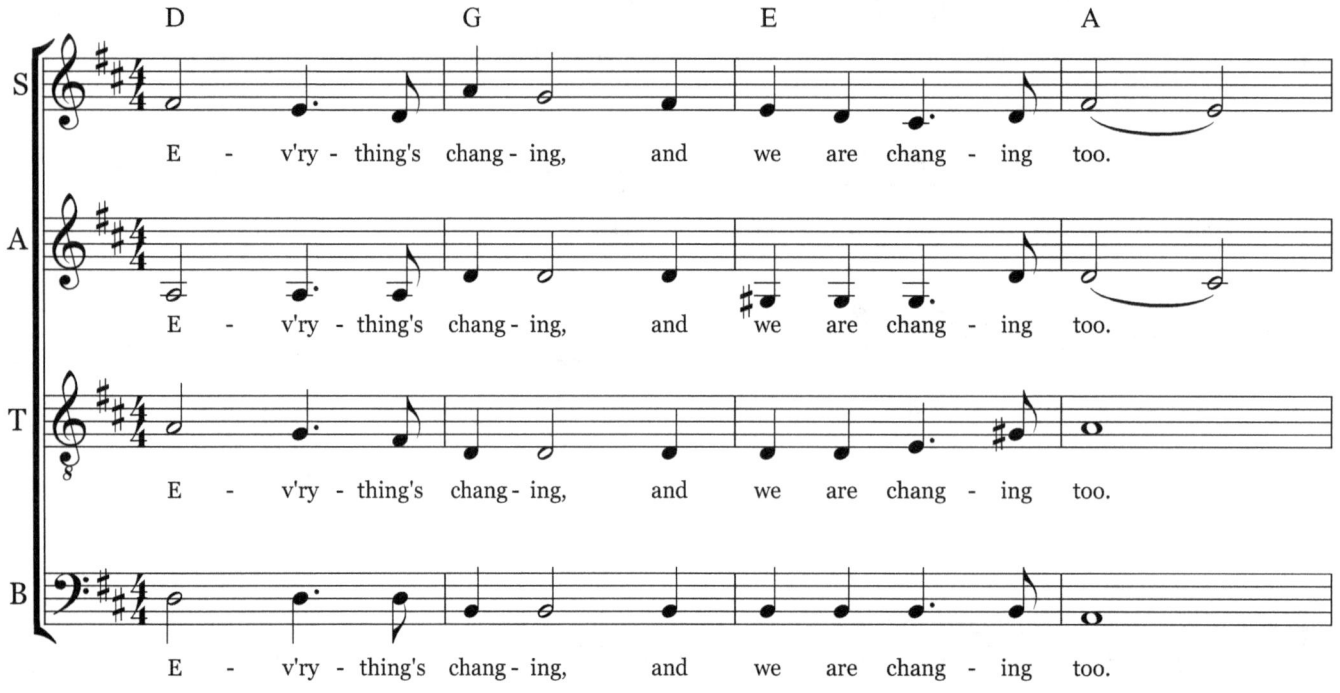

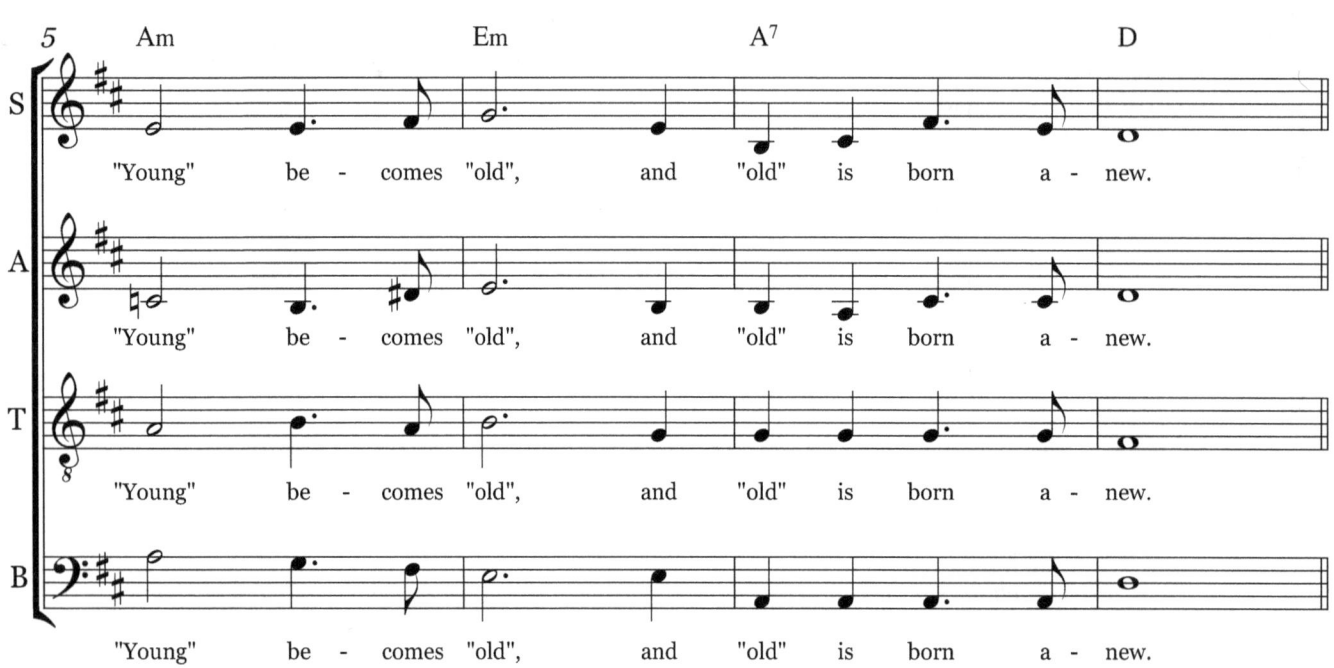

All works by Secretary Michael have been placed in the Public Domain. They may be freely copied and performed.

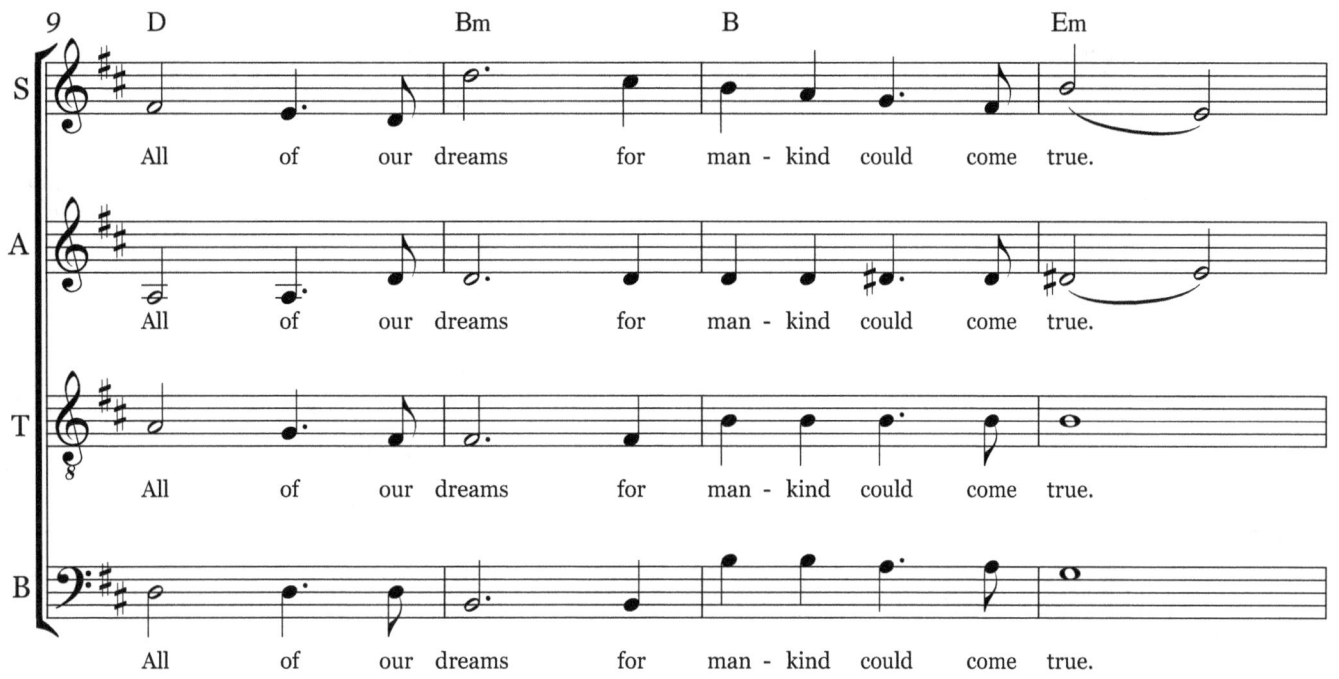
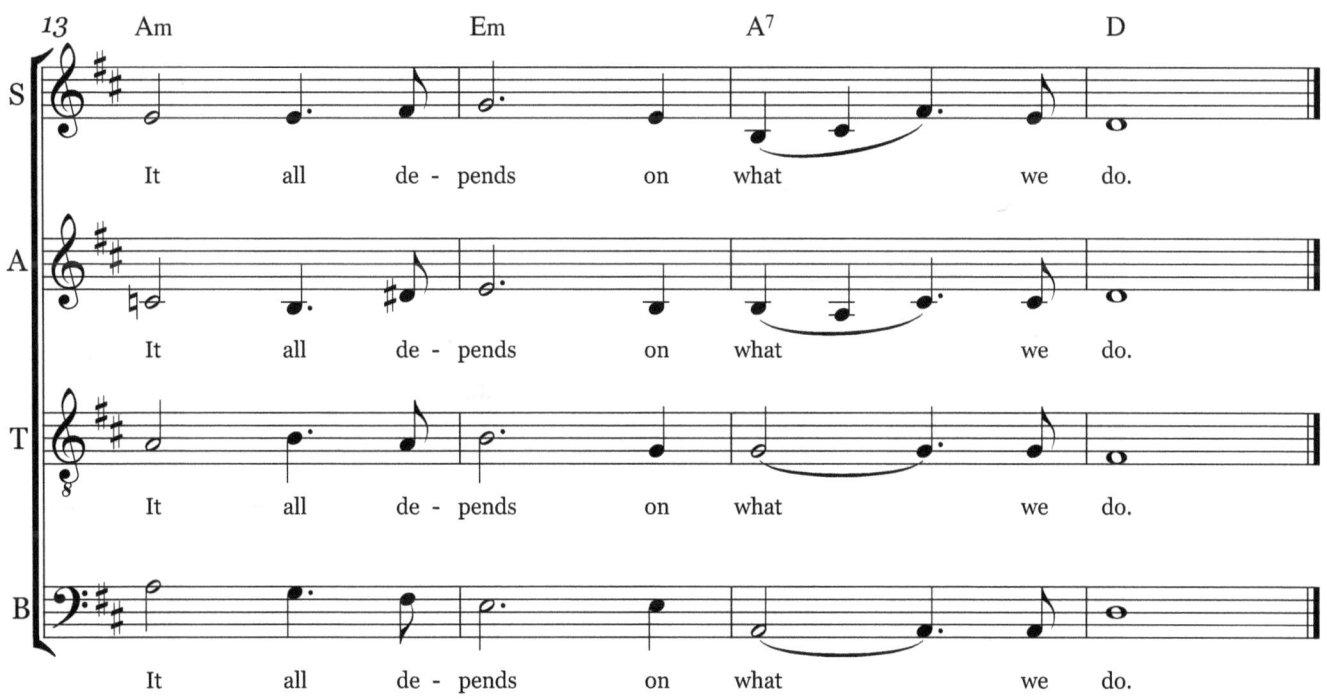

(Note: chord symbols support the soprano melody, not necessarily the SATB harmony)

29. For Those Who Have Beliefs Bizarre

(From the Secular Hymnal)

Words: Secretary Michael

Music: "Ye Banks and Braes" - a Scottish folk melody
SATB arrangement by Secretary Michael
(traditional hymn: "We Cannot Measure How You Heal")

All works by Secretary Michael have been placed in the Public Domain. They may be freely copied and performed.

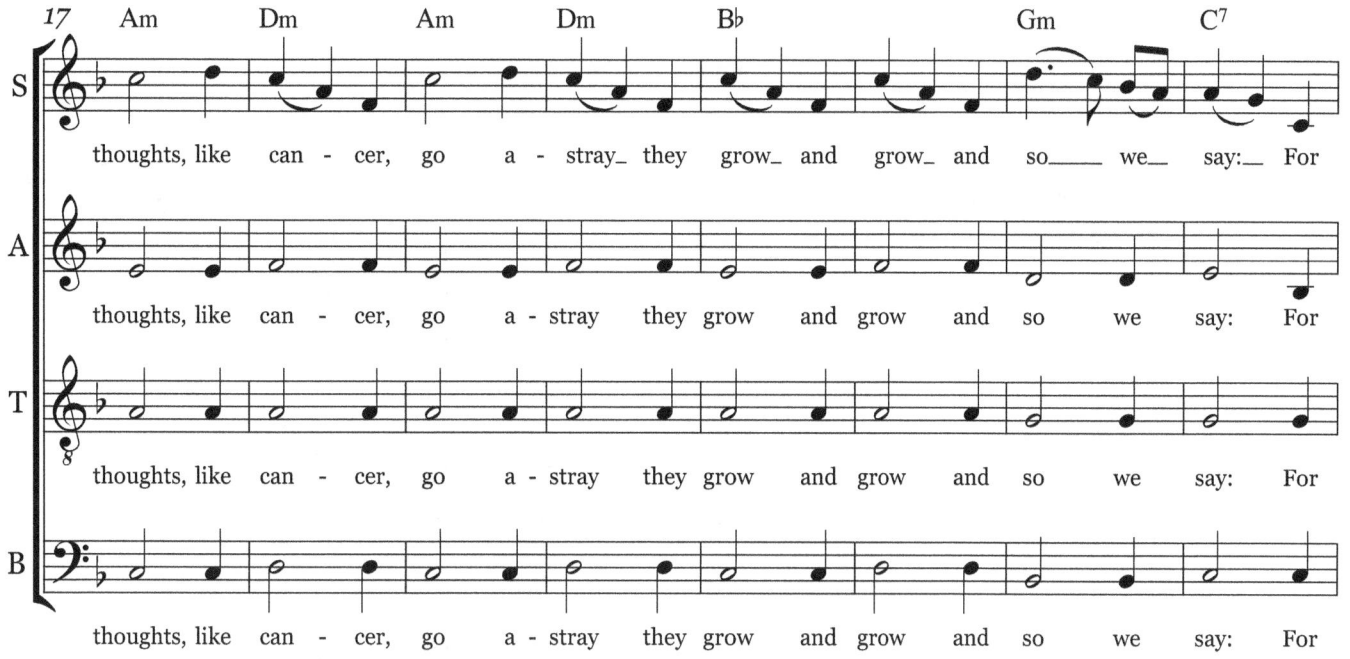

30. For What I've Done
(From the Secular Hymnal)

Words: Secretary Michael

Music: Louis Lambillotte, c. 1840
(traditional hymn: "Come Holy Ghost")

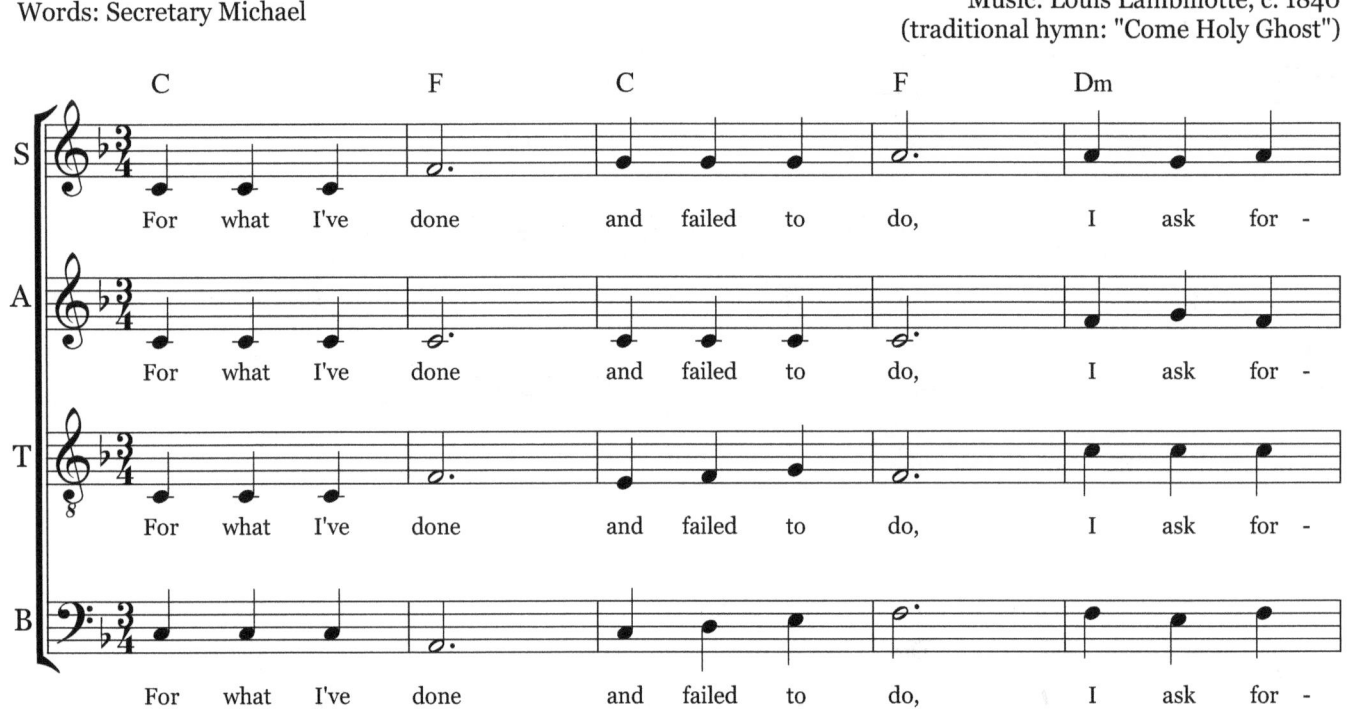

All works by Secretary Michael have been placed in the Public Domain. They may be freely copied and performed.

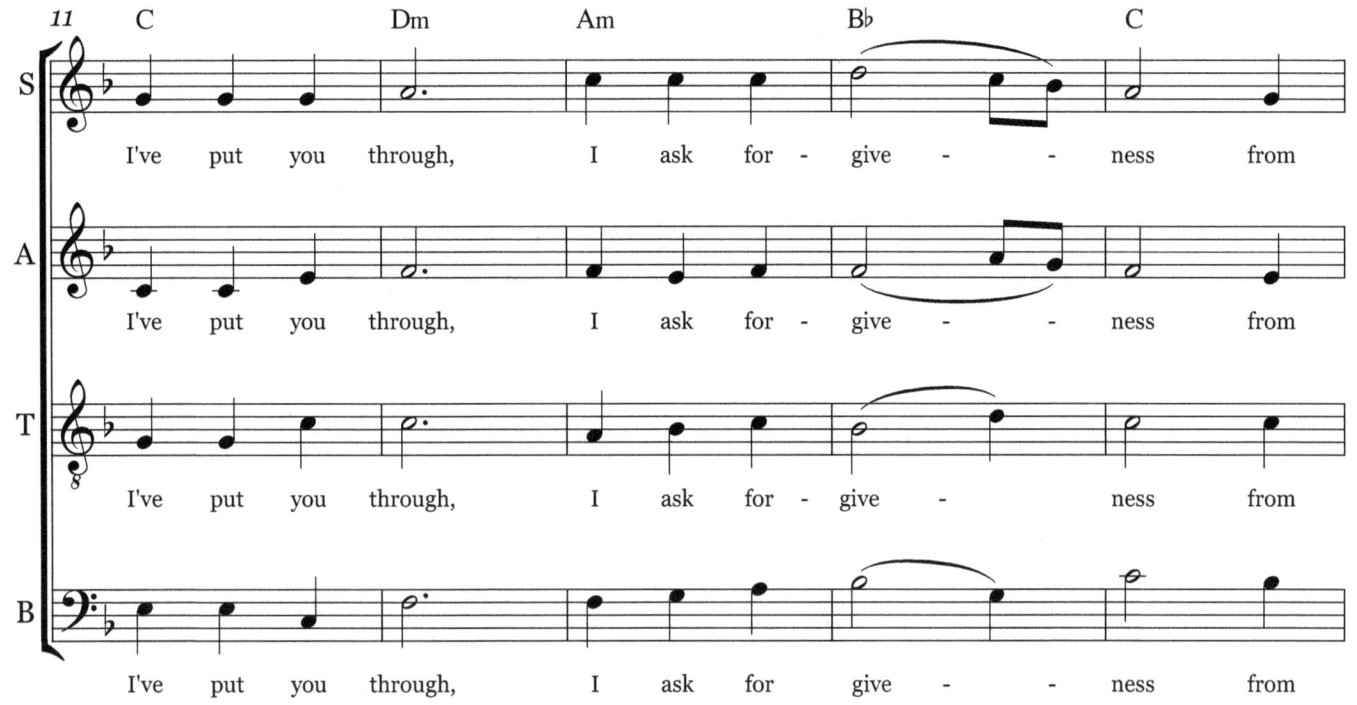

(Note: chord symbols support the soprano melody, not necessarily the SATB harmony)

31. Go Further Farther

(From the Secular Hymnal)

Words: Secretary Michael

Music: "Dundee" from the Scottish Psalter, 1615
Harmonized by Thomas Ravenscroft (1592-1635)
(traditional hymn: "O God of Bethel By Whose Hand")

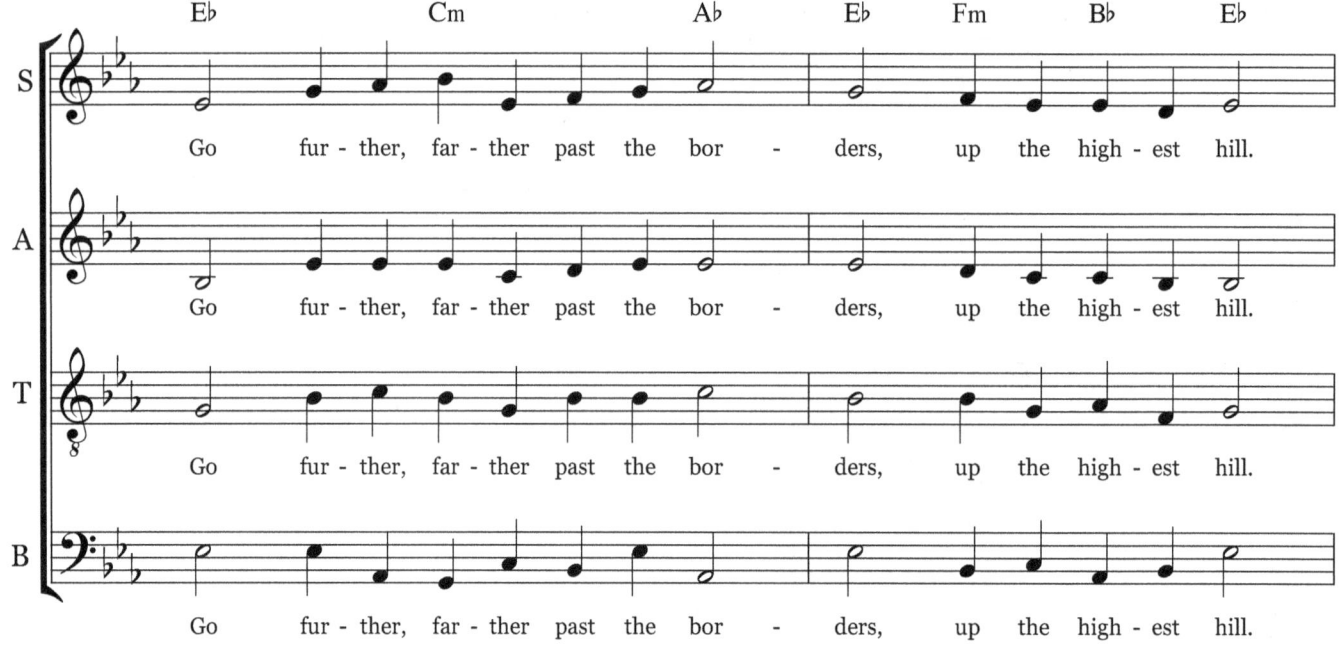

All works by Secretary Michael have been placed in the Public Domain. They may be freely copied and performed.

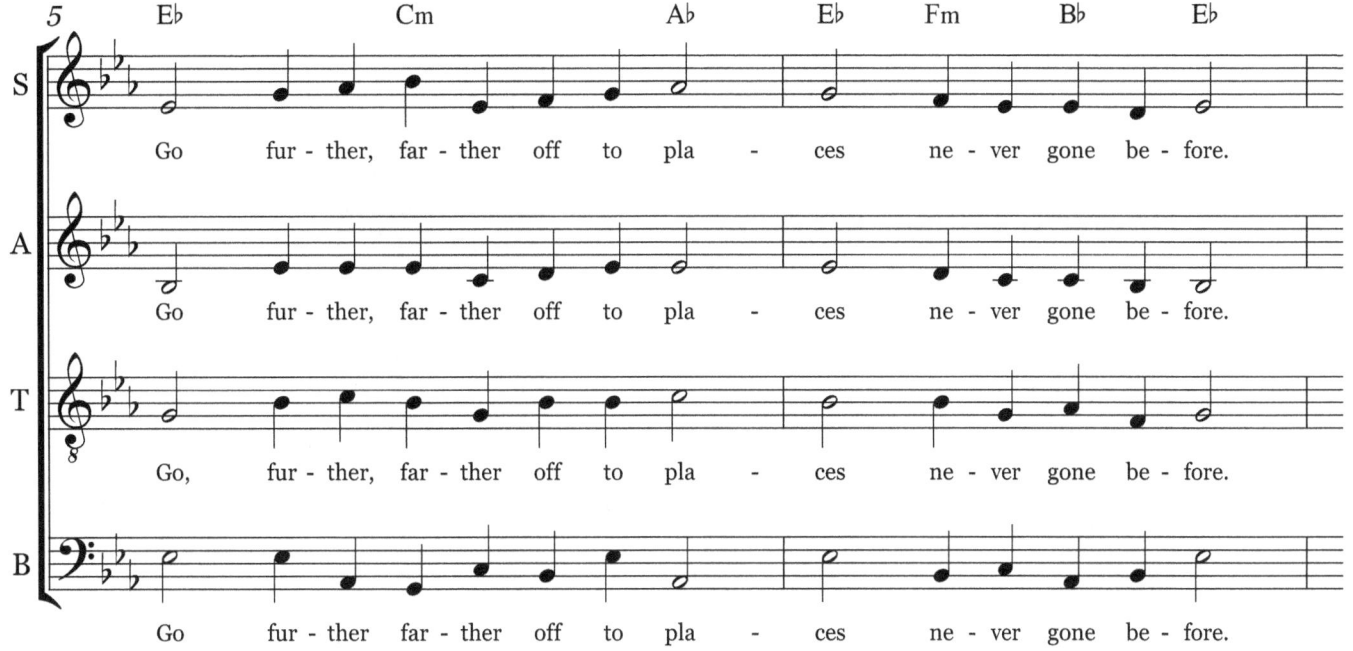

(Note: chord symbols support the soprano melody, not necessarily the SATB harmony)

32. Going Up, Going Up

(From the Secular Hymnal)

Words: Secretary Michael

Music: "McDaniel" by Charles Hutchinson Gabriel, 1914
(traditional hymn: "Since Jesus Came Into My Heart")

All works by Secretary Michael have been placed in the Public Domain. They may be freely copied and performed.

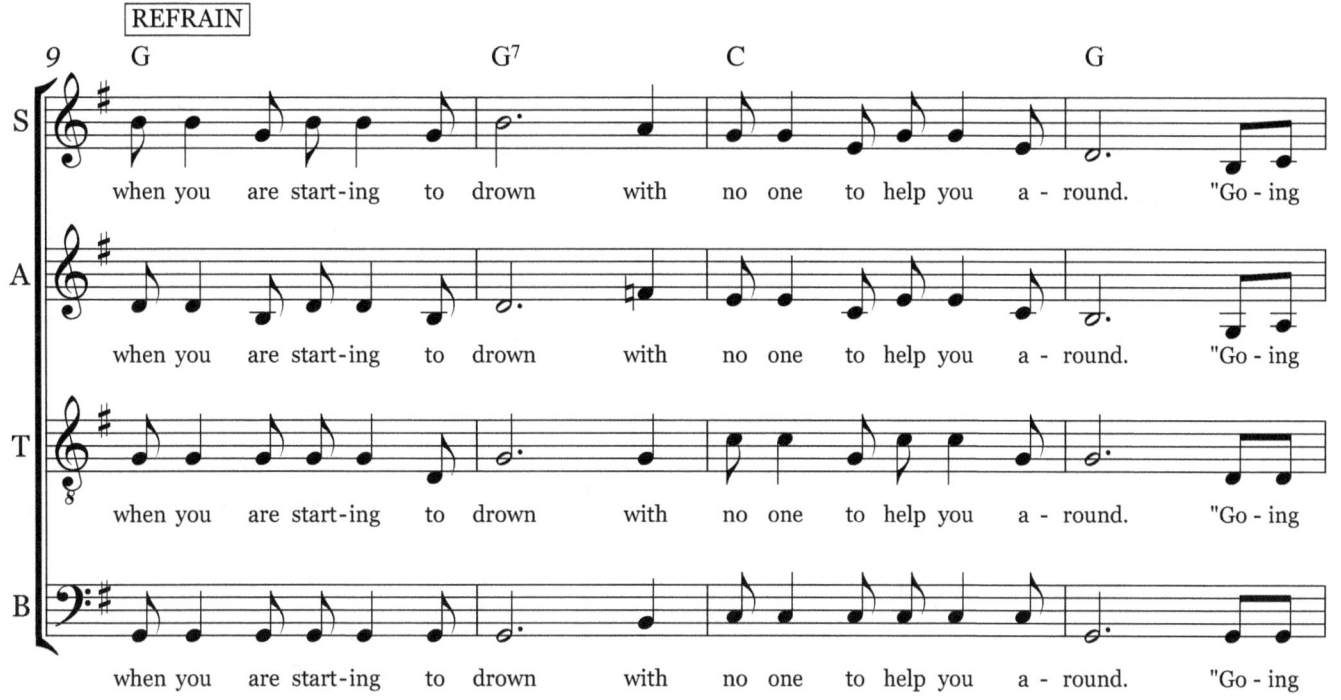
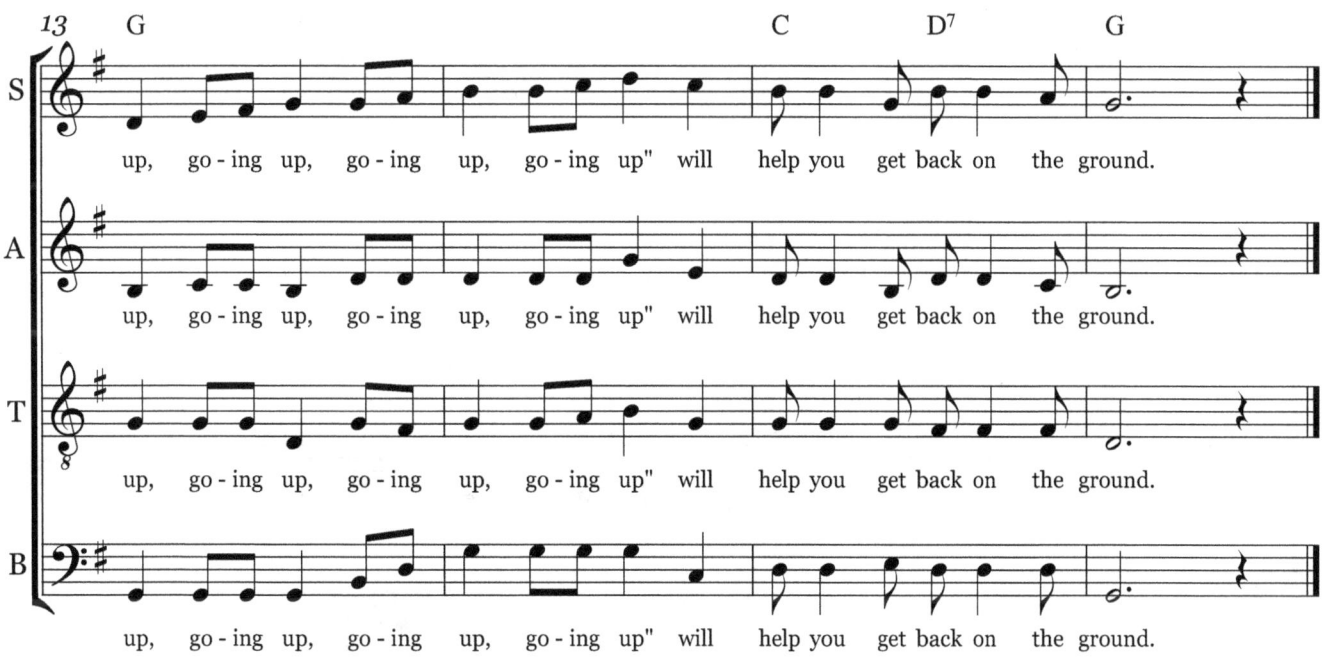

(Note: chord symbols support the soprano melody, not necessarily the SATB harmony)

33. Grief Has Got To Take Its Time

(From the Secular Hymnal)

Words: Secretary Michael

Music: "Toplady" by Thomas Hastings, 1830
(traditional hymn: "Rock of Ages")

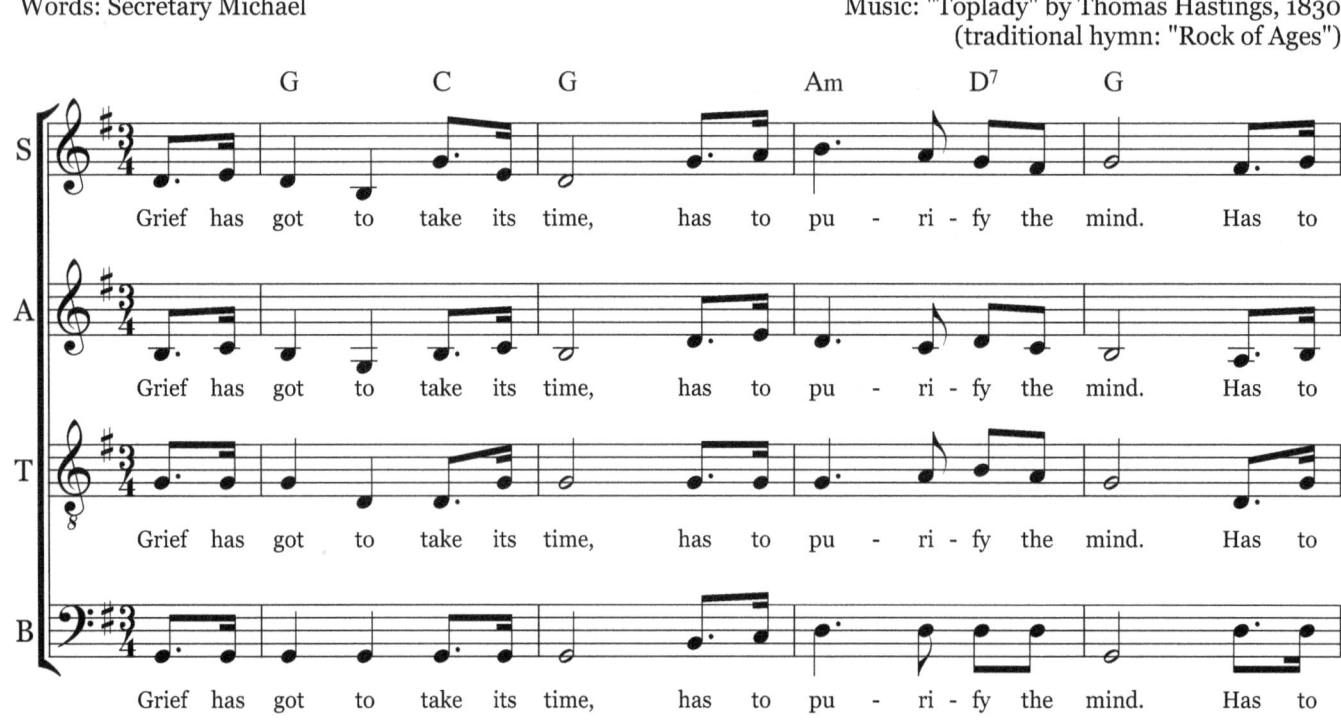

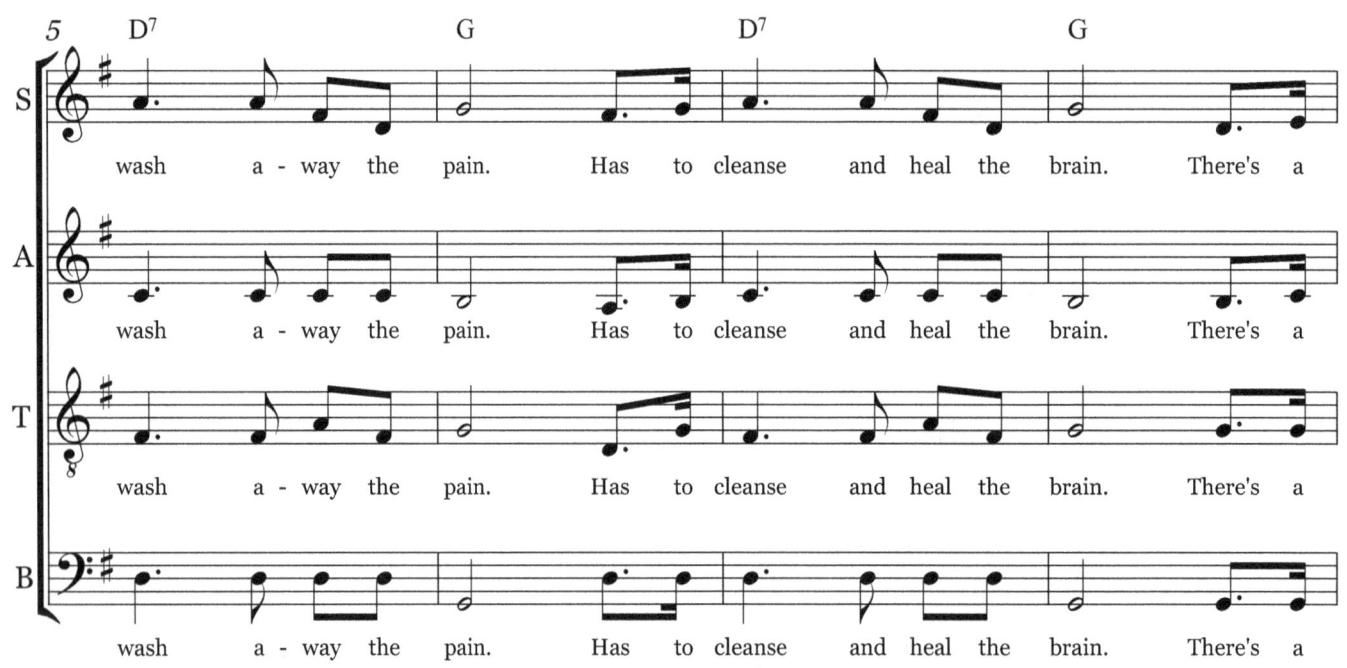

All works by Secretary Michael have been placed in the Public Domain. They may be freely copied and performed.

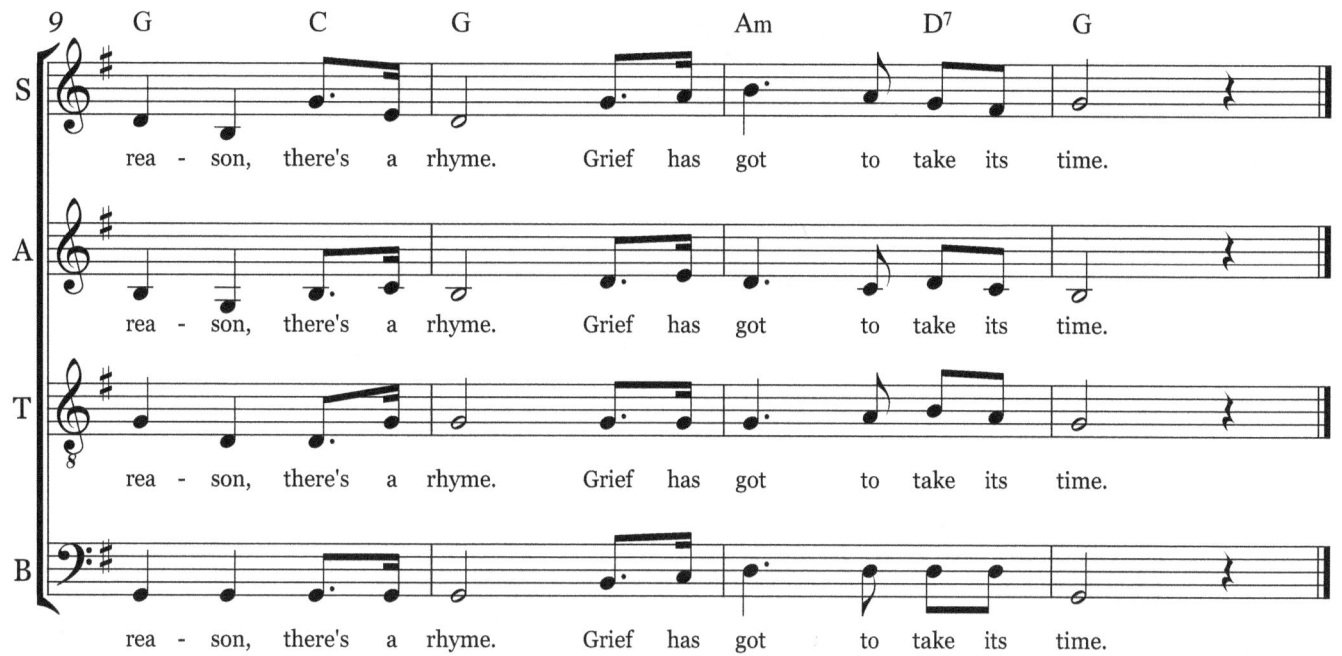

(Note: chord symbols support the soprano melody, not necessarily the SATB harmony)

34. Happy Be
(From the Secular Hymnal)

Words: Secretary Michael

Music: "Trust in Jesus" by William James Kirkpatrick, 1882
(traditional hymn: "Tis So Sweet To Trust In Jesus")

All works by Secretary Michael have been placed in the Public Domain. They may be freely copied and performed.

(Note: chord symbols support the soprano melody, not necessarily the SATB harmony)

35. Harvesting Hunger
(From the Secular Hymnal)

Words: Secretary Michael

Music: "Arizona" by Robert Henry Earnshaw (1856-1929)
(traditional hymn: "Lord Of All Being")

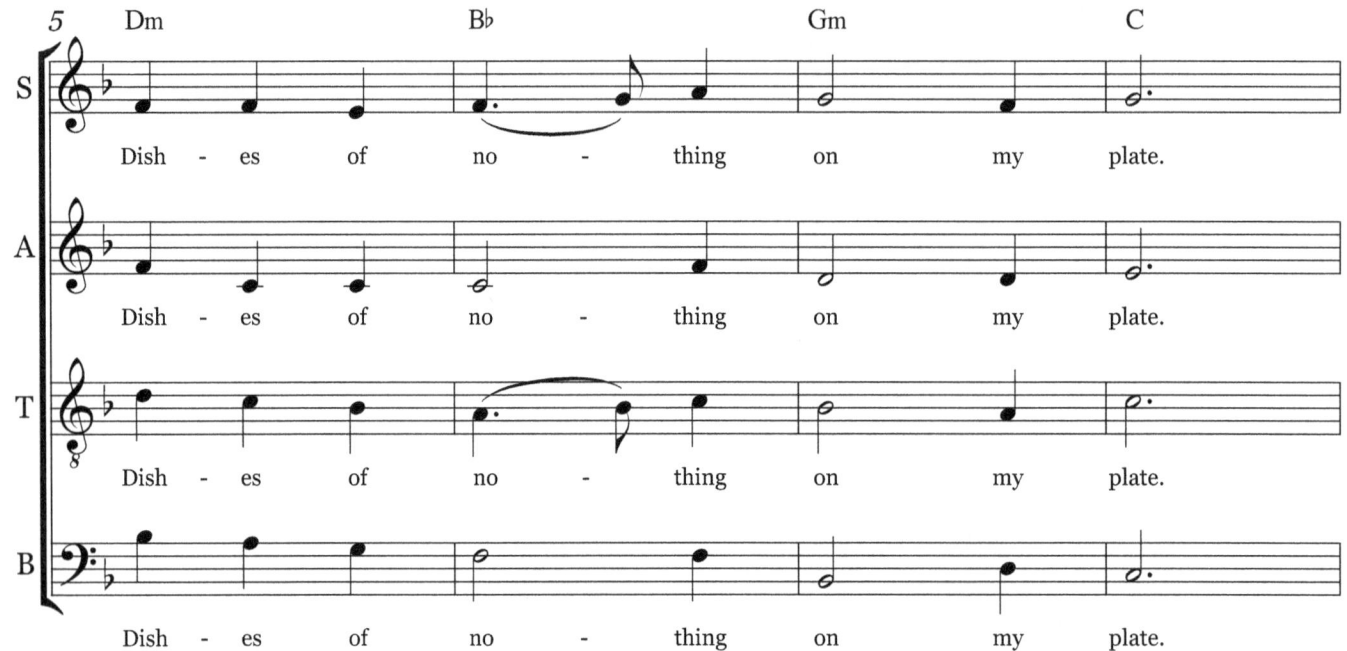

All works by Secretary Michael have been placed in the Public Domain. They may be freely copied and performed.

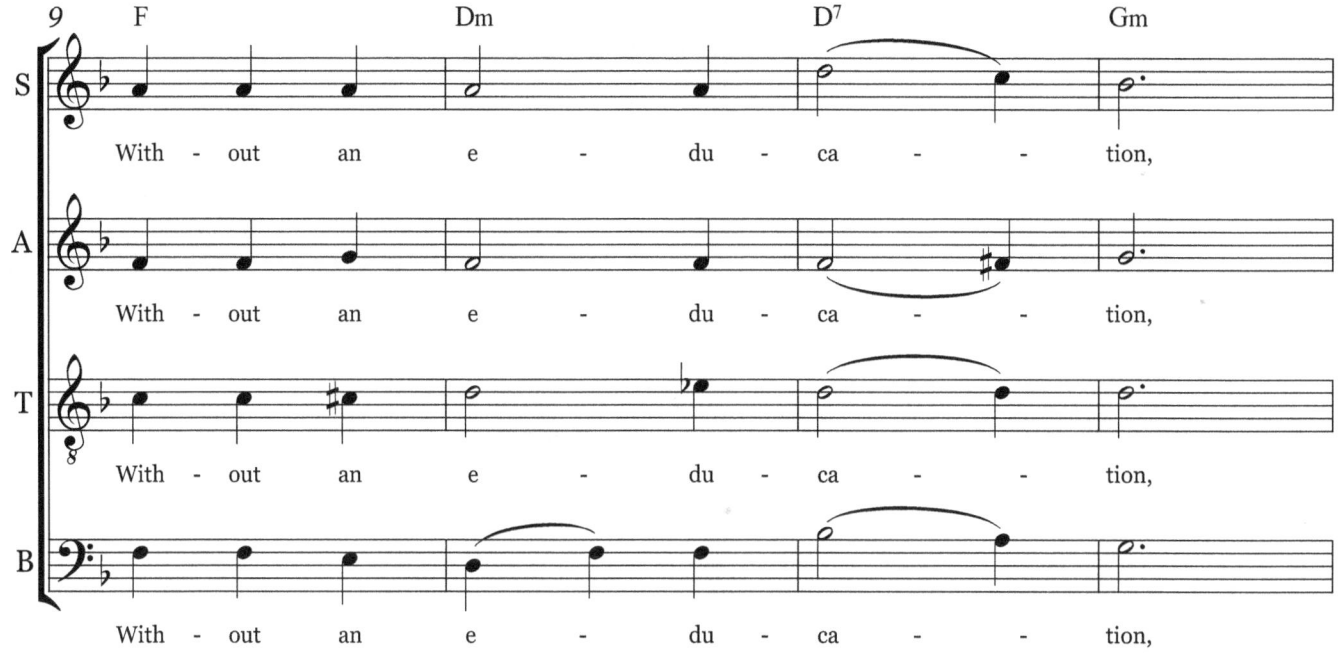

(Note: chord symbols support the soprano melody, not necessarily the SATB harmony)

36. I am a Terrorist
(From the Secular Hymnal)

Words: Secretary Michael

Music: "Trentham" by Robert Jackson, 1888
(traditional hymn: "Breathe On Me")

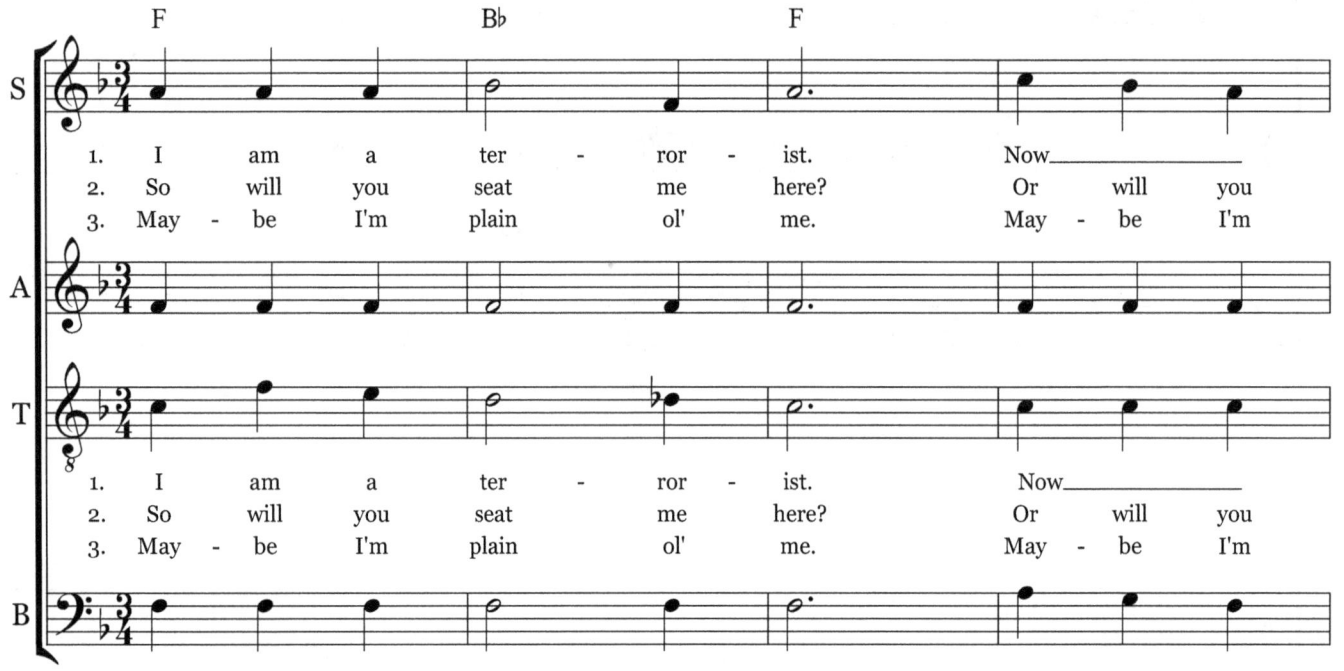

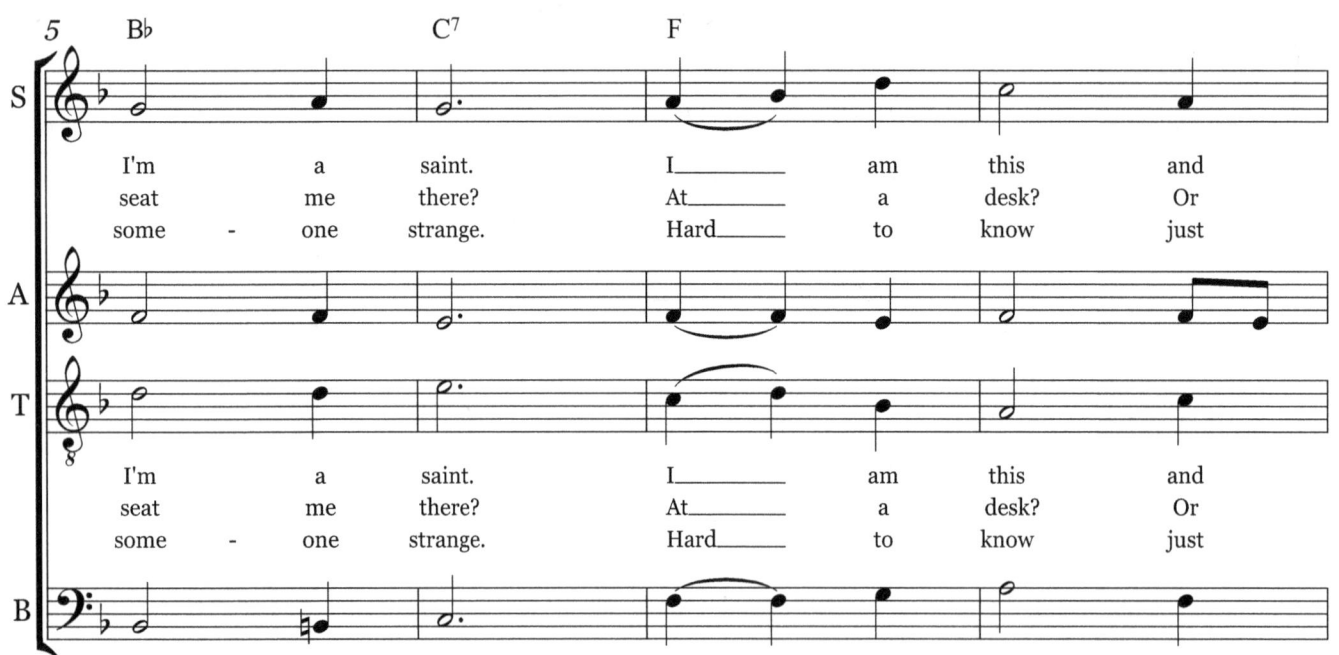

All works by Secretary Michael have been placed in the Public Domain. They may be freely copied and performed.

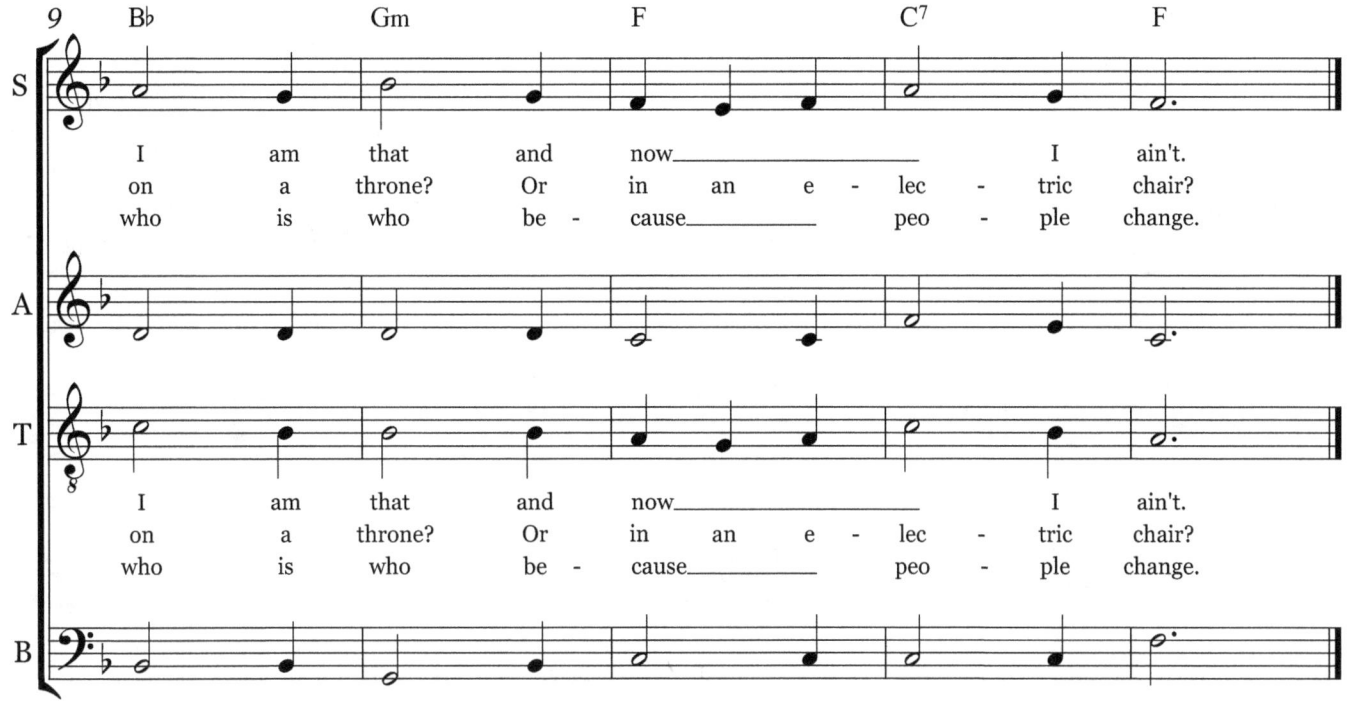

(Note: chord symbols support the soprano melody, not necessarily the SATB harmony)

37. I am the Captain of My Boat
(From the Secular Hymnal)

Words: Secretary Michael

Melody by George Coles, 1883
SATB Arrangement: Secretary Michael
(traditional hymn: "A Poor Wayfaring Man of Grief")

1. I am the captain of my boat on a calm, a calm and peaceful sea. I am the captain of my boat on a calm, a calm and peaceful sea. With stormy seas with wind and hail the boats get smashed and captains jailed. There are

2. There are equal captains, equal boats that never sail and never float. On stormy seas with wind and hail the boats get smashed and captains jailed. There are

All works by Secretary Michael have been placed in the Public Domain. They may be freely copied and performed.

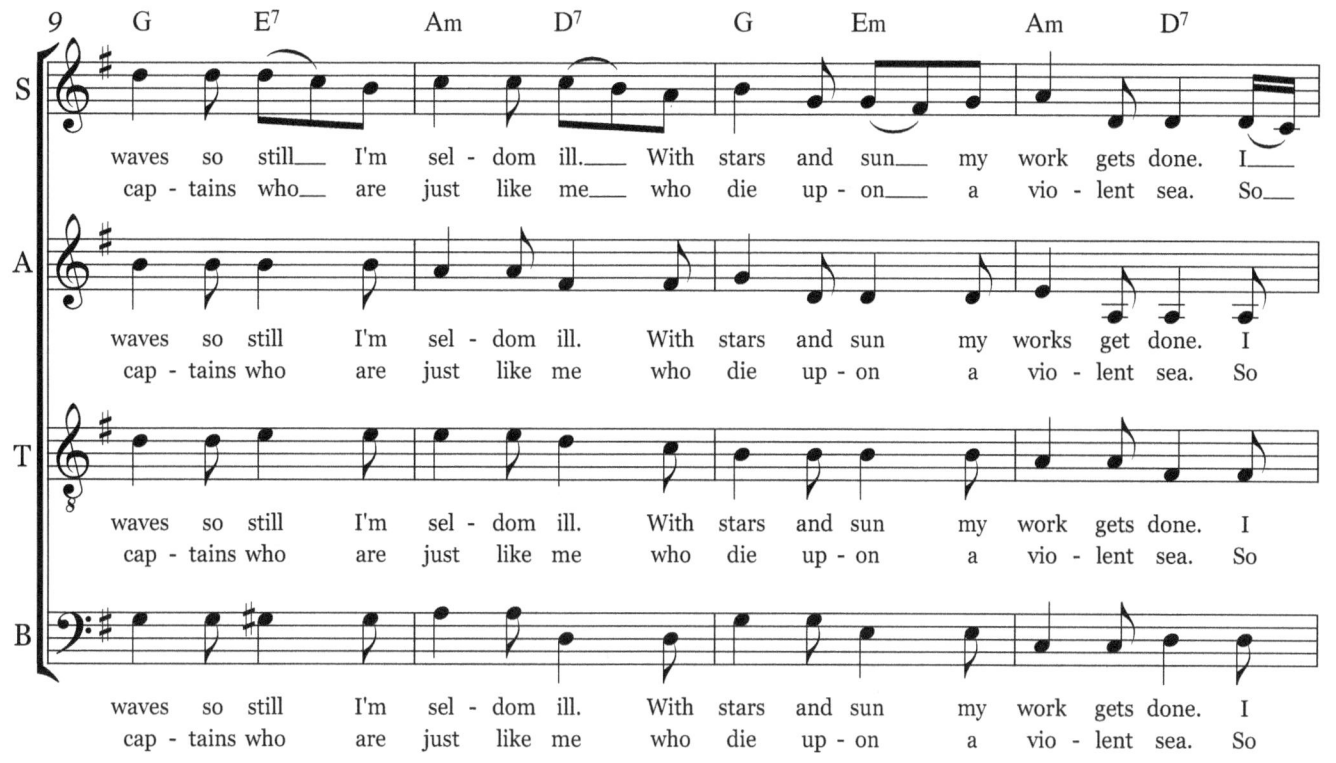
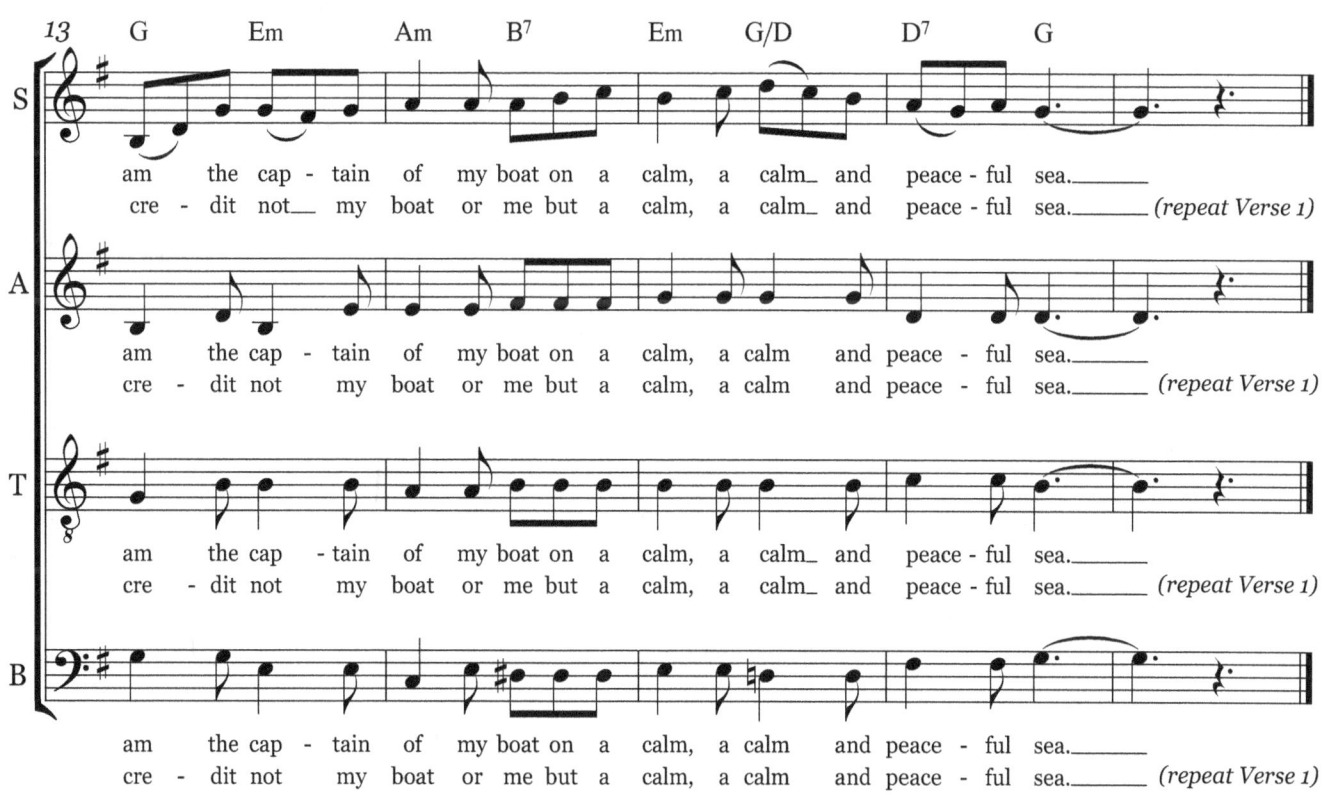

(Note: chord symbols support the soprano melody, not necessarily the SATB harmony)

38. I Declare A Brand-New Me

(From the Secular Hymnal)

Words: Secretary Michael

Music: "Cymraeg" by Robert Lowry, 1876
(traditional hymn: "Here Is Love Vast As the Ocean")

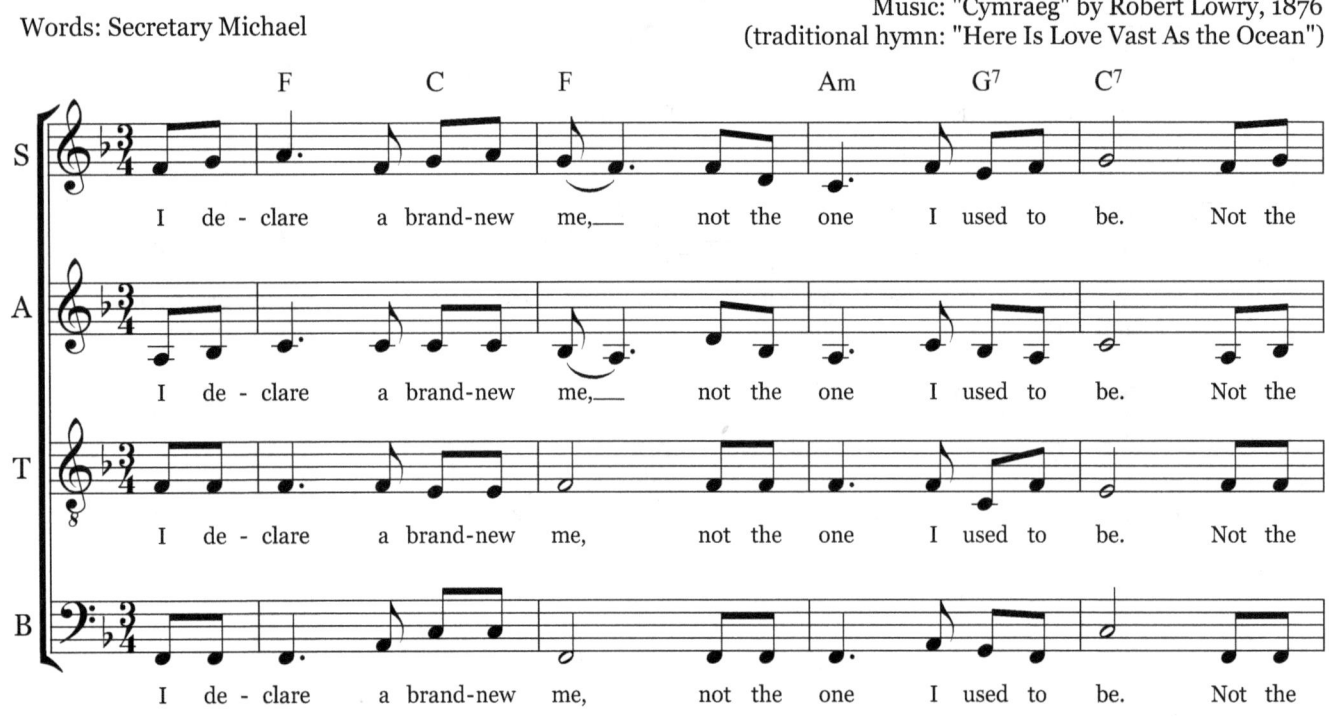
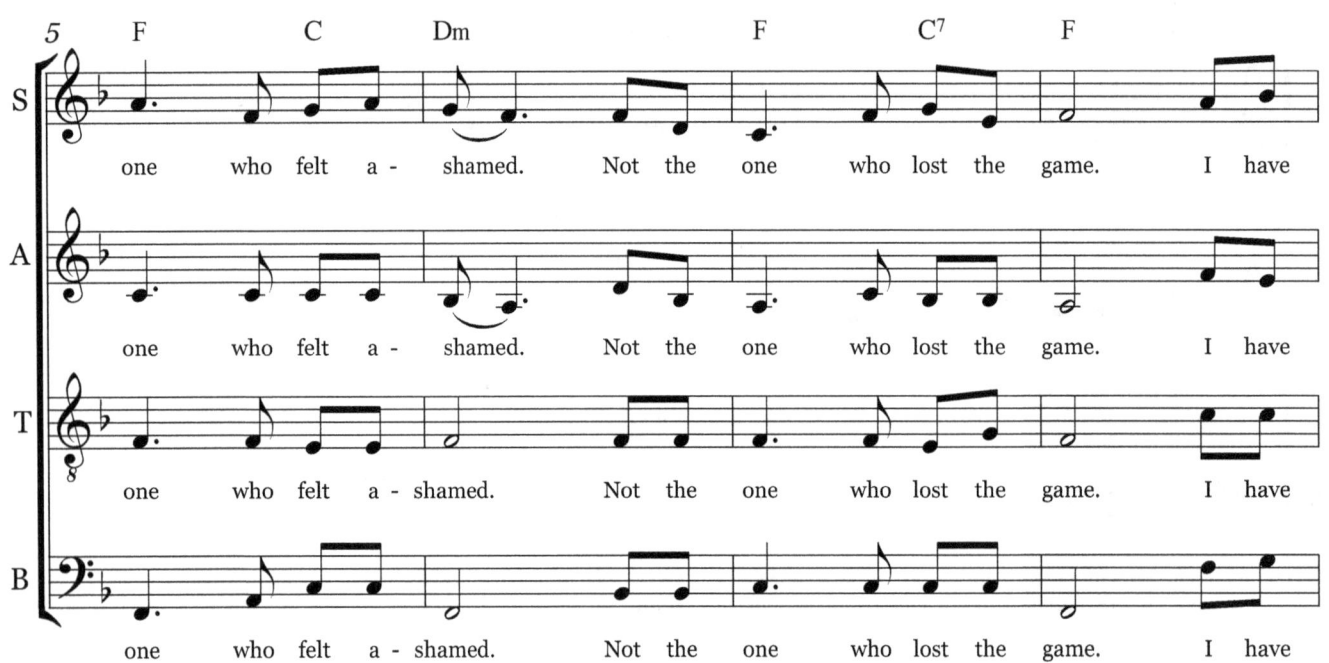

All works by Secretary Michael have been placed in the Public Domain. They may be freely copied and performed.

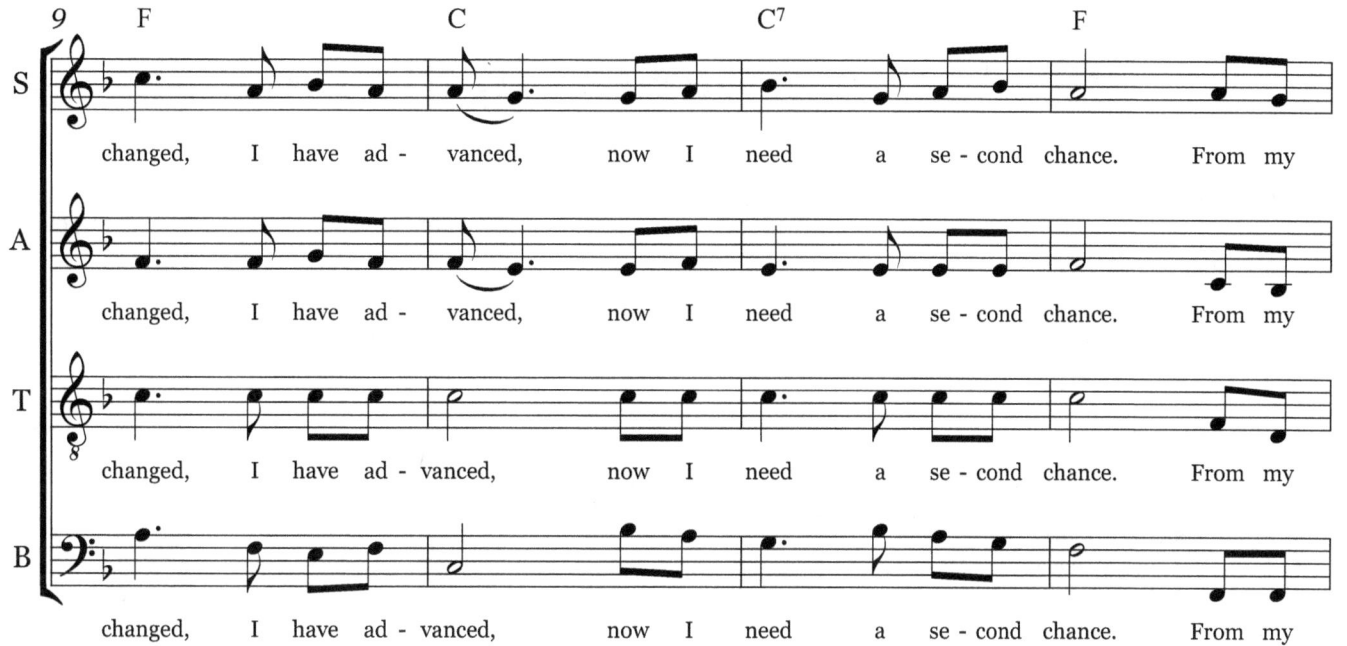
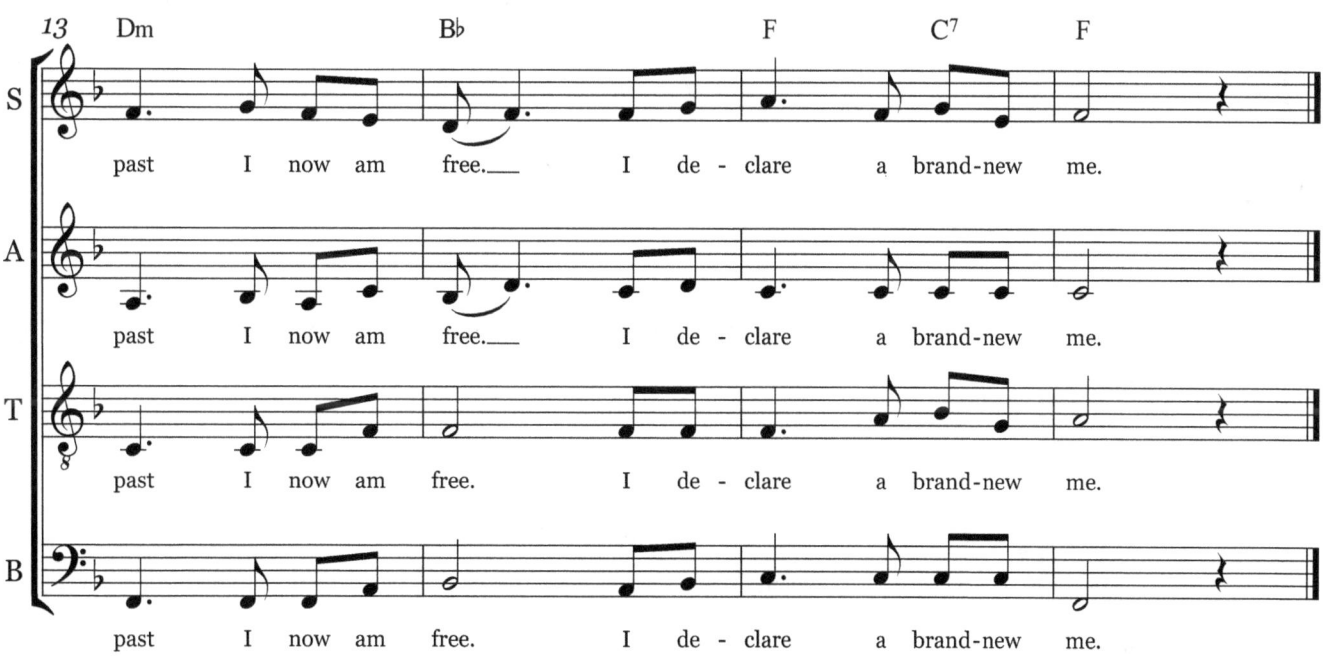

(Note: chord symbols support the soprano melody, not necessarily the SATB harmony)

39. I Have a Garden in the Park
(From the Secular Hymnal)

Words: Secretary Michael

Music: "Solid Rock" by William Batchelder Bradbury, 1863
(traditional hymn: "My Hope Is Built On Nothing Less")

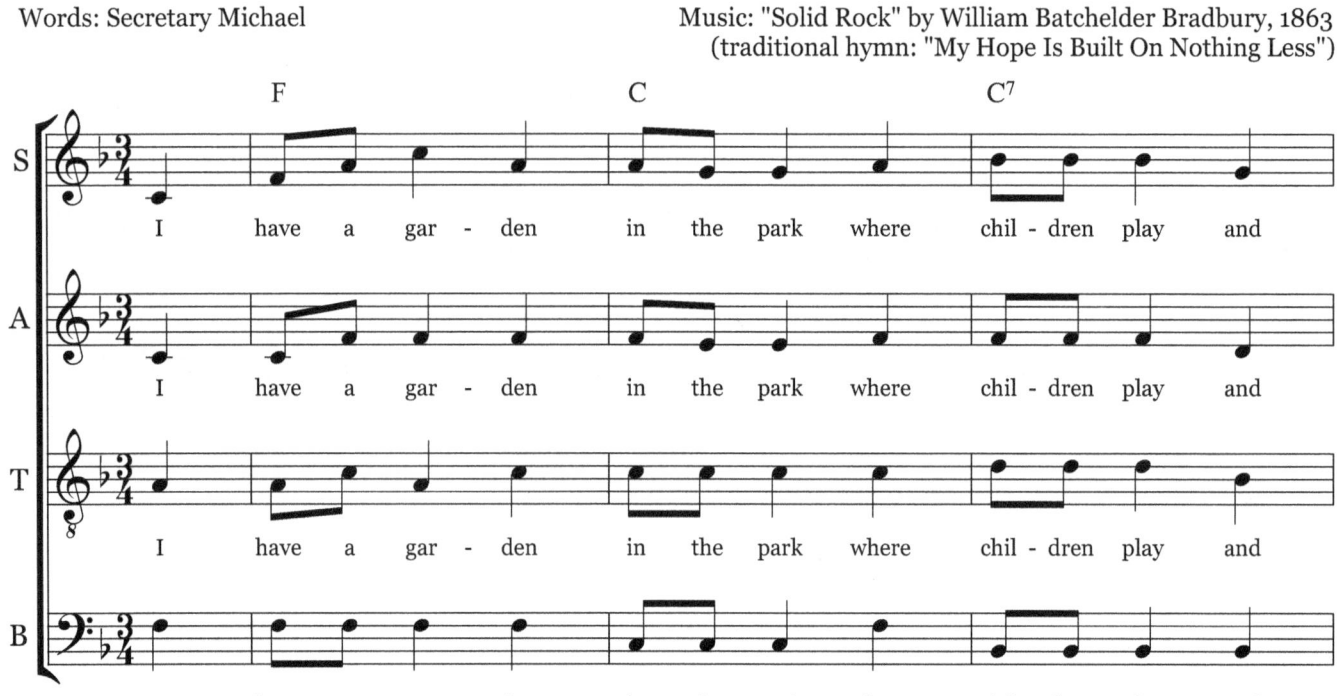

All works by Secretary Michael have been placed in the Public Domain. They may be freely copied and performed.

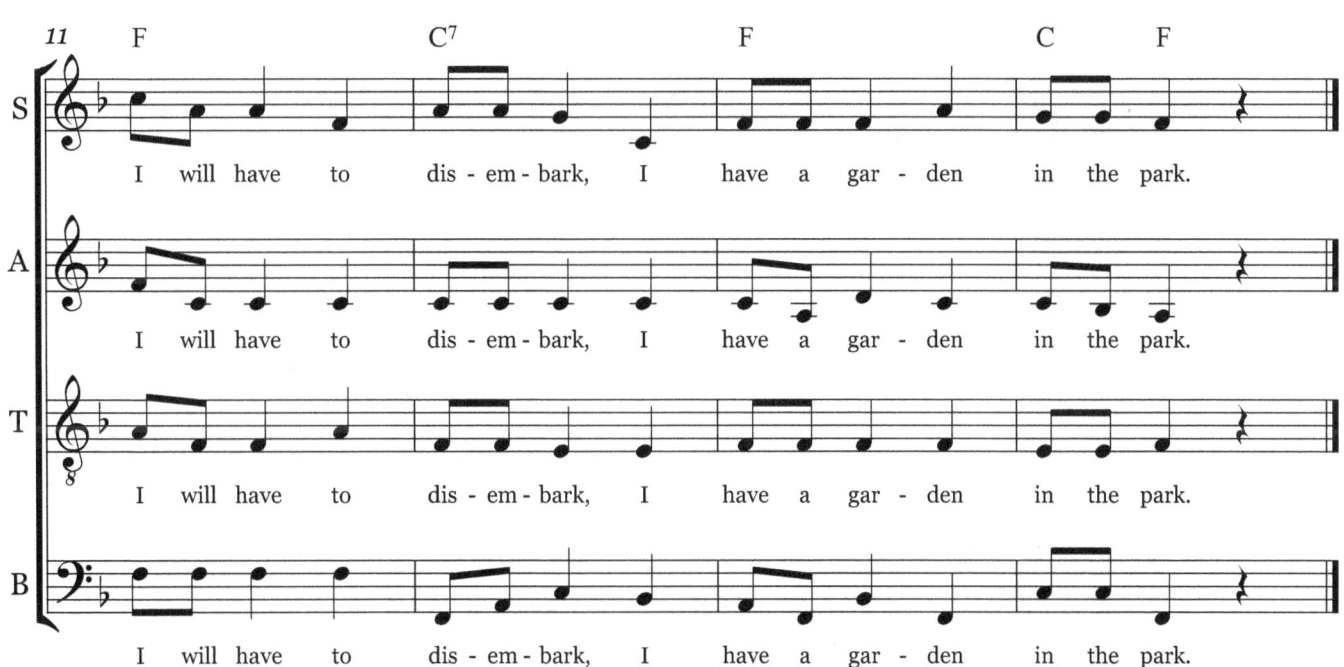

(Note: chord symbols support the soprano melody, not necessarily the SATB harmony)

40. I Have a Puzzle of the World
(From the Secular Hymnal)

Words: Secretary Michael

Music: "St. Peter" by Alexander Robert Reinagle, 1836
(traditional hymn: "How Sweet the Name of Jesus Sounds")

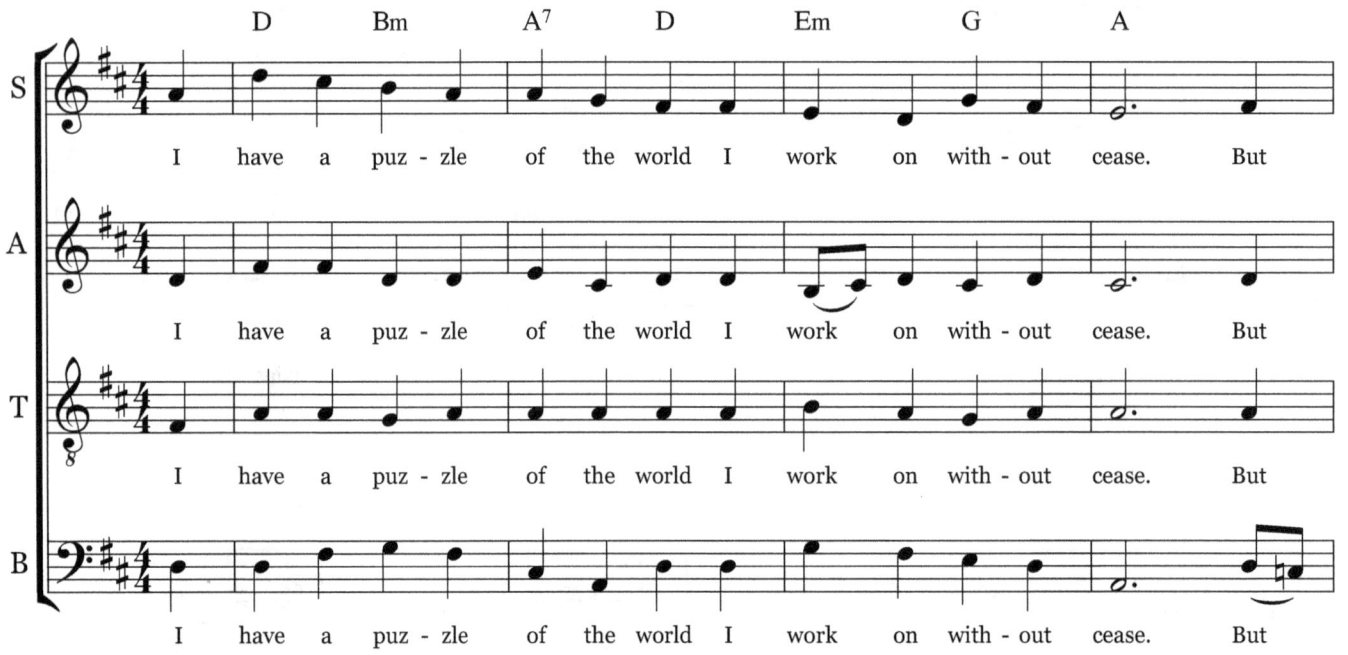

All works by Secretary Michael have been placed in the Public Domain. They may be freely copied and performed.

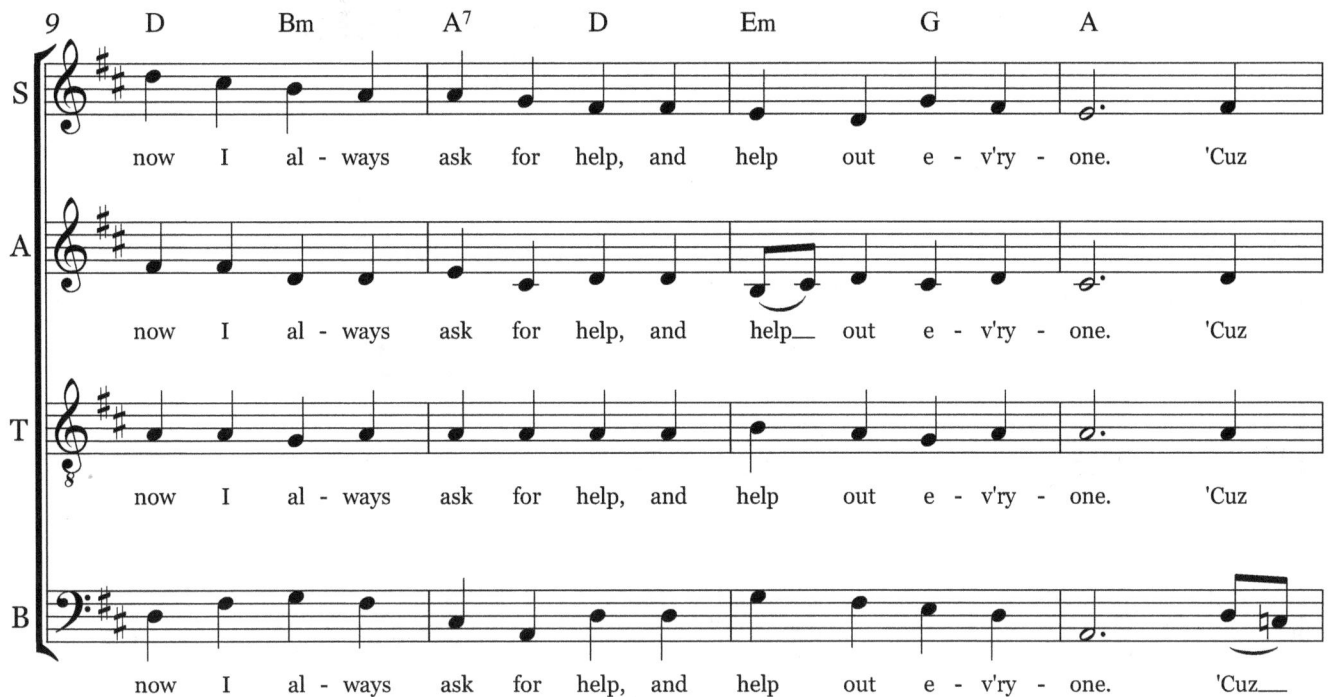
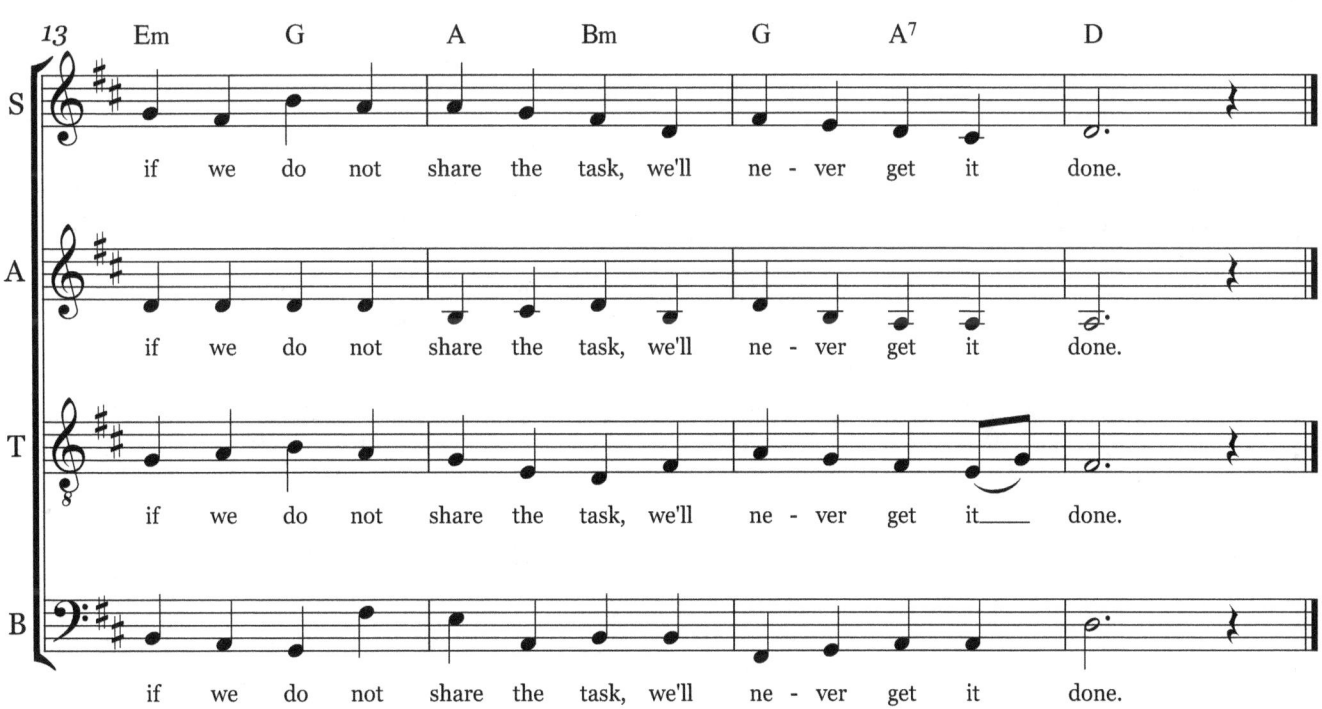

(Note: chord symbols support the soprano melody, not necessarily the SATB harmony)

41. I Once Was So Certain
(From the Secular Hymnal)

Words: Secretary Michael

Music: "Lourdes Hymn"
(traditional hymn: "Immaculate Mary")

1. I once was so certain, so righteous, so strong. But now I can see that I had it all wrong. All
2. Today I'm not certain, not righteous, not strong. The world would be better if you came along. A-

All works by Secretary Michael have been placed in the Public Domain. They may be freely copied and performed.

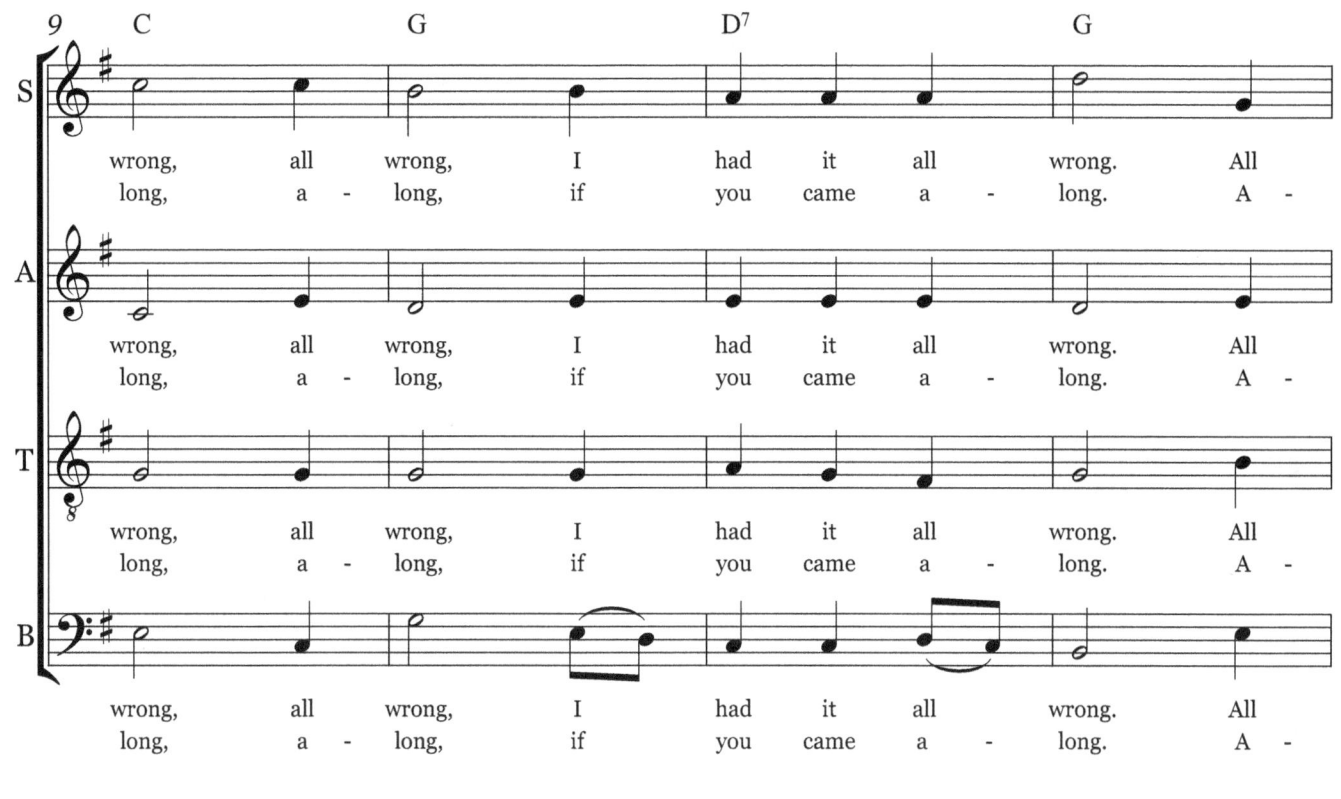

(Note: chord symbols support the soprano melody, not necessarily the SATB harmony)

(Note: chord symbols support the soprano melody, not necessarily the SATB harmony)

(Note: chord symbols support the soprano melody, not necessarily the SATB harmony)

44. I Think I'm Right

(From the Secular Hymnal)

Words: Secretary Michael

Music: George Frederick Root, 1870
(traditional hymn: "Come to the Savior, Make No Delay")

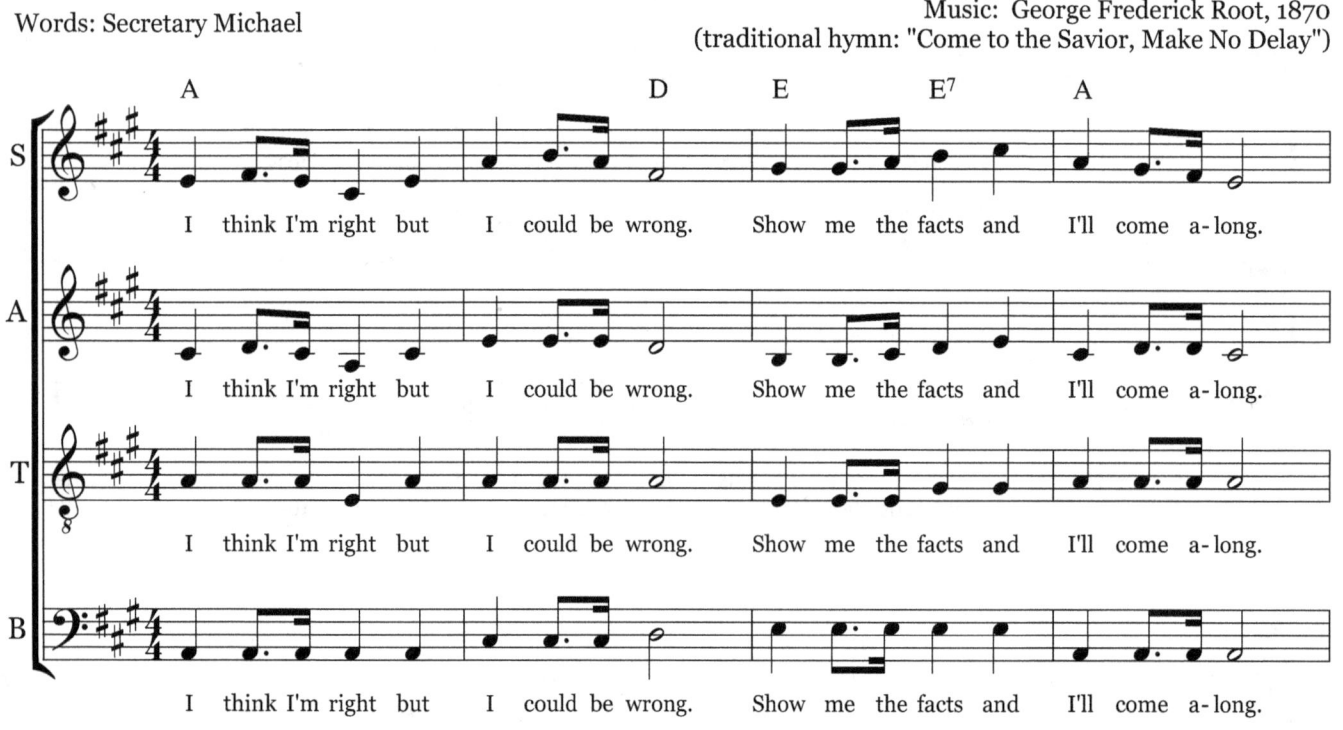

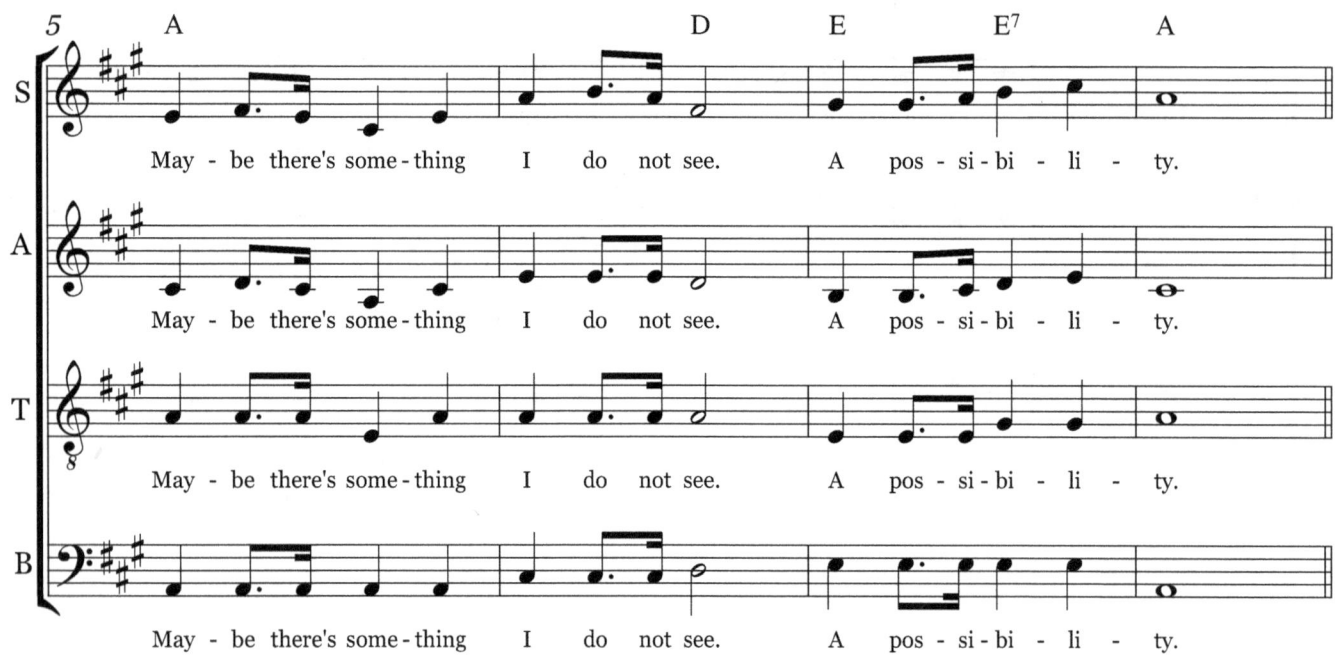

All works by Secretary Michael have been placed in the Public Domain. They may be freely copied and performed.

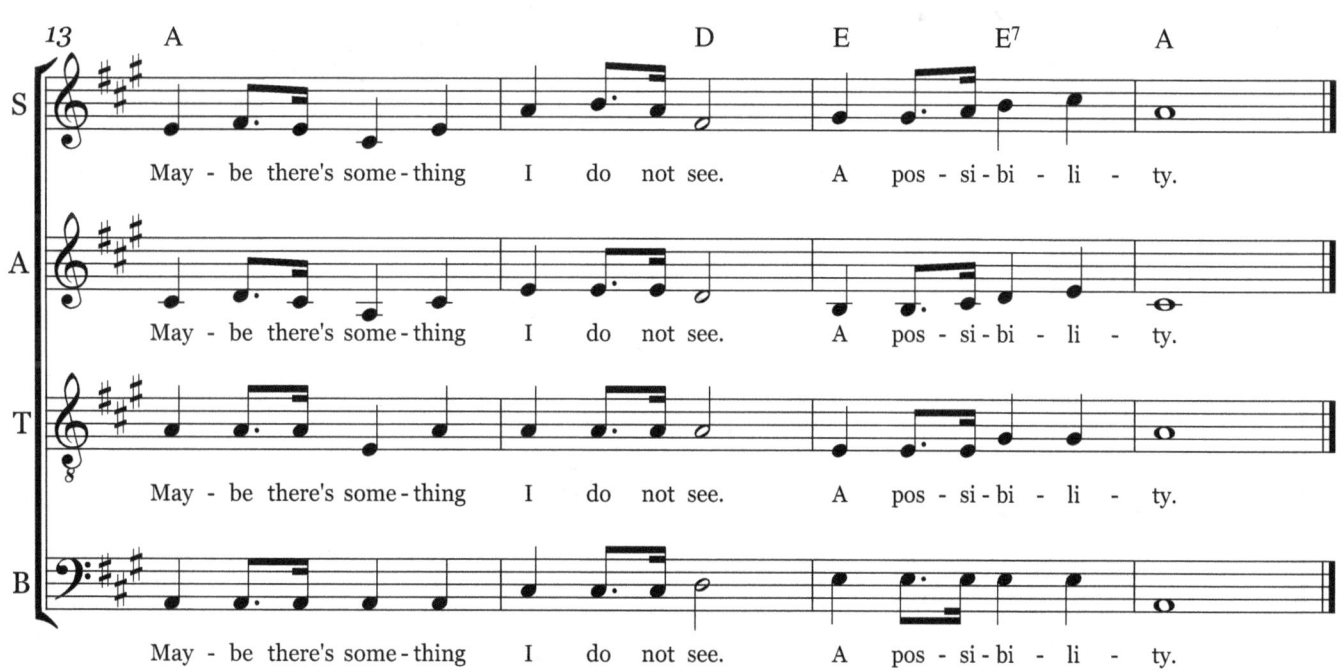

(Note: chord symbols support the soprano melody, not necessarily the SATB harmony)

45. I Will Look and I Will See

(From the Secular Hymnal)

Words: Secretary Michael

Music: "Sagina" by Thomas Campbell, 1825
(traditional hymn: "And Can It Be?")

All works by Secretary Michael have been placed in the Public Domain. They may be freely copied and performed.

(Note: chord symbols support the soprano melody, not necessarily the SATB harmony)

46. If We're Not the Ones

(From the Secular Hymnal)

Words: Secretary Michael

Music: "Hanson Place" by Robert Lowry, 1864
(traditional hymn: "Shall We Gather at the River")

All works by Secretary Michael have been placed in the Public Domain. They may be freely copied and performed.

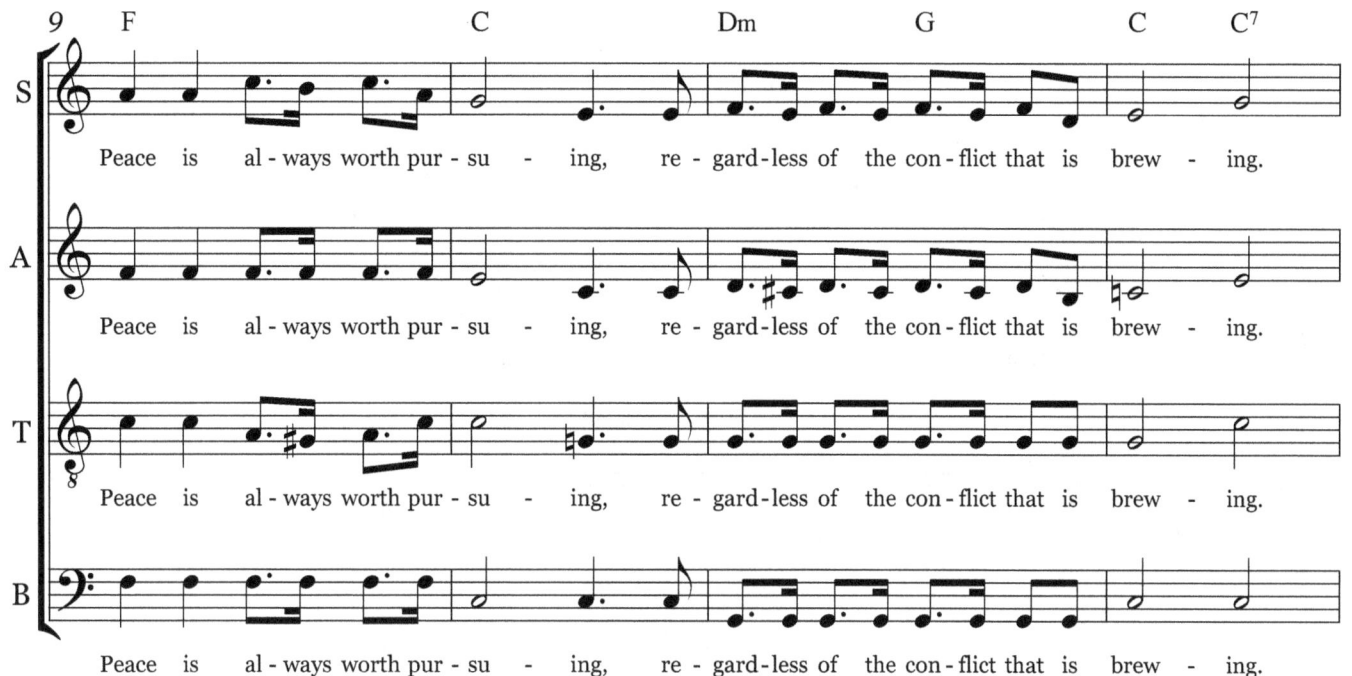

(Note: chord symbols support the soprano melody, not necessarily the SATB harmony)

(Note: chord symbols support the soprano melody, not necessarily the SATB harmony)

(Note: chord symbols support the soprano melody, not necessarily the SATB harmony)

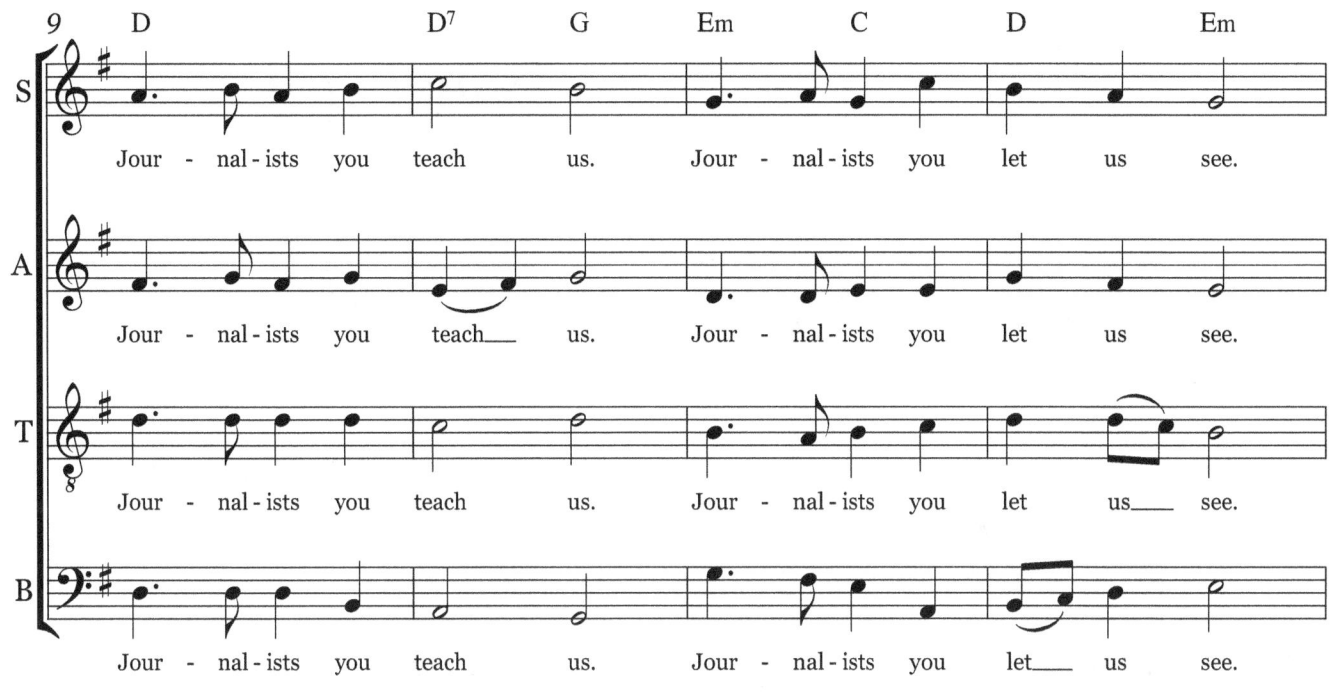
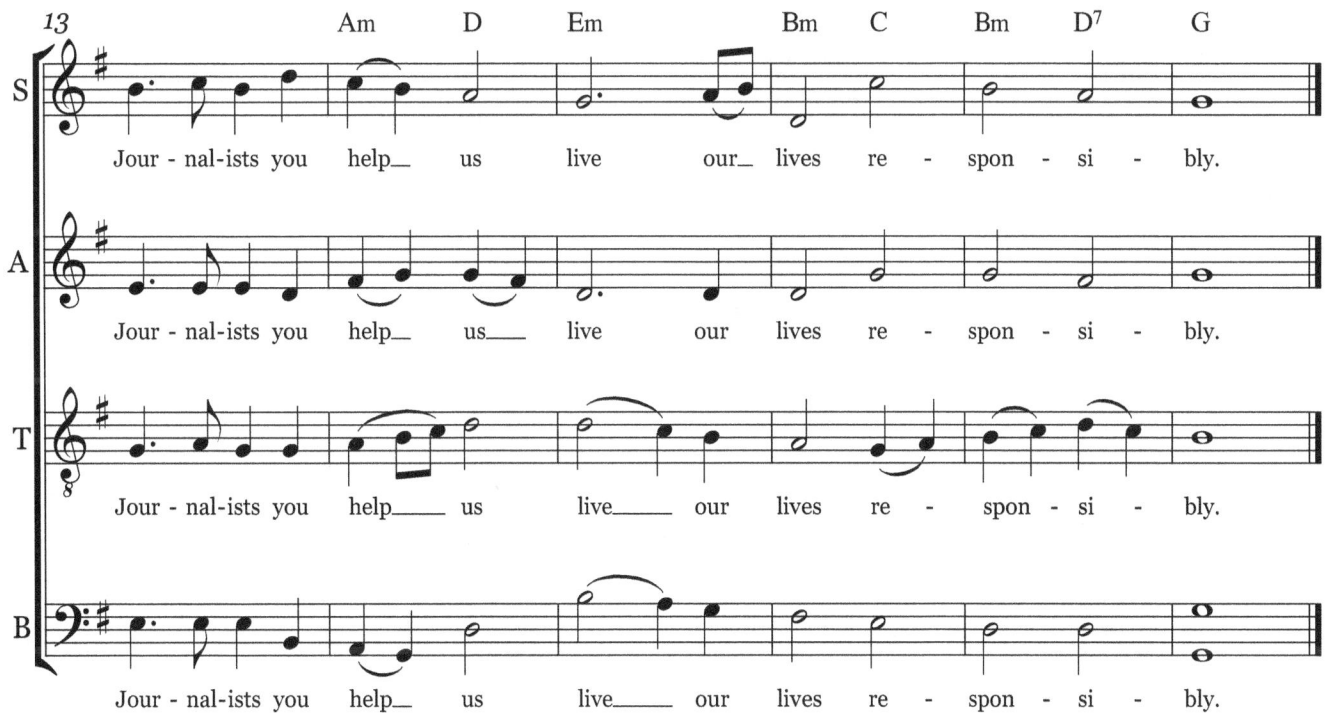

(Note: chord symbols support the soprano melody, not necessarily the SATB harmony)

50. Injustice To You Is Injustice To Me

(From the Secular Hymnal)

Words: Secretary Michael

Music: "St. Clement" by Clement Cotterill Scholefield, 1874
(traditional hymn: "The Day Thou Gavest Lord Is Ended")

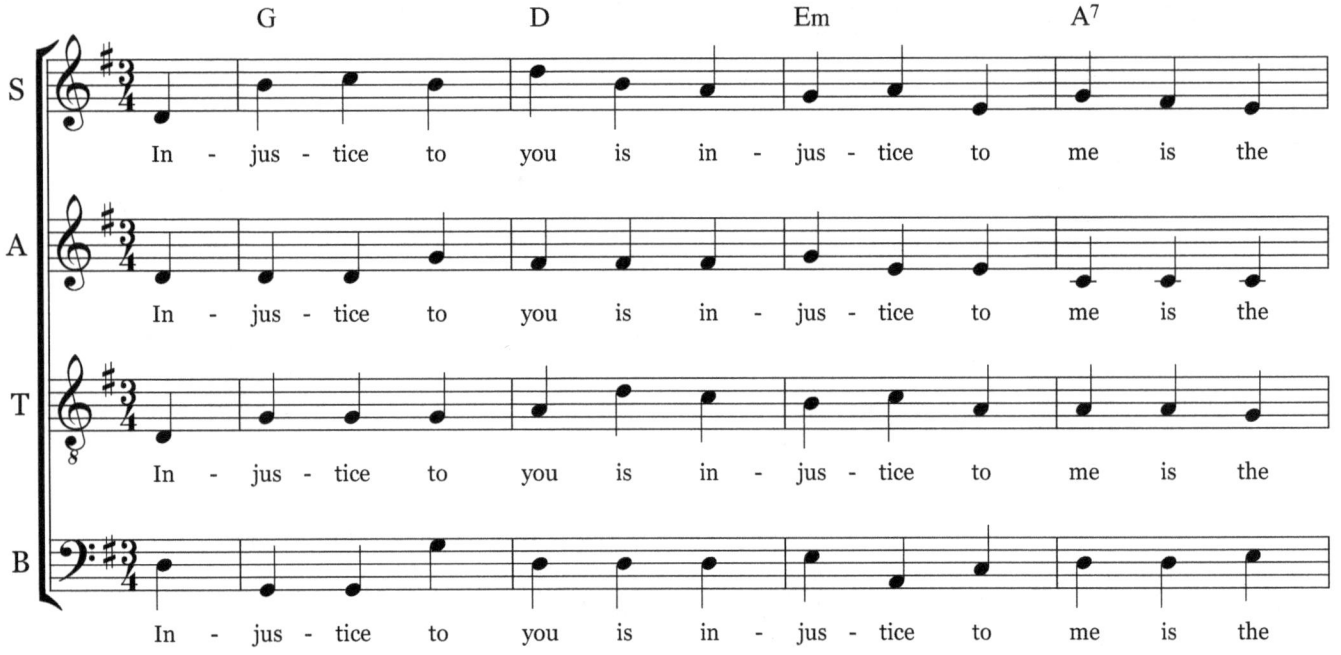

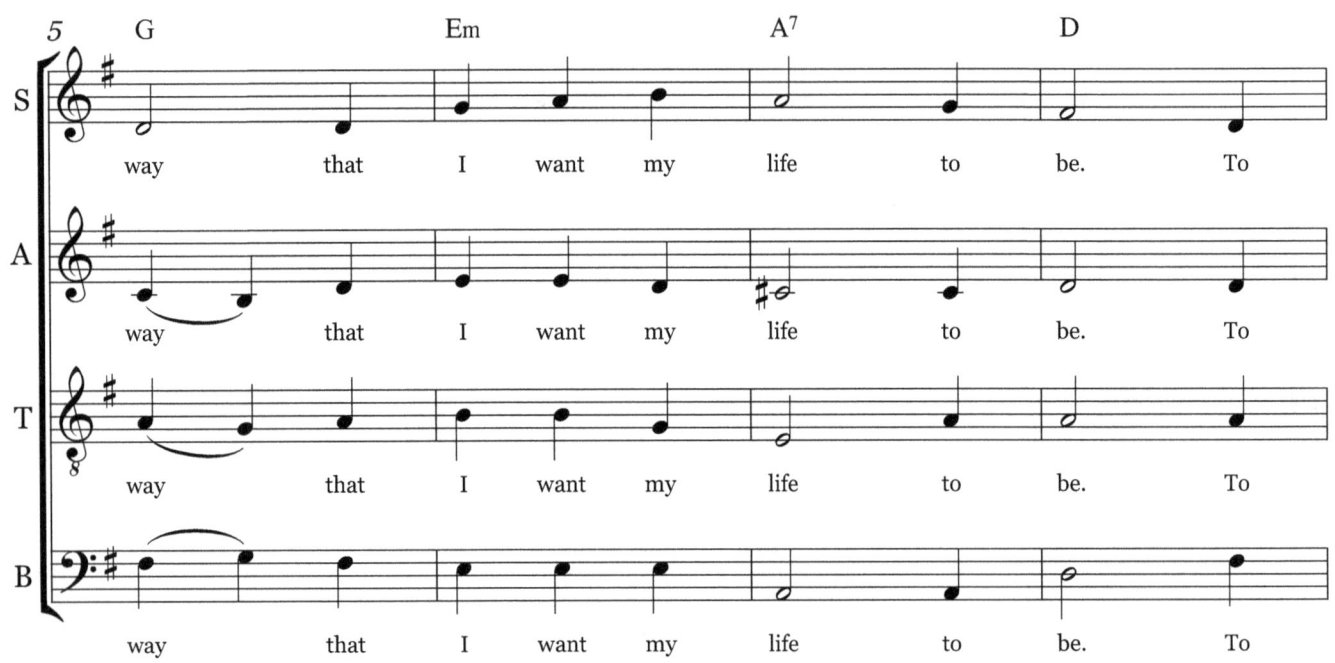

All works by Secretary Michael have been placed in the Public Domain. They may be freely copied and performed.

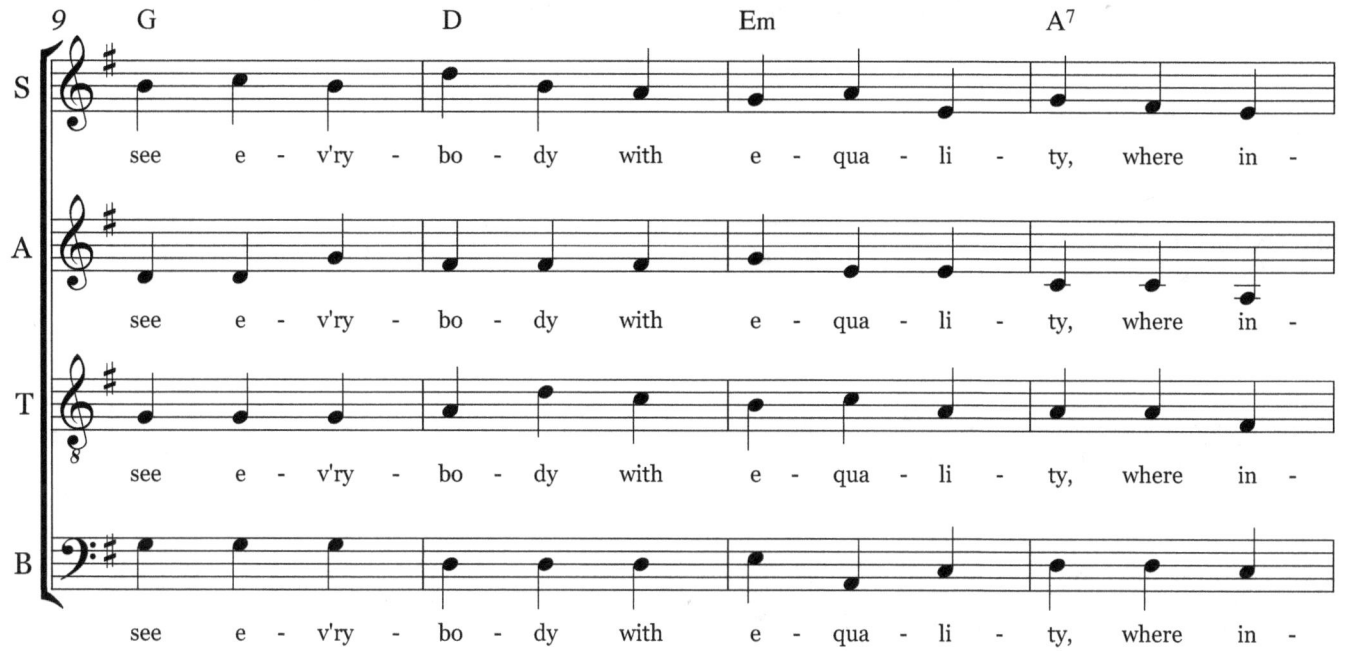

(Note: chord symbols support the soprano melody, not necessarily the SATB harmony)

51. Intelligence is a Bouquet

(From the Secular Hymnal)

Words: Secretary Michael

Music: "St. Margaret" by Albert Lister Peace
(traditional hymn: "O Love That Will Not Let Me Go")

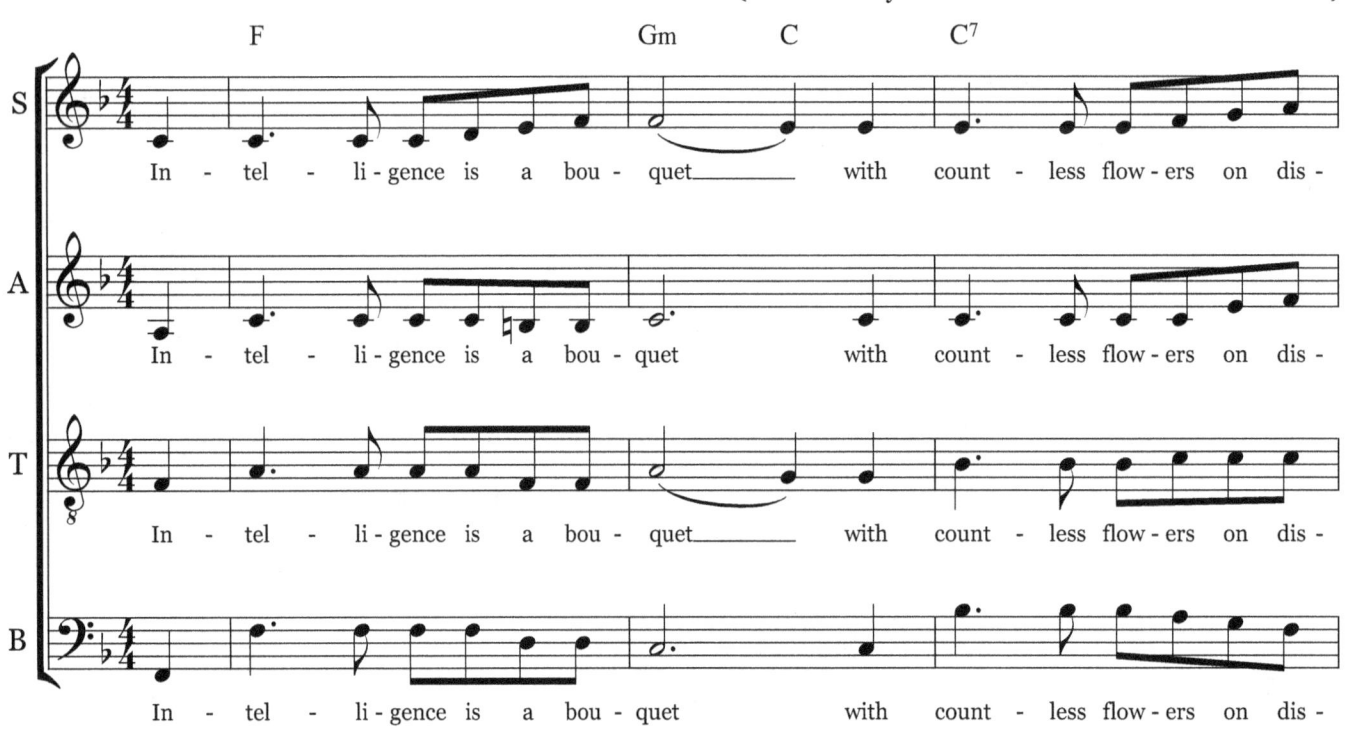

All works by Secretary Michael have been placed in the Public Domain. They may be freely copied and performed.

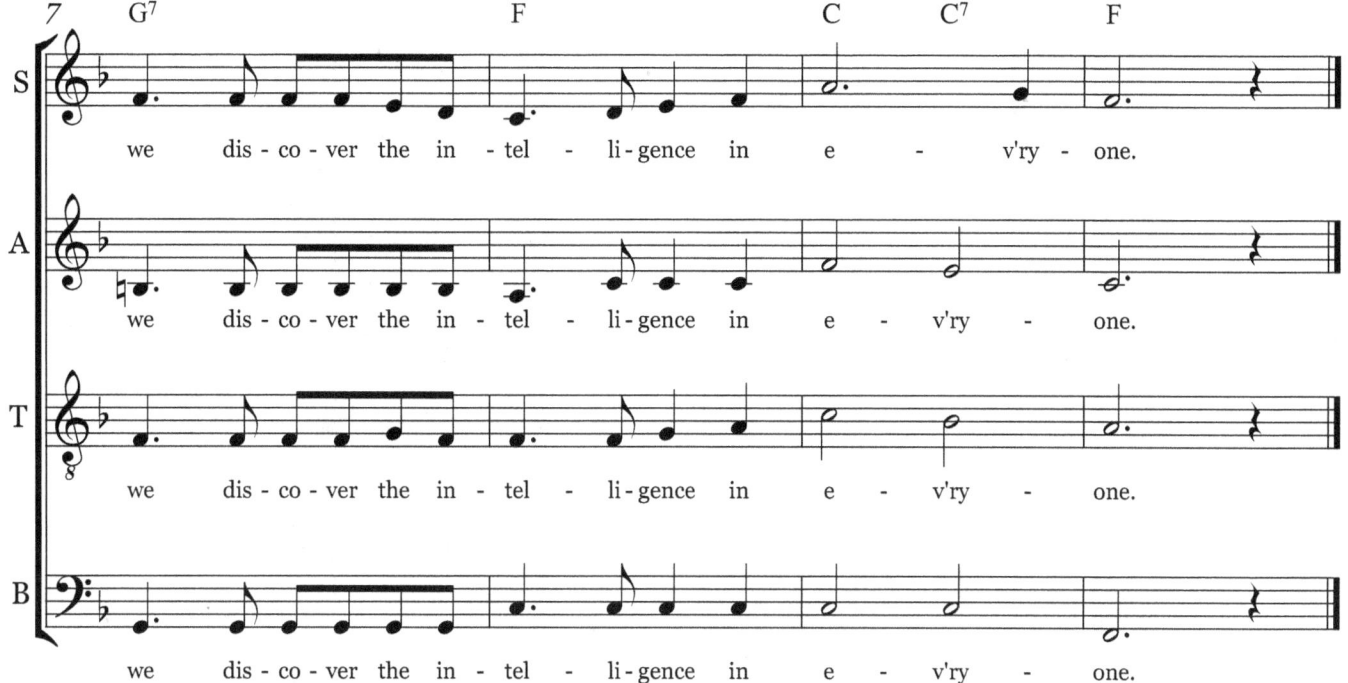

(Note: chord symbols support the soprano melody, not necessarily the SATB harmony)

52. It's Great To Know Some Things By Heart

(From the Secular Hymnal)

Words: Secretary Michael

Tune: "Repton" by Charles Hubert Hastings Parry, 1888
SATB Arrangement: Secretary Michael
(traditional hymn: "Dear Lord and Father of Mankind")

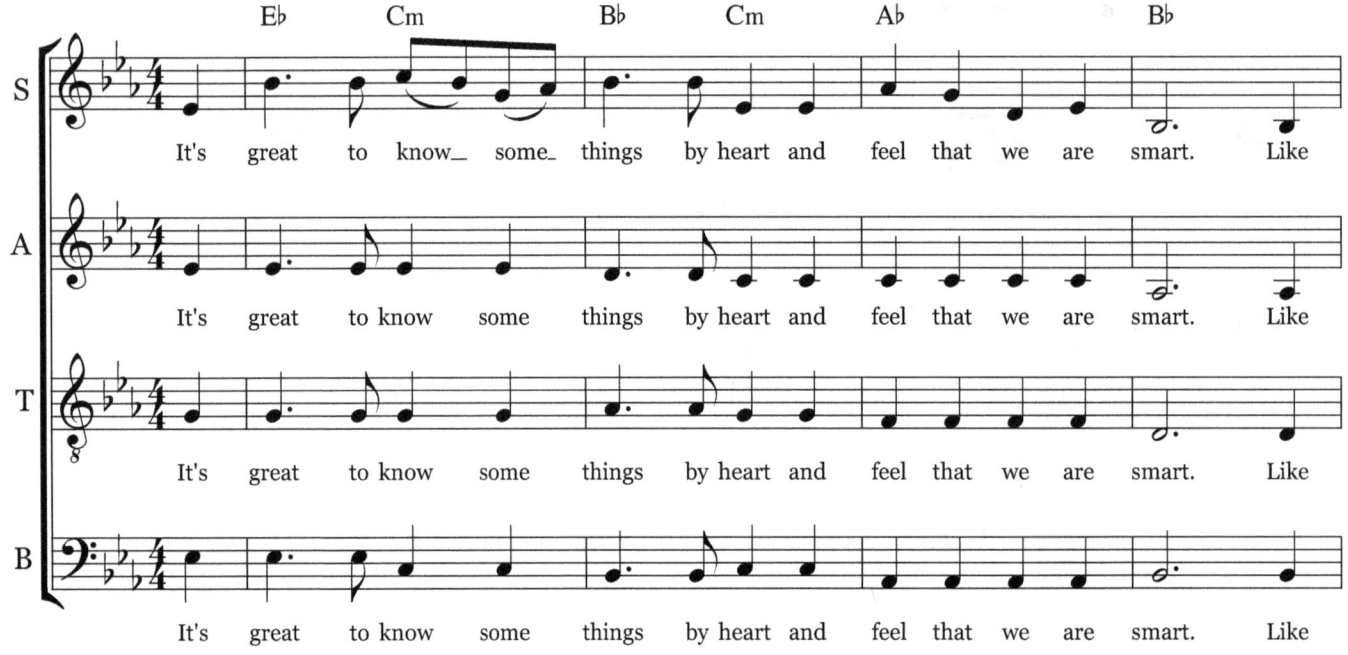

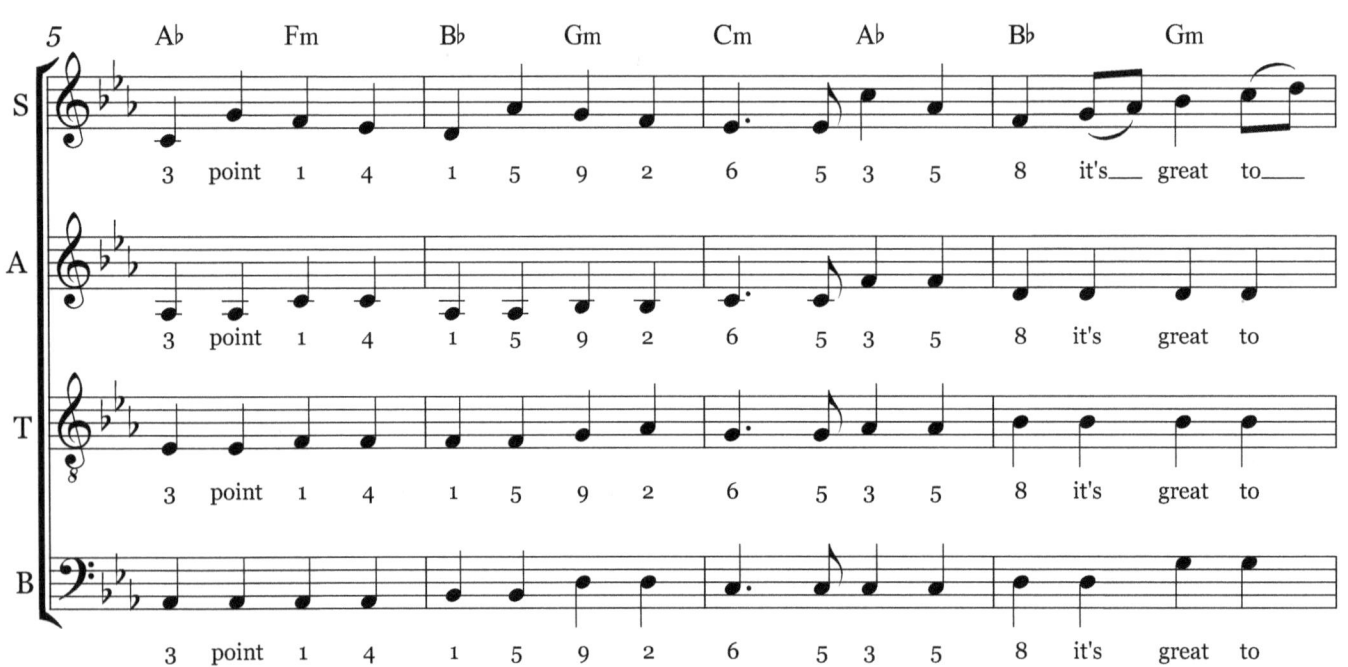

All works by Secretary Michael have been placed in the Public Domain. They may be freely copied and performed.

The song calculates Pi to 11 decimals.
Pi calculated to 100 decimals is:
3.1415926535897932384626433
8327950288419716939937510
5820974944592307816406286
20899862803482534211706 79...

53. I've Never Known a Sinner

(From the Secular Hymnal)

Words: Secretary Michael

Music: "Azmon" by Carl Gotthelf Glaser, 1828
Arranged by Lowell Mason, 1839
(traditional hymn: "O for a Thousand Tongues to Sing")

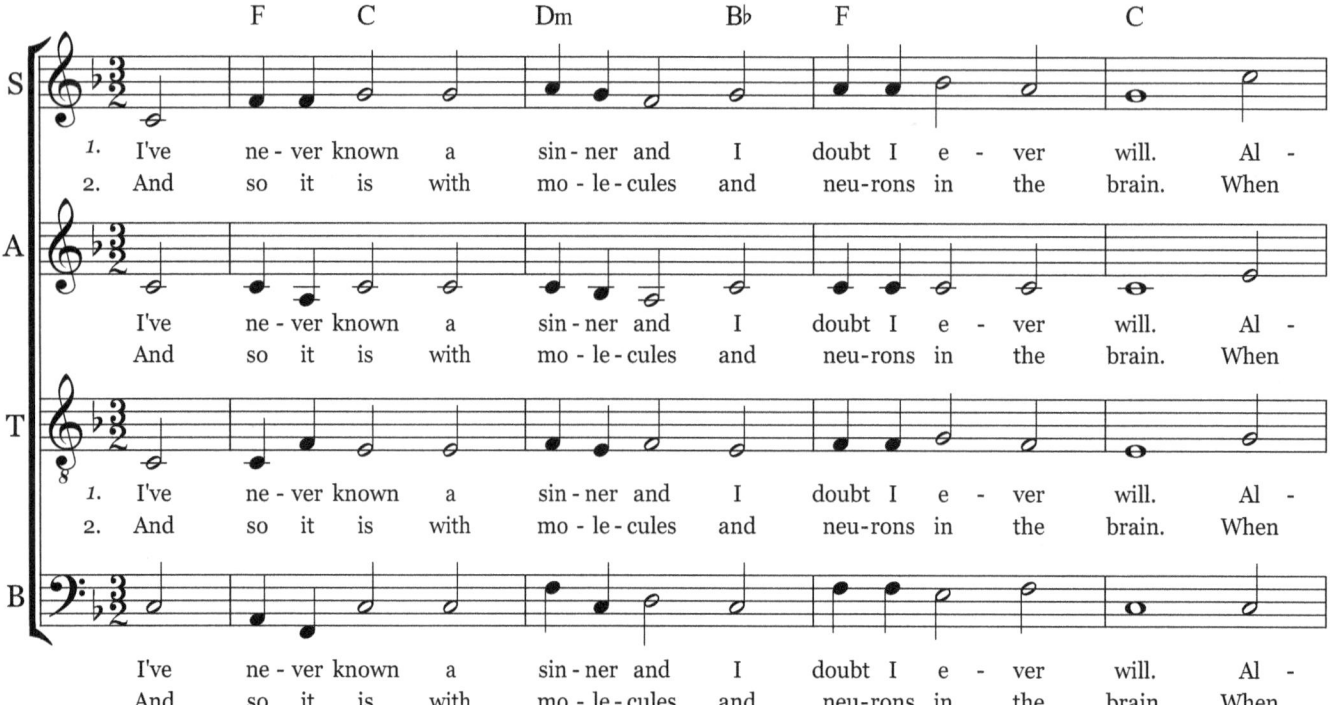

1. I've ne-ver known a sin-ner and I doubt I e-ver will. Al-
2. And so it is with mo-le-cules and neu-rons in the brain. When

though I know of those who lie, and those who steal and kill. A
one will bump a-no-ther one, the next must do the same. I've

All works by Secretary Michael have been placed in the Public Domain. They may be freely copied and performed.

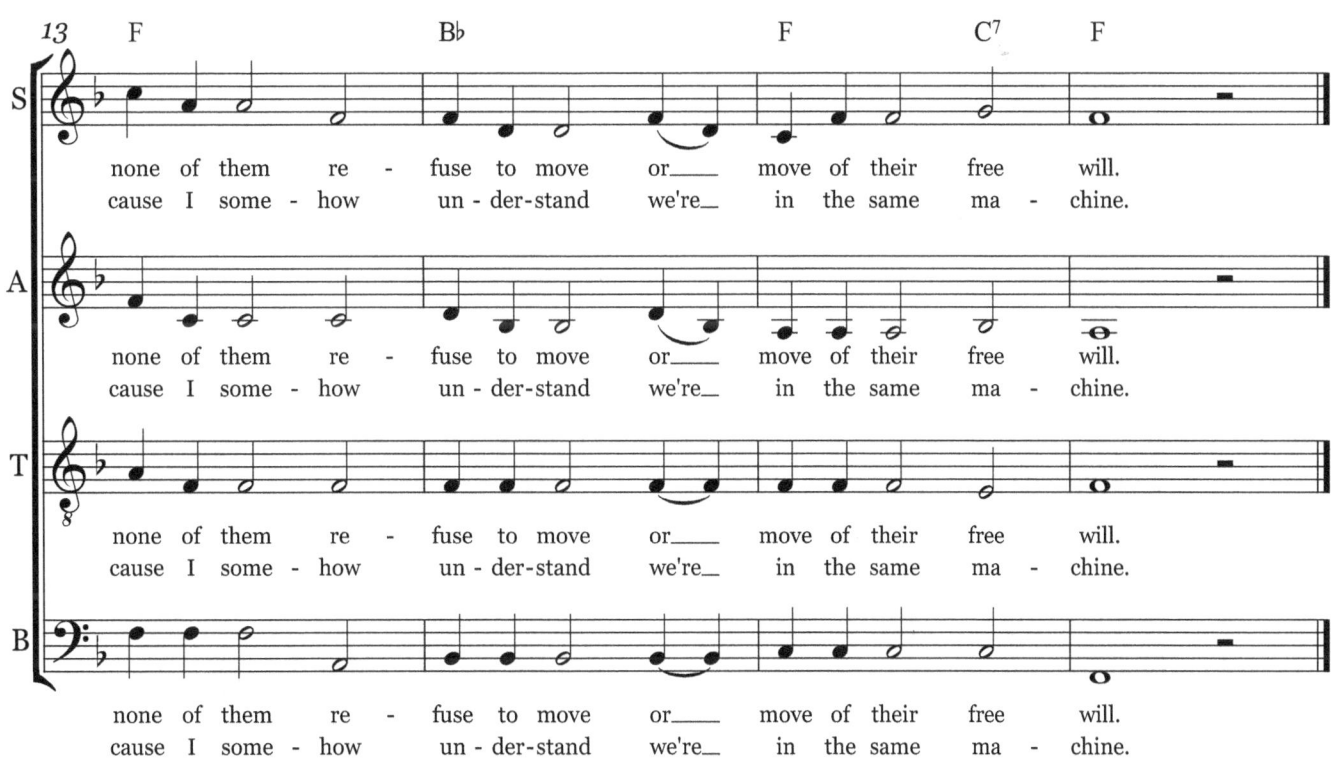

(Note: chord symbols support the soprano melody, not necessarily the SATB harmony)

54. Journey Forward

(From the Secular Hymnal)

Words: Secretary Michael

Music: William Tomer, 1880
(traditional hymn: "God Be With You Till We Meet Again")

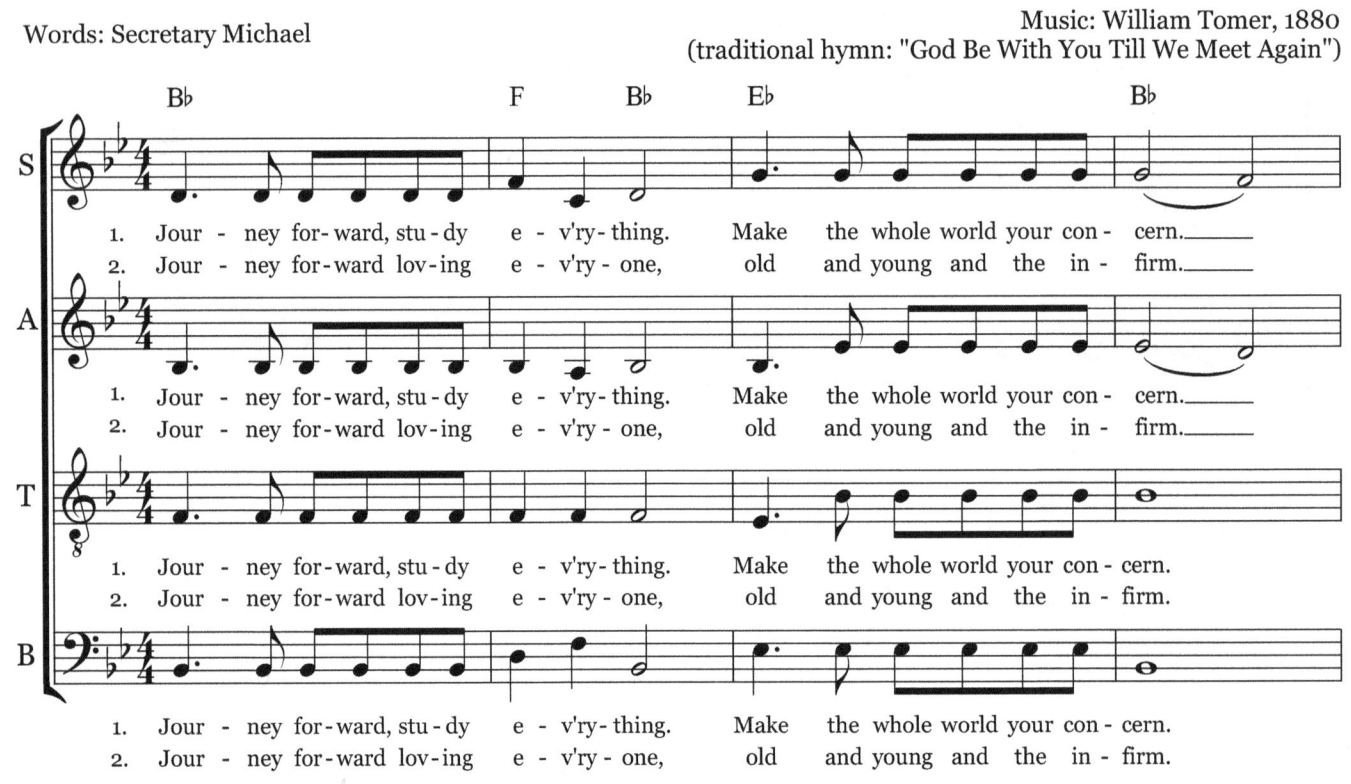

PD *All works by Secretary Michael have been placed in the Public Domain. They may be freely copied and performed.*

(Note: chord symbols support the soprano melody, not necessarily the SATB harmony)

(Note: chord symbols support the soprano melody, not necessarily the SATB harmony)

(Note: chord symbols support the soprano melody, not necessarily the SATB harmony)

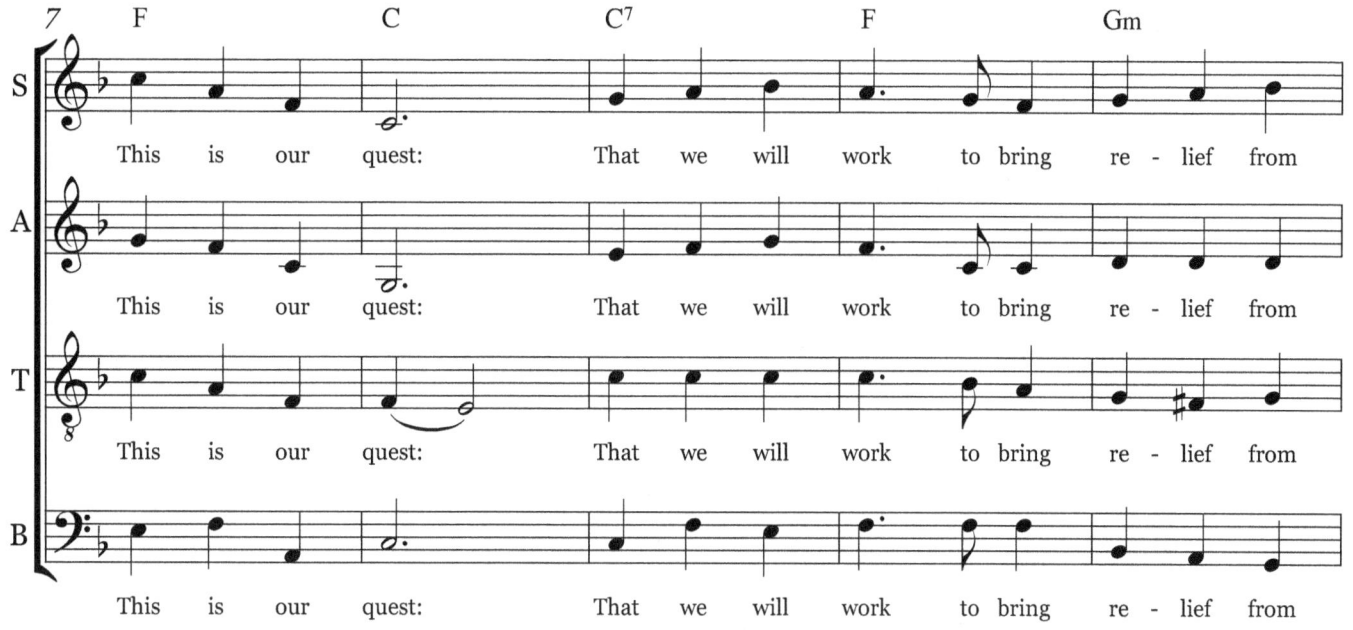
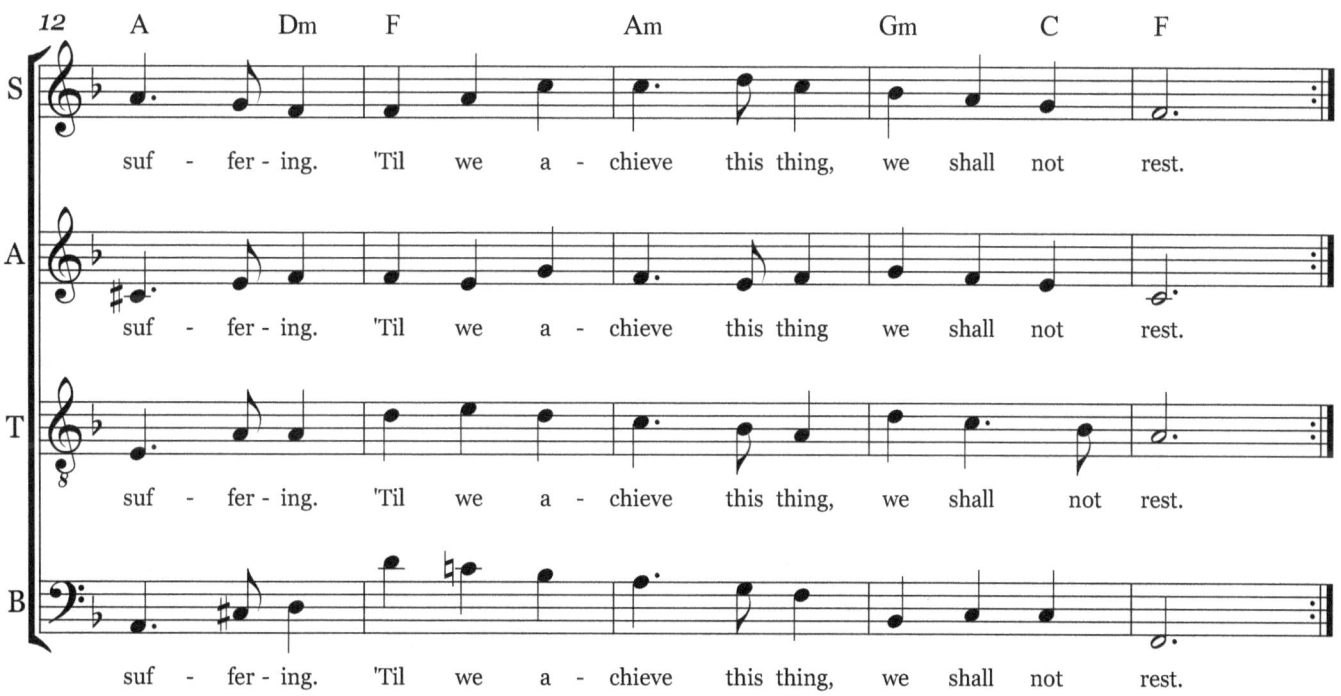

(Note: chord symbols support the soprano melody, not necessarily the SATB harmony)

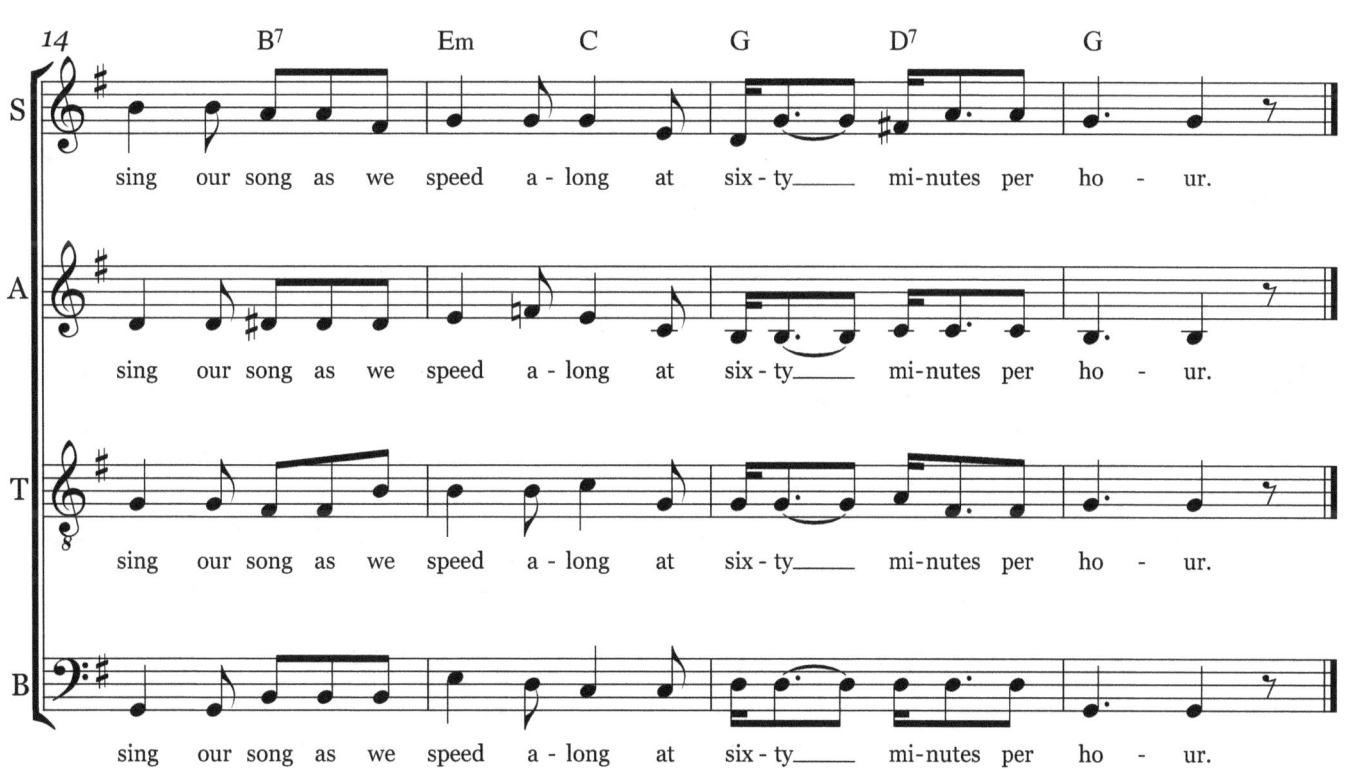

(Note: chord symbols support the soprano melody, not necessarily the SATB harmony)

59. Let's Start a Big Commotion

(From the Secular Hymnal)

Words: Secretary Michael

Music: "Thaxted" by Gustaf T. Holst, 1921
(traditional hymn: "I Vow to Thee, My Country")

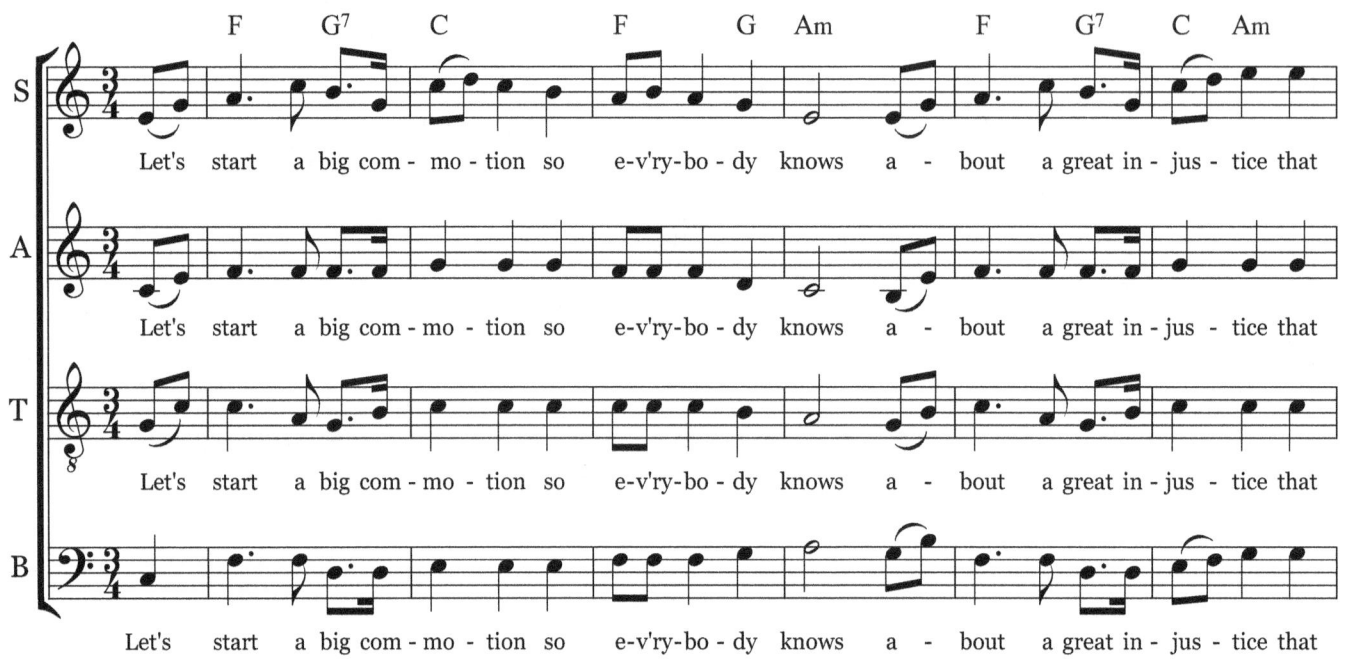

Let's start a big com-mo-tion so ev'ry-bo-dy knows a-bout a great in-jus-tice that

they can help op-pose. Let's shake the foun-da-tions, let's shout and bang the drums, be-cause

All works by Secretary Michael have been placed in the Public Domain. They may be freely copied and performed.

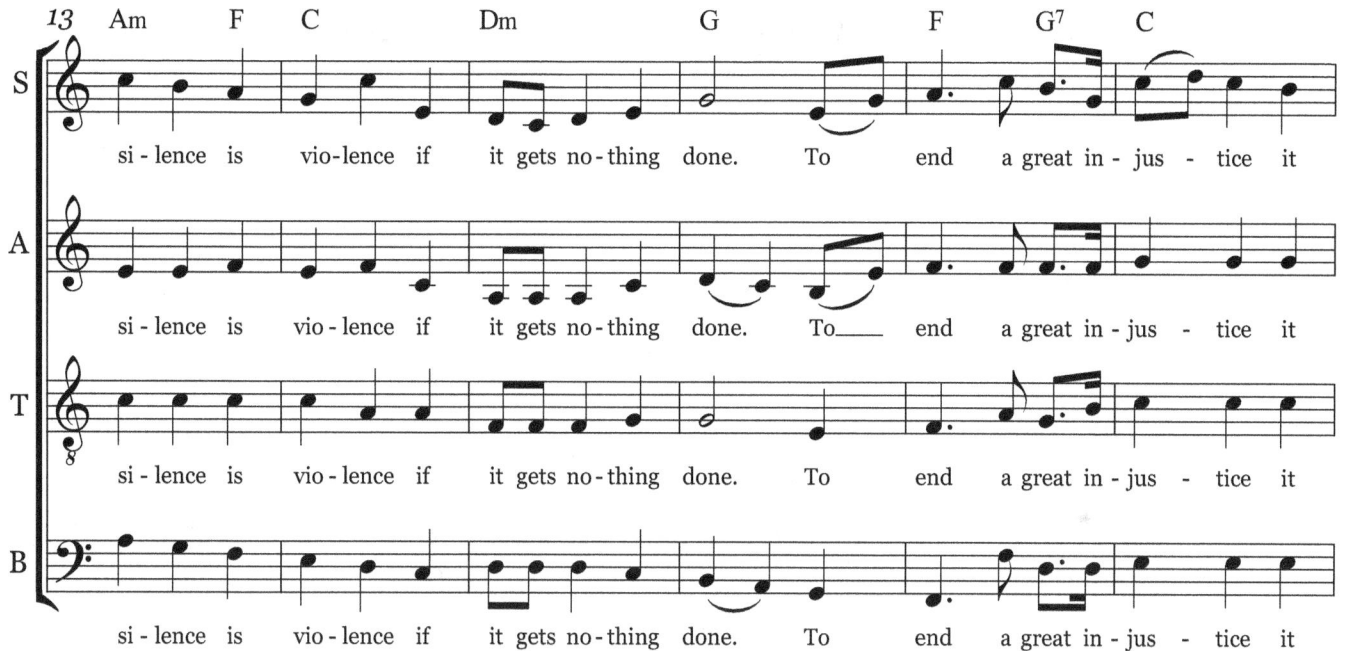
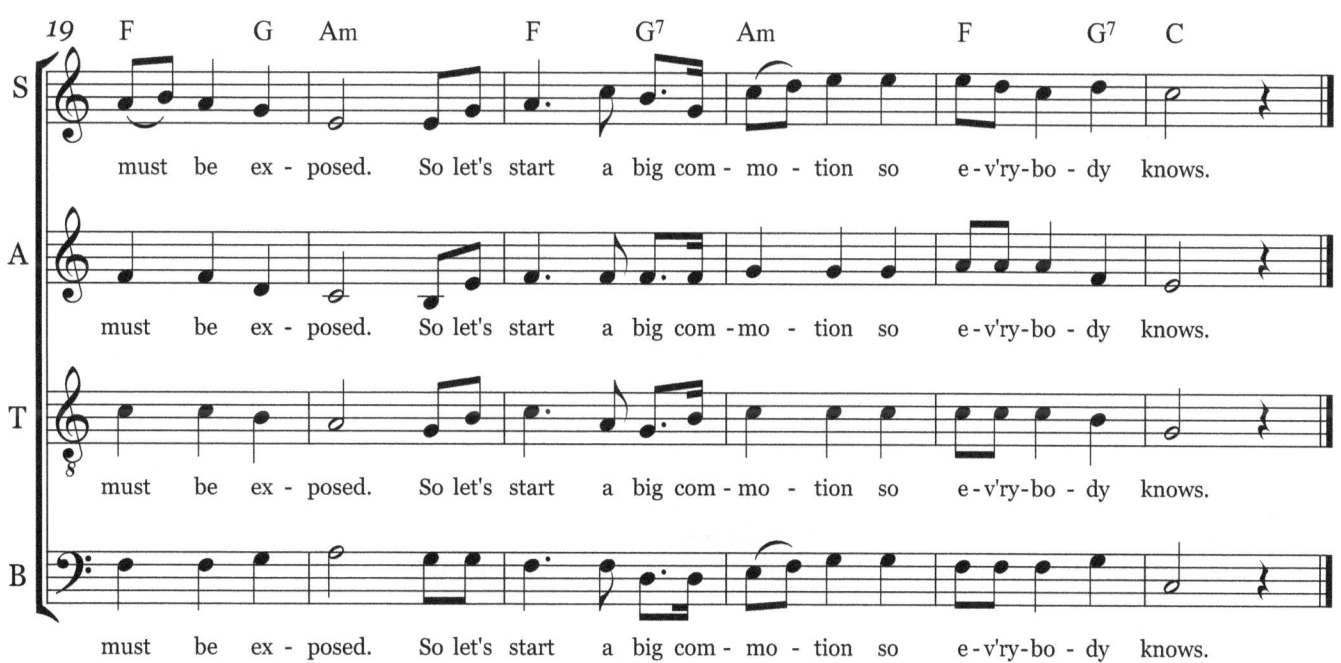

(Note: chord symbols support the soprano melody, not necessarily the SATB harmony)

60. Let's Stop Making Weapons

(From the Secular Hymnal)

Words: Secretary Michael

Music: "Sparrow" by Charles Hutchinson Gabriel, 1905
(traditional hymn: "His Eye Is on the Sparrow")

All works by Secretary Michael have been placed in the Public Domain. They may be freely copied and performed.

(Note: chord symbols support the soprano melody, not necessarily the SATB harmony)

61. Let's Try Something Different
(From the Secular Hymnal)

Words: Secretary Michael

Music: "Evangel" by William Howard Doane, 1867
(traditional hymn: "Tell Me the Old, Old Story")

All works by Secretary Michael have been placed in the Public Domain. They may be freely copied and performed.

(Note: chord symbols support the soprano melody, not necessarily the SATB harmony)

62. Long Road
(From the Secular Hymnal)

Words (and music alteration): Secretary Michael

Music: "Meine Hoffnung Stehet Feste" by J.Neander, 1680
Harmonized by J.S.Bach (Cantata 40), 1723
(traditional hymn:"All My Hope On God Is Founded")

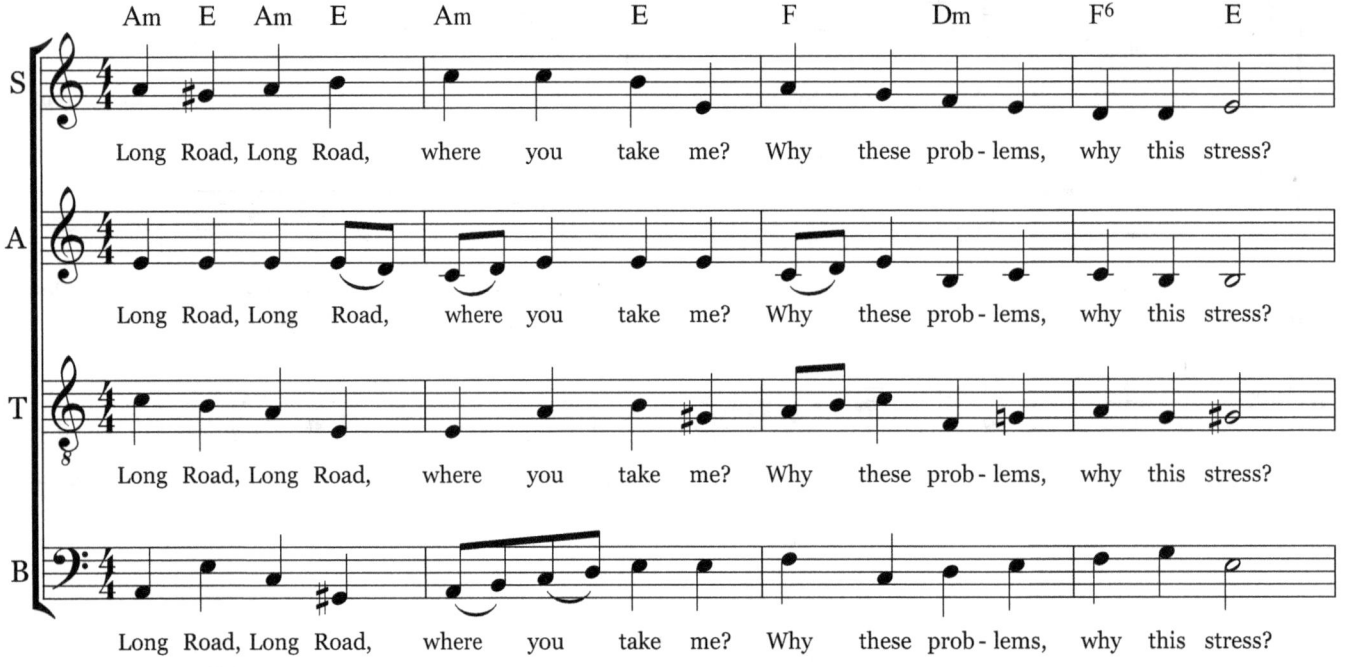

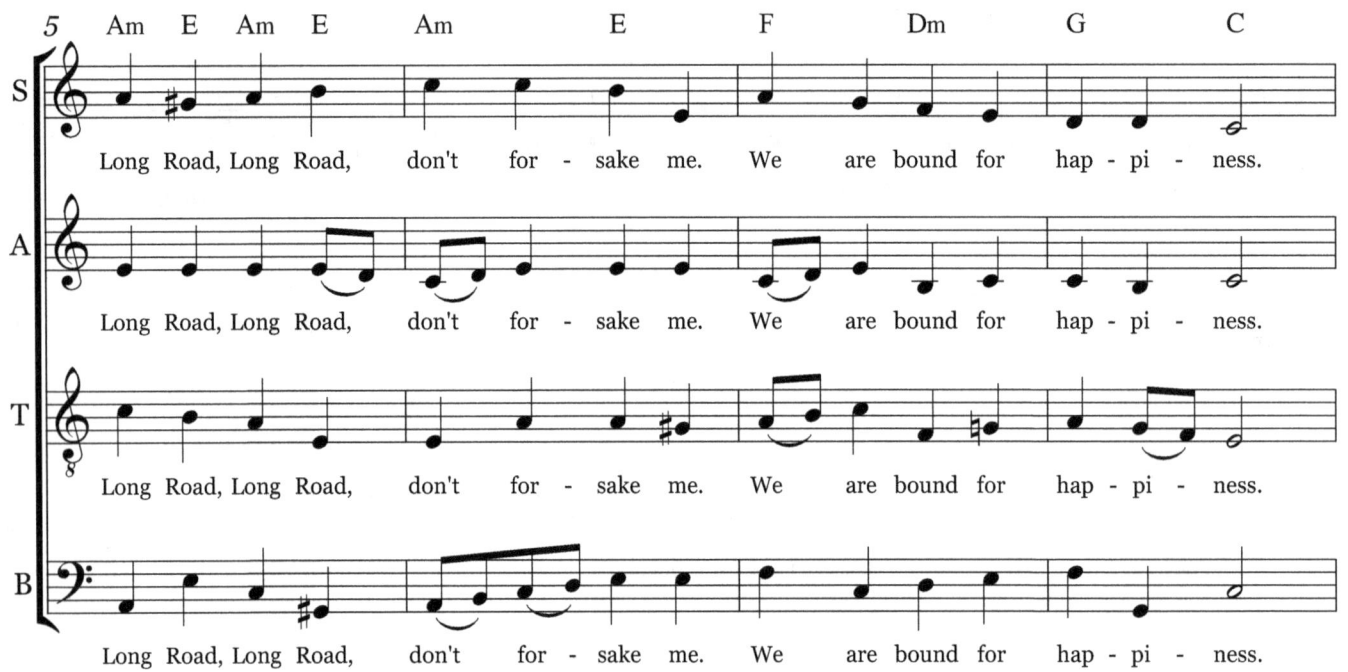

All works by Secretary Michael have been placed in the Public Domain. They may be freely copied and performed.

(Note: chord symbols support the soprano melody, not necessarily the SATB harmony)

63. Make Just One Brand-New Friend

(From the Secular Hymnal)

Words: Secretary Michael

Music: "Foundation" by Joseph Funk, 1832
(traditional hymn: "How Firm a Foundation")

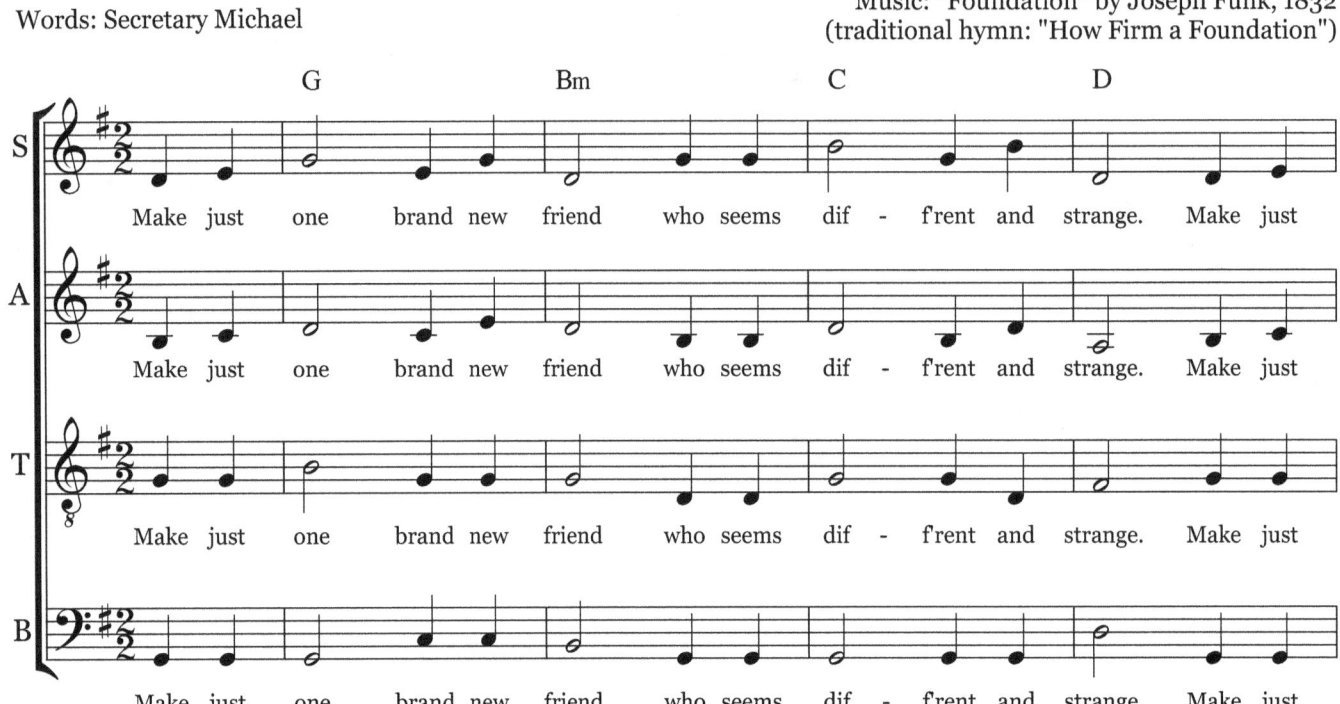

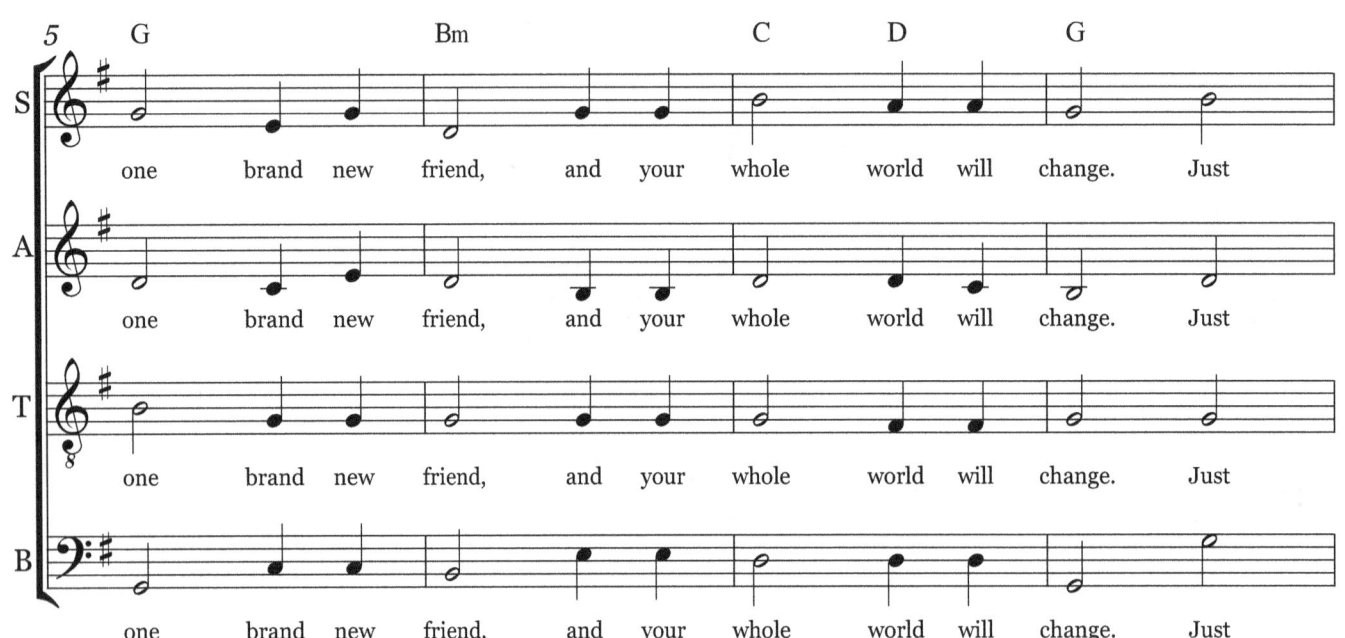

All works by Secretary Michael have been placed in the Public Domain. They may be freely copied and performed.

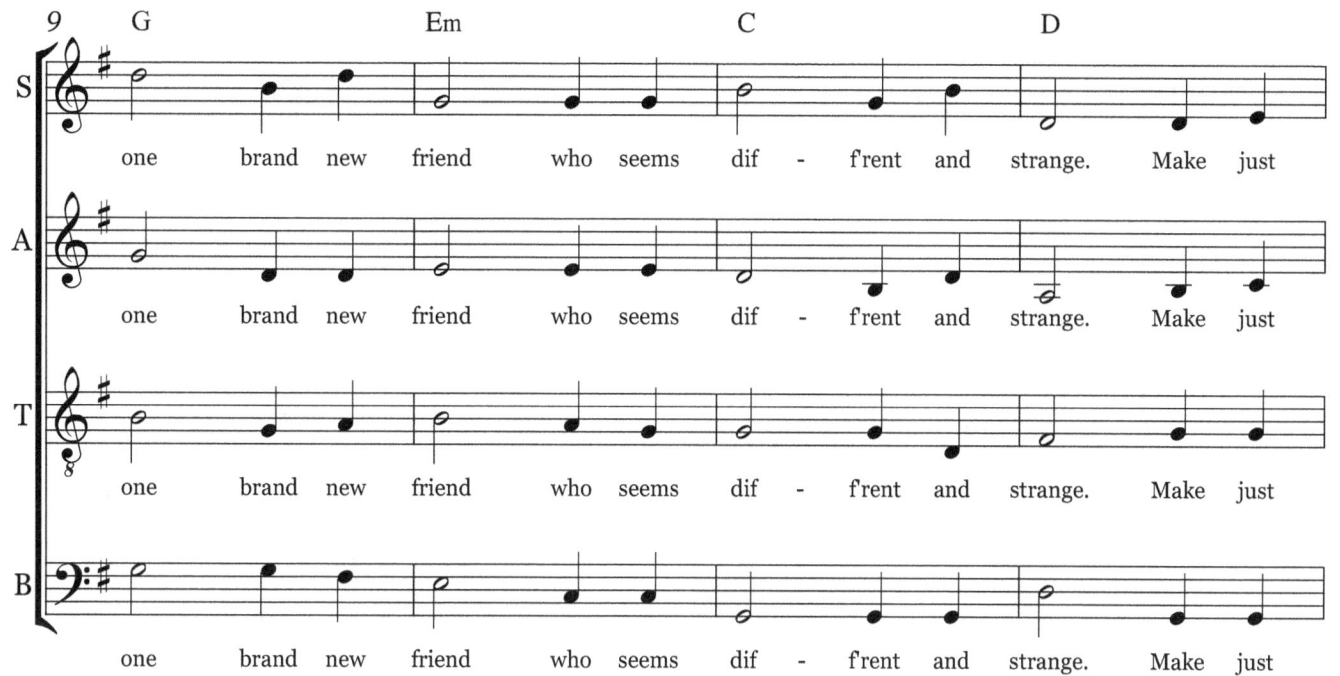
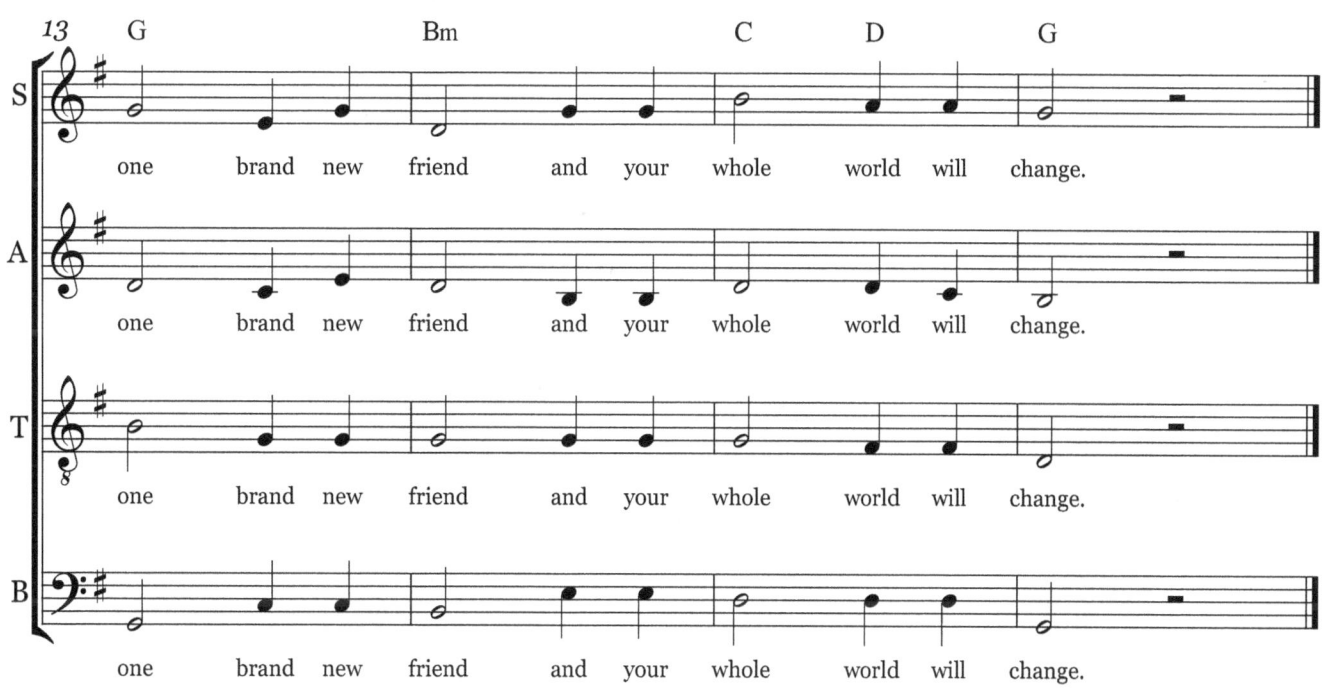

(Note: chord symbols support the soprano melody, not necessarily the SATB harmony)

64. May We Make Moments of Peace

(From the Secular Hymnal)

Words: Secretary Michael

Music: "Duke Street" by John Hatton, 1793
(traditional hymn: "Jesus Shall Reign, Where'er the Sun")

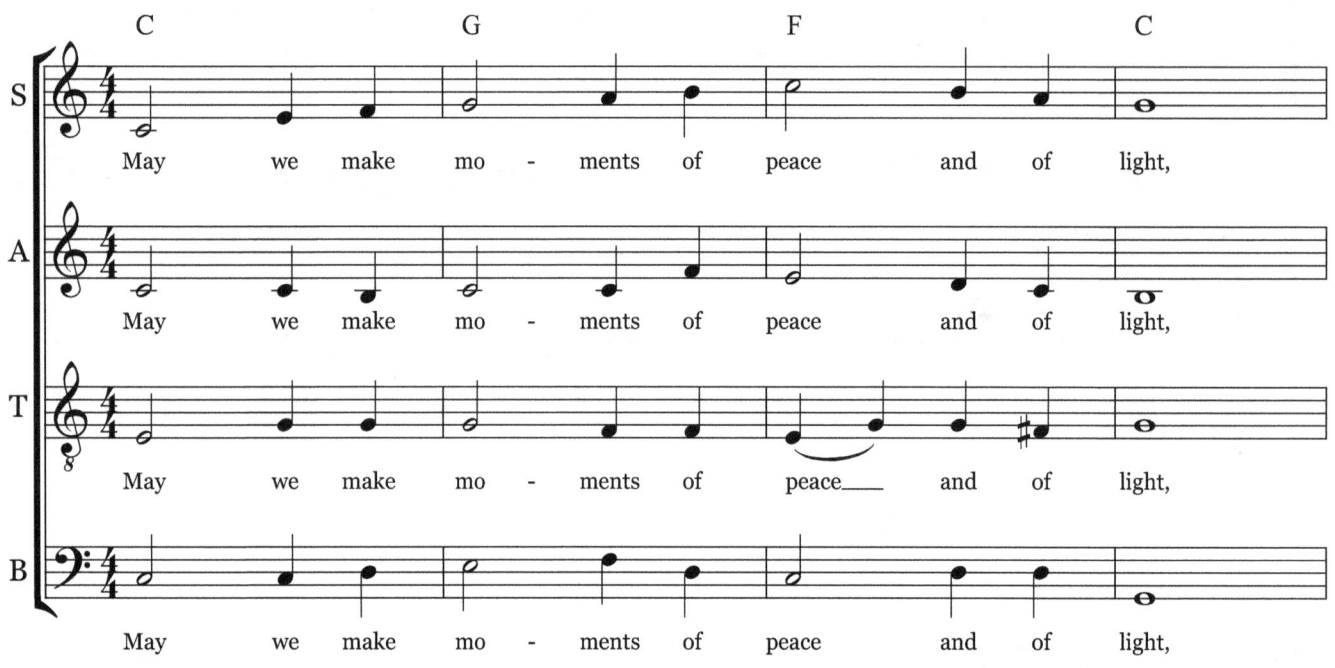

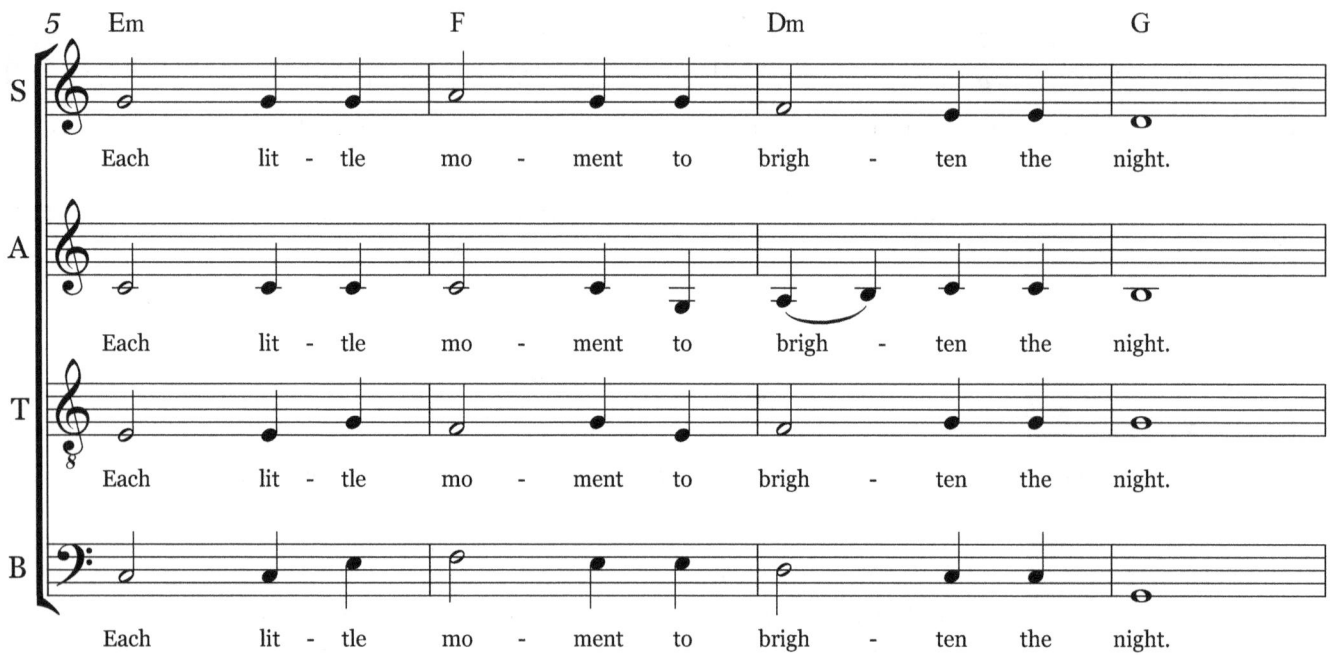

All works by Secretary Michael have been placed in the Public Domain. They may be freely copied and performed.

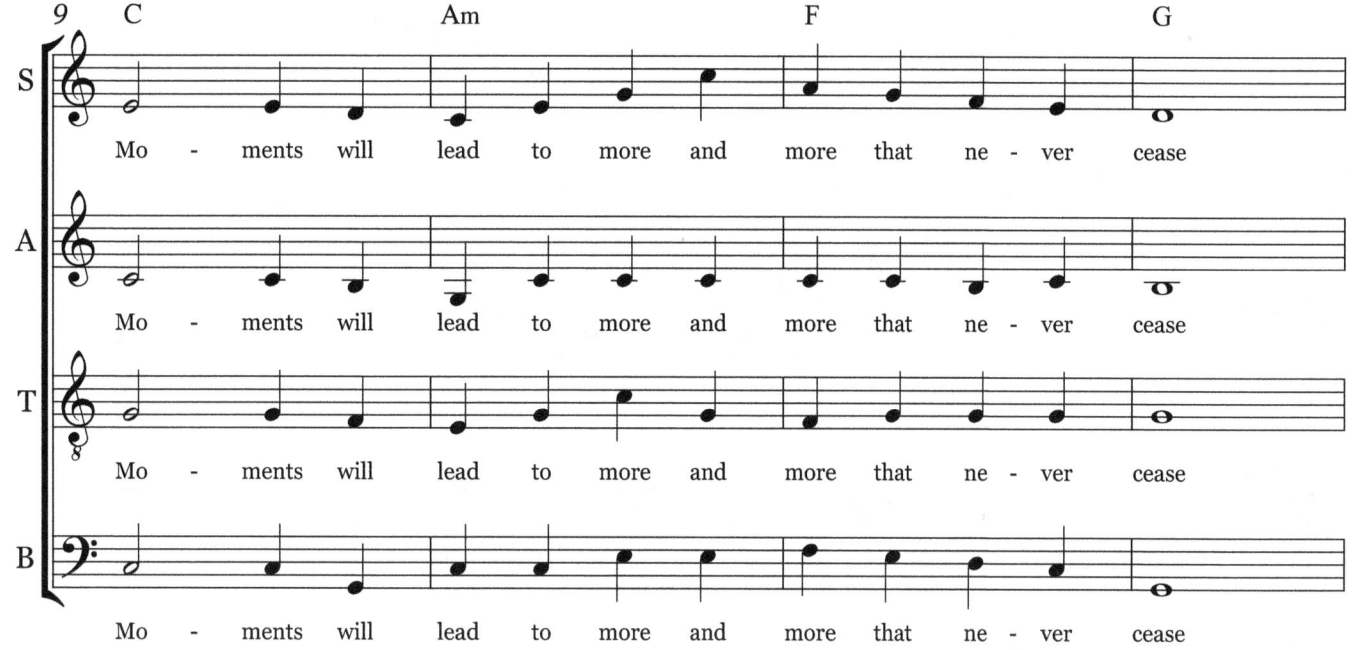
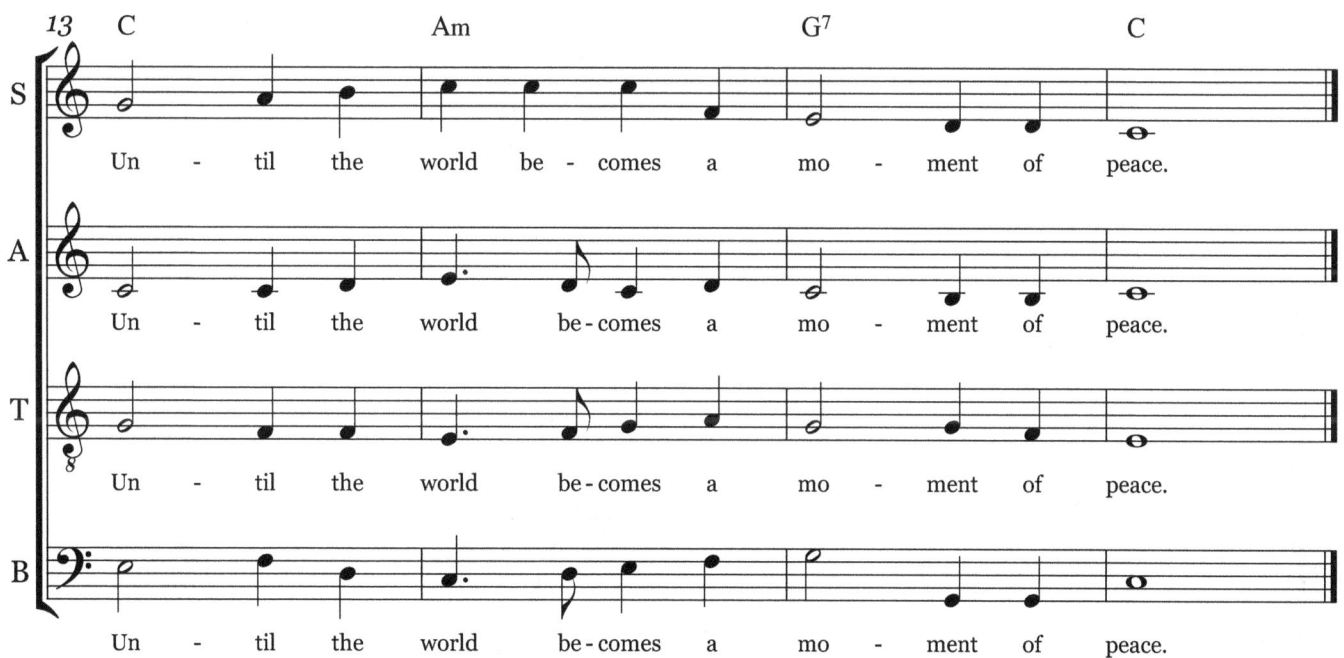

(Note: chord symbols support the soprano melody, not necessarily the SATB harmony)

65. No Cheers For David

(From the Secular Hymnal)

Words: Secretary Michael

Music: "O Perfect Love" by Joseph Barnby, 1889
Arranged by John Stainer, 1898
(traditional hymn: "O Perfect Love")

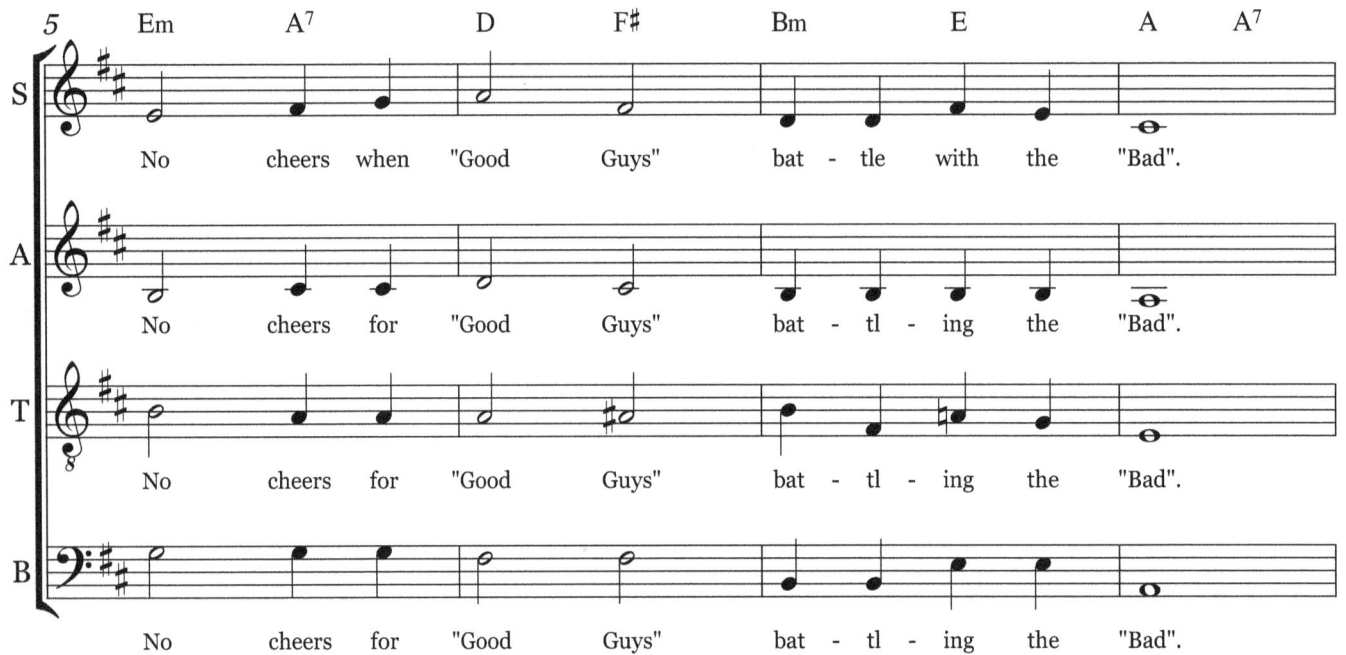

All works by Secretary Michael have been placed in the Public Domain. They may be freely copied and performed.

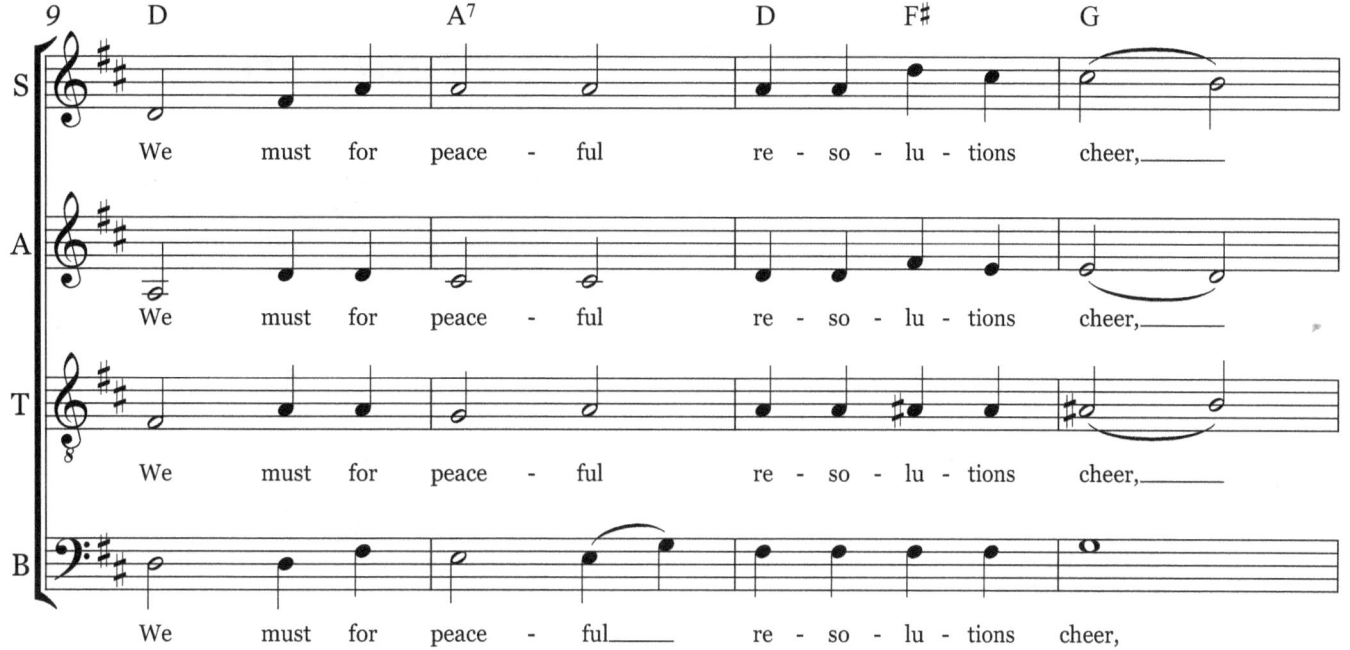
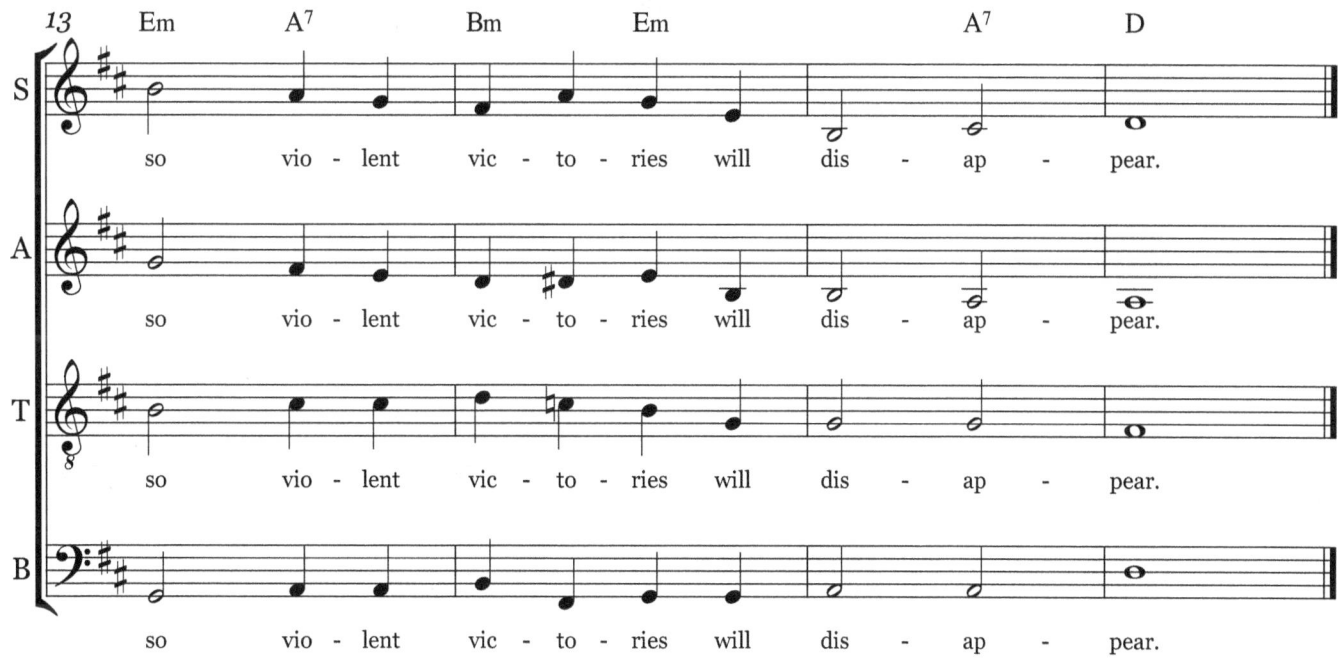

(Note: chord symbols support the soprano melody, not necessarily the SATB harmony)

66. No Need to Sing the Same Notes

(From the Secular Hymnal)

Words: Secretary Michael

Music: "Wir Pflugen" (We Plow) by Johann A.P. Schulz, 1800
(traditional hymn: "We Plow the Fields and Scatter")

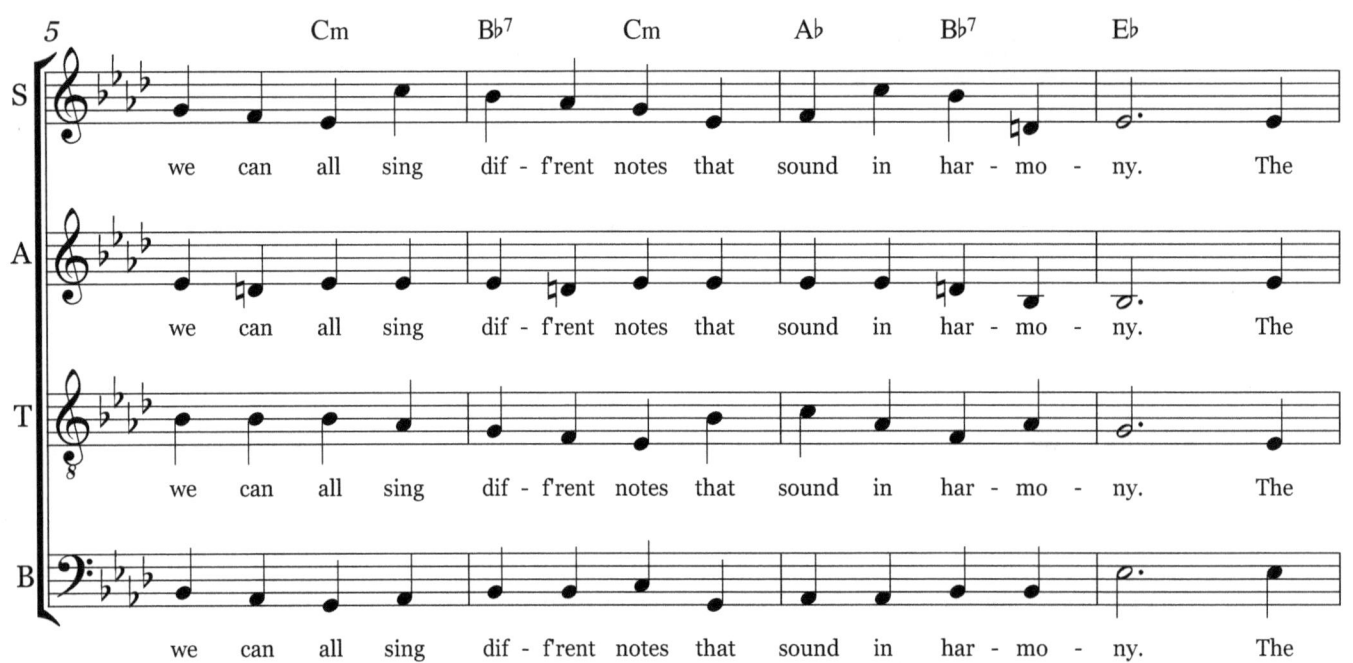

All works by Secretary Michael have been placed in the Public Domain. They may be freely copied and performed.

(Note: chord symbols support the soprano melody, not necessarily the SATB harmony)

67. Nonviolence May Take a Long Time

(From the Secular Hymnal)

Words: Secretary Michael

Music: "Redeemed" by William James Kirkpatrick, 1882
(traditional hymn: "Redeemed")

All works by Secretary Michael have been placed in the Public Domain. They may be freely copied and performed.

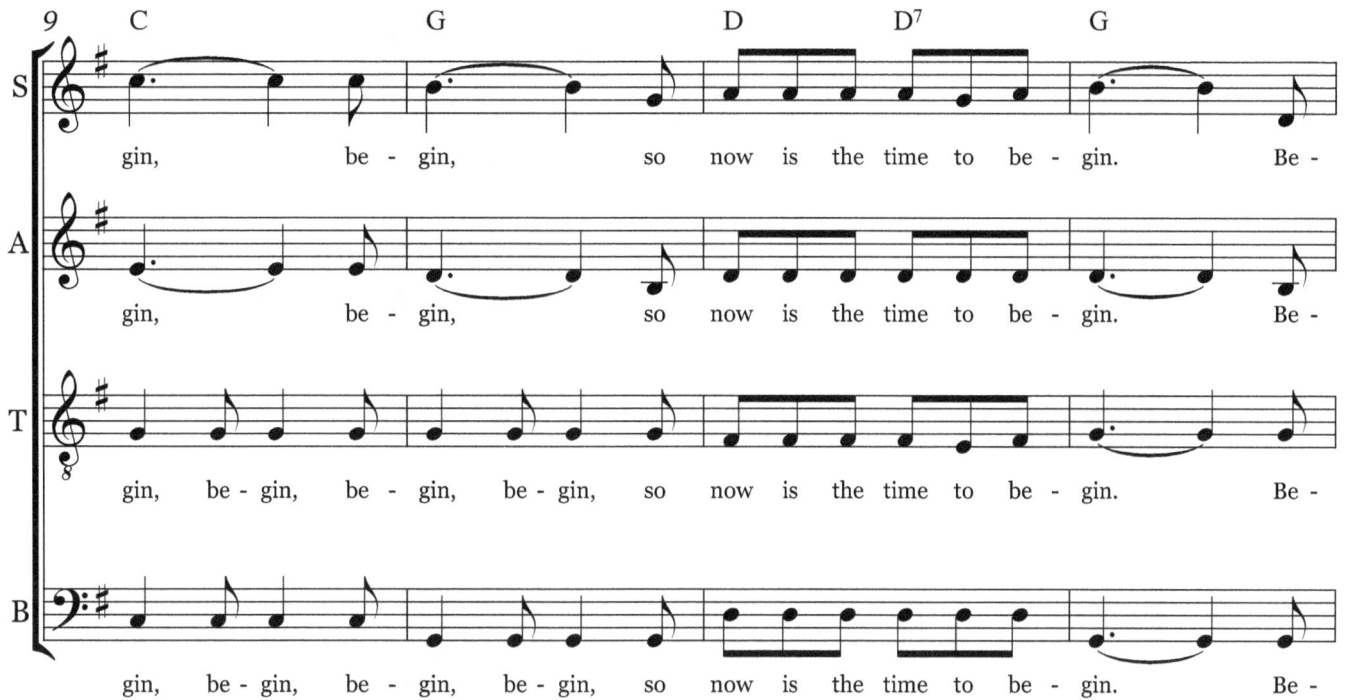

(Note: chord symbols support the soprano melody, not necessarily the SATB harmony)

68. Nonviolence Must Be Taught
(From the Secular Hymnal)

Words: Secretary Michael

Melody: "All in the April Evening" by Hugh S. Roberton, 1911
SATB arrangement: Secretary Michael
(traditional hymn: "All in the April Evening")

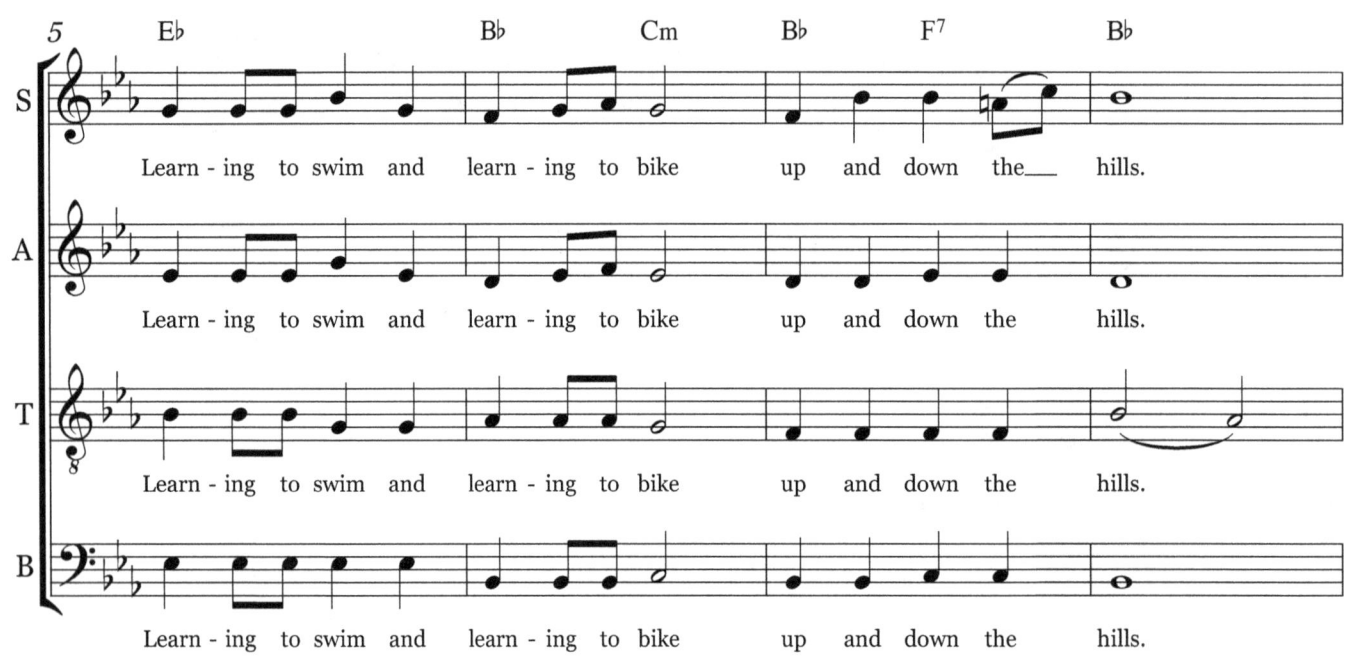

All works by Secretary Michael have been placed in the Public Domain. They may be freely copied and performed.

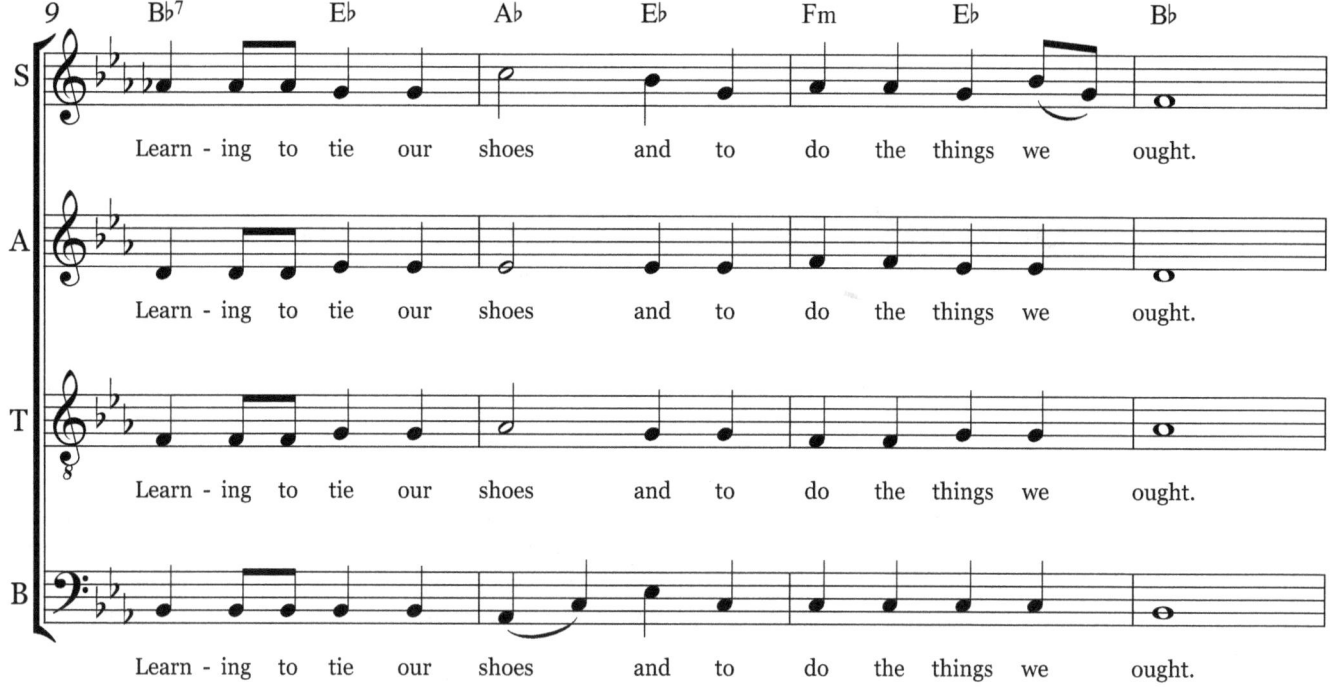
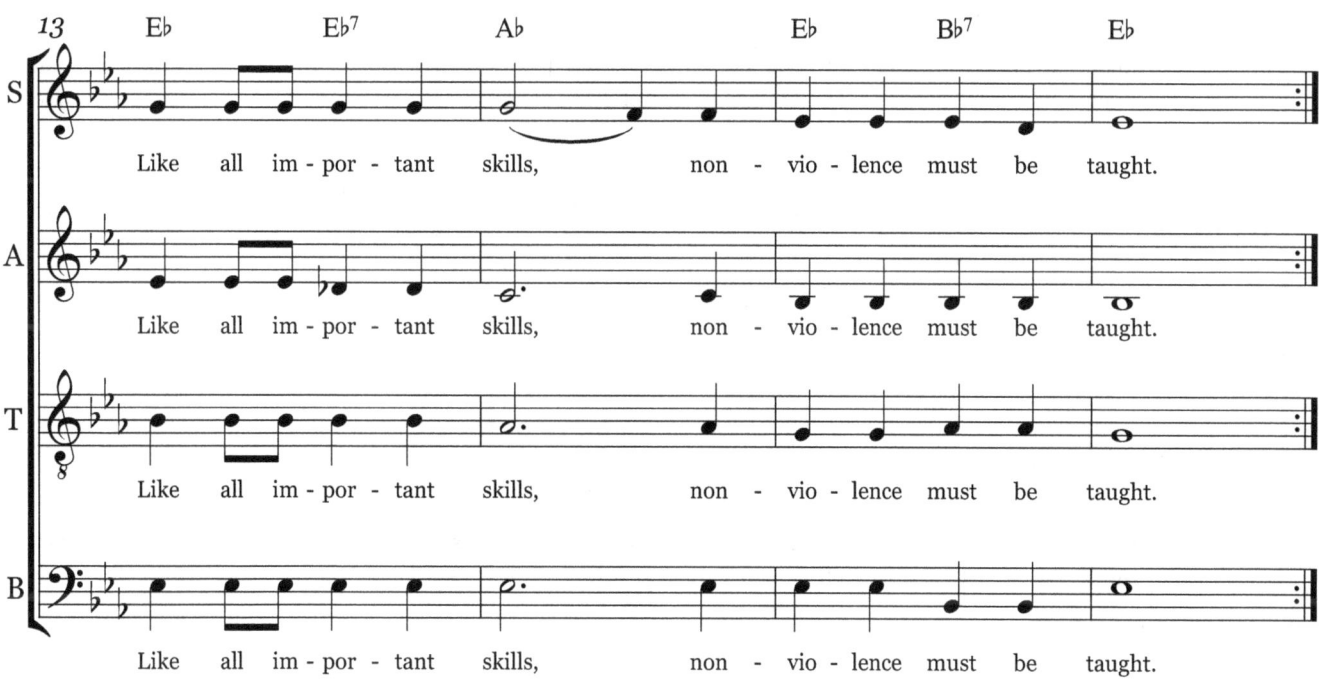

(Note: chord symbols support the soprano melody, not necessarily the SATB harmony)

69. Nothing's Heavy With Lots of Hands
(From the Secular Hymnal)

Words: Secretary Michael

Music: "Hendon" by Henri Abraham Cesar Malan, 1827
Harmony: Lowell Mason, 1841
(traditional hymn: "Take My Life and Let It Be")

1. No-thing's heavy with lots of hands shar-ing bur-dens, shar-ing plans. A-ny-thing that
2. No-thing's stuck with lots of feet mov-ing 'til the job's com-plete. Step by step and
3. No-thing's hard with lots of minds, not just yours and not just mine. All the peo-ple

All works by Secretary Michael have been placed in the Public Domain. They may be freely copied and performed.

(Note: chord symbols support the soprano melody, not necessarily the SATB harmony)

70. Oh Child Do Not Despair

(From the Secular Hymnal)

Words: Secretary Michael

Tune: "St. Thomas" by Aaron Williams (c. 1770)
SATB Arrangement: Secretary Michael
(traditional hymn: "O Bless the Lord, My Soul")

All works by Secretary Michael have been placed in the Public Domain. They may be freely copied and performed.

(Note: chord symbols support the soprano melody, not necessarily the SATB harmony)

71. Ojalá
(From the Secular Hymnal)

Words: Secretary Michael

Music: *Katholisches Gesangbuch* (Vienna) 1686
(traditional hymn: "Holy God, We Praise Thy Name")

All works by Secretary Michael have been placed in the Public Domain. They may be freely copied and performed.

Ohalá (pronounced: *Oh-ha-LAH*) is the beautiful Spanish word meaning "let us hope"

(Note: chord symbols support the soprano melody, not necessarily the SATB harmony)

72. Onward Upward
(From the Secular Hymnal)

Words: Secretary Michael

Music: "St. Gertrude" by Arthur Seymour Sullivan, 1871
(traditional hymn: "Onward Christian Soldiers")

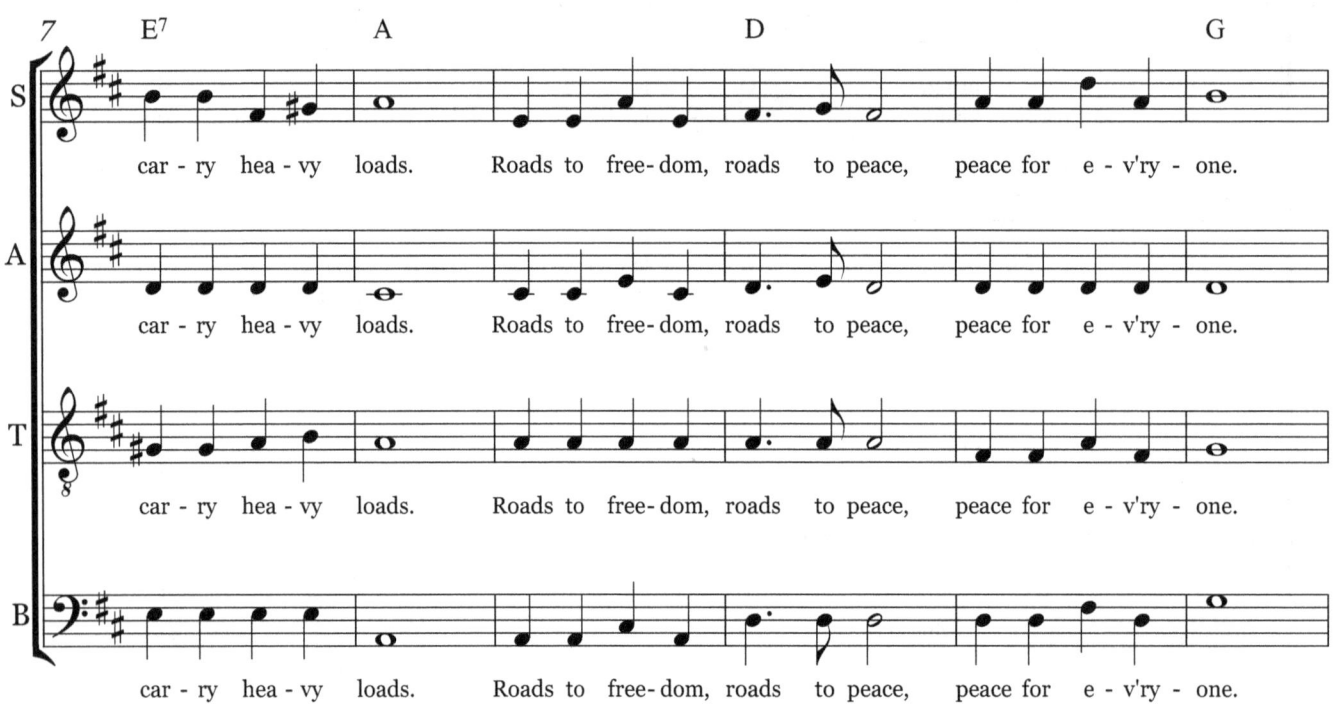

All works by Secretary Michael have been placed in the Public Domain. They may be freely copied and performed.

(Note: chord symbols support the soprano melody, not necessarily the SATB harmony)

73. Open Open Up the Window

(From the Secular Hymnal)

Words: Secretary Michael

Music: "Austrian Hymn" by Franz Joseph Hayden, 1797
(traditional hymn: "Glorious Things of Thee Are Spoken")

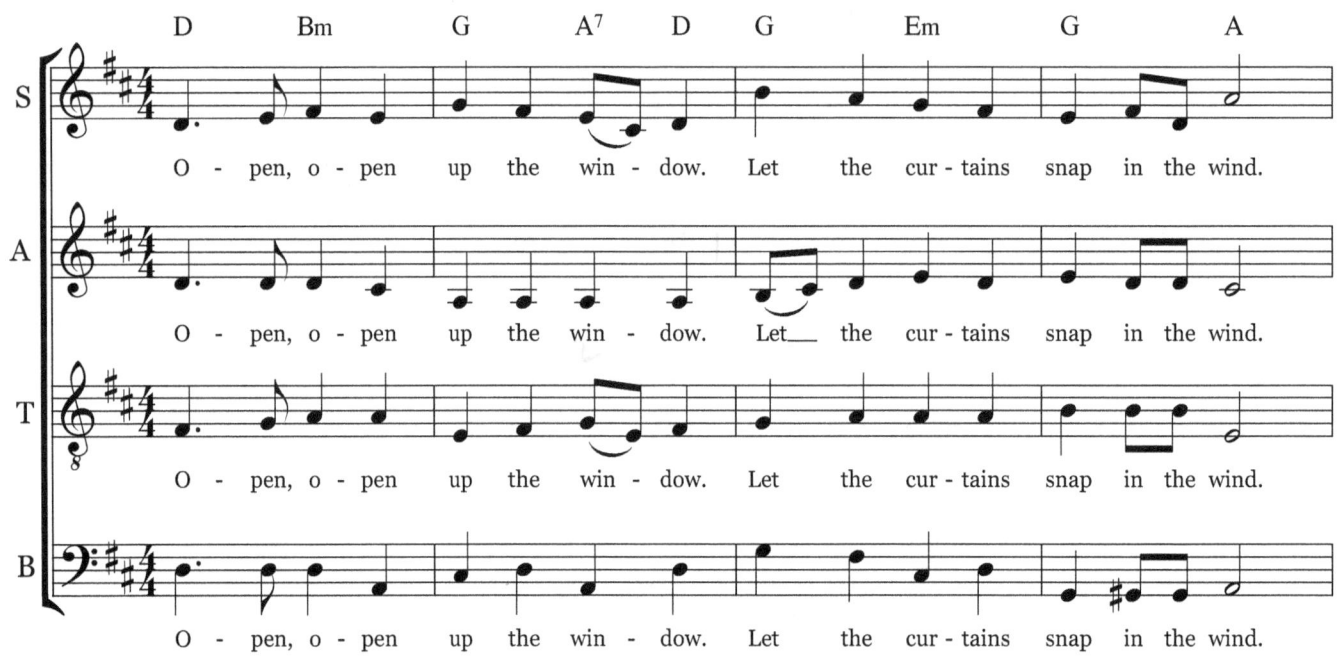

 *All works by Secretary Michael have been placed in the Public Domain. They may be freely copied and performed.*

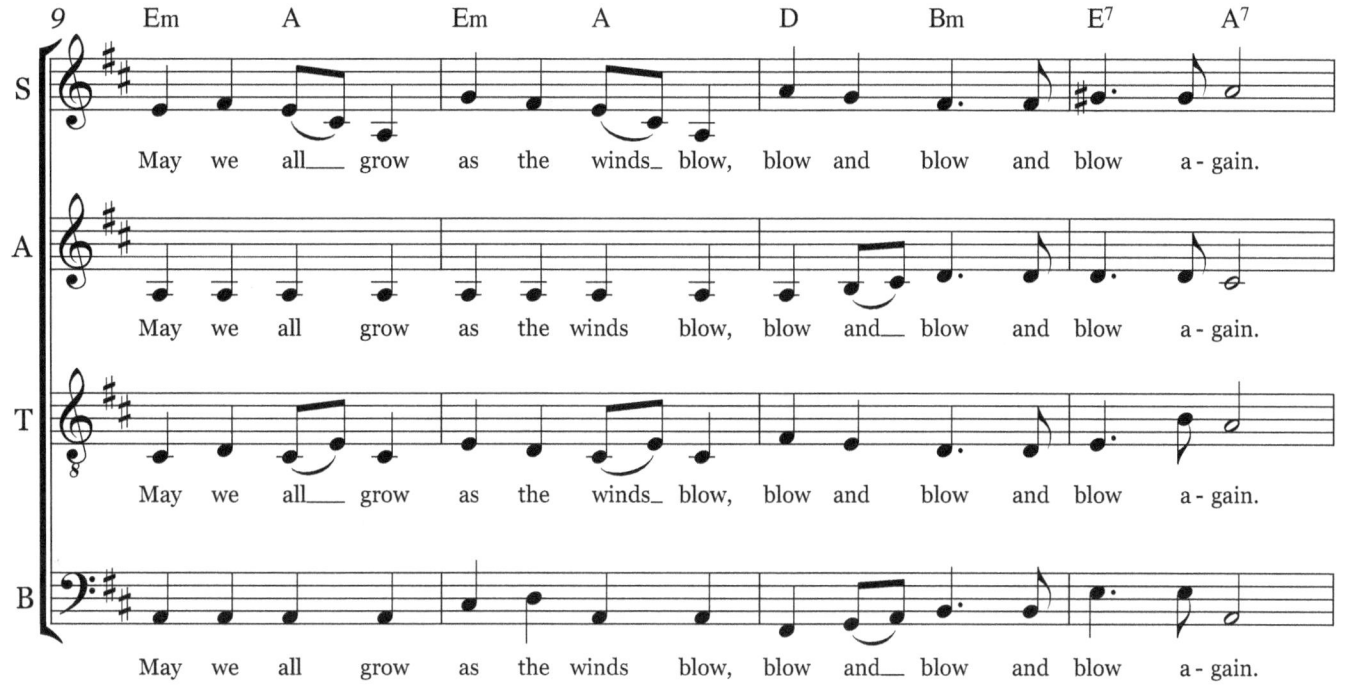
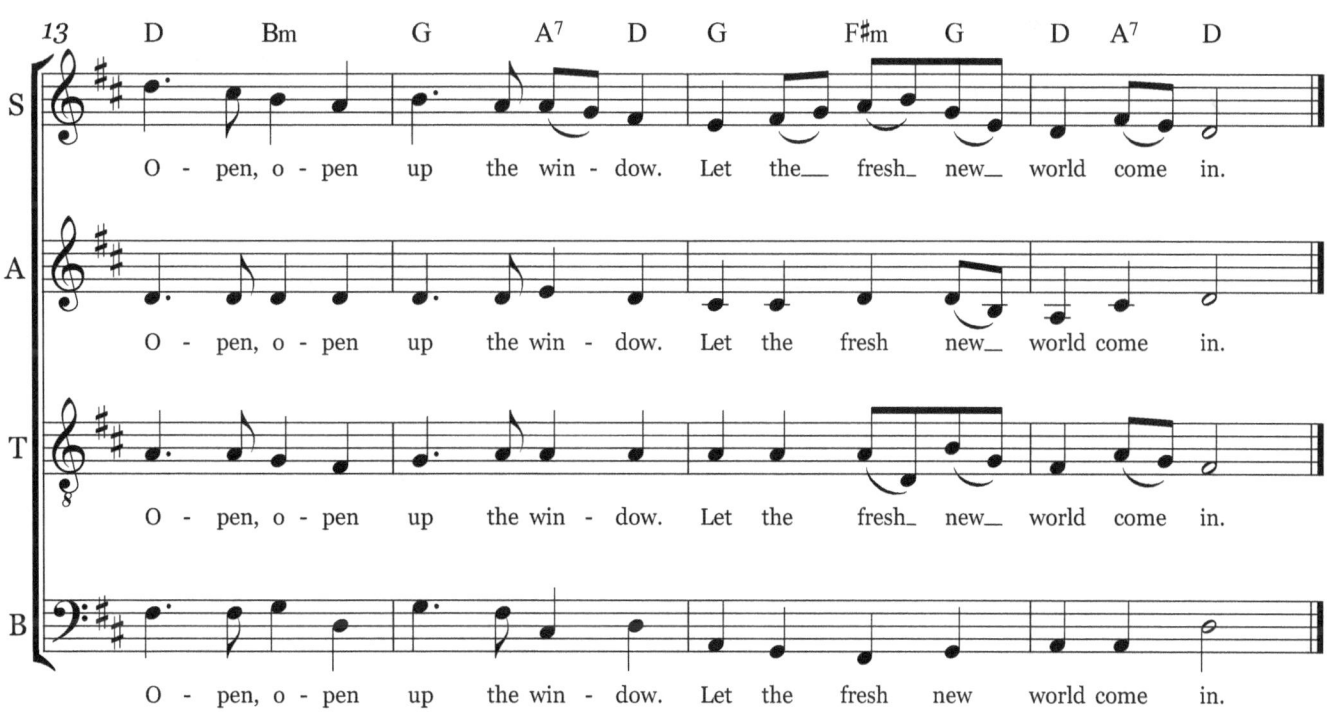

(Note: chord symbols support the soprano melody, not necessarily the SATB harmony)

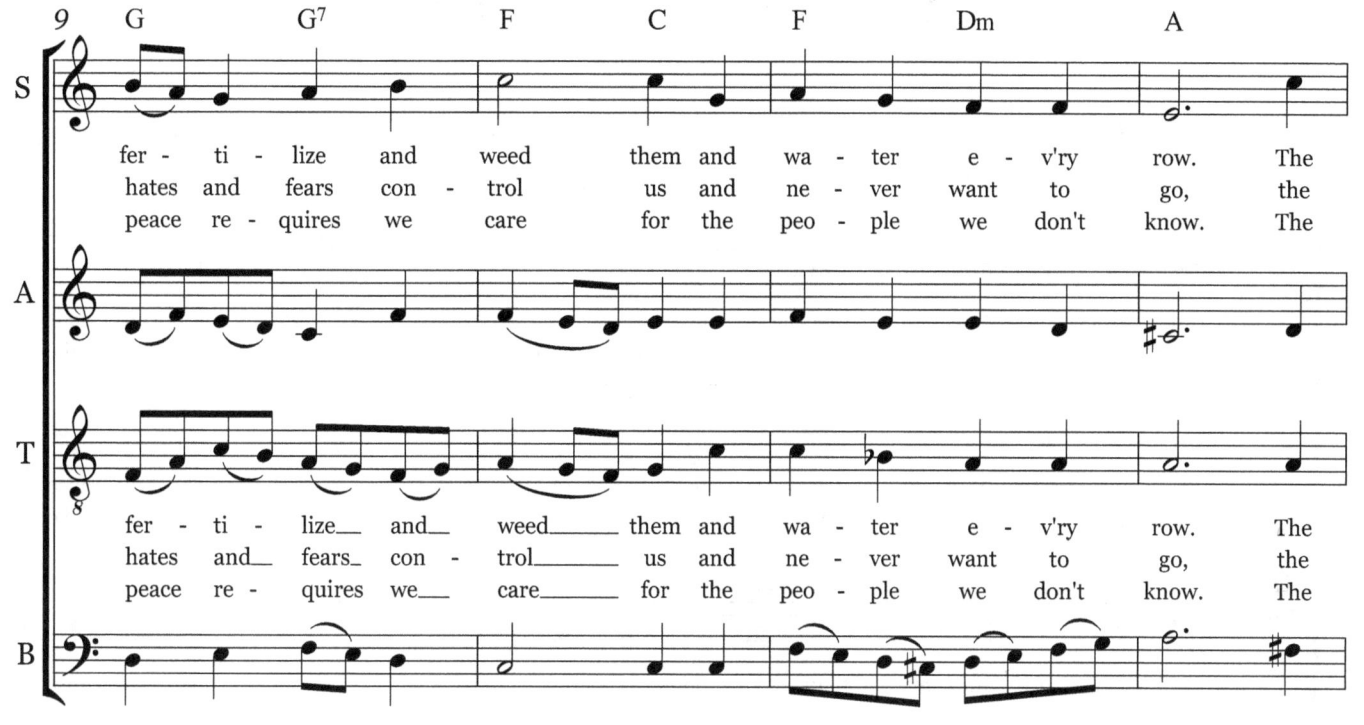
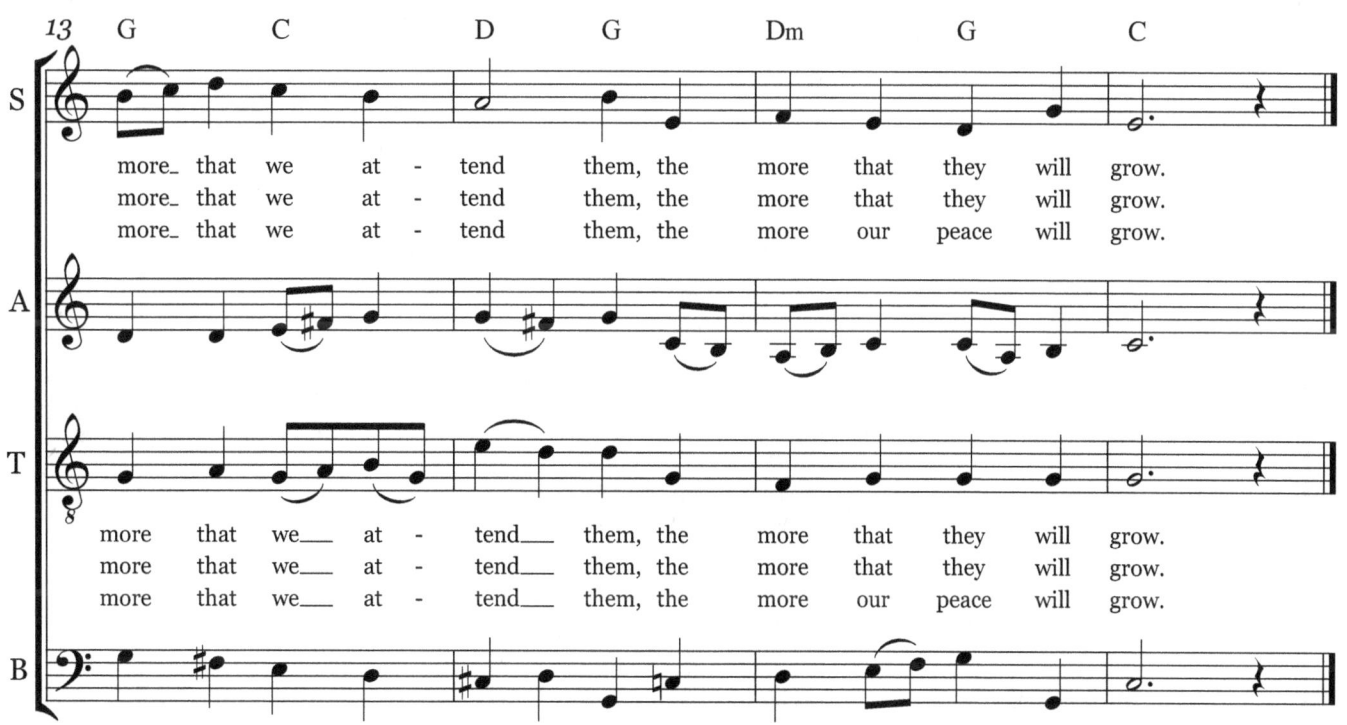

(Note: chord symbols support the soprano melody, not necessarily the SATB harmony)

75. Pain Can Cause
(From the Secular Hymnal)

All works by Secretary Michael have been placed in the Public Domain. They may be freely copied and performed.

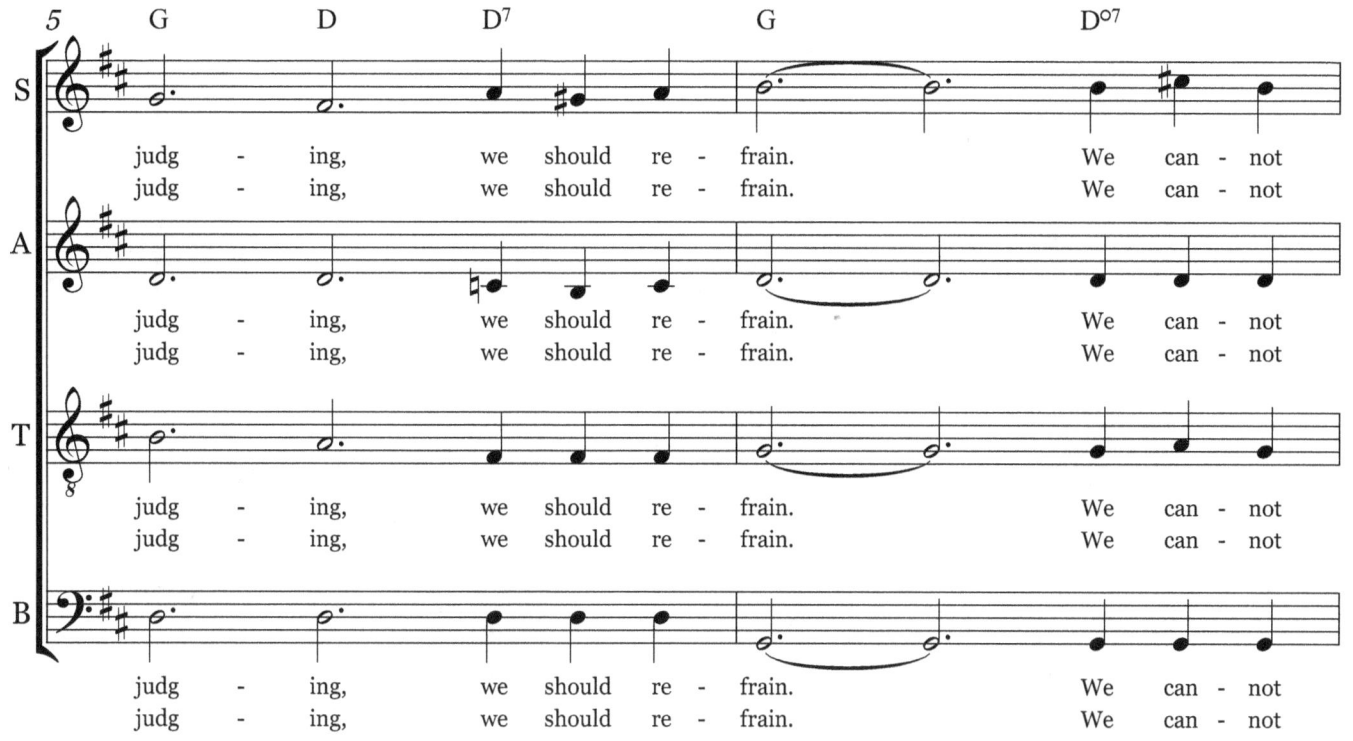
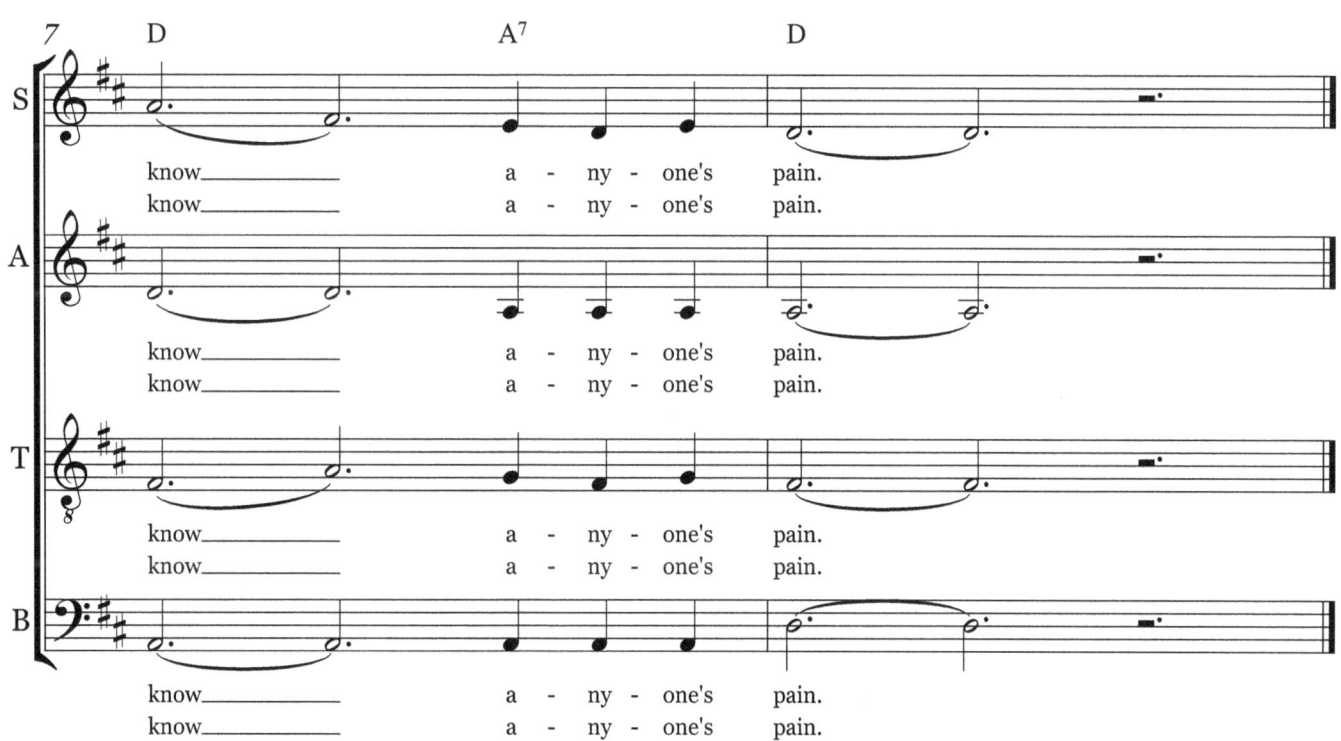

(Note: chord symbols support the soprano melody, not necessarily the SATB harmony)

76. Parents Gone
(From the Secular Hymnal)

Words: Secretary Michael

Music: "Wondrous Love" from *Southern Harmony*, 1835
(traditional hymn: "What Wondrous Love Is This")

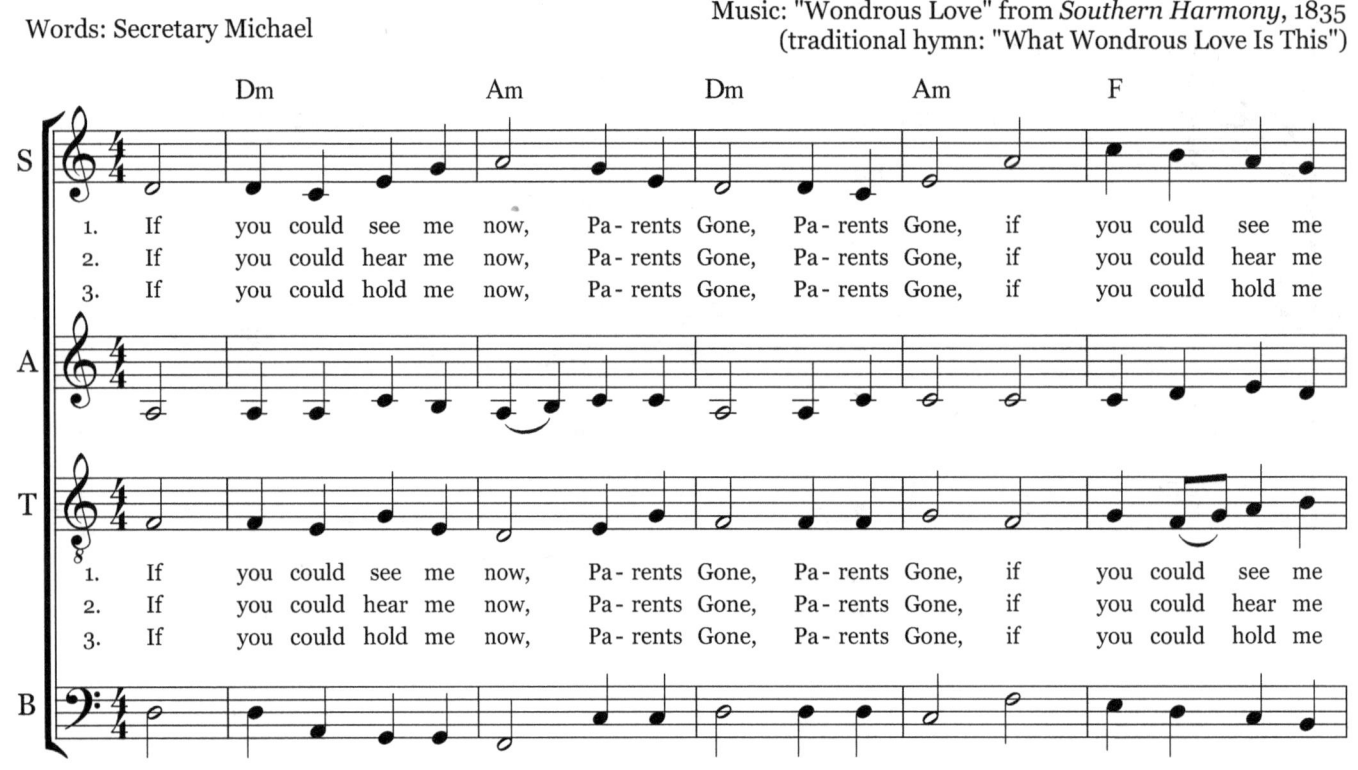

All works by Secretary Michael have been placed in the Public Domain. They may be freely copied and performed.

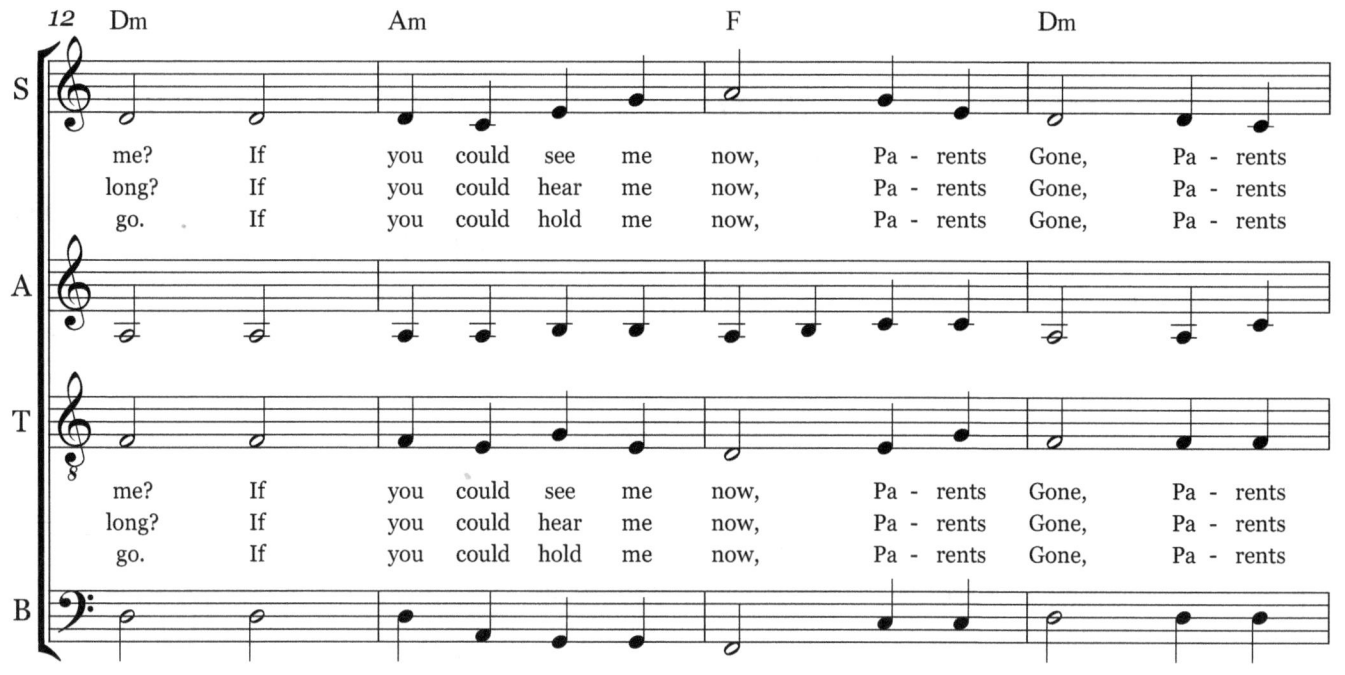
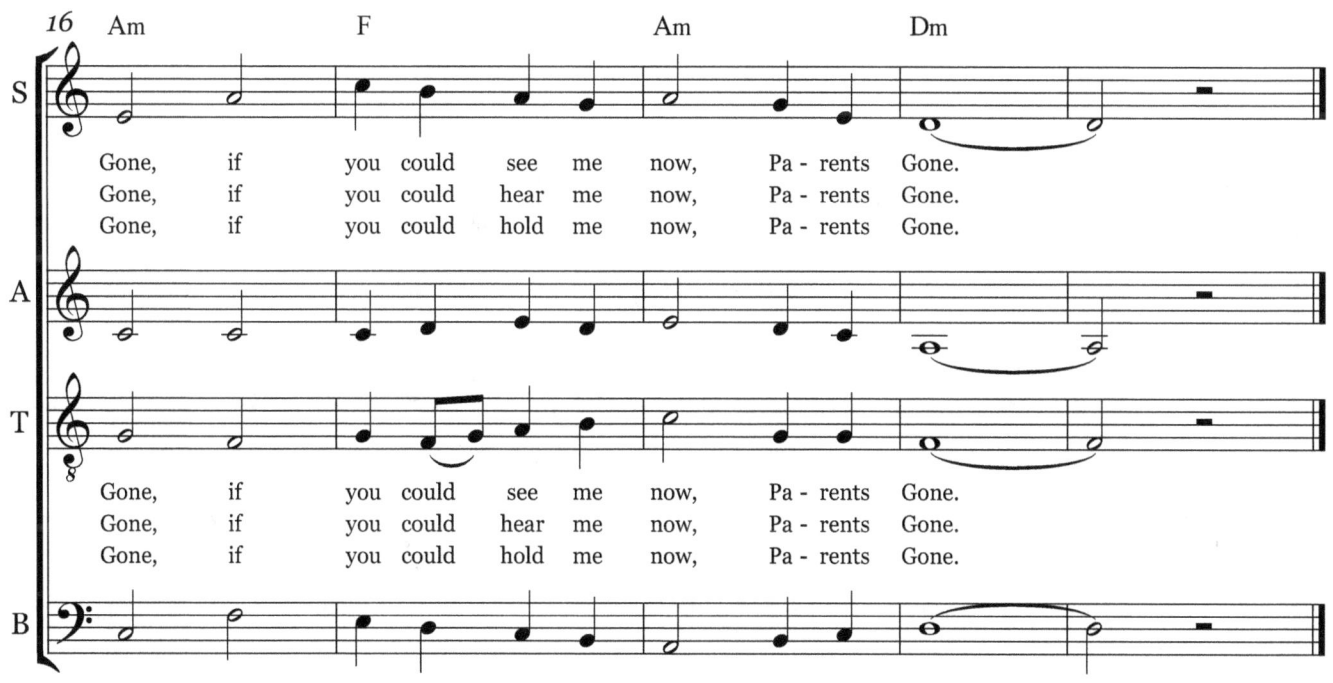

(Note: chord symbols support the soprano melody, not necessarily the SATB harmony)

77. Past Performance is No Guarantee
(From the Secular Hymnal)

Words: Secretary Michael

Music: "Mannheim" by Friedrich Filitz, 1847
(traditional hymn: "Lead Us Heavenly Father Lead Us")

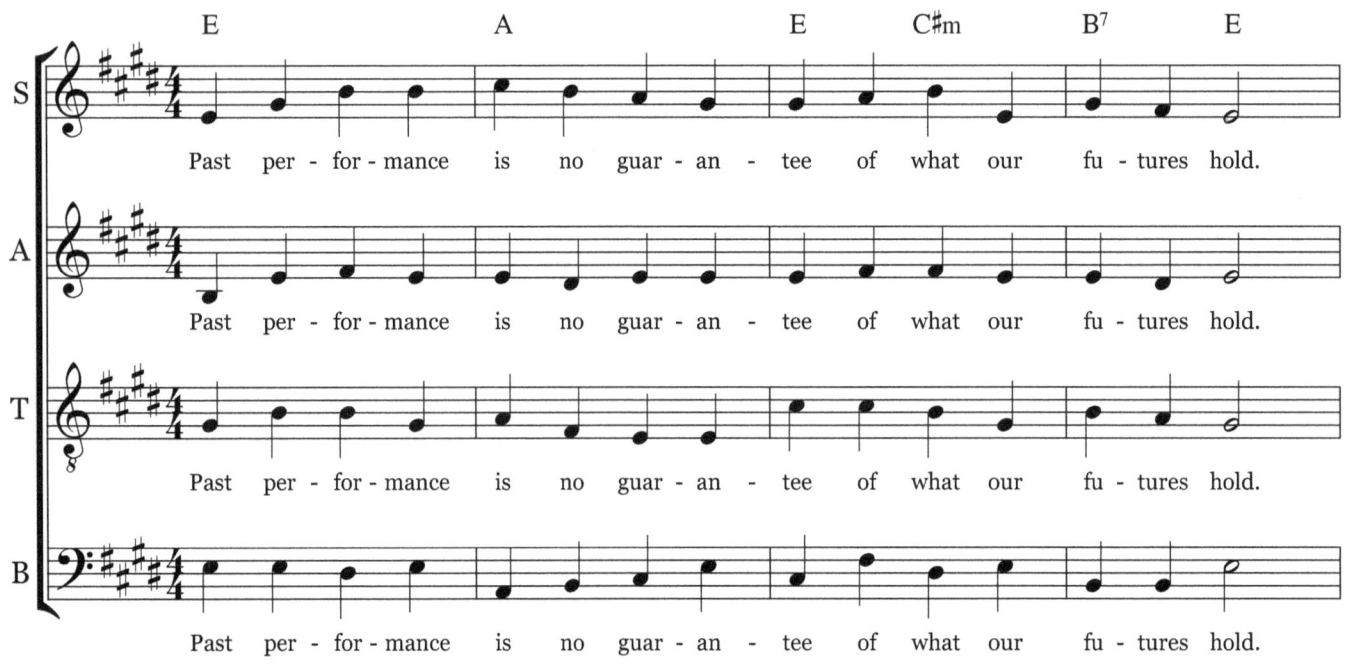

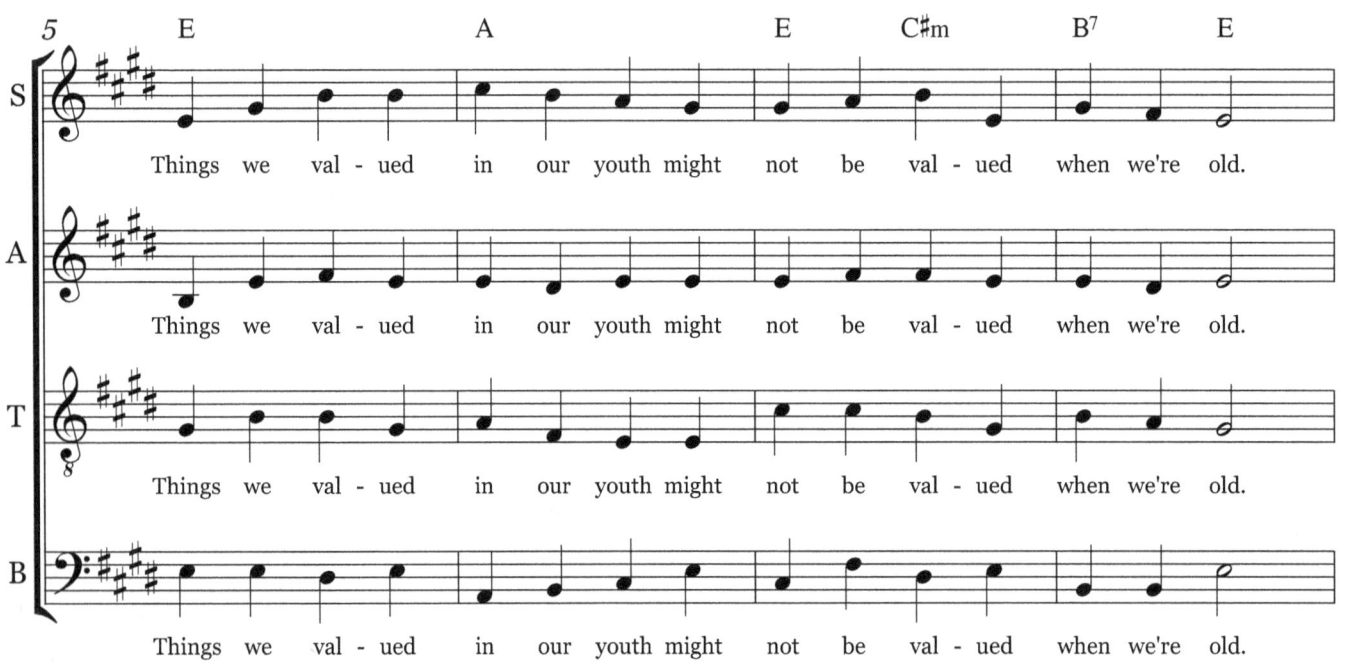

All works by Secretary Michael have been placed in the Public Domain. They may be freely copied and performed.

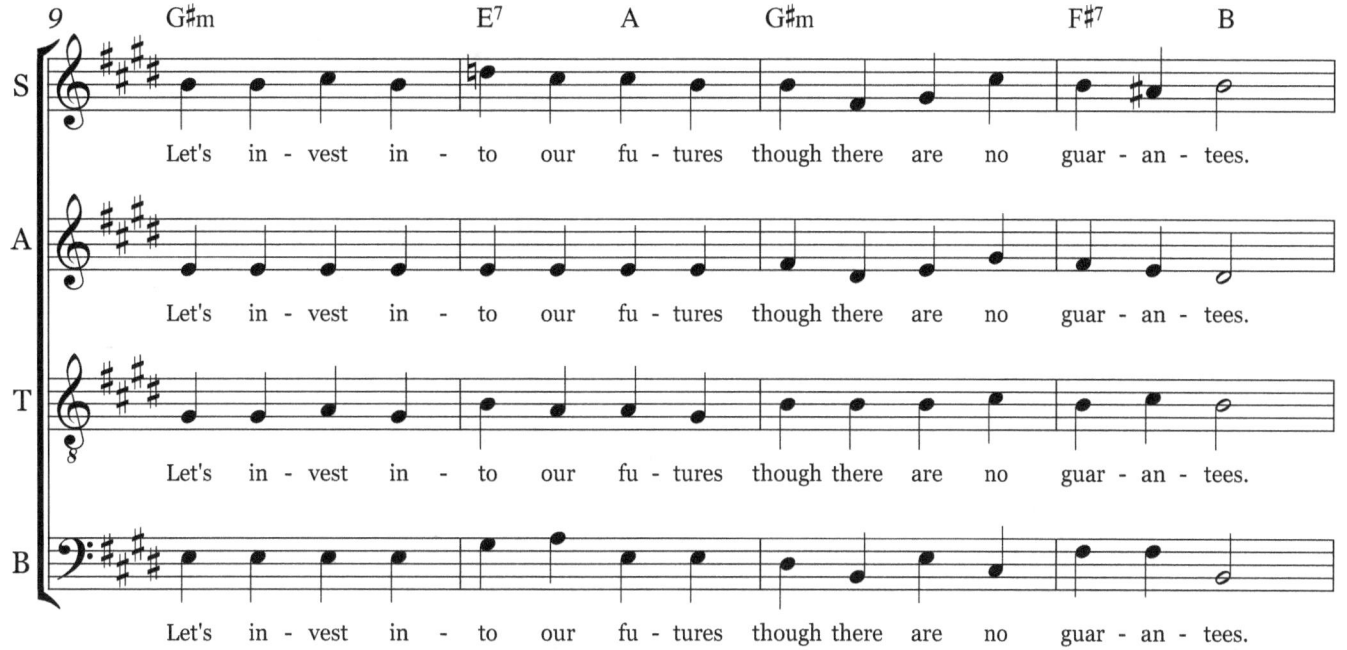

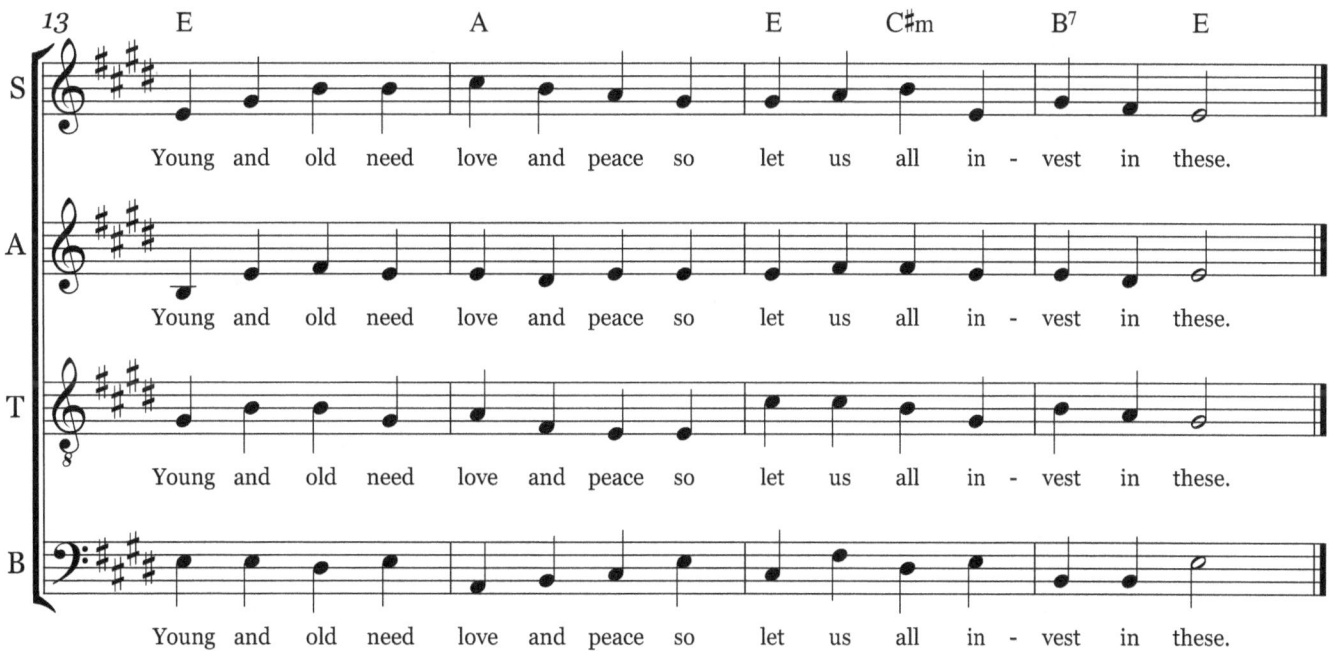

(The title [and first line] of this Secular Hymn comes from a common disclaimer that investment companies use: "Past Performance is No Guarantee of Future Results")

(Note: chord symbols support the soprano melody, not necessarily the SATB harmony)

78. Peace is Not What I Looked For
(From the Secular Hymnal)

Words: Secretary Michael

Music: Charles Crozat Converse, 1868
(traditional hymn: "What a Friend We Have In Jesus")

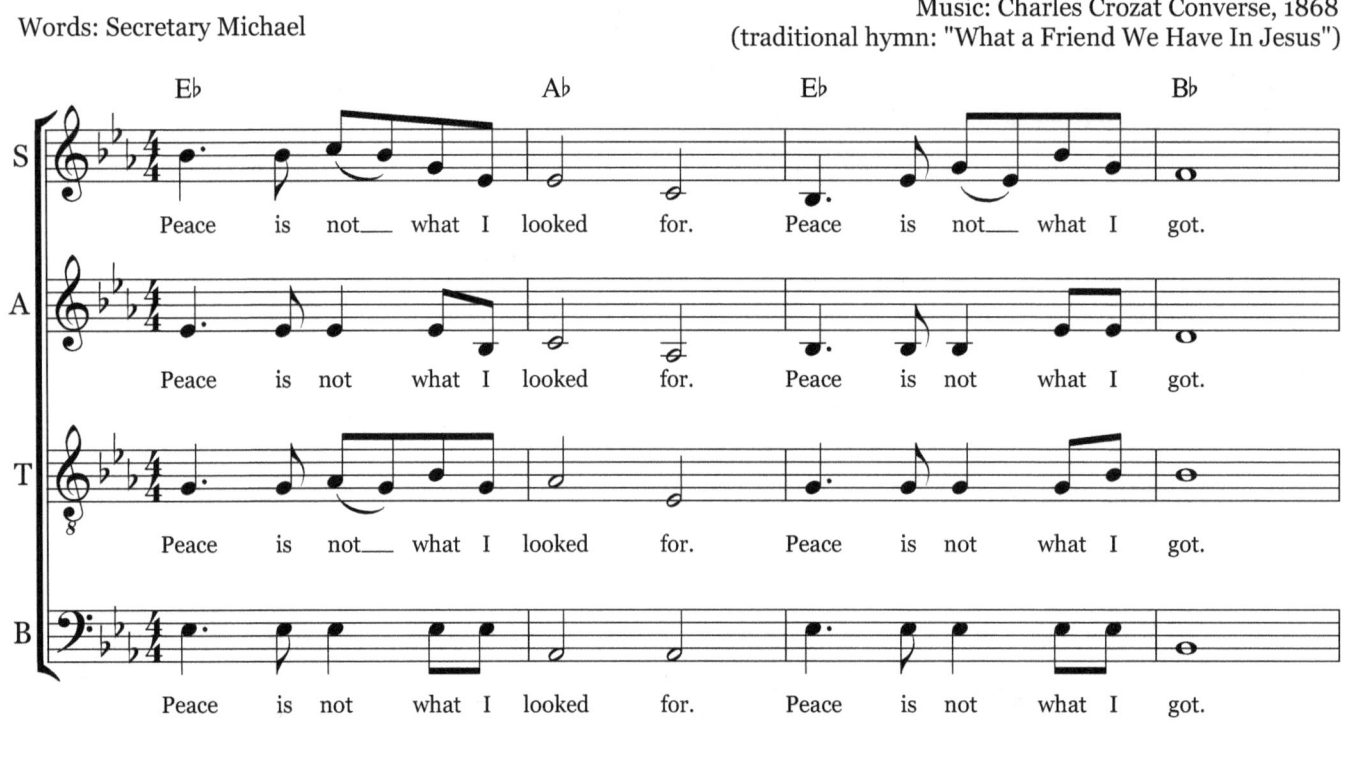

All works by Secretary Michael have been placed in the Public Domain. They may be freely copied and performed.

(Note: chord symbols support the soprano melody, not necessarily the SATB harmony)

79. Peace Like a River

(From the Secular Hymnal)

Words and Music: traditional American
Adapted by Secretary Michael
(traditional hymn: "I've Got Peace Like a River")

(Substitute this rhythm for all similar 4th-verse occurrences)

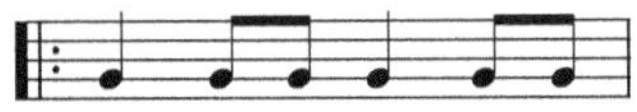

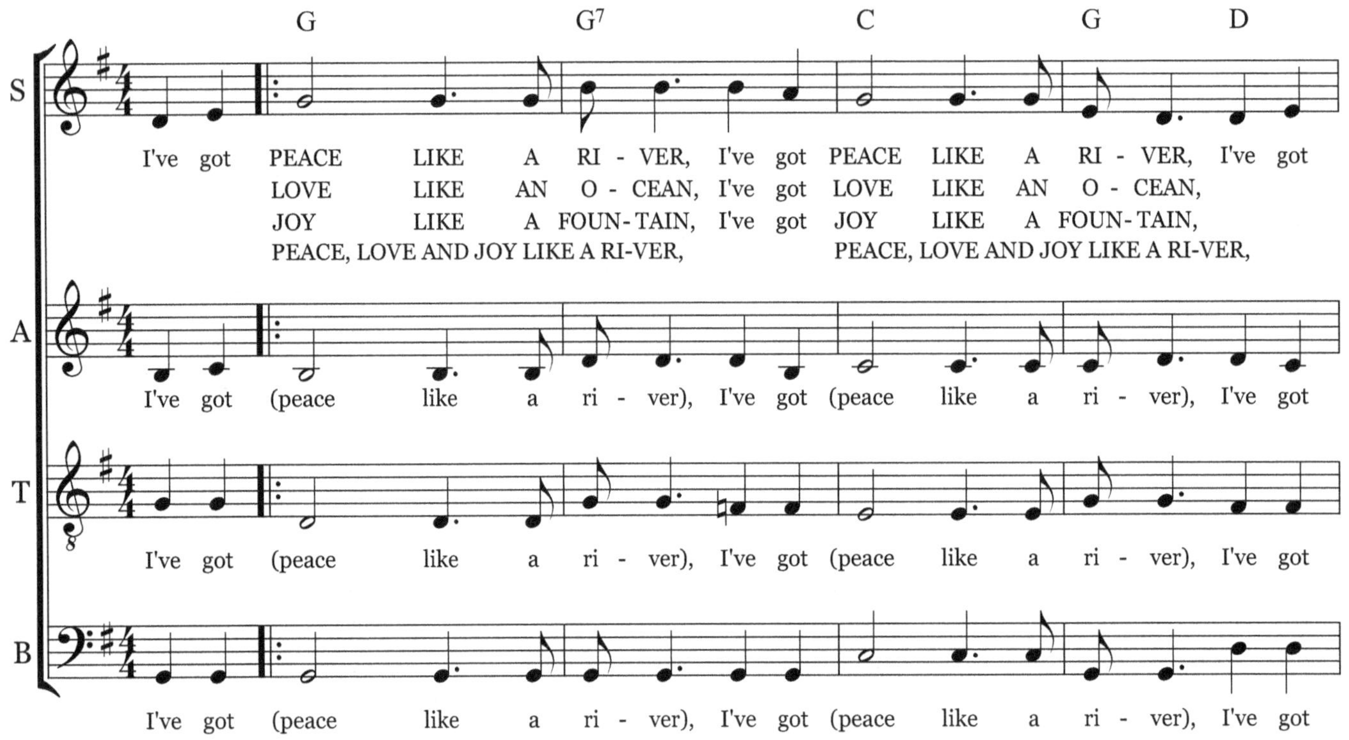

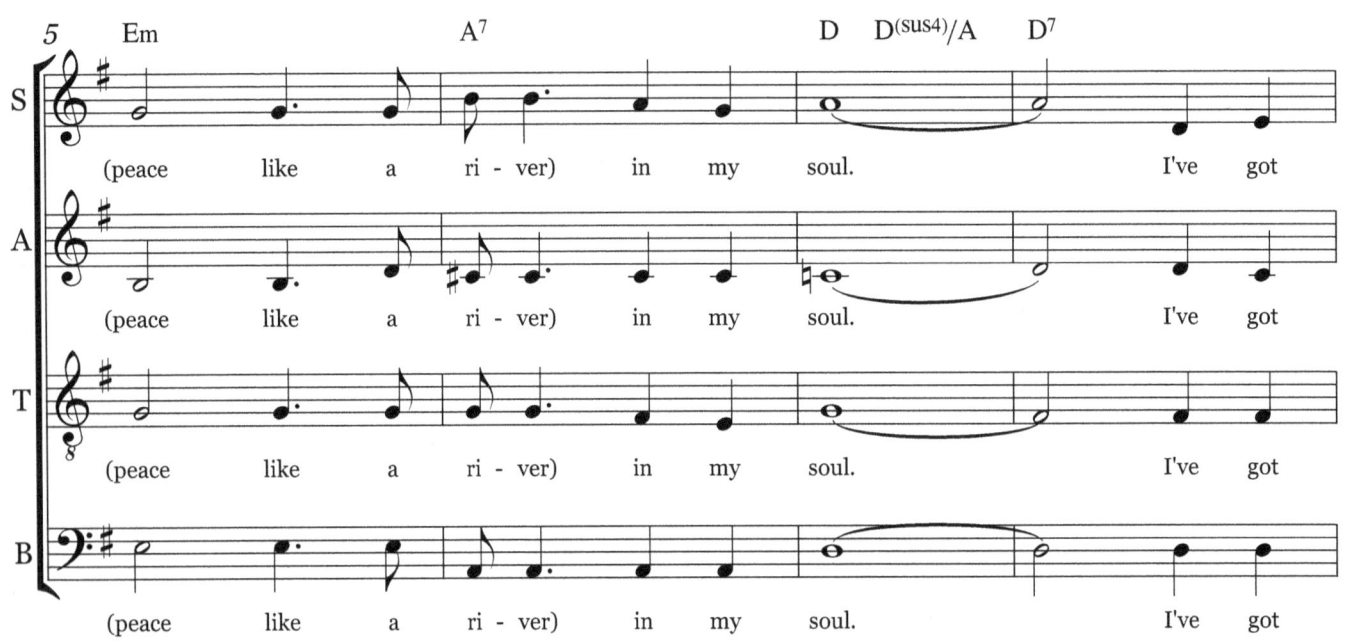

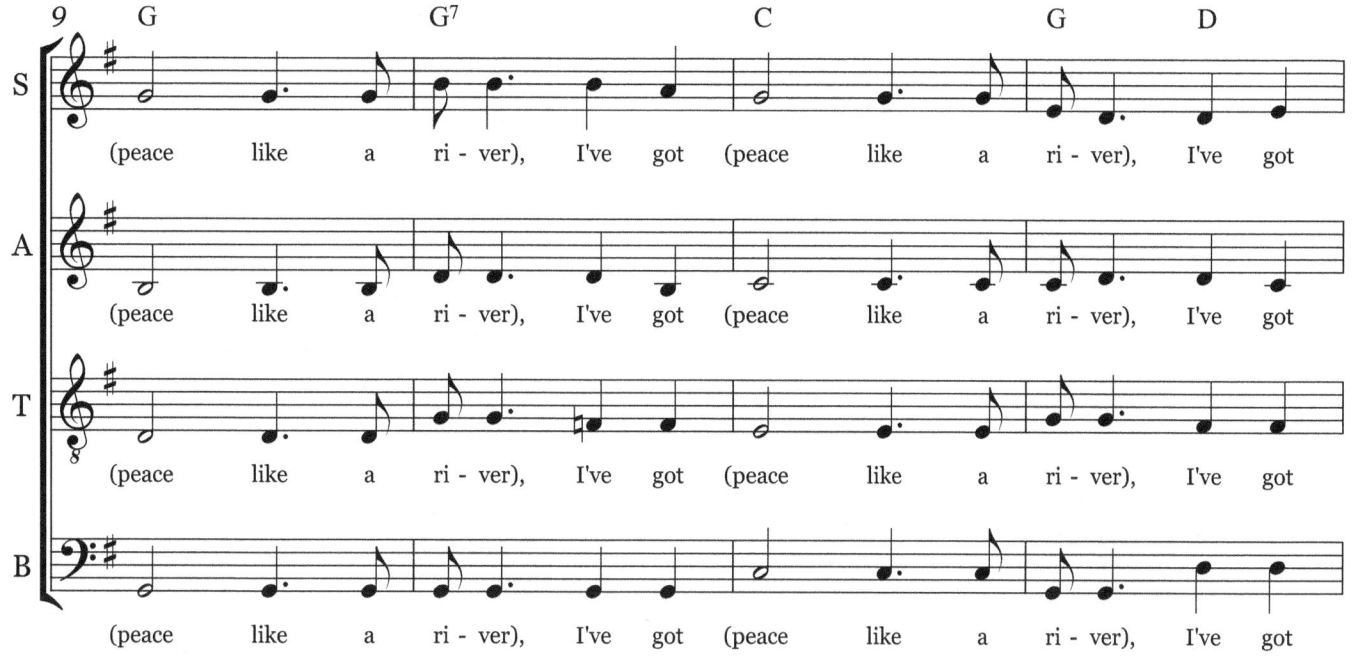
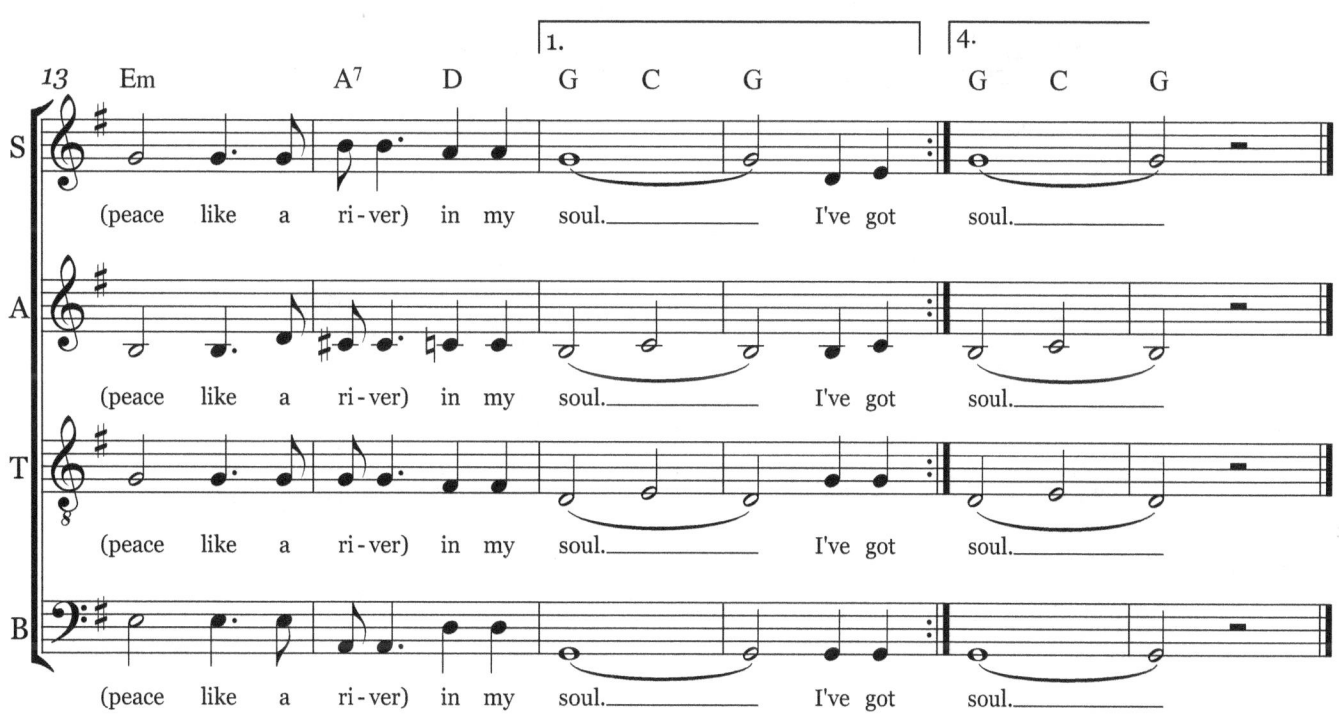

(Note: chord symbols support the soprano melody, not necessarily the SATB harmony)

80. People Are More

(From the Secular Hymnal)

Words: Secretary Michael

Music: "Aberystwyth" by Joseph Parry, 1879
(traditional hymn: "Jesus Lover Of My Soul")

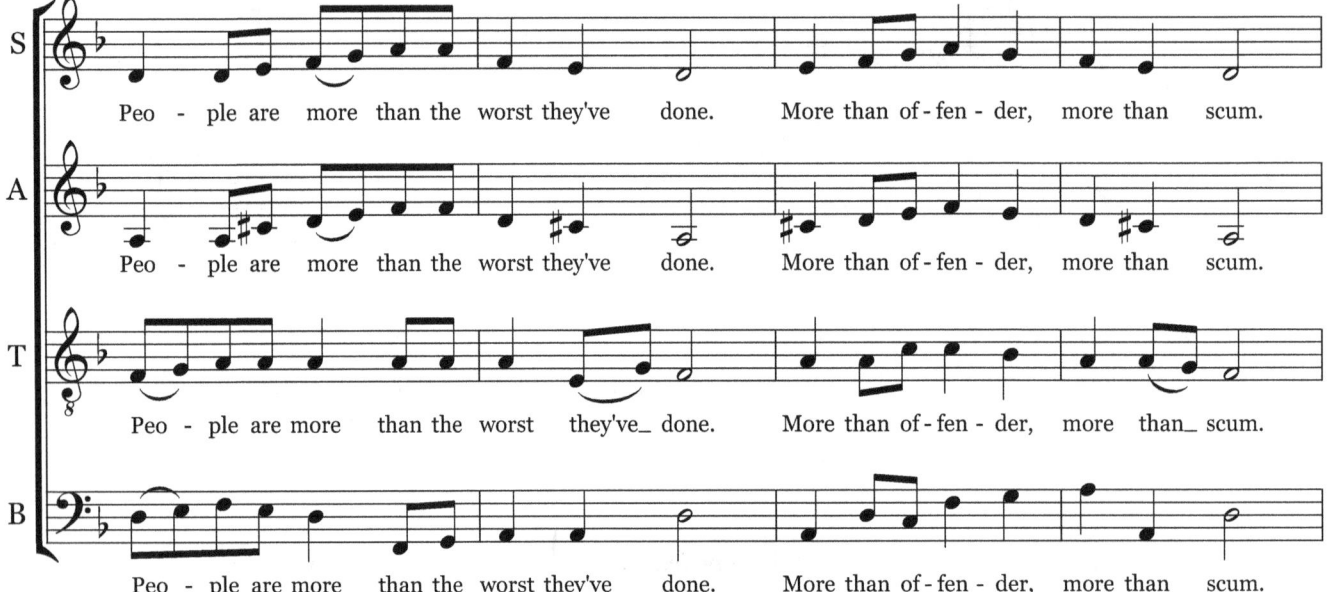

All works by Secretary Michael have been placed in the Public Domain. They may be freely copied and performed.

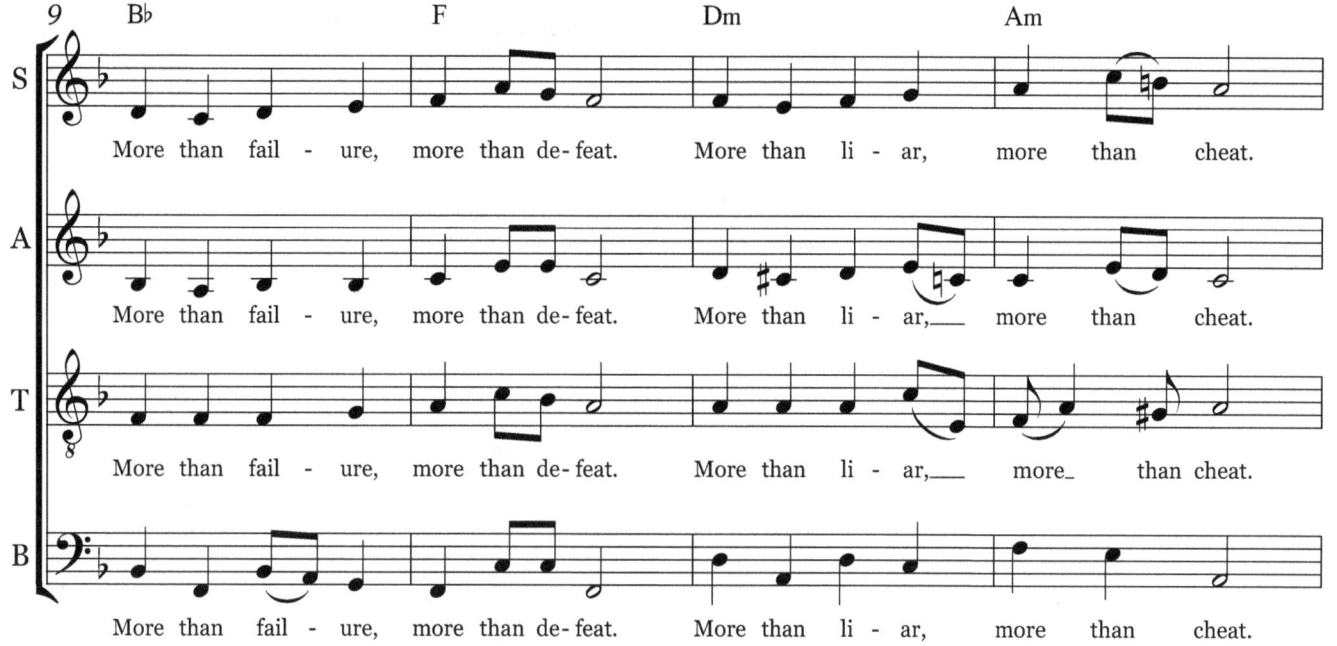

(Note: chord symbols support the soprano melody, not necessarily the SATB harmony)

81. People We Need to Meet

(From the Secular Hymnal)

All works by Secretary Michael have been placed in the Public Domain. They may be freely copied and performed.

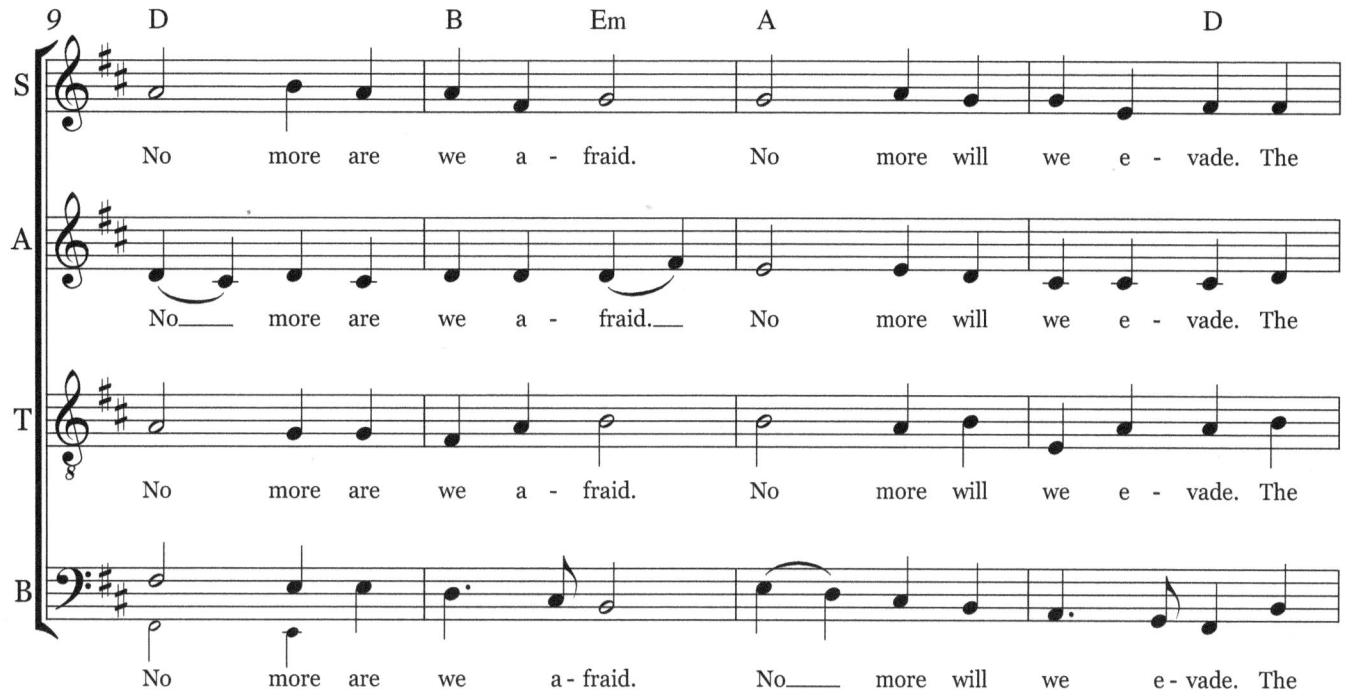
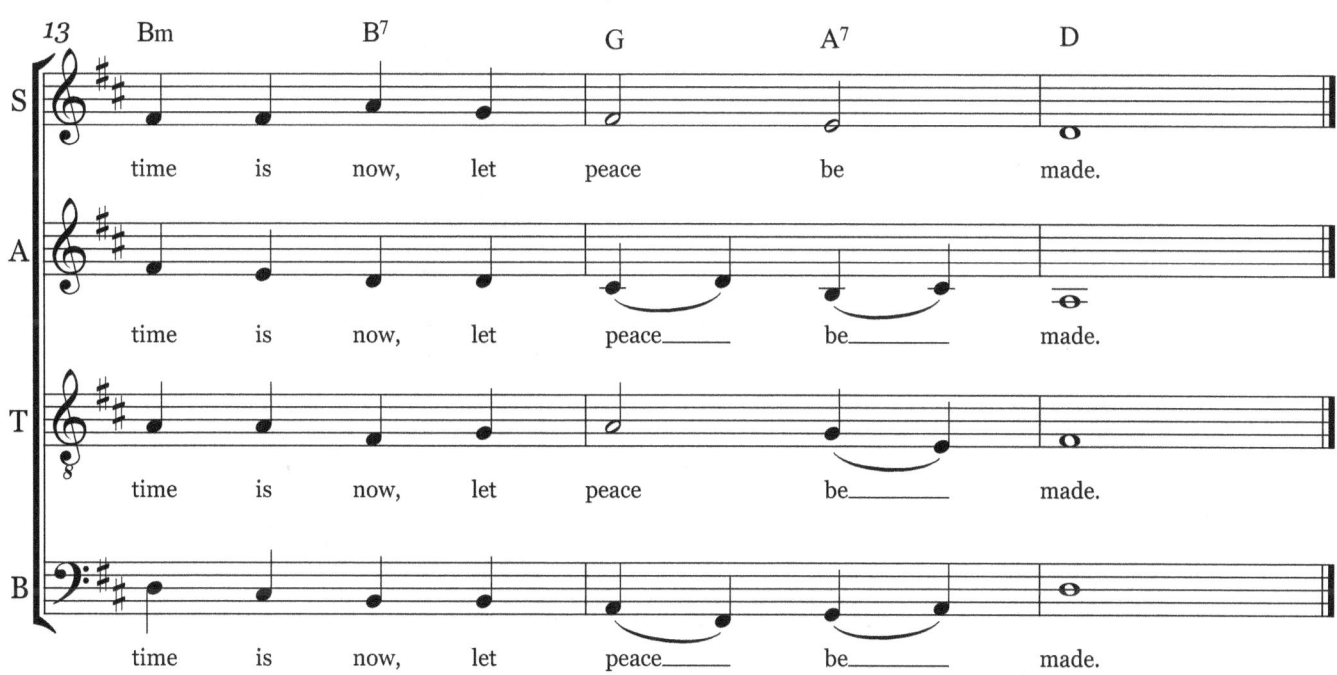

(Note: chord symbols support the soprano melody, not necessarily the SATB harmony)

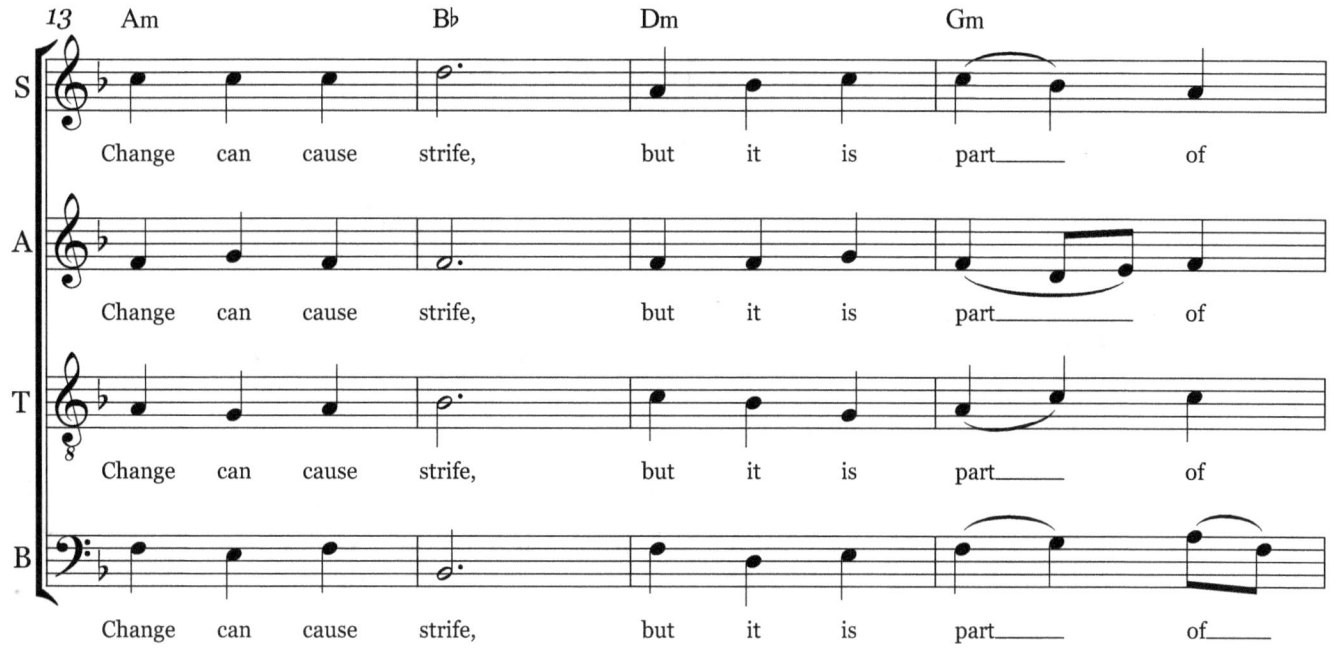

(Note: chord symbols support the soprano melody, not necessarily the SATB harmony)

83. Relieving Suffering

(From the Secular Hymnal)

Words: Secretary Michael

Music: "Need" by Robert Lowry, 1872
(traditional hymn: "I Need Thee Every Hour")

All works by Secretary Michael have been placed in the Public Domain. They may be freely copied and performed.

(Note: chord symbols support the soprano melody, not necessarily the SATB harmony)

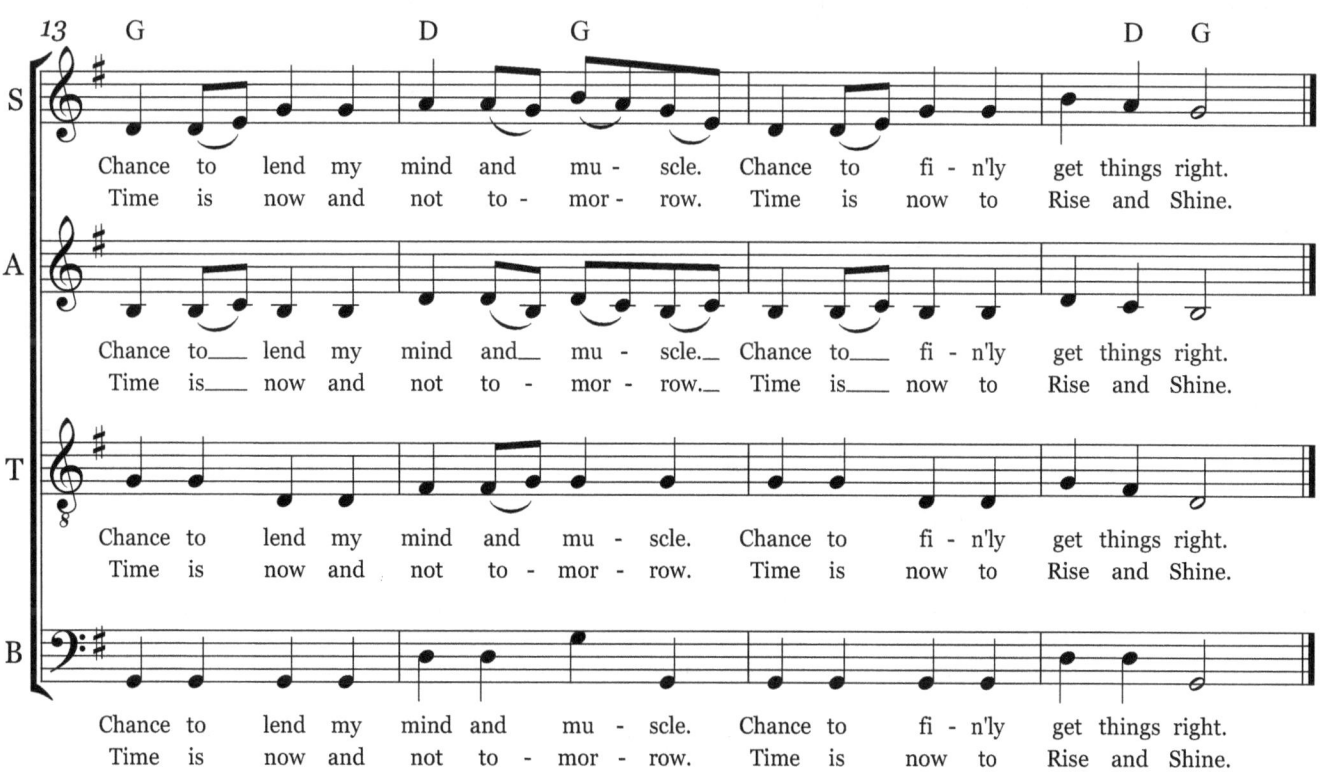

(Note: chord symbols support the soprano melody, not necessarily the SATB harmony)

85. Seen, Heard and Understood
(From the Secular Hymnal)

Words: Secretary Michael

Music: "Bethany" by Lowell Mason, 1856
(traditional hymn: "Nearer My God, To Thee")

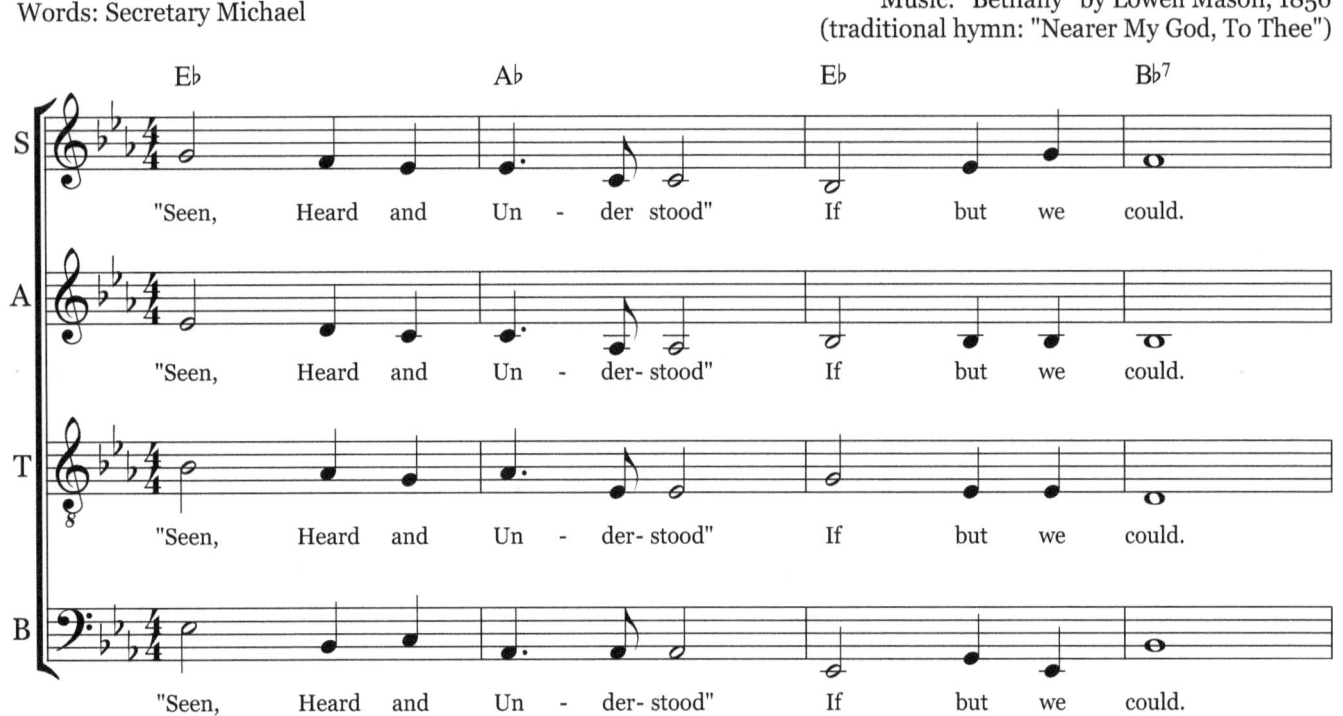

All works by Secretary Michael have been placed in the Public Domain. They may be freely copied and performed.

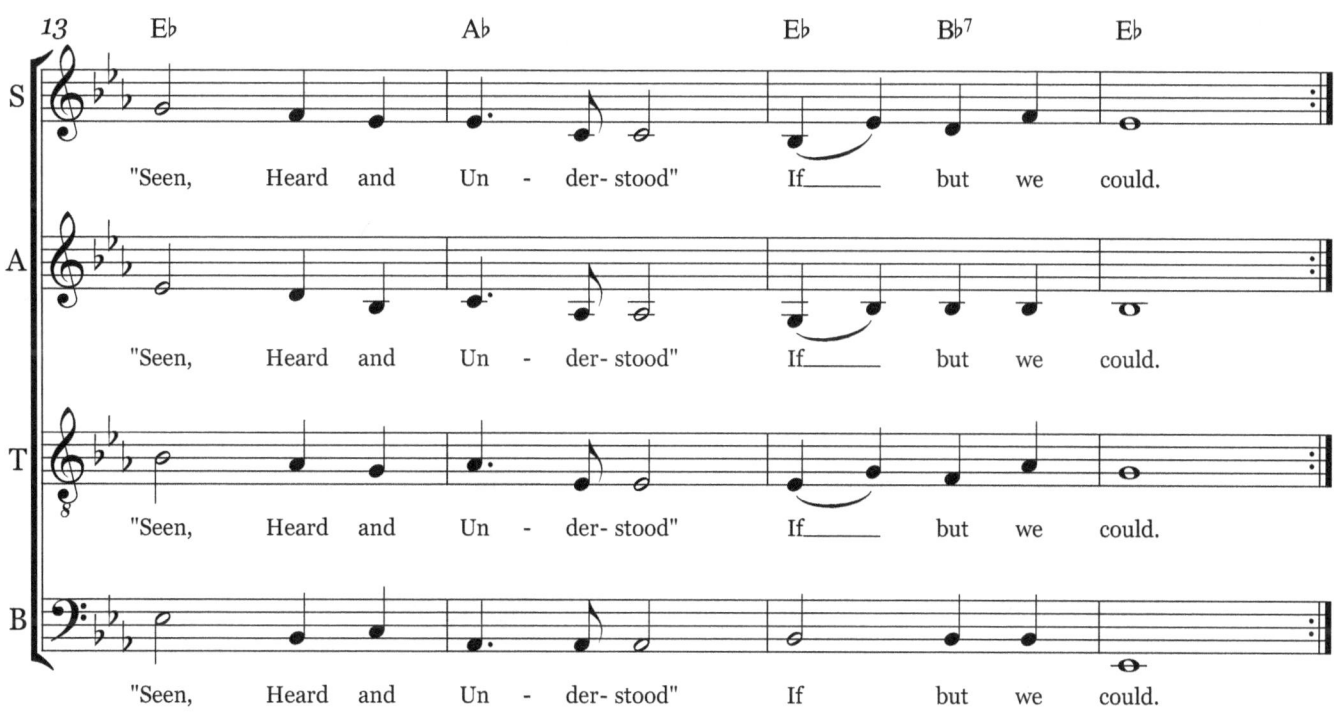

(Note: chord symbols support the soprano melody, not necessarily the SATB harmony)

86. Skating, Skating

(From the Secular Hymnal)

Words: Secretary Michael

Music: "Westminster Abbey" by Henry Purcell, c.1680
(traditional hymn: "Christ is Made the Sure Foundation")

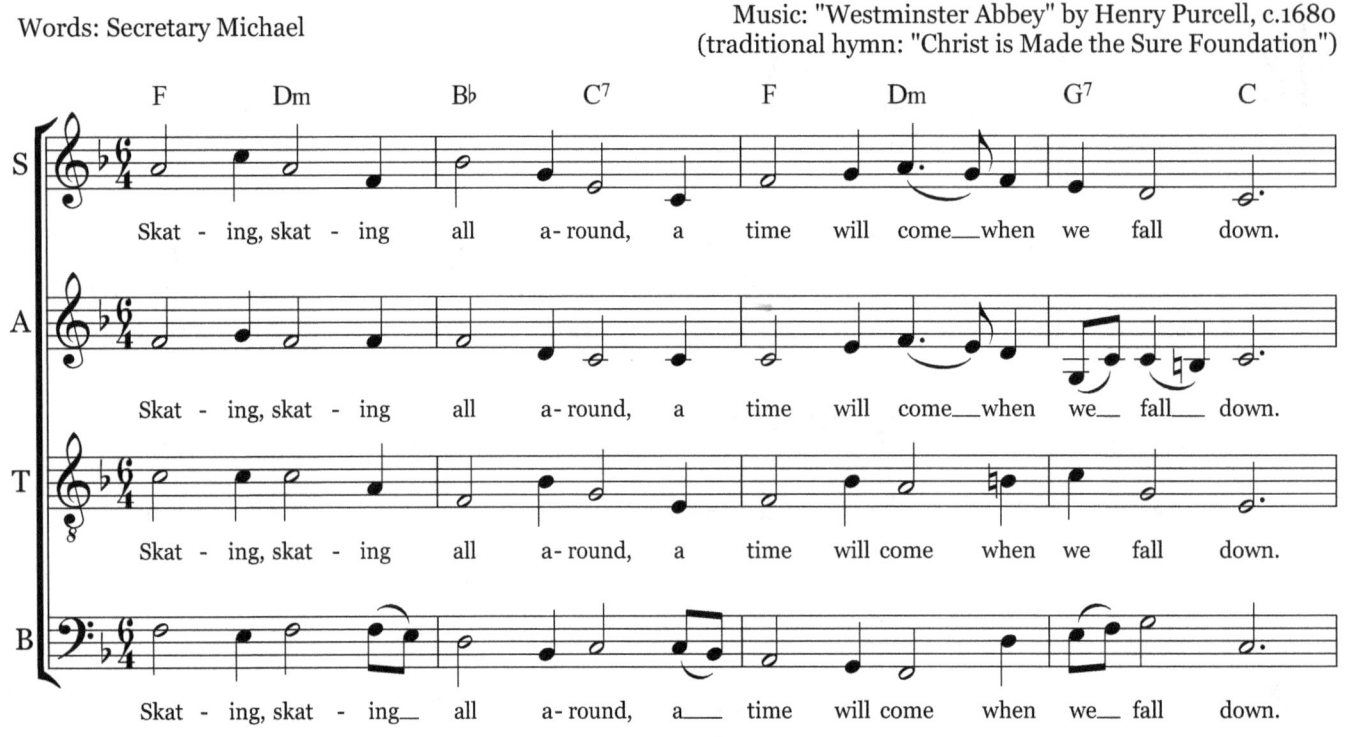

All works by Secretary Michael have been placed in the Public Domain. They may be freely copied and performed.

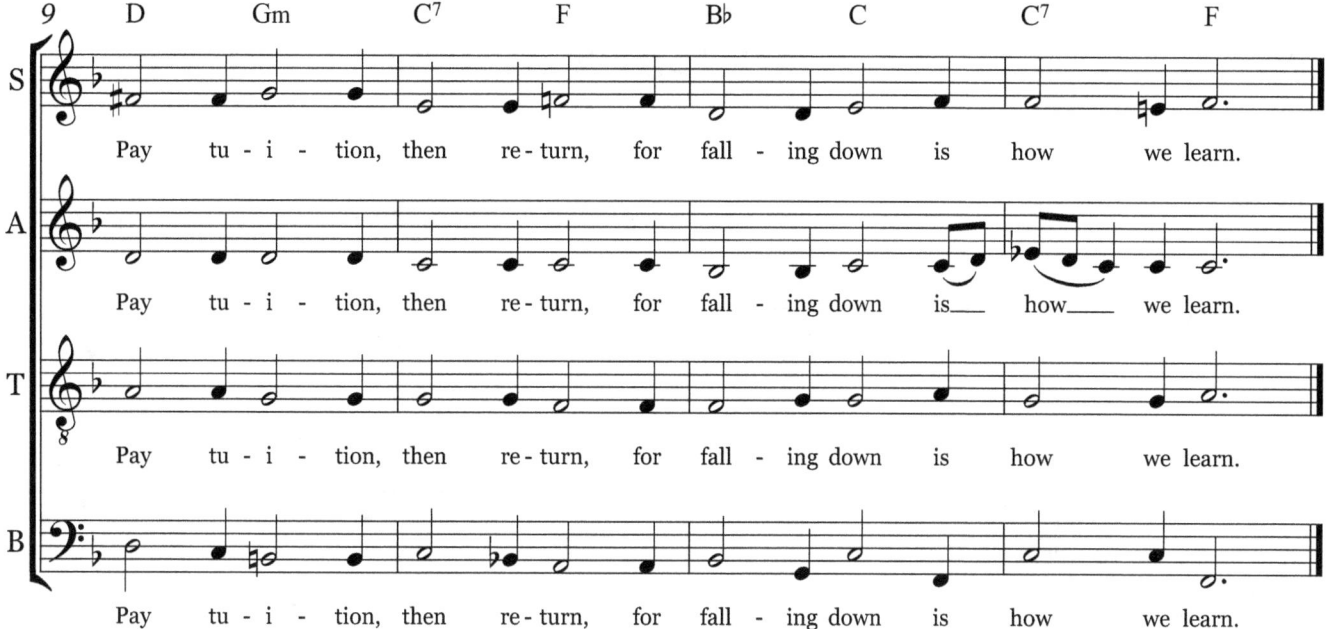

(Note: chord symbols support the soprano melody, not necessarily the SATB harmony)

87. So Many Ways

(From the Secular Hymnal)

Words: Secretary Michael

Music: "Billing" by Sir Richard Runciman Terry, 1912
(traditional hymn: "Praise to the Holiest in the Height")

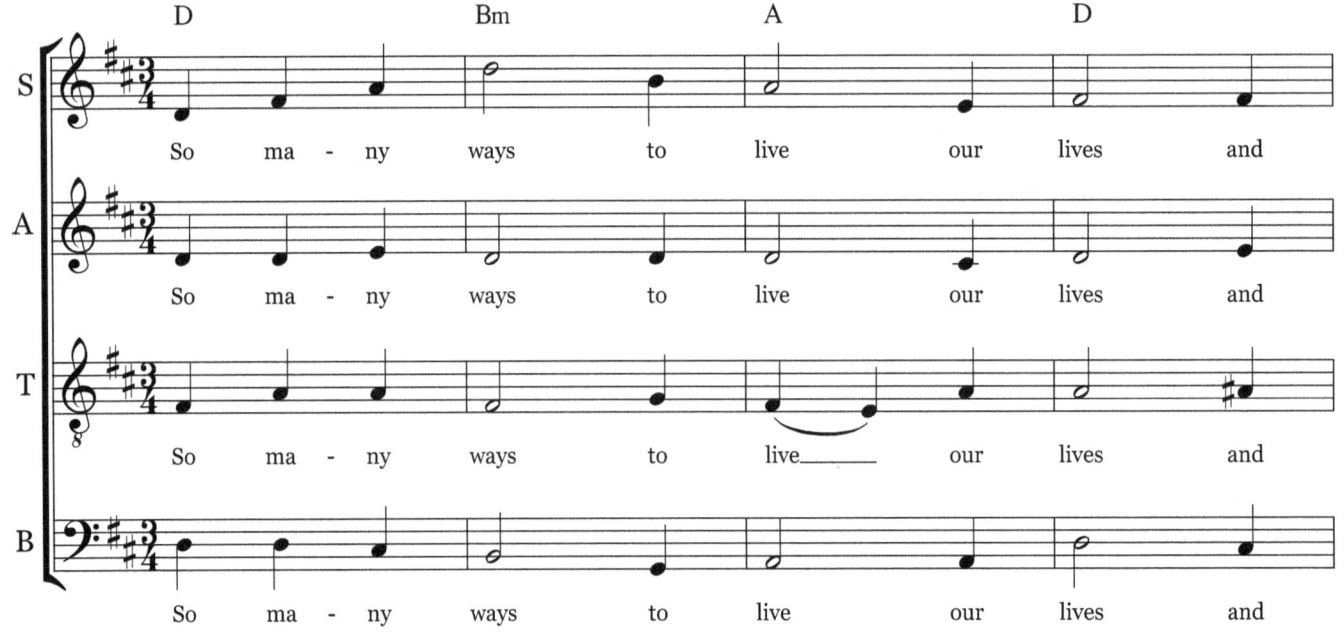

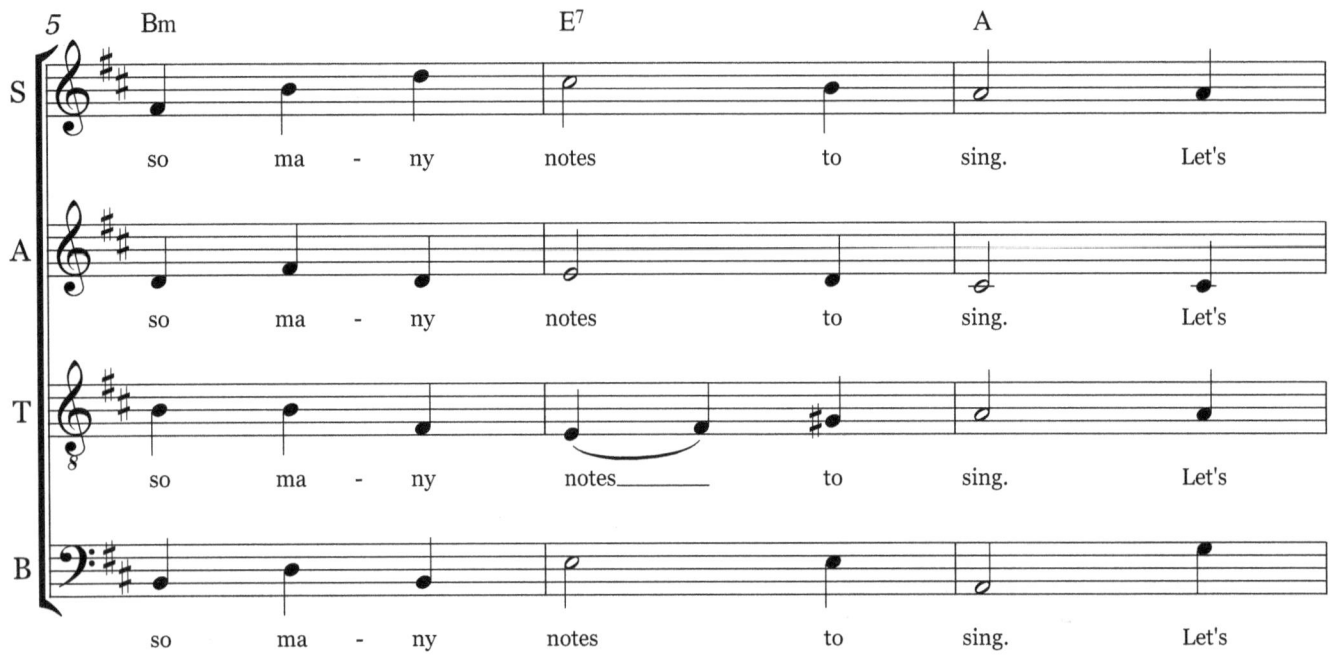

All works by Secretary Michael have been placed in the Public Domain. They may be freely copied and performed.

(Note: chord symbols support the soprano melody, not necessarily the SATB harmony)

88. Some Are Young, Some Old

(From the Secular Hymnal)

Words: Secretary Michael

Music: "Anchor" by William James Kirkpatrick, 1882
(traditional hymn: "Will Your Anchor Hold?")

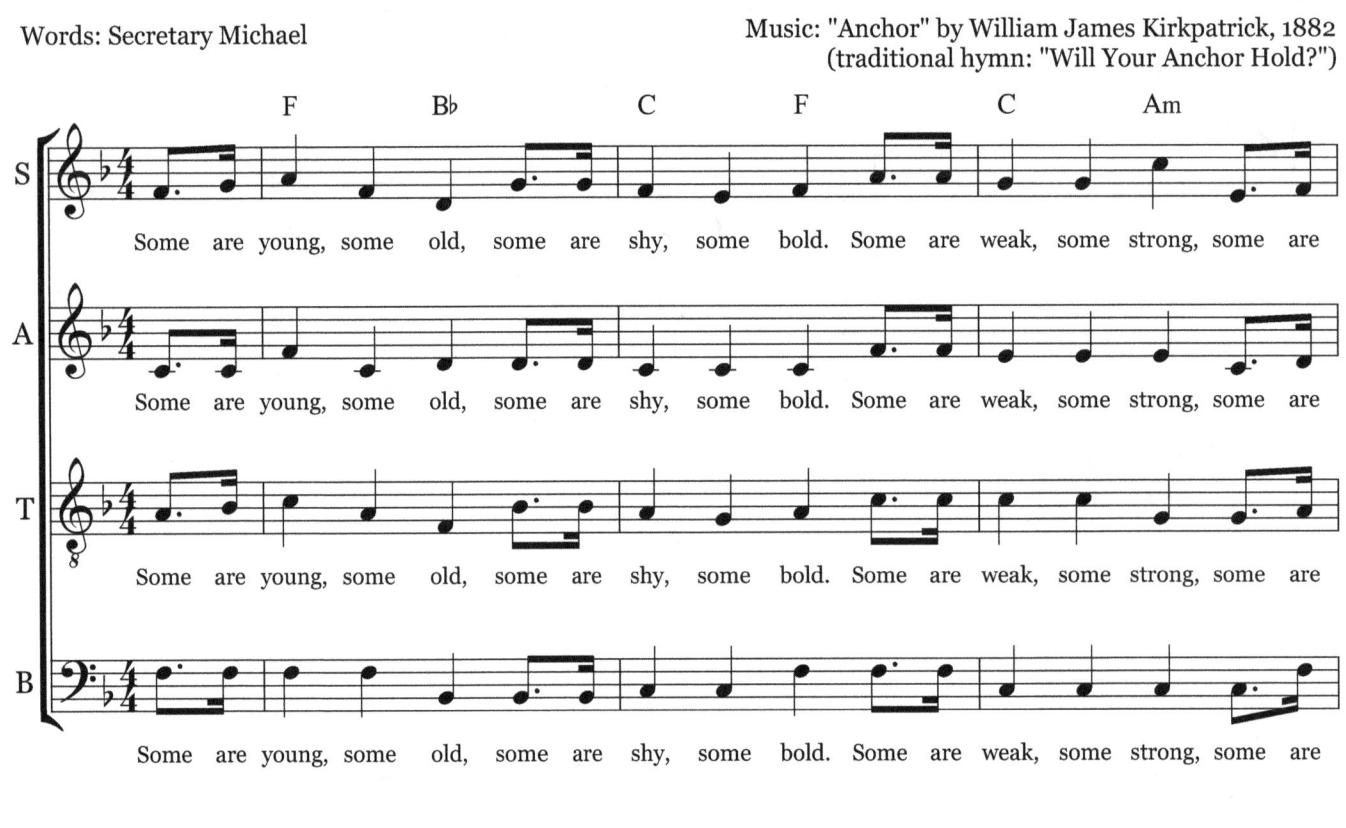

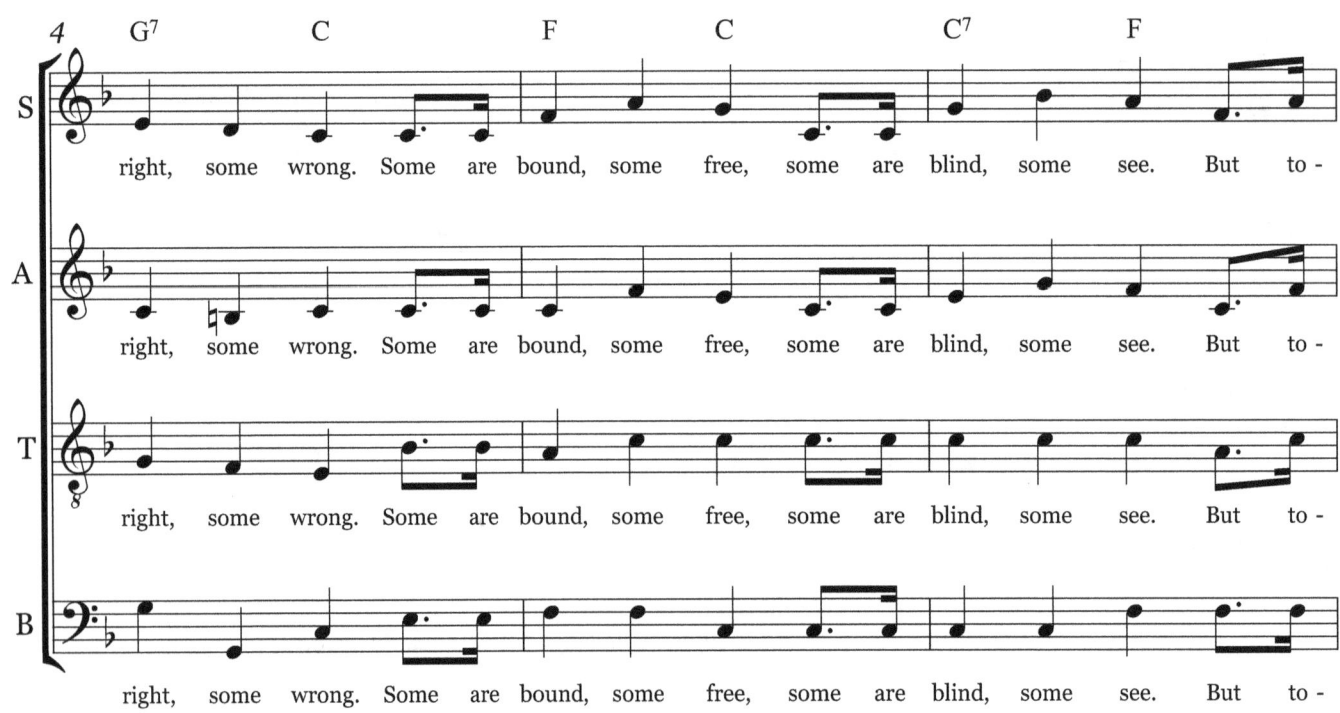

All works by Secretary Michael have been placed in the Public Domain. They may be freely copied and performed.

(Note: chord symbols support the soprano melody, not necessarily the SATB harmony)

89. Someday When Guns Are Gone

(From the Secular Hymnal)

Words: Secretary Michael

Music: "Dennis" by Johann Georg Nageli
Arranged by Lowell Mason, 1845
(traditional hymn: "Blest Be the Tie That Binds")

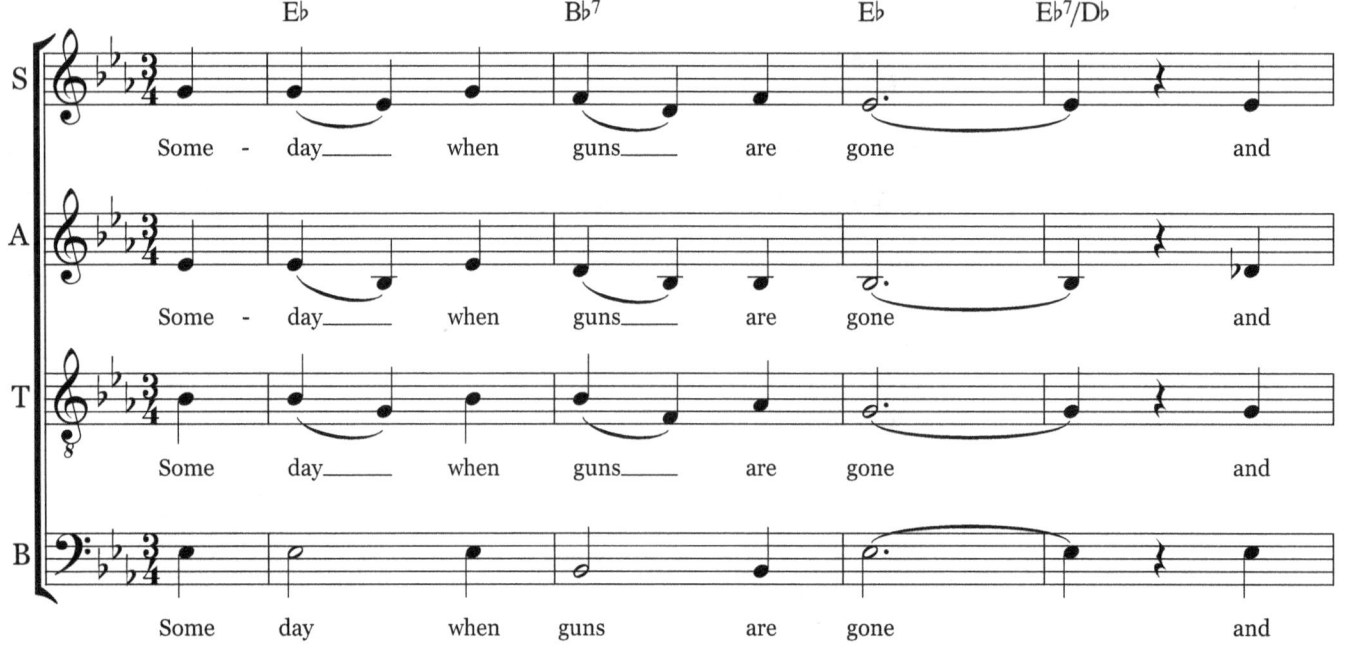

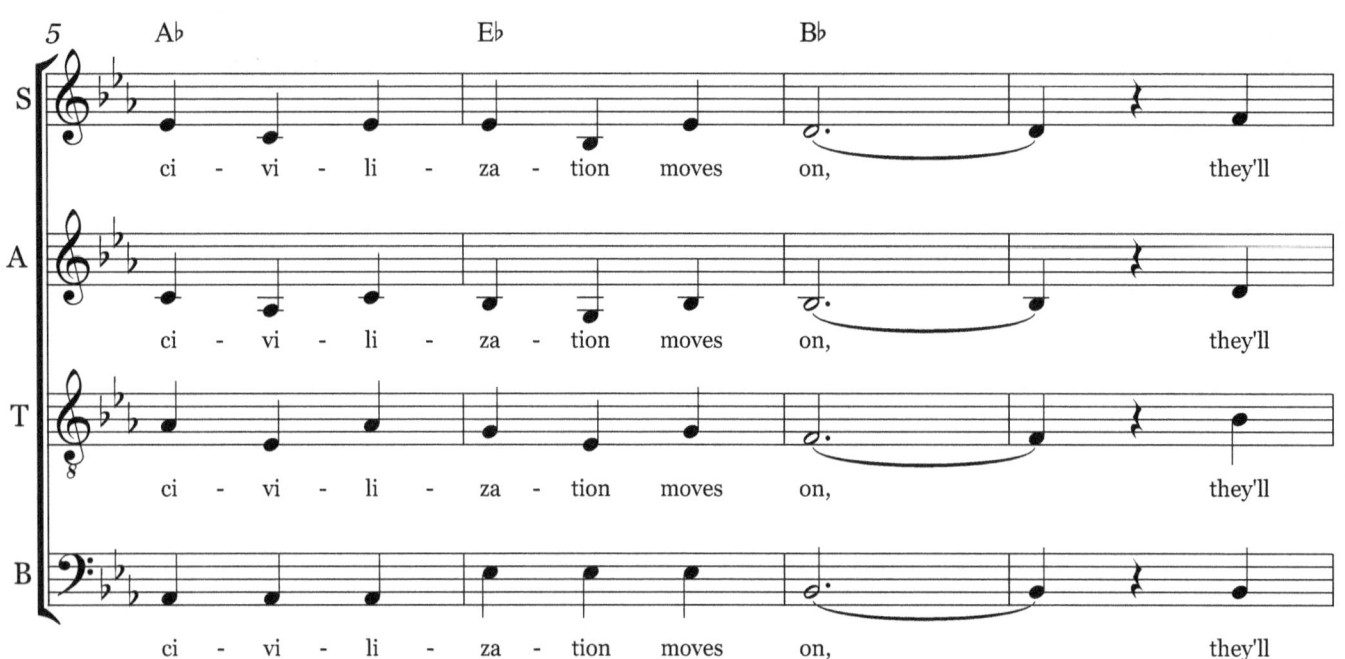

All works by Secretary Michael have been placed in the Public Domain. They may be freely copied and performed.

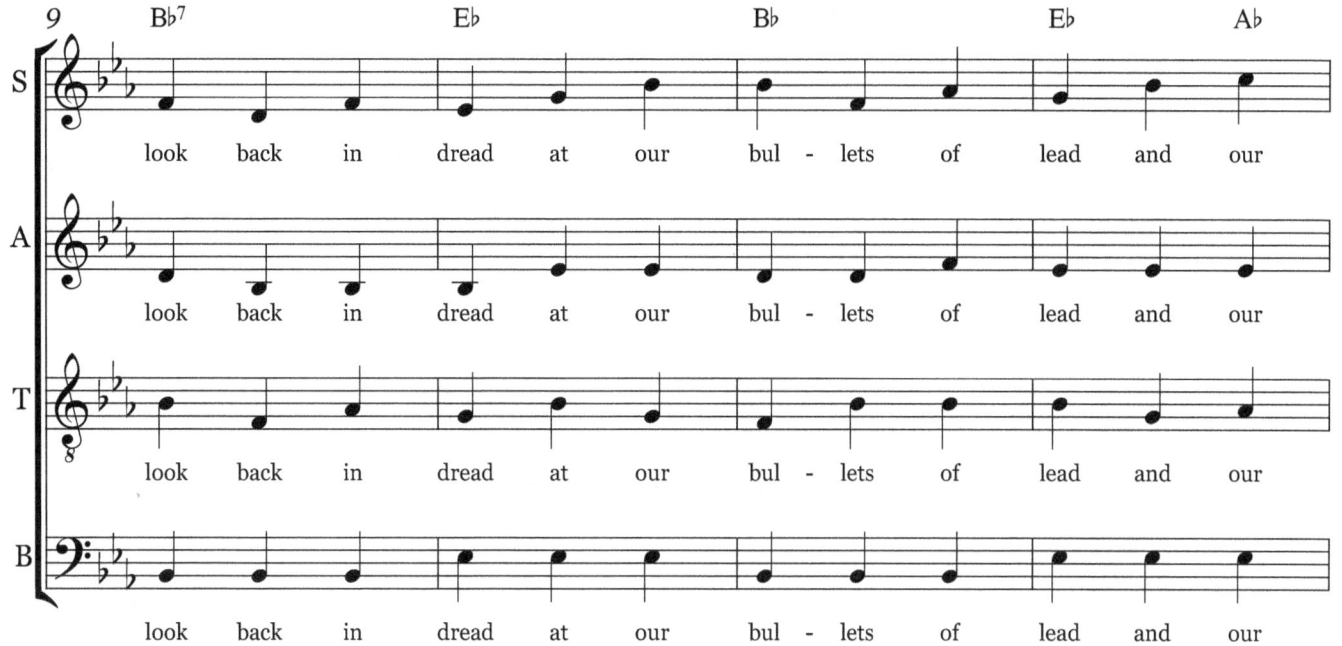
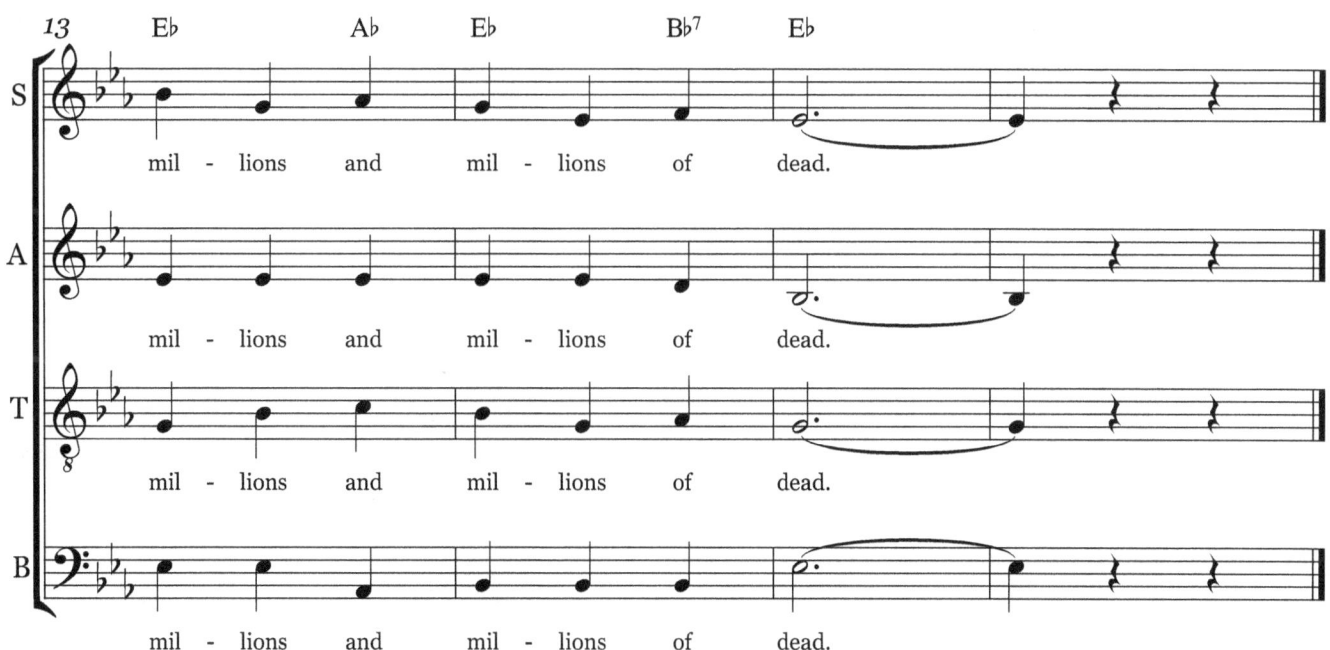

(Note: chord symbols support the soprano melody, not necessarily the SATB harmony)

90. Someone Should

(From the Secular Hymnal)

Words: Secretary Michael

Music: "Cwm Rhondda" by John Hughes, 1907
(traditional hymn: "Guide Me, O Thou Great Jehovah")

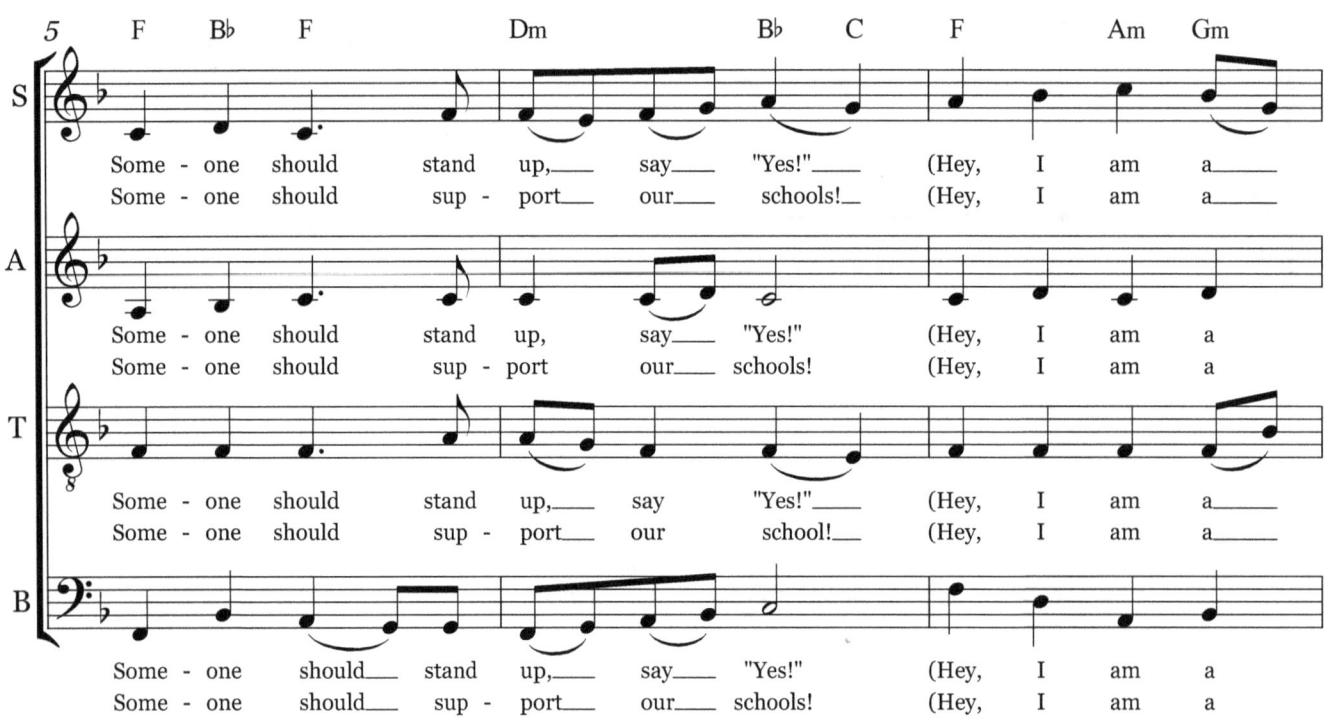

All works by Secretary Michael have been placed in the Public Domain. They may be freely copied and performed.

(Note: chord symbols support the soprano melody, not necessarily the SATB harmony)

91. Spent Our Treasure

(From the Secular Hymnal)

Words: Secretary Michael

Tune: "Were You There?" (traditional African-American spiritual)
Arranged by C. Winfred Douglas, 1940 (P.D.)
(traditional hymn: "Were You There When They Crucified My Lord?")

All works by Secretary Michael have been placed in the Public Domain. They may be freely copied and performed.

(Explanation: U-235 is bomb-grade uranium which is refined from common uranium through expensive processing)

(Note: chord symbols support the soprano melody, not necessarily the SATB harmony)

92. Standing At Bat

(From the Secular Hymnal)

Words: Secretary Michael

Music: "Hamburg" by Lowell Mason, 1824
(traditional hymn: "When I Survey the Wondrous Cross")

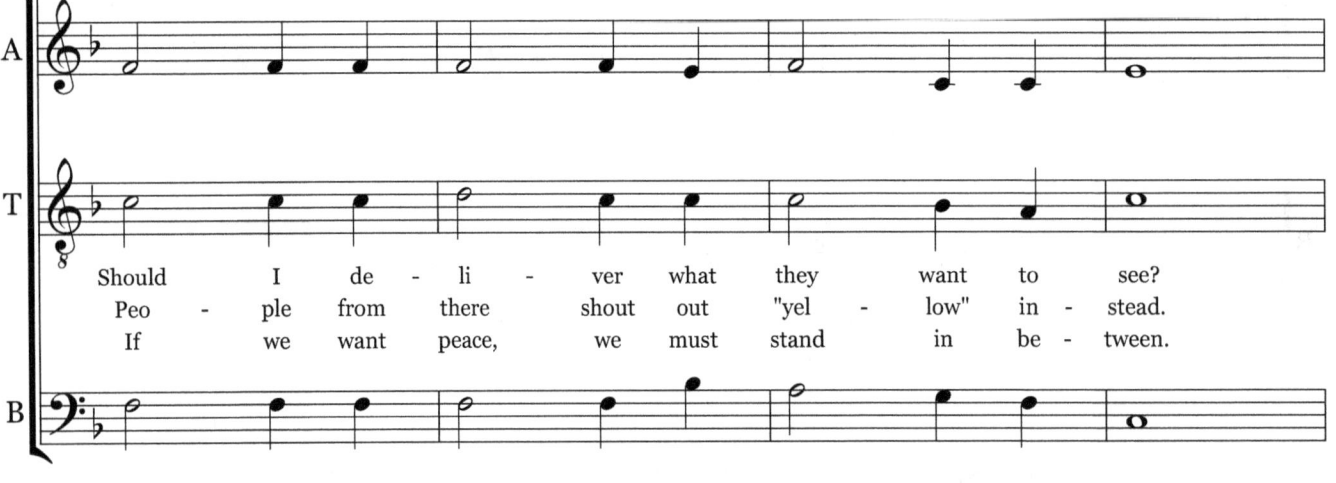

1. Stand - ing at bat as the teams look at me.
2. Peo - ple from here say to fight for the "red".
3. Why in the world should I fight for a team?

Should I de - li - ver what they want to see?
Peo - ple from there shout out "yel - low" in - stead.
If we want peace, we must stand in be - tween.

(PD) *All works by Secretary Michael have been placed in the Public Domain. They may be freely copied and performed.*

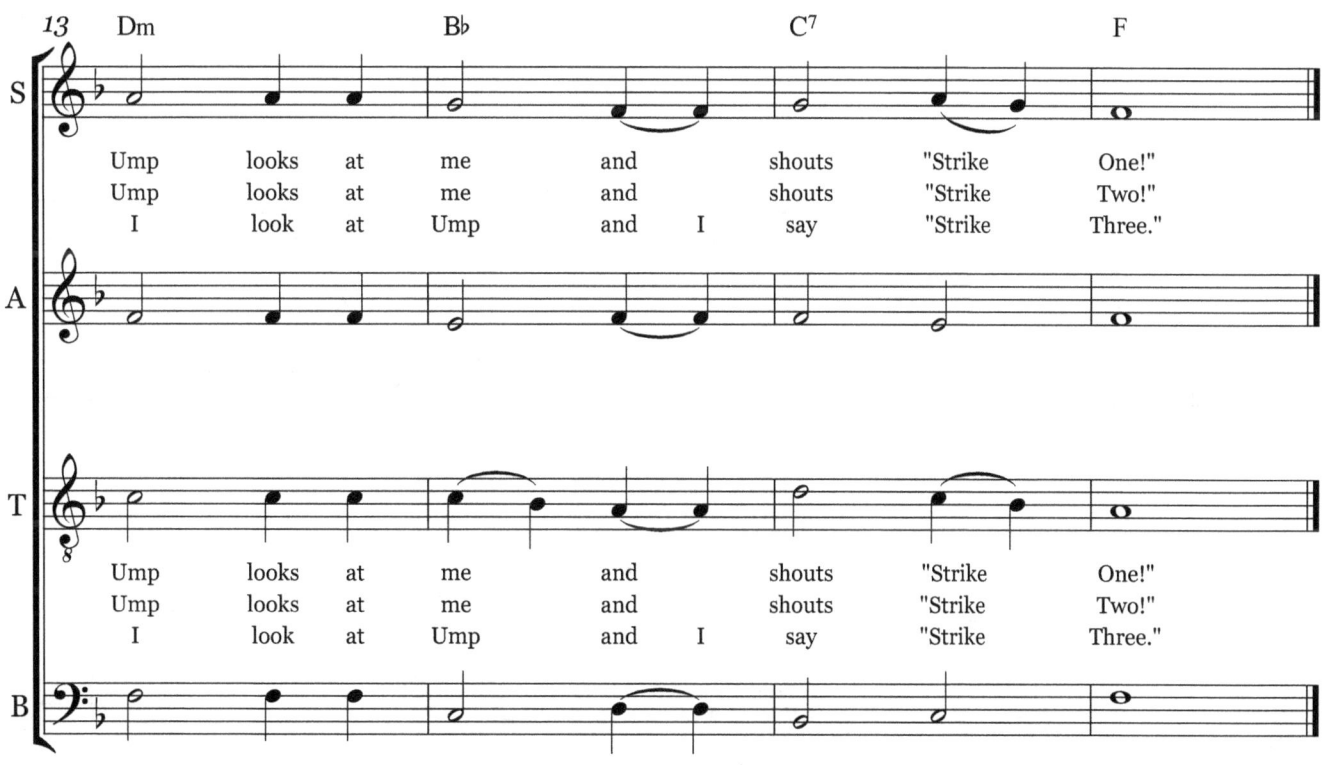

(Note: chord symbols support the soprano melody, not necessarily the SATB harmony)

93. Step by Step

(From the Secular Hymnal)

Words: Secretary Michael

Music: "China" by William Batchelder Bradbury, 1862
(traditional hymn: "Jesus Loves Me, This I Know")

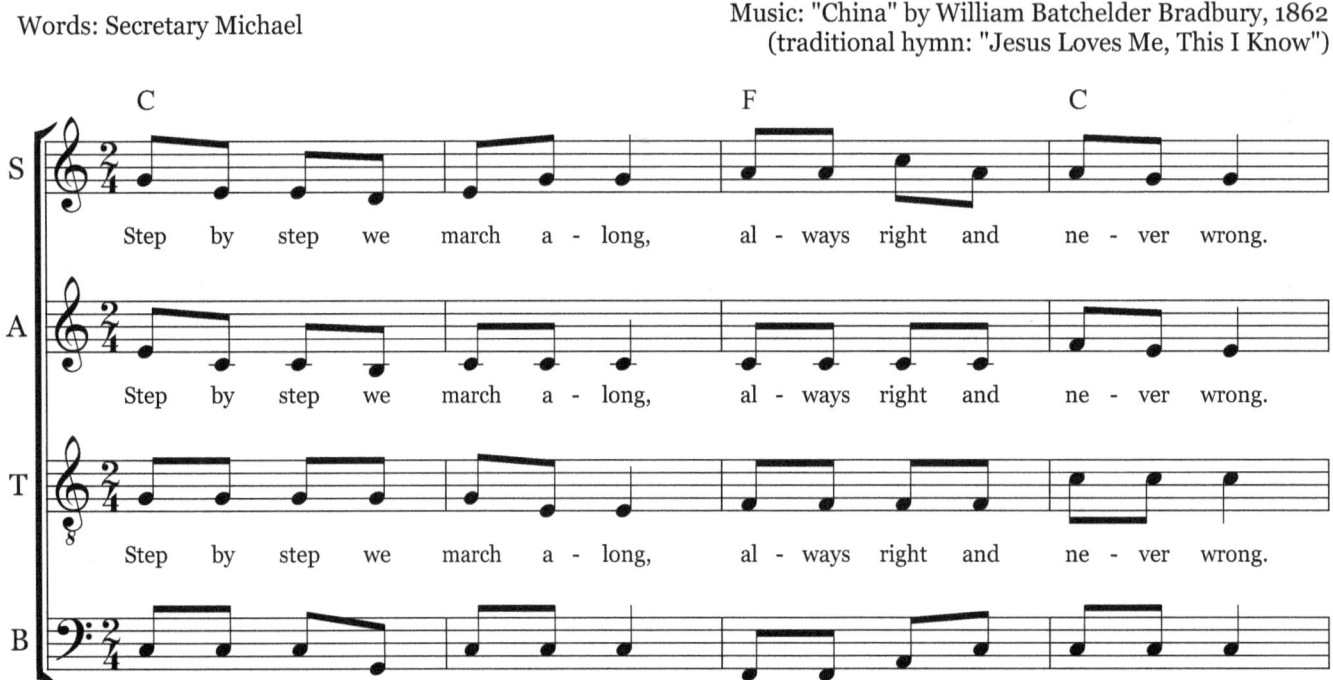

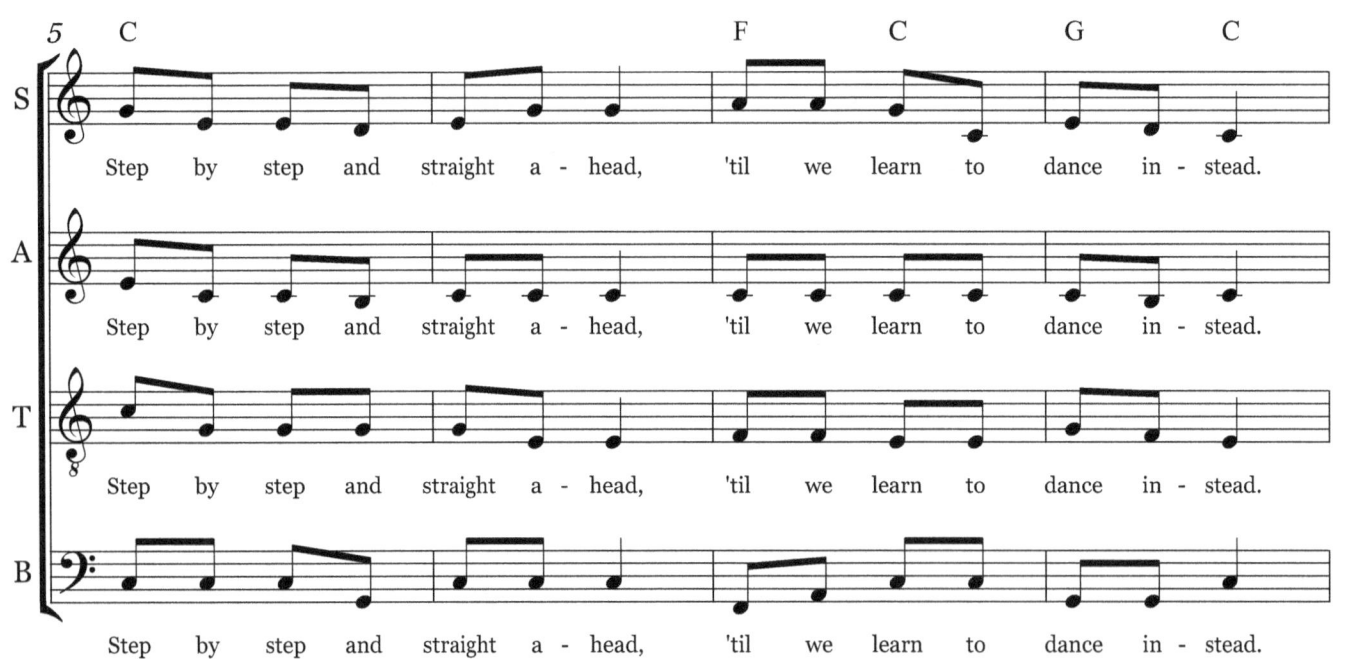

All works by Secretary Michael have been placed in the Public Domain. They may be freely copied and performed.

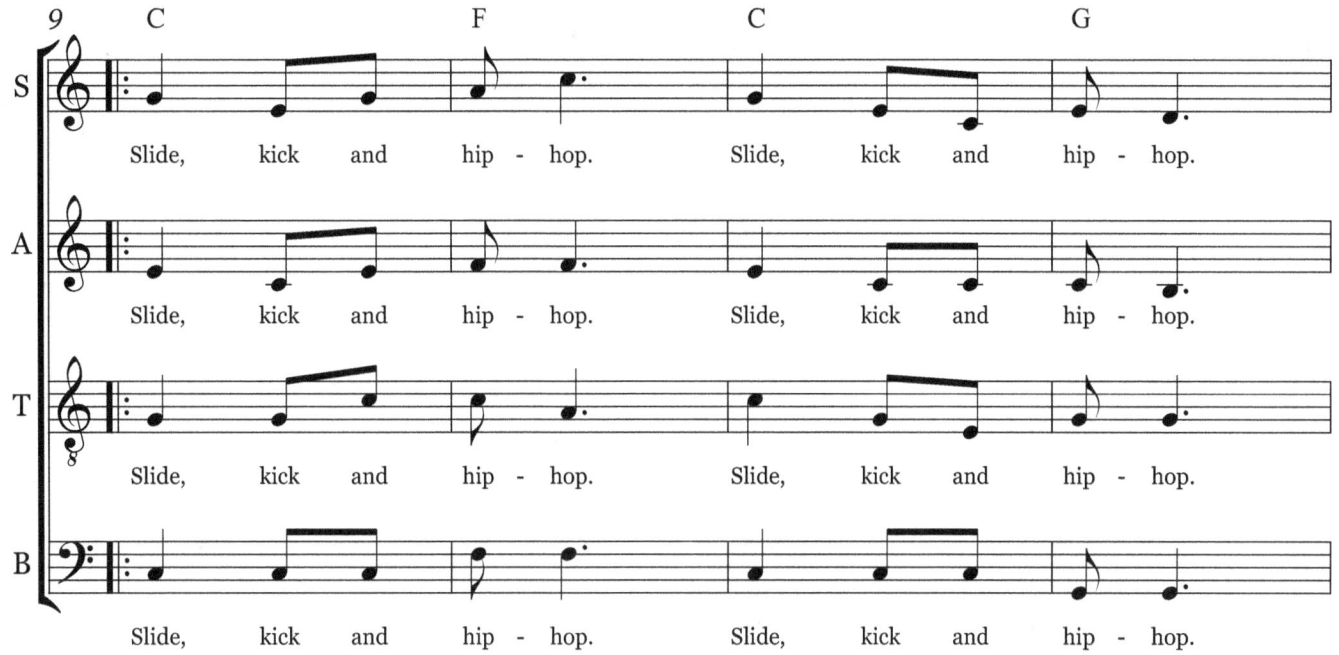

(Note: chord symbols support the soprano melody, not necessarily the SATB harmony)

94. Storms Will Come

(From the Secular Hymnal)

Words: Secretary Michael

Music: "St. Helen" by Sir George C Martin, 1889
(traditional hymn: "Lord Enthroned in Heavenly Splendor")

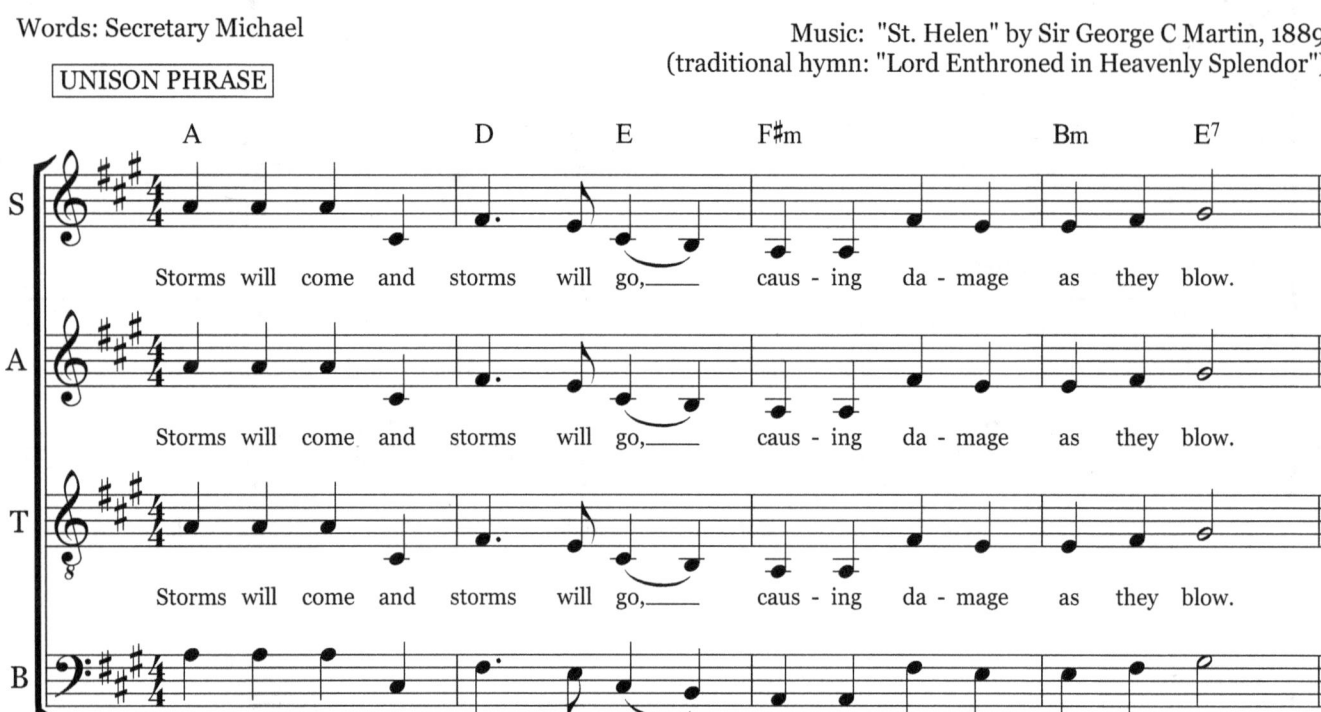

All works by Secretary Michael have been placed in the Public Domain. They may be freely copied and performed.

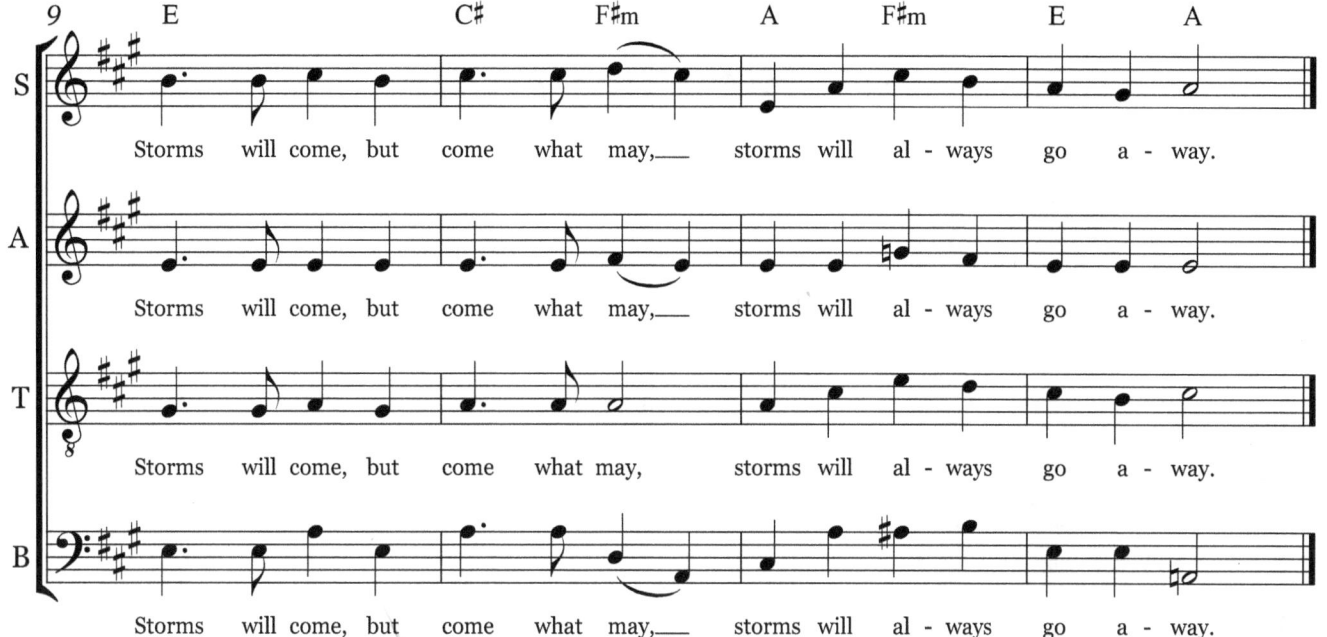

(Note: chord symbols support the soprano melody, not necessarily the SATB harmony)

95. Striving To Be

(From the Secular Hymnal)

Words: Secretary Michael

Music: "Pentecost" by William Boyd, 1868
(traditional hymn: "Fight the Good Fight")

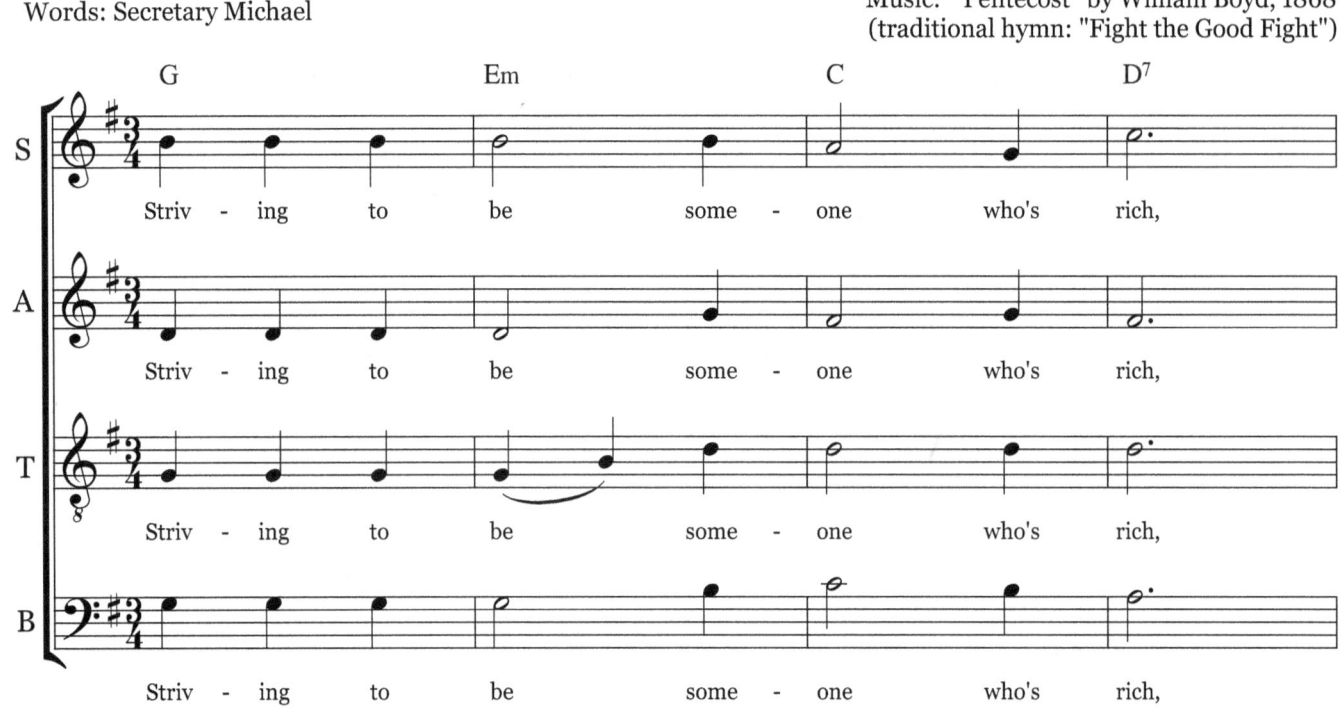

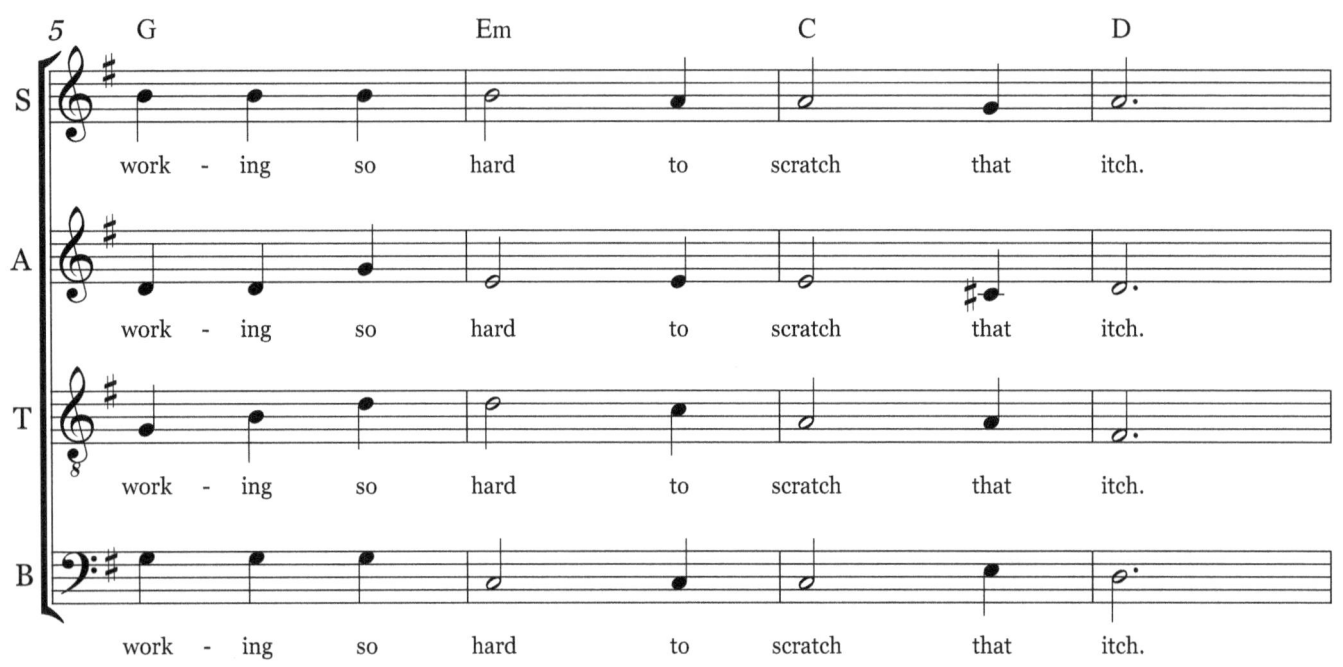

All works by Secretary Michael have been placed in the Public Domain. They may be freely copied and performed.

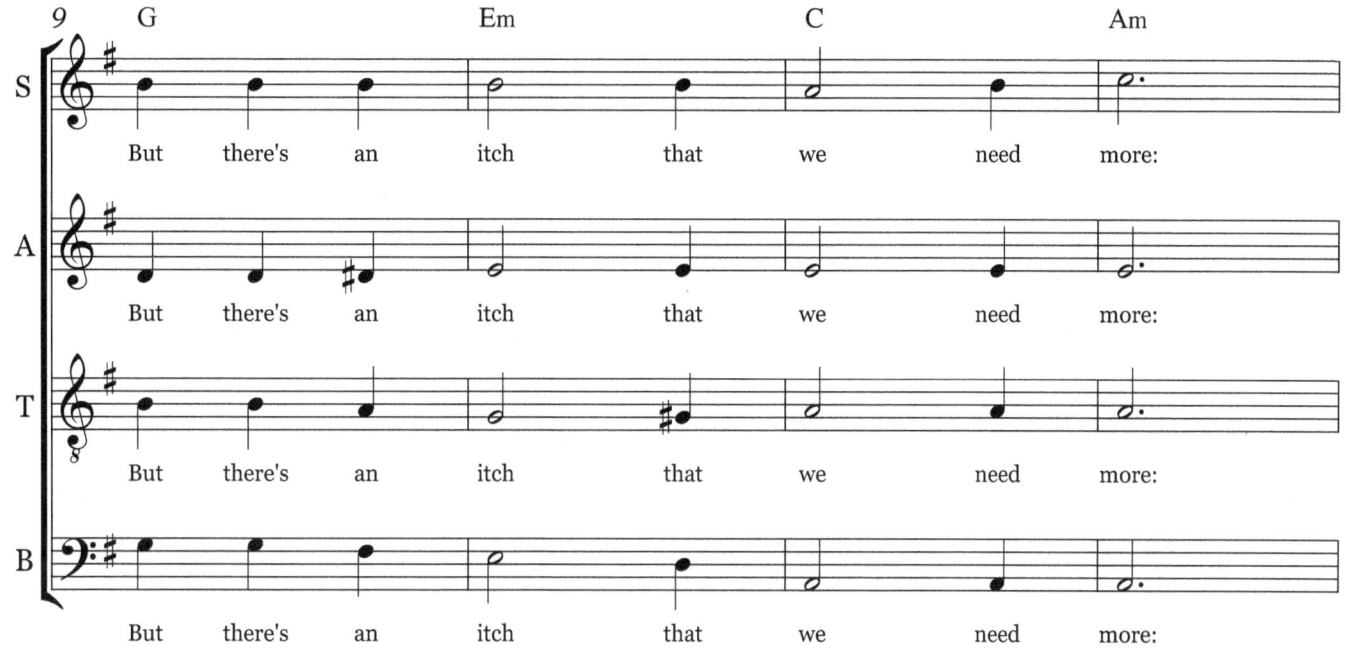
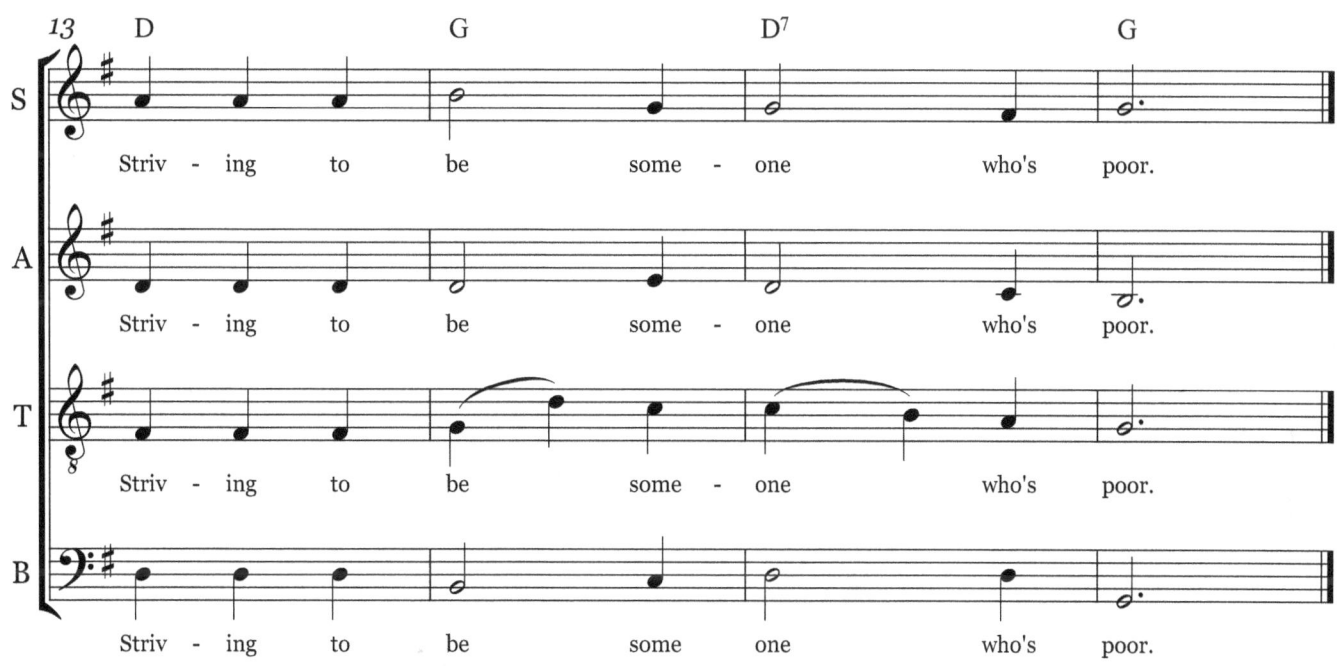

(Note: chord symbols support the soprano melody, not necessarily the SATB harmony)

96. Swapping Shoes
(From the Secular Hymnal)

Words: Secretary Michael

Music: "Dix" by Conrad Kocher, 1838
Arranged by William Henry Monk, 1865
(traditional hymn: "For the Beauty of the Earth")

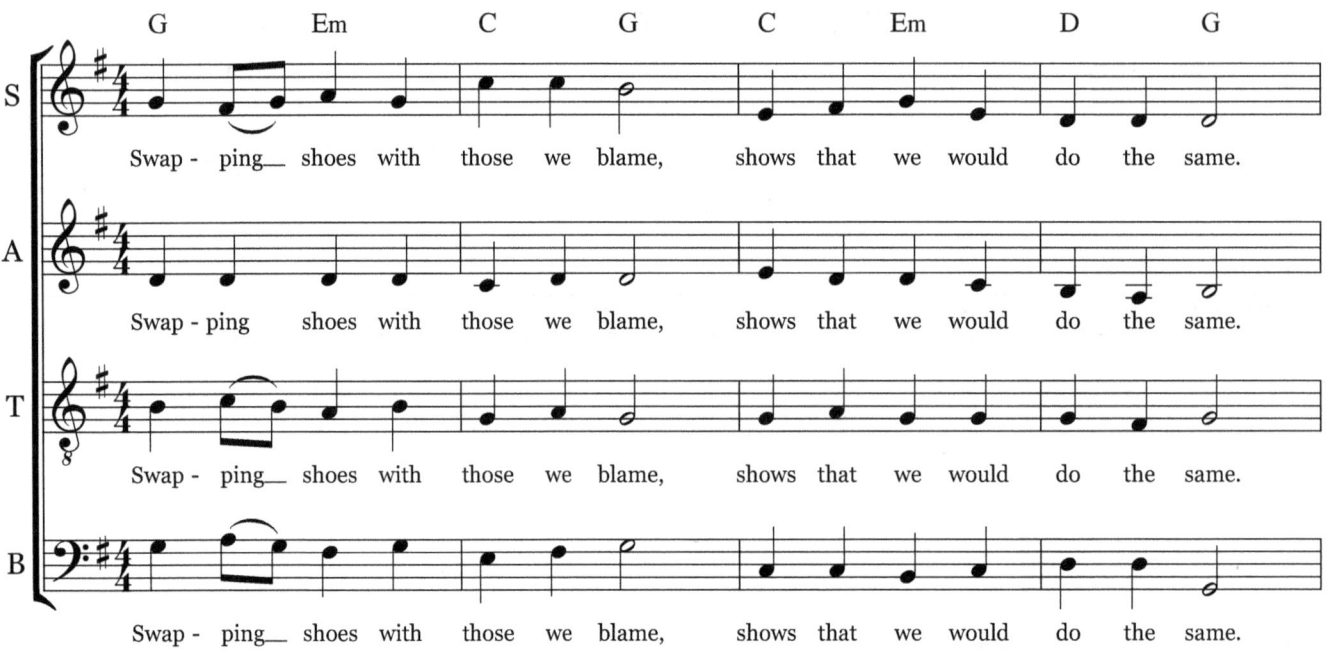

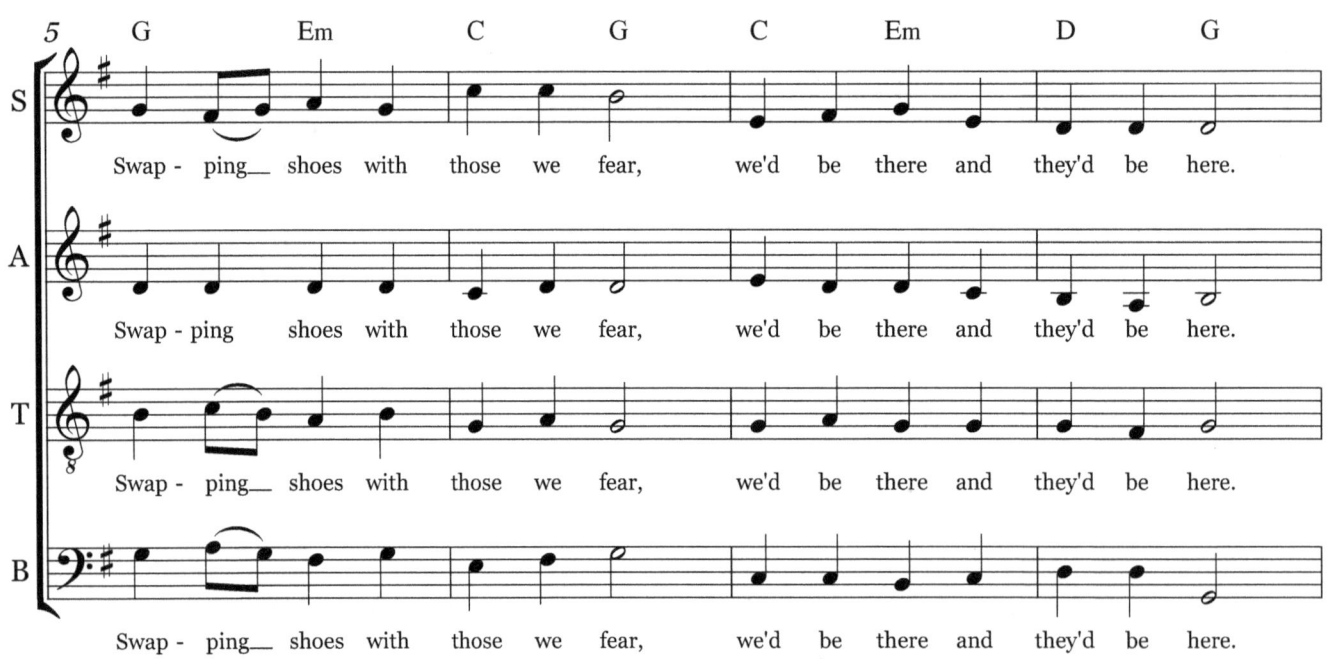

All works by Secretary Michael have been placed in the Public Domain. They may be freely copied and performed.

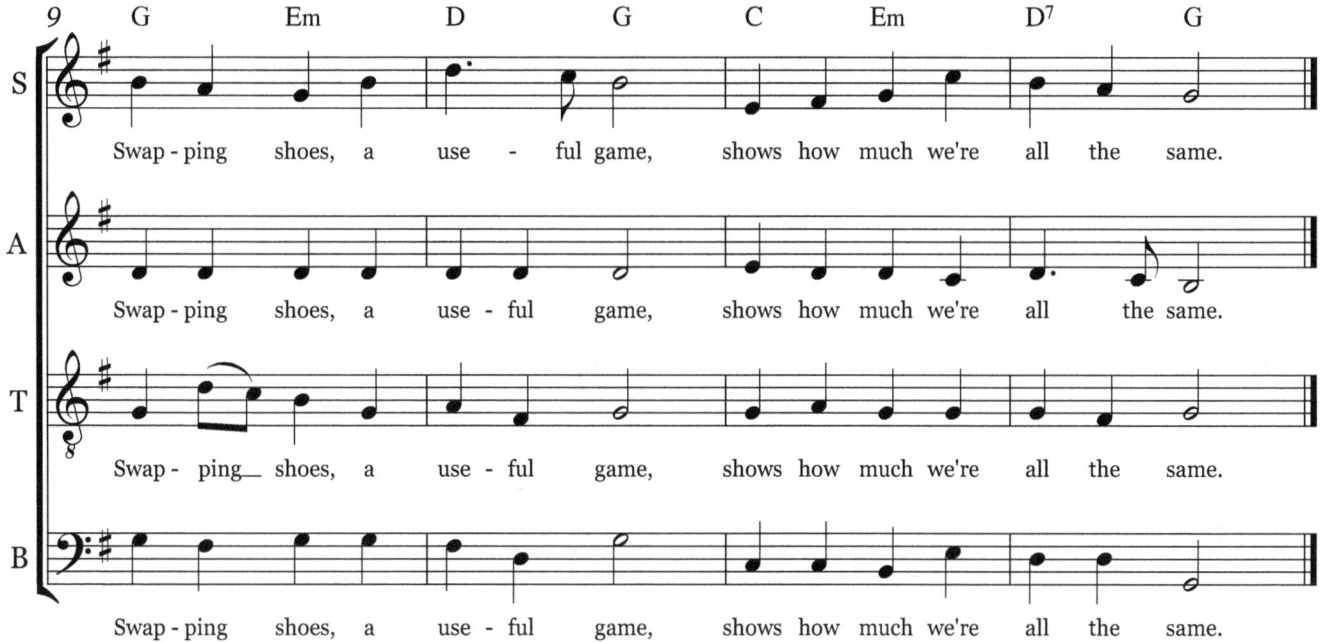

(Note: chord symbols support the soprano melody, not necessarily the SATB harmony)

97. Tall Oaks From Little Acorns Grow

(From the Secular Hymnal)

Words: Secretary Michael

Music: "St. Columba" (traditional Irish melody)
Harmonized by Charles Villiers Stanford, 1906
(traditional hymn: "The King of Love My Shepherd Is")

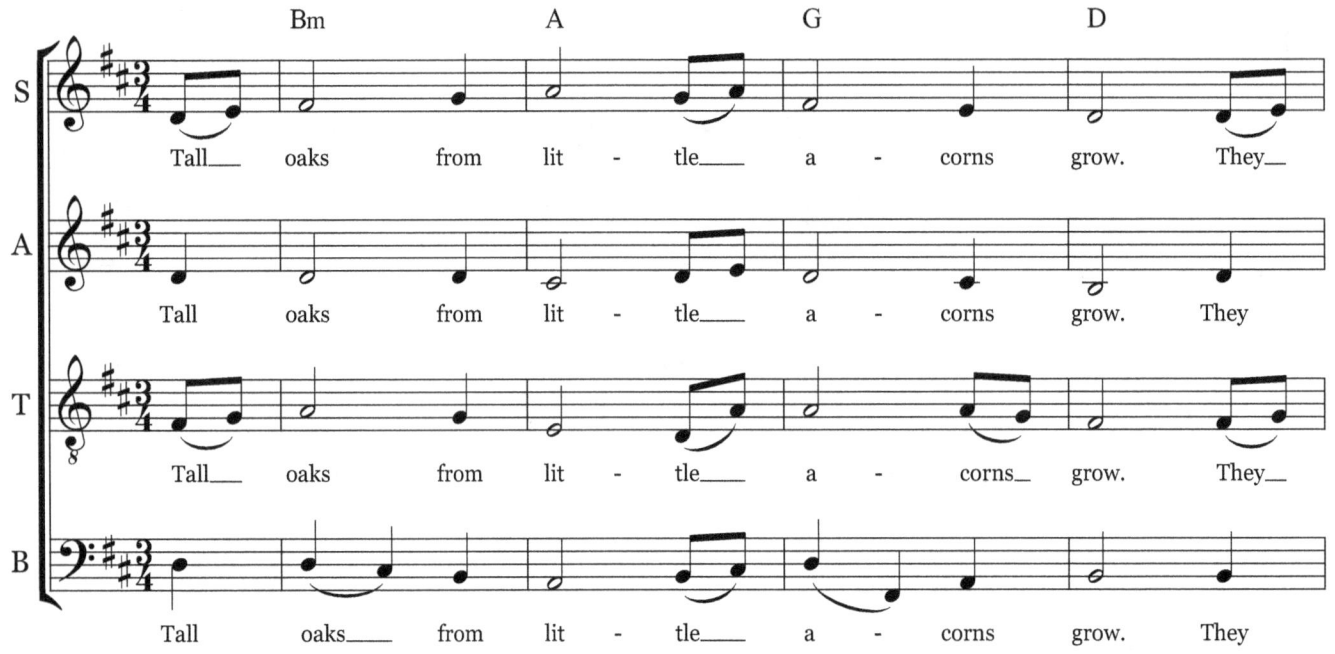

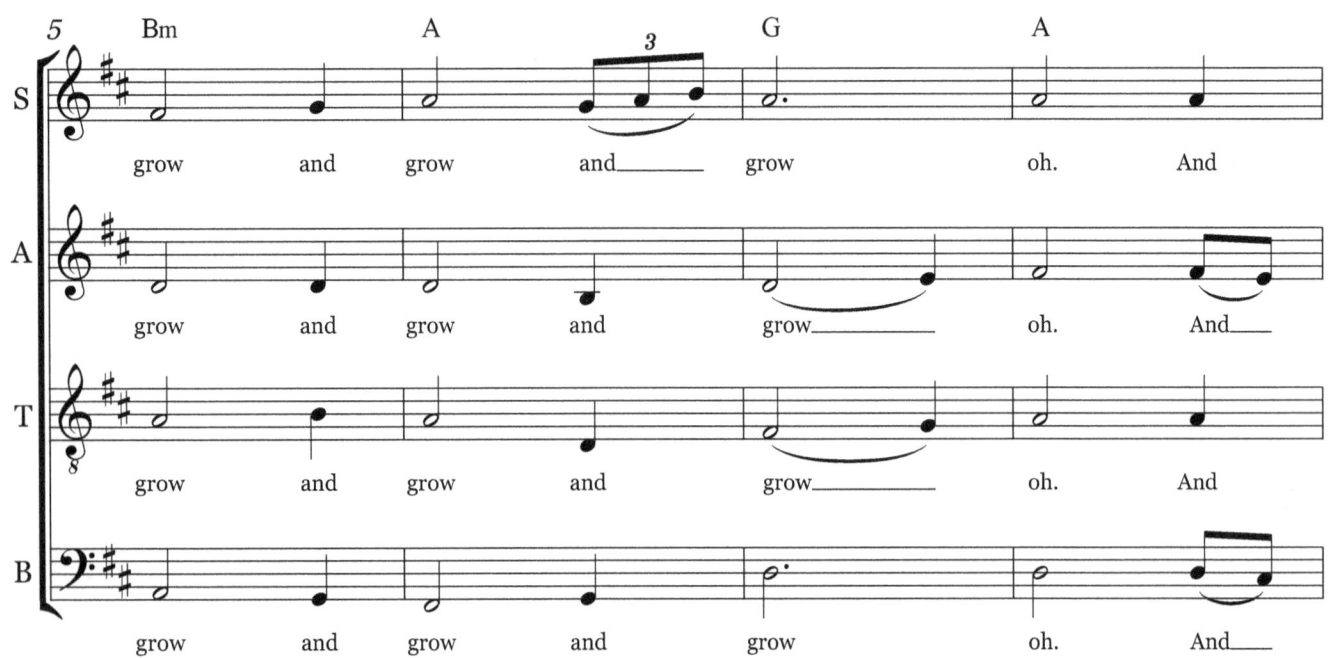

All works by Secretary Michael have been placed in the Public Domain. They may be freely copied and performed.

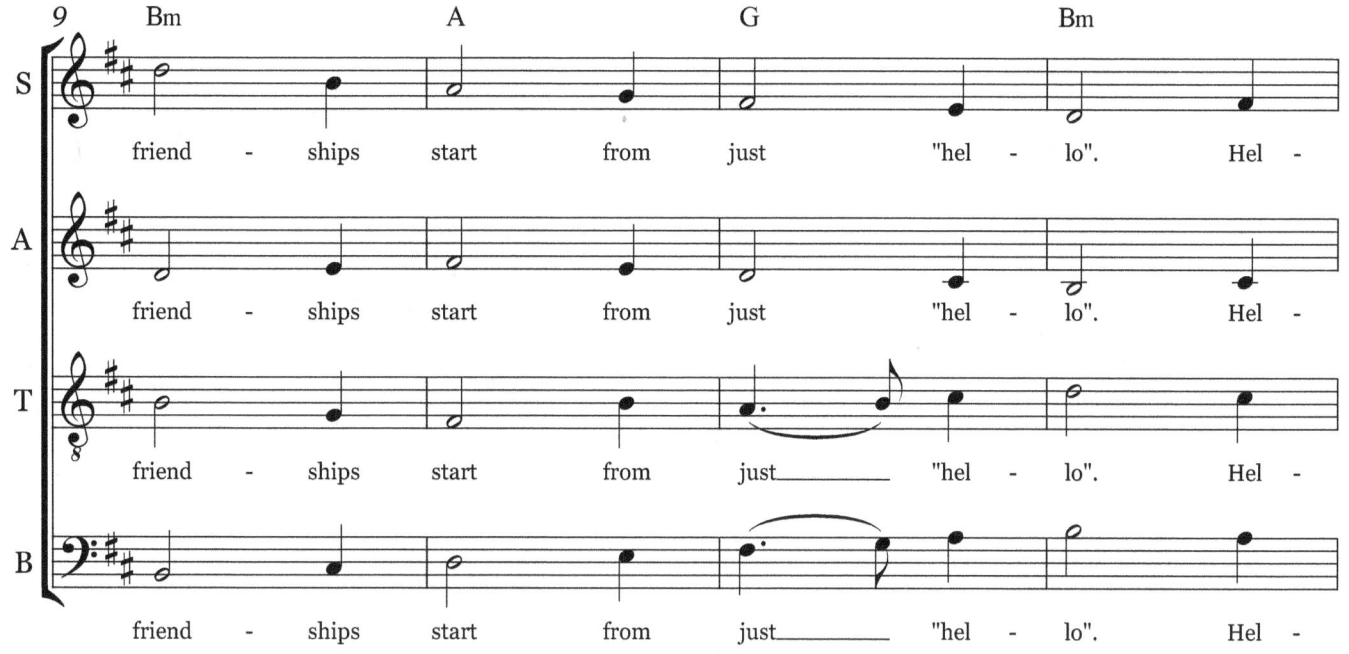
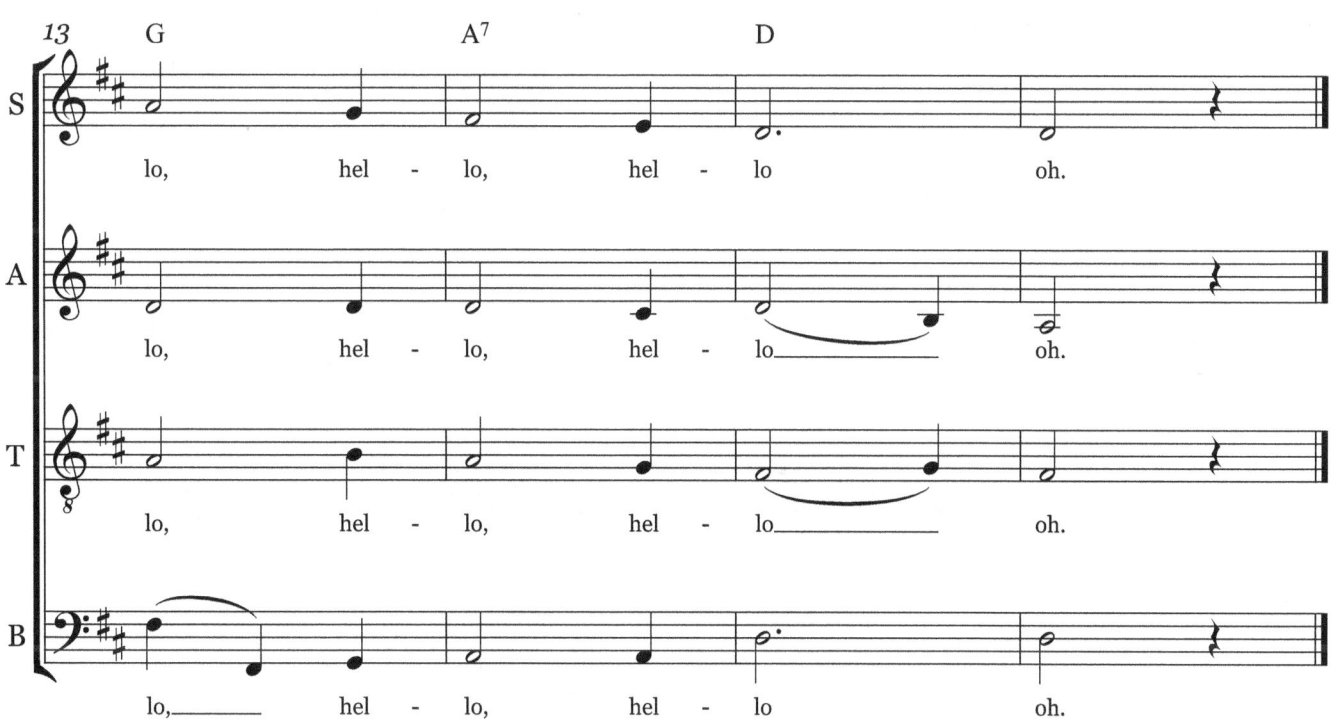

(Note: chord symbols support the soprano melody, not necessarily the SATB harmony)

98. The Greatest Walk
(From the Secular Hymnal)

Words: Secretary Michael

Melody: Sir Hubert Parry, 1916
SATB Arrangement: Secretary Michael
(traditional hymn: "Jerusalem")

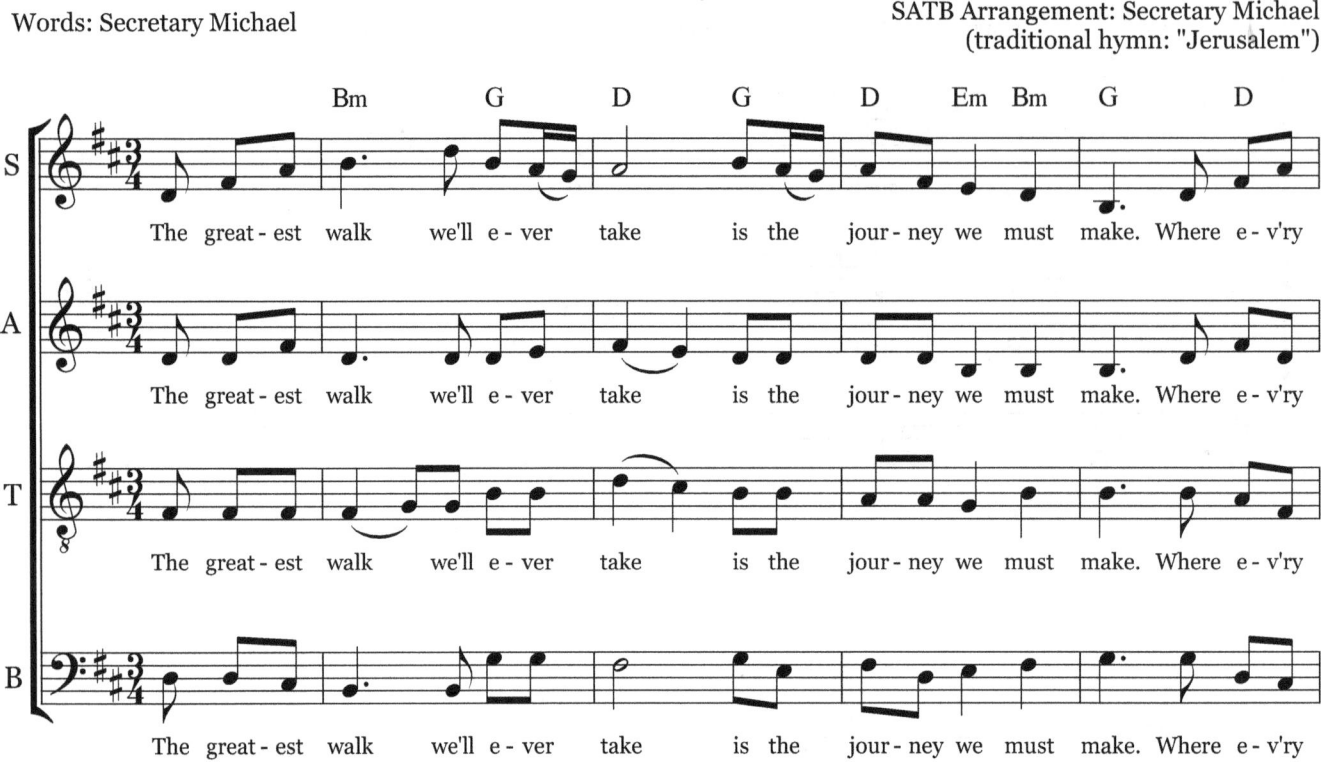

PD *All works by Secretary Michael have been placed in the Public Domain. They may be freely copied and performed.*

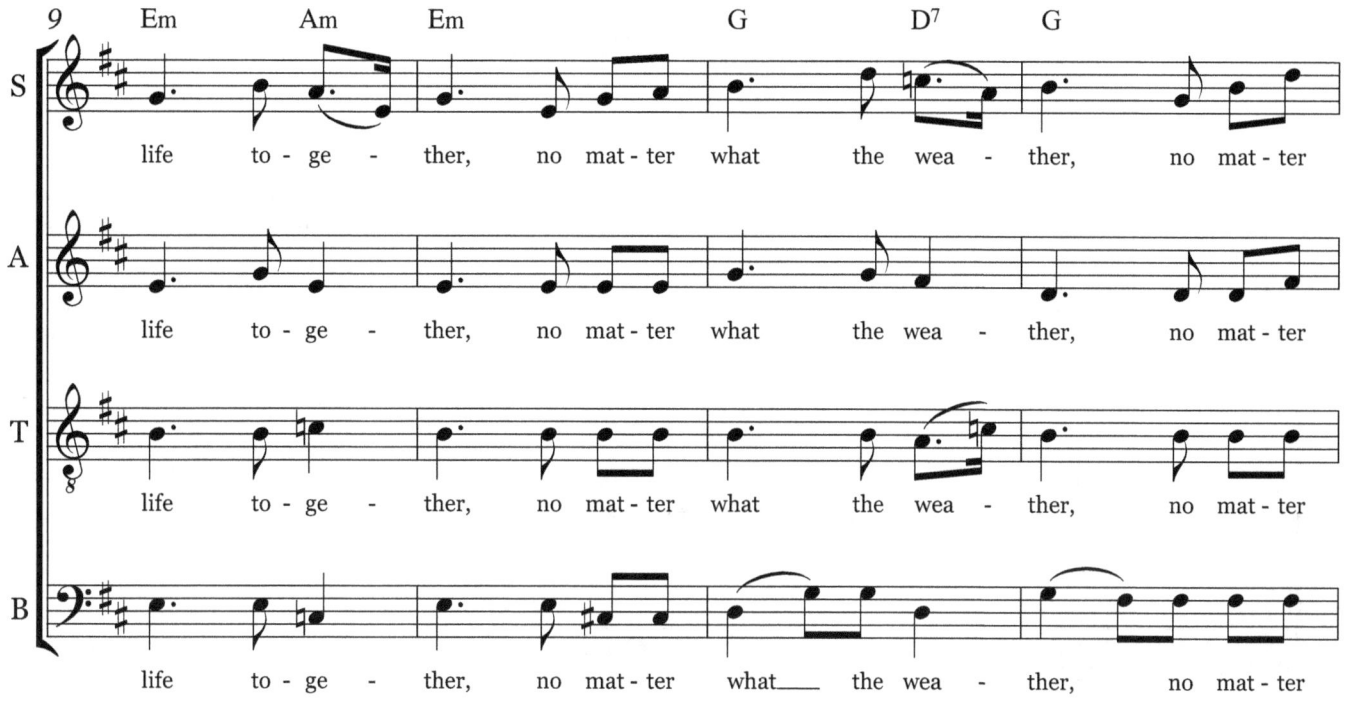
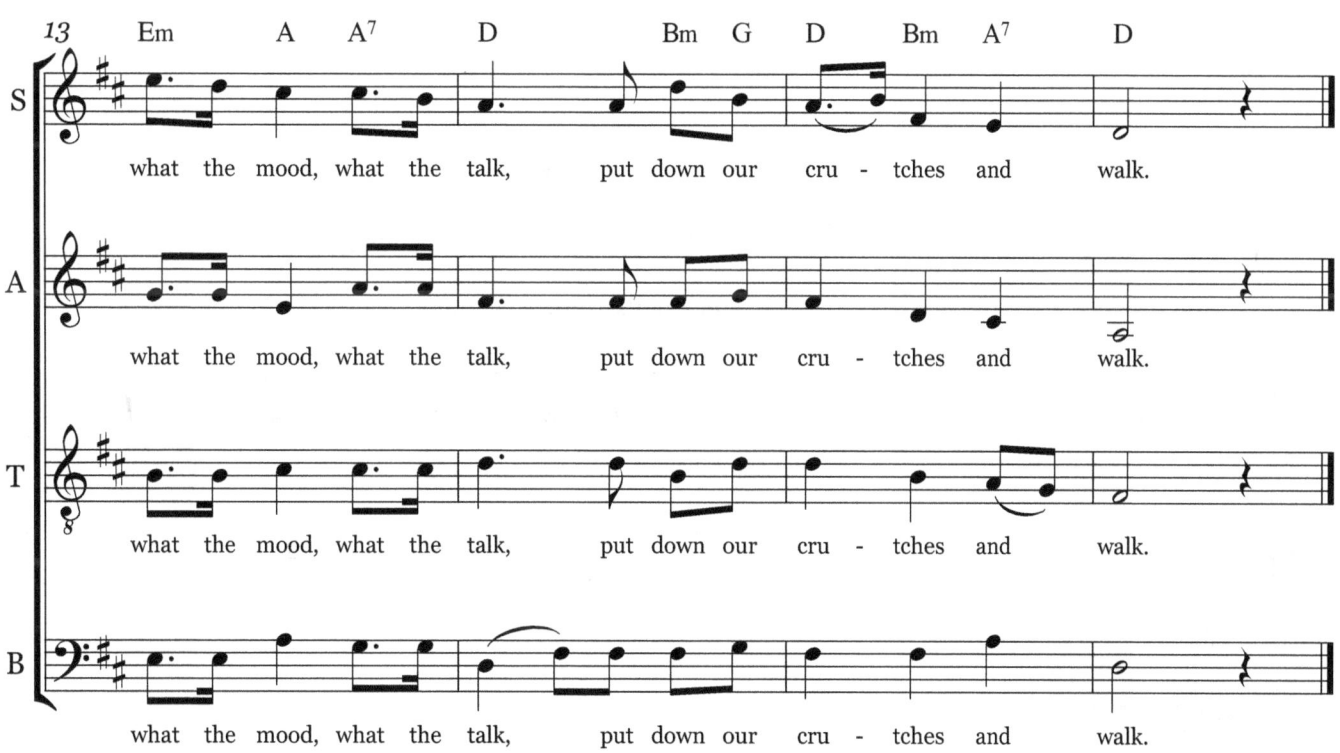

(Note: chord symbols support the soprano melody, not necessarily the SATB harmony)

99. The Many Truths

(From the Secular Hymnal)

Words: Secretary Michael

Music: *Finlandia* by Jean Sibelius, 1899
SATB Arrangement: Secretary Michael
(traditional hymn: "Be Still My Soul")

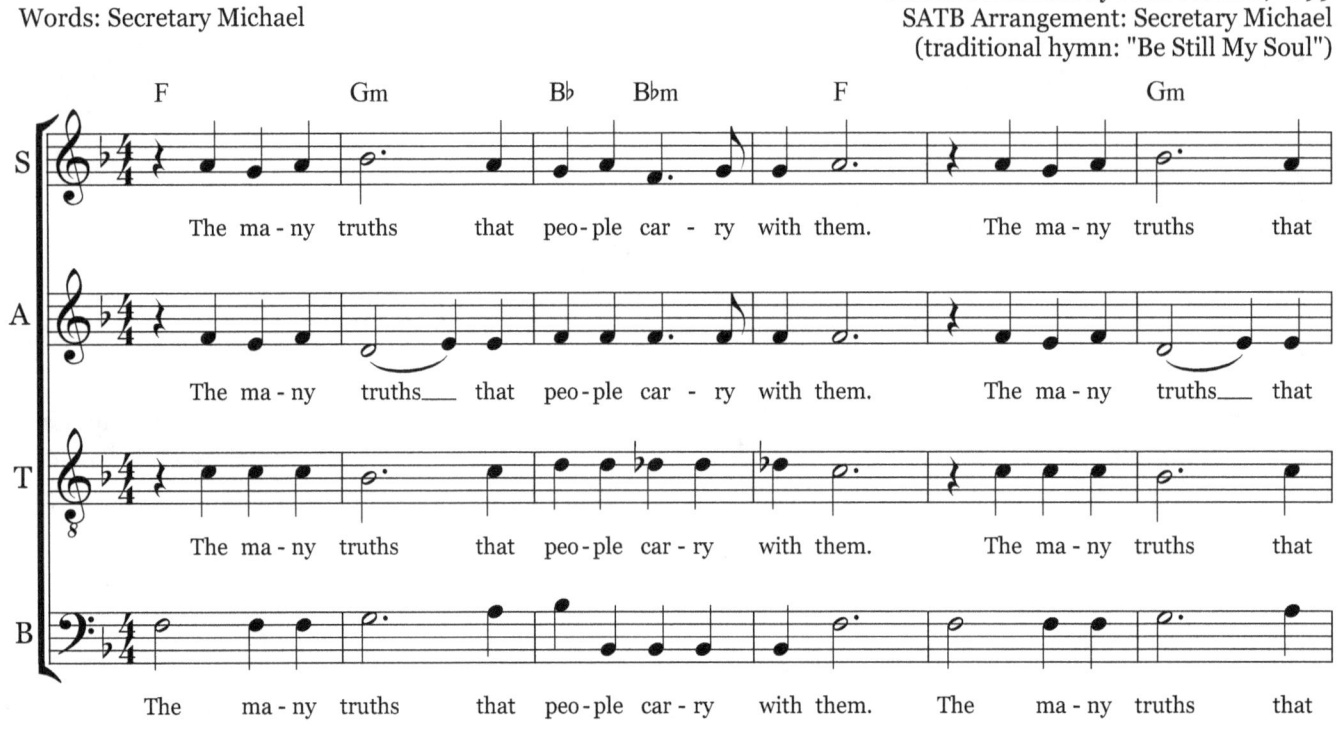

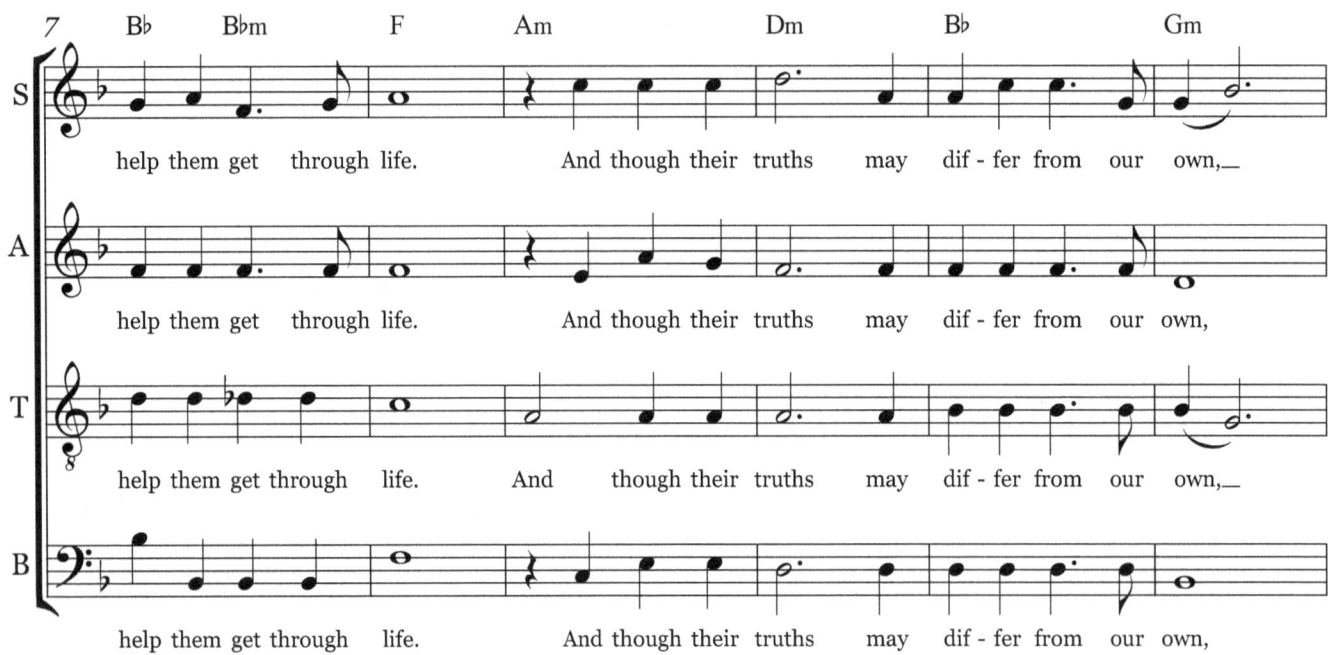

All works by Secretary Michael have been placed in the Public Domain. They may be freely copied and performed.

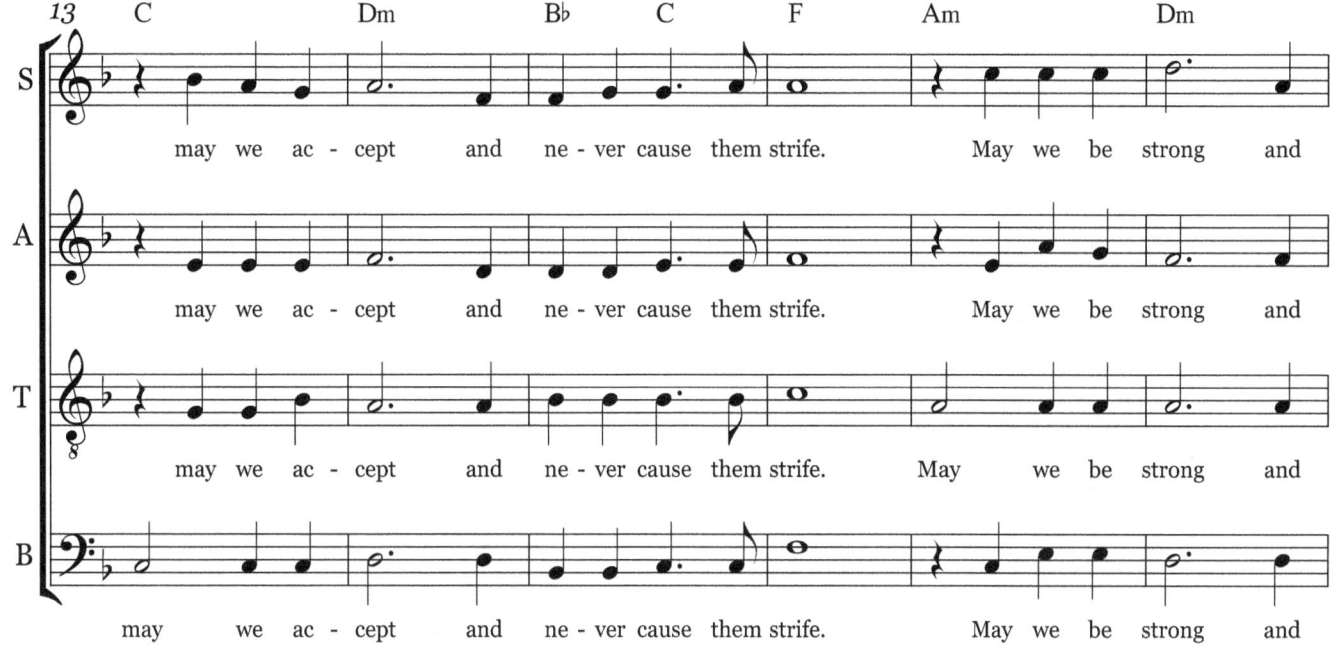
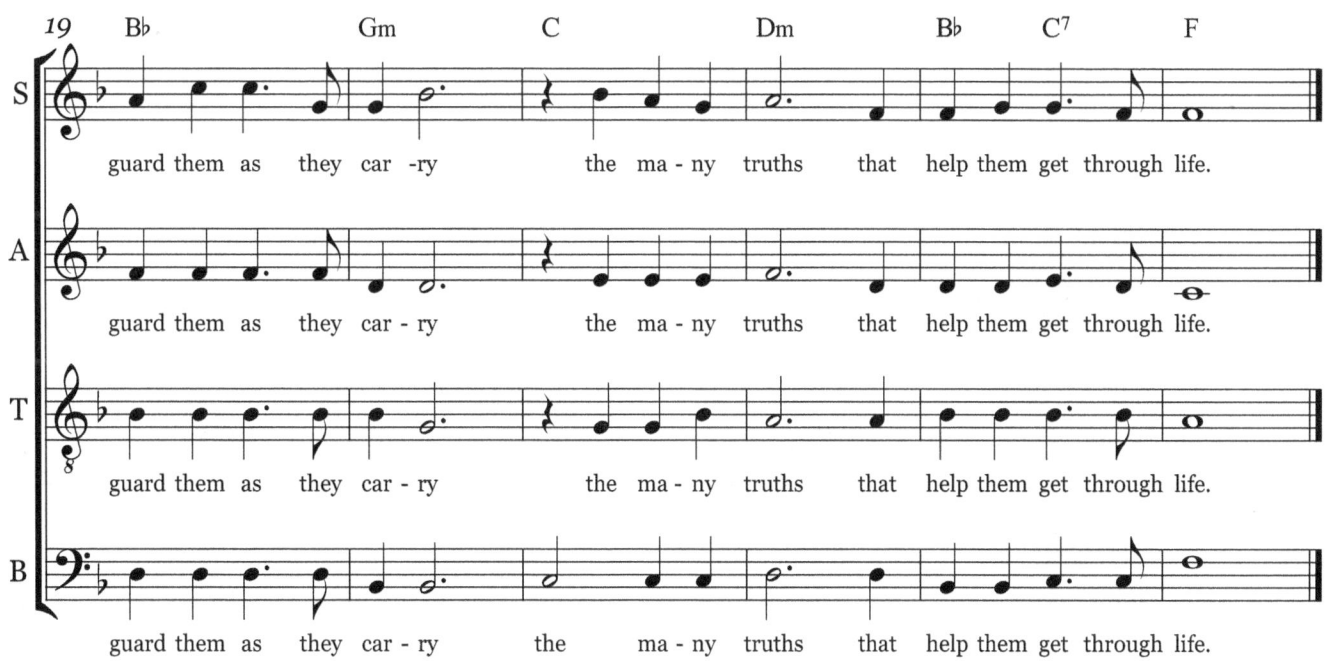

(Note: chord symbols support the soprano melody, not necessarily the SATB harmony)

100. The Only Path to Peace is Peace

(From the Secular Hymnal)

Words: Secretary Michael

Music: "St. Anne" by William Croft, 1708
(traditional hymn: "Our God Our Help in Ages Past")

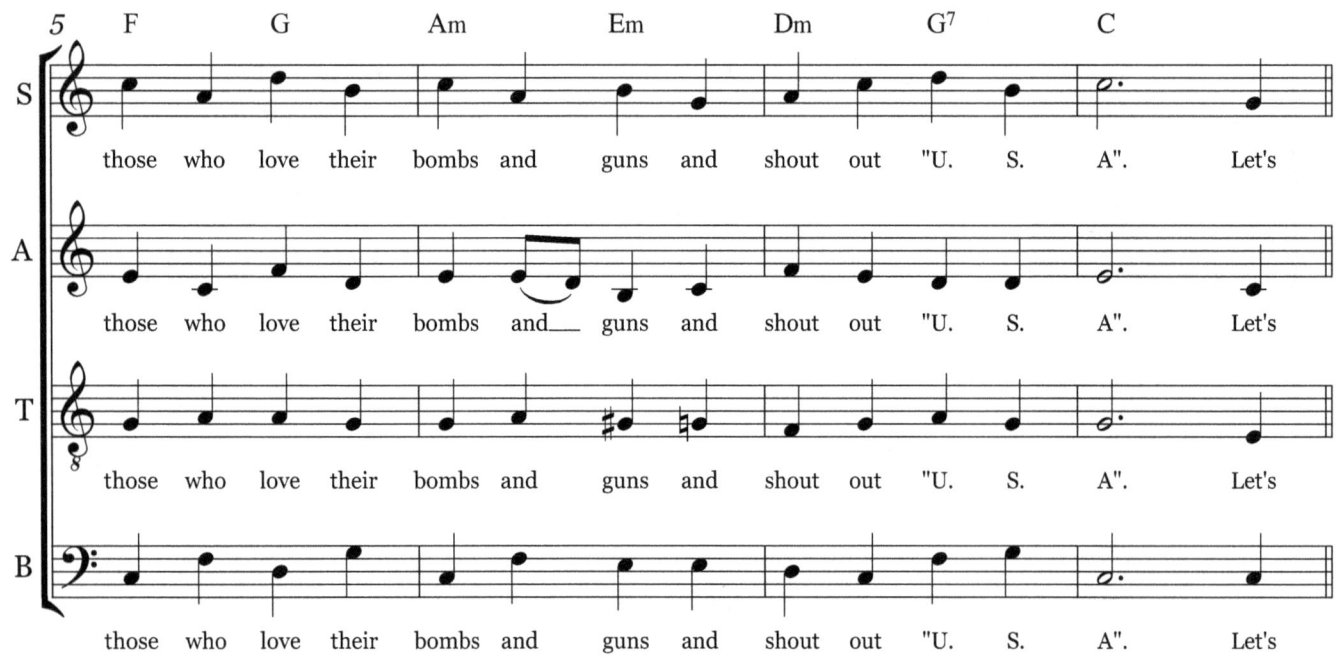

All works by Secretary Michael have been placed in the Public Domain. They may be freely copied and performed.

(Note: chord symbols support the soprano melody, not necessarily the SATB harmony)

(Note: chord symbols support the soprano melody, not necessarily the SATB harmony)

102. There are Times

(From the Secular Hymnal)

Words: Secretary Michael

Music: "All To Christ" by John Thomas Grape, 1868
(traditional hymn: "Jesus Paid It All")

1. There are times I want to stop, and times I want to go. But I always want to be the person that I know.
2. There are times when I am fast, and times when I am slow. But I always want to be the person that I know.
3. There are times when I am high, and times when I am low. But I always want to be the person that I know.

All works by Secretary Michael have been placed in the Public Domain. They may be freely copied and performed.

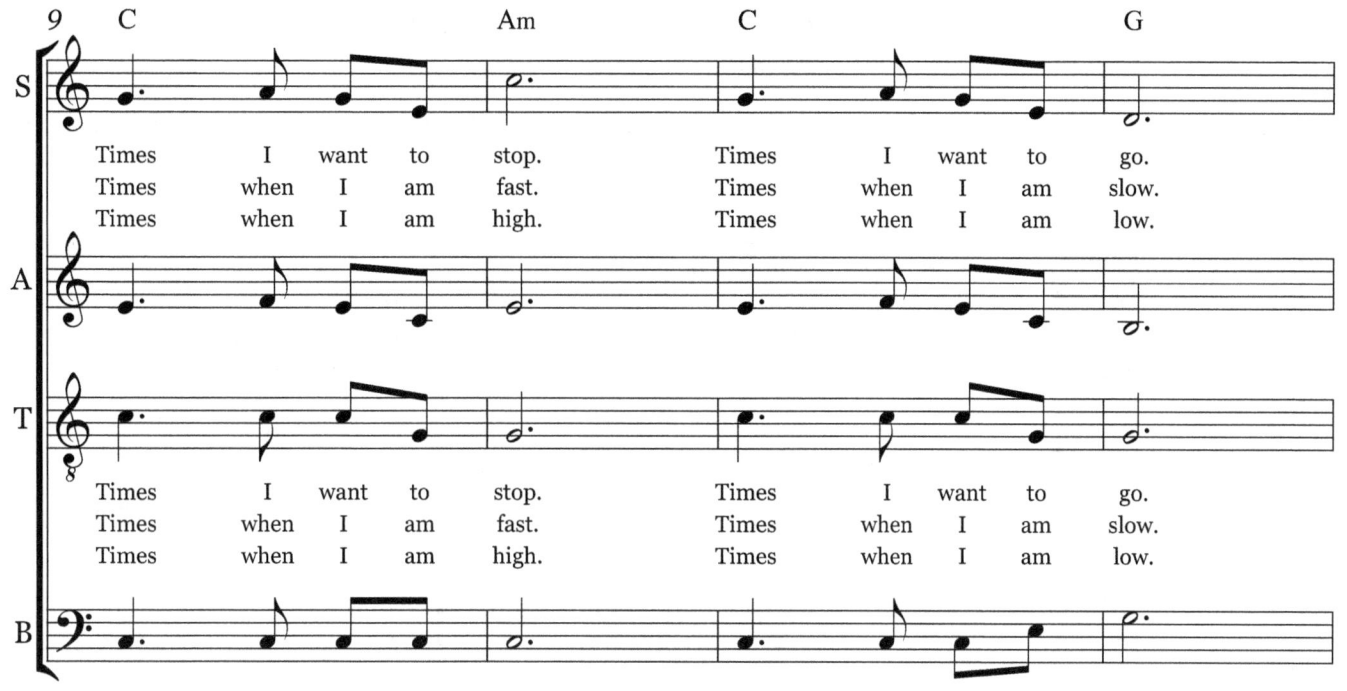
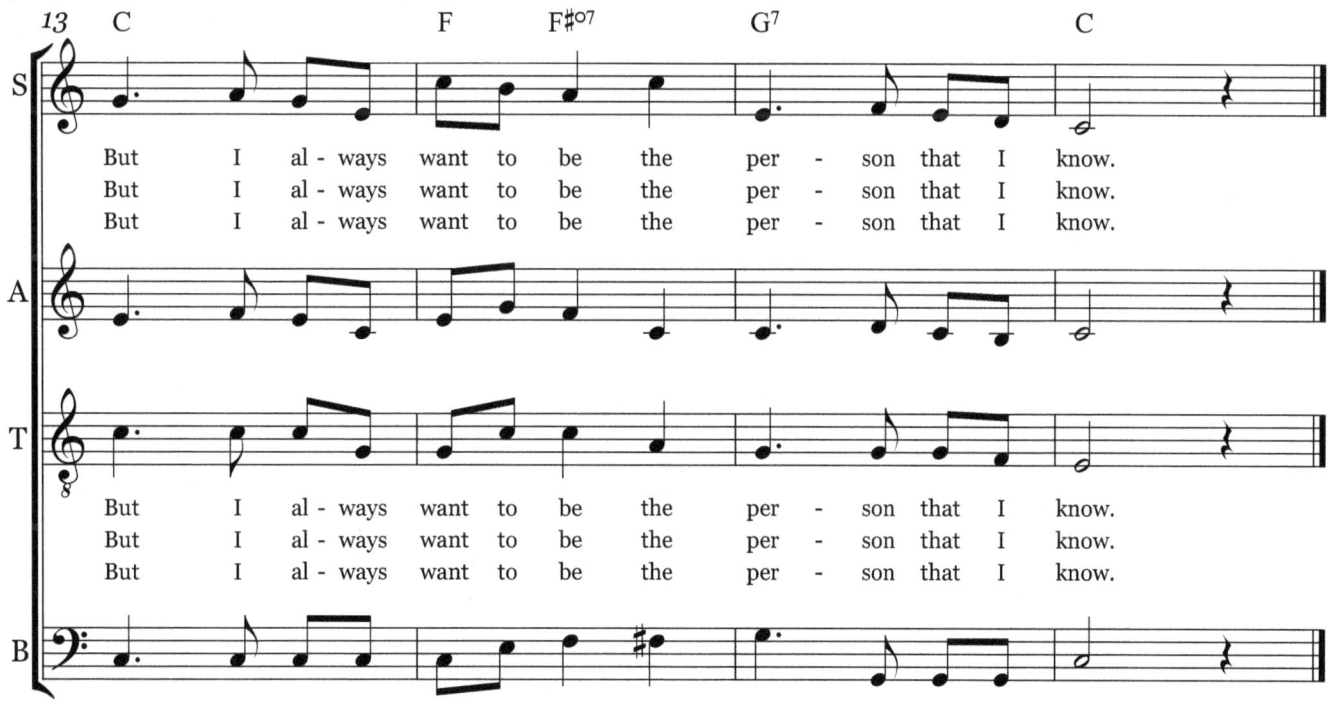

(Note: chord symbols support the soprano melody, not necessarily the SATB harmony)

103. There is a Game
(From the Secular Hymnal)

Words: Secretary Michael

Music: "Bring Them In" by William Augustine Ogden, 1885
(traditional hymn: "Bring Them In")

All works by Secretary Michael have been placed in the Public Domain. They may be freely copied and performed.

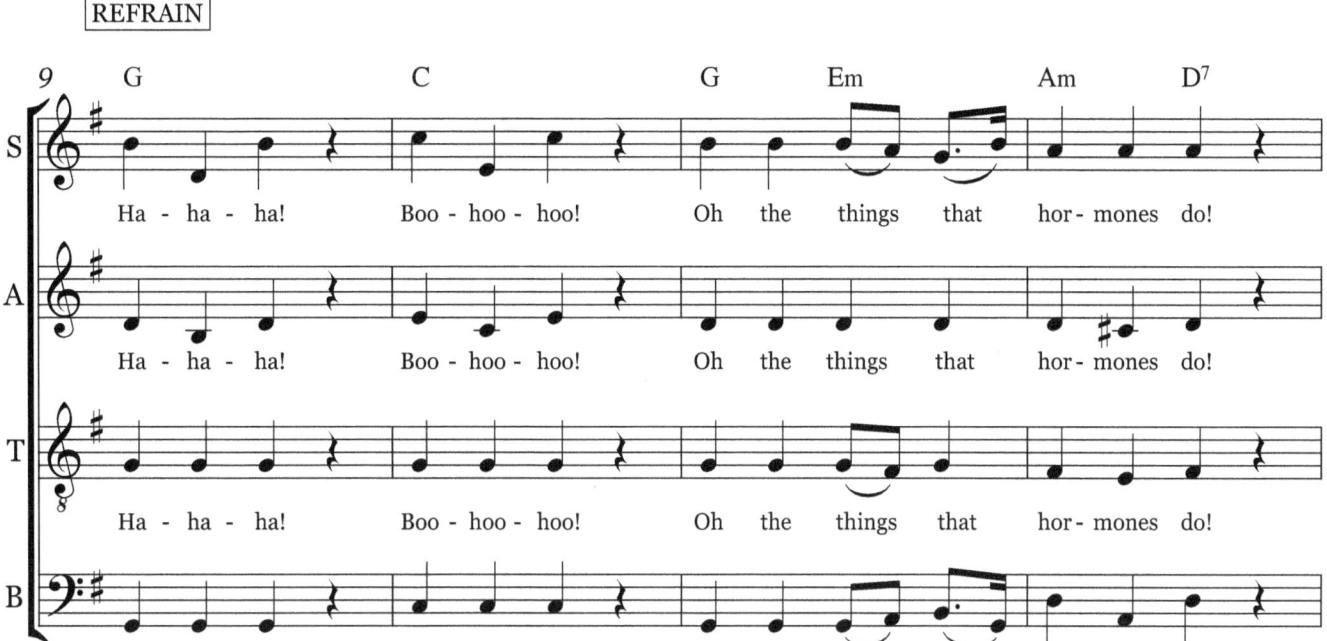
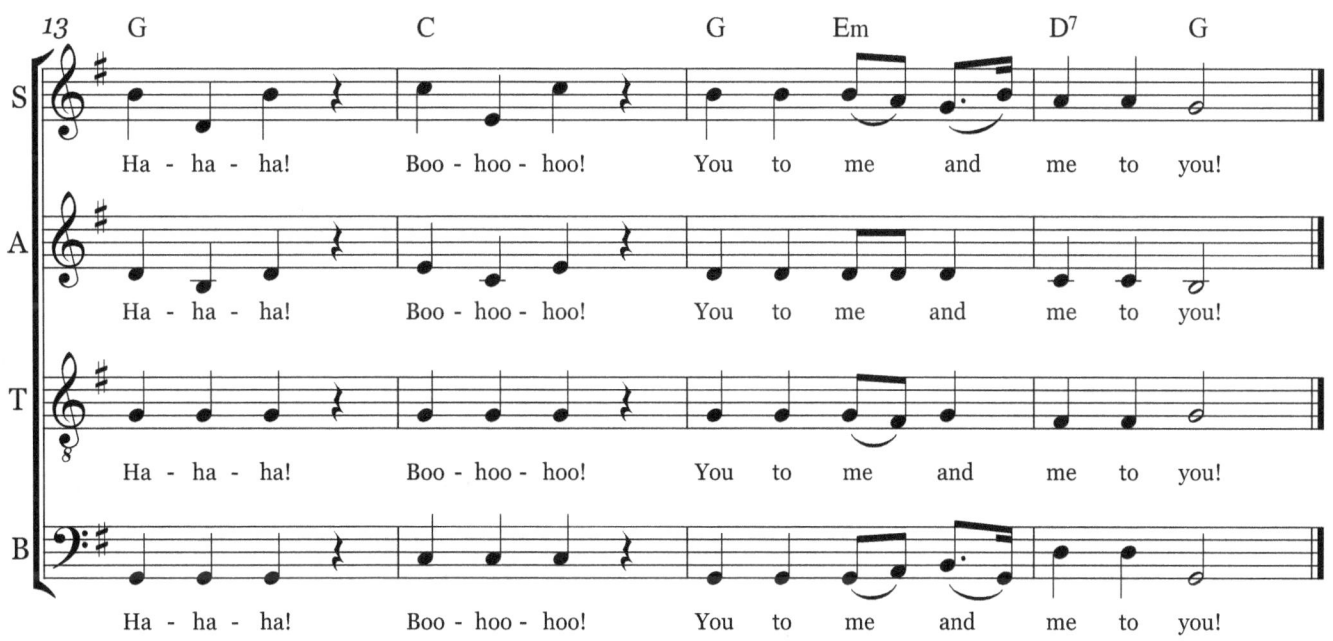

(Note: chord symbols support the soprano melody, not necessarily the SATB harmony)

104. There is a Rule of Thumb

(From the Secular Hymnal)

Words: Secretary Michael

Music: "Diademata" by George J. Elvey, 1868
(traditional hymn: "Crown Him With Many Crowns")

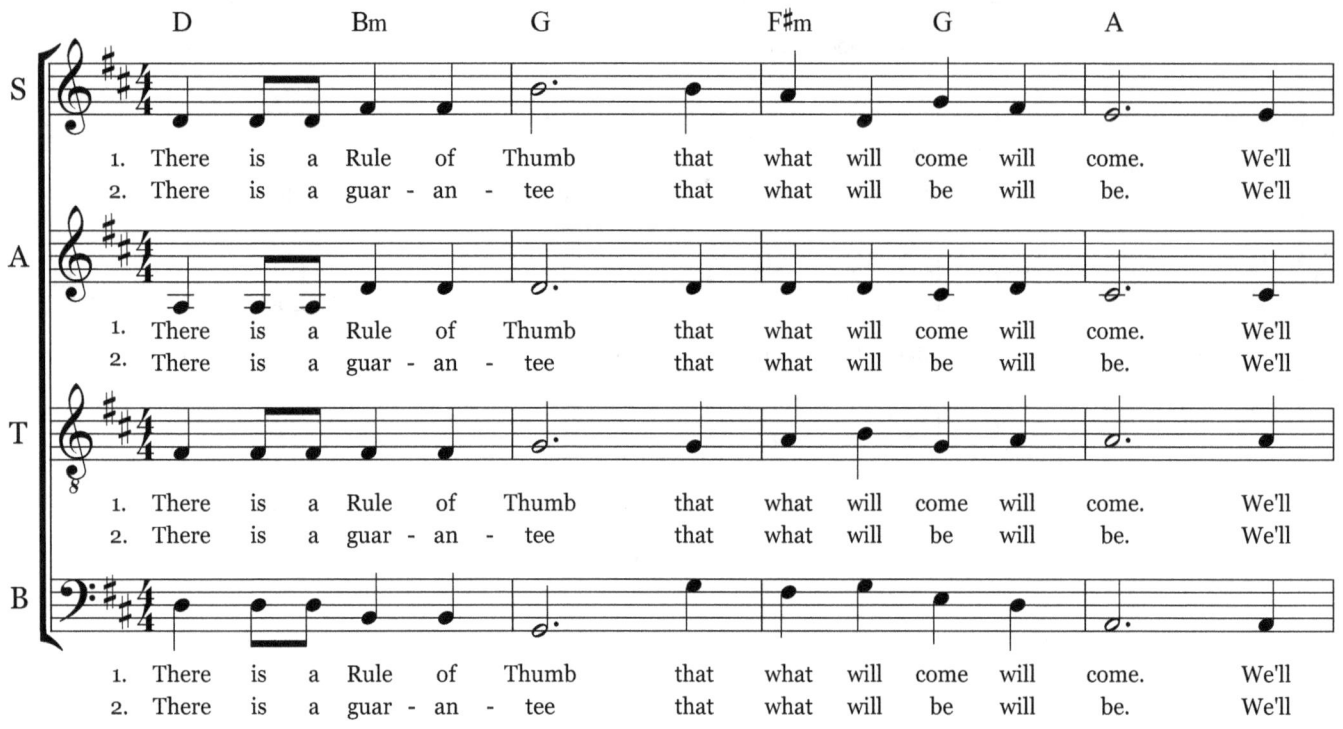

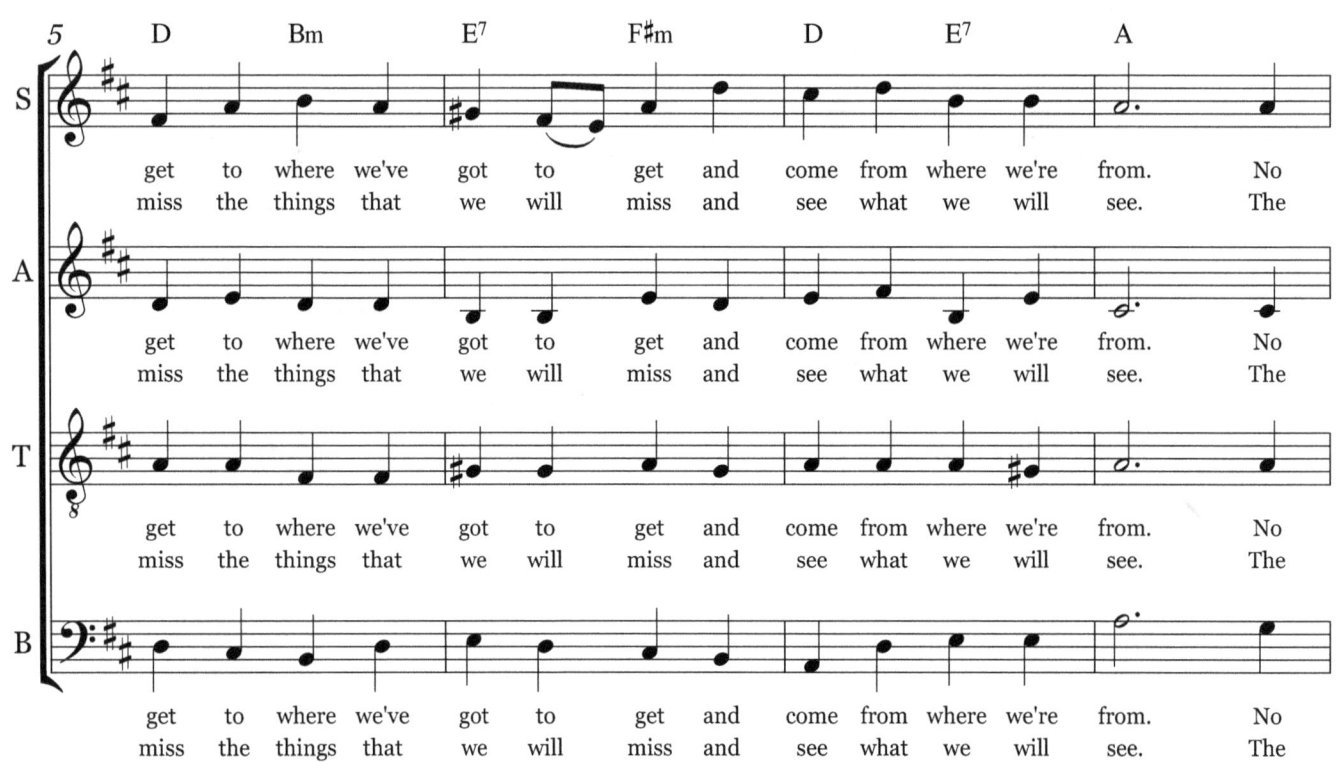

All works by Secretary Michael have been placed in the Public Domain. They may be freely copied and performed.

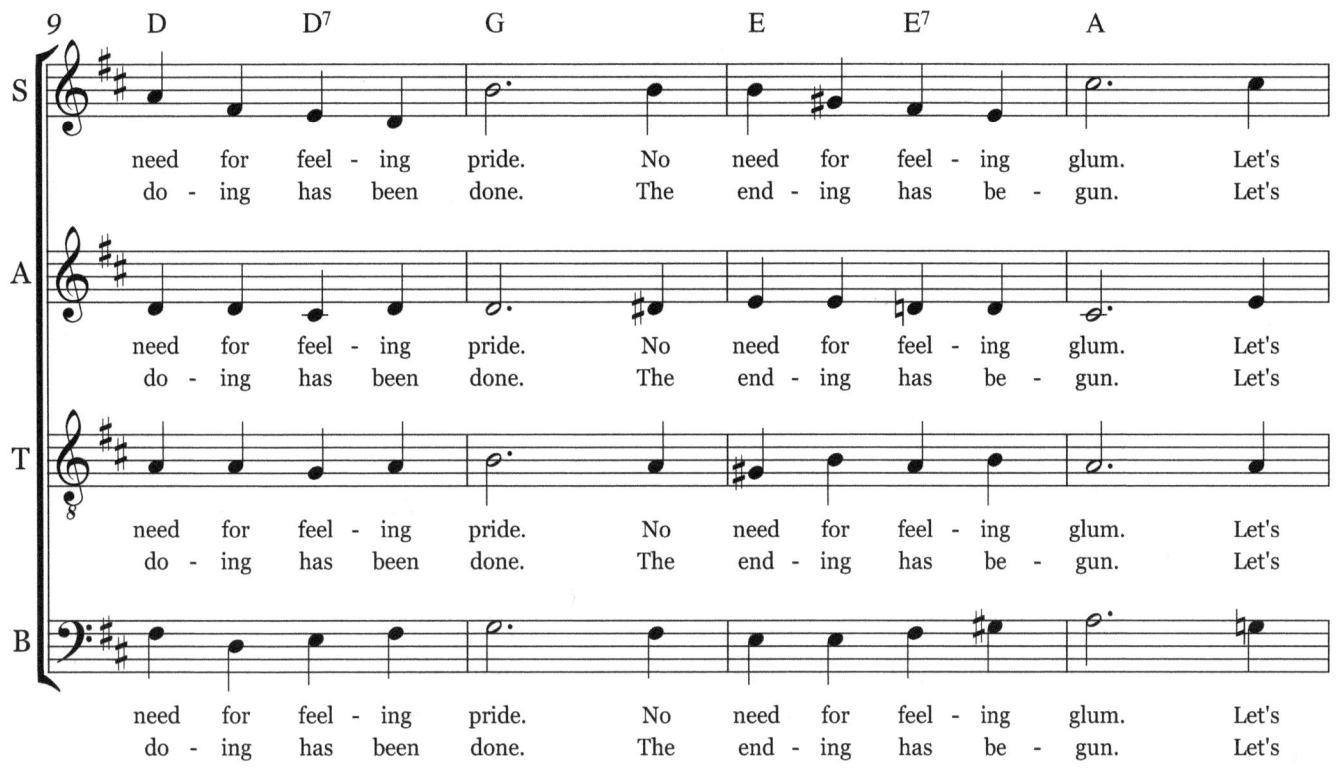
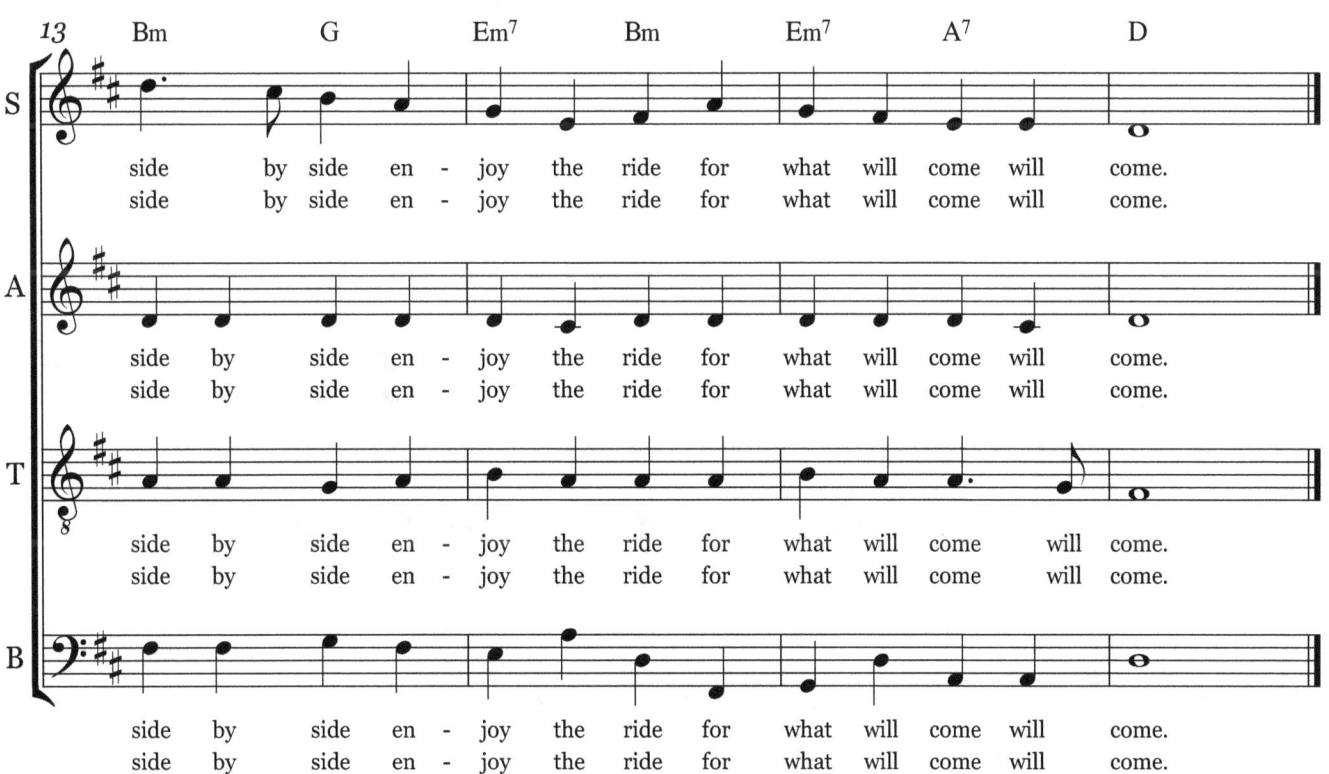

(Note: chord symbols support the soprano melody, not necessarily the SATB harmony)

105. There is an Empty Box

(From the Secular Hymnal)

Words: Secretary Michael

Music: "Aurelia" by Samuel Sebastian Wesley, 1864
(traditional hymn: "The Church's One Foundation")

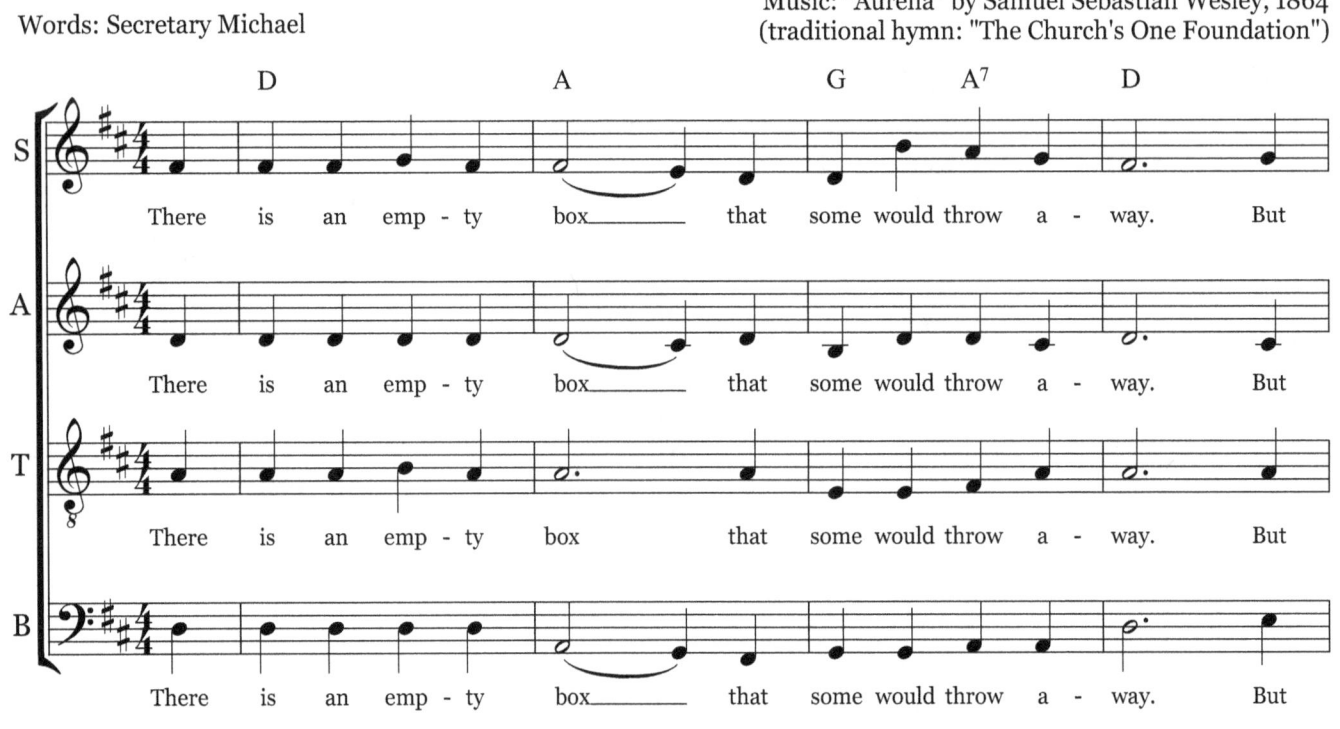

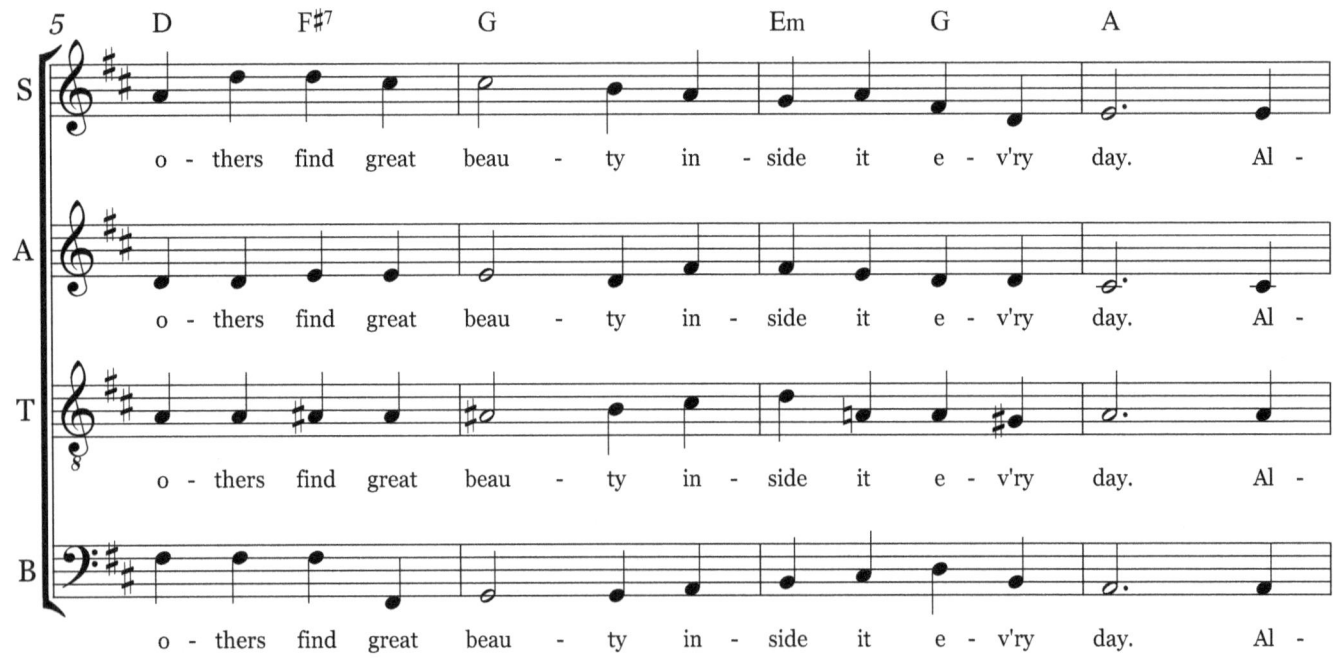

All works by Secretary Michael have been placed in the Public Domain. They may be freely copied and performed.

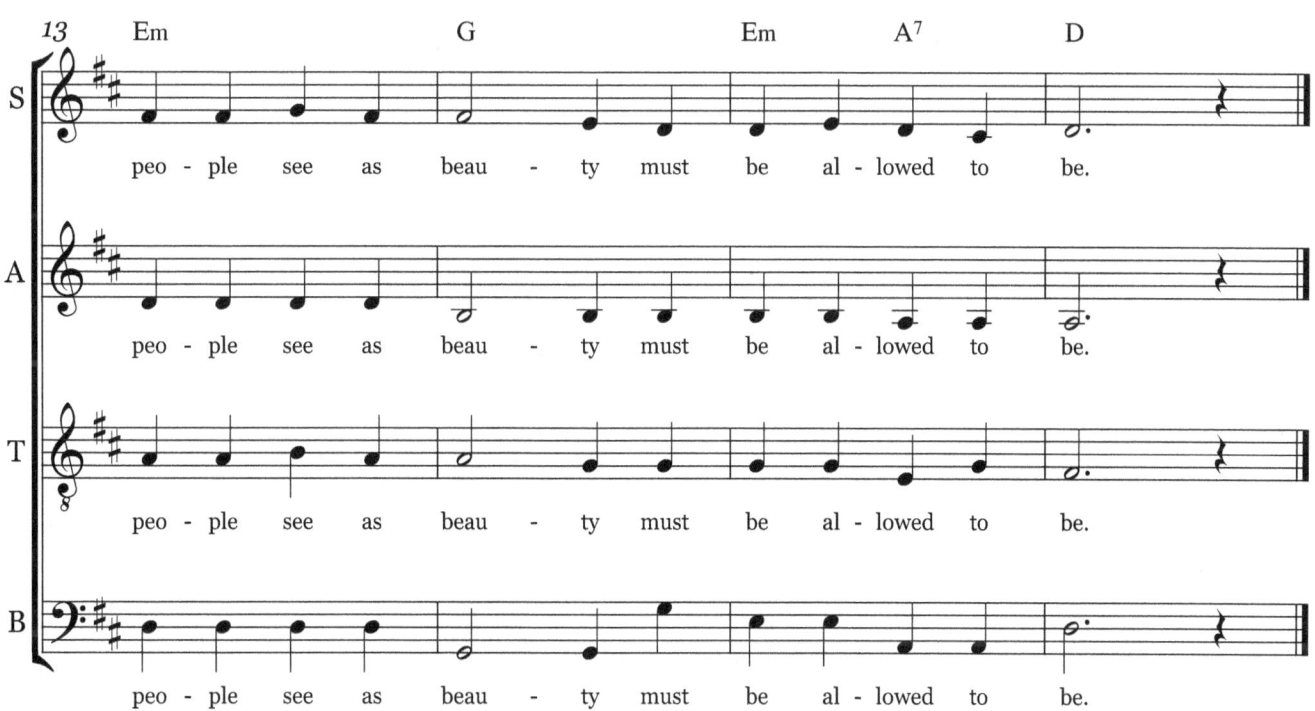

(Note: chord symbols support the soprano melody, not necessarily the SATB harmony)

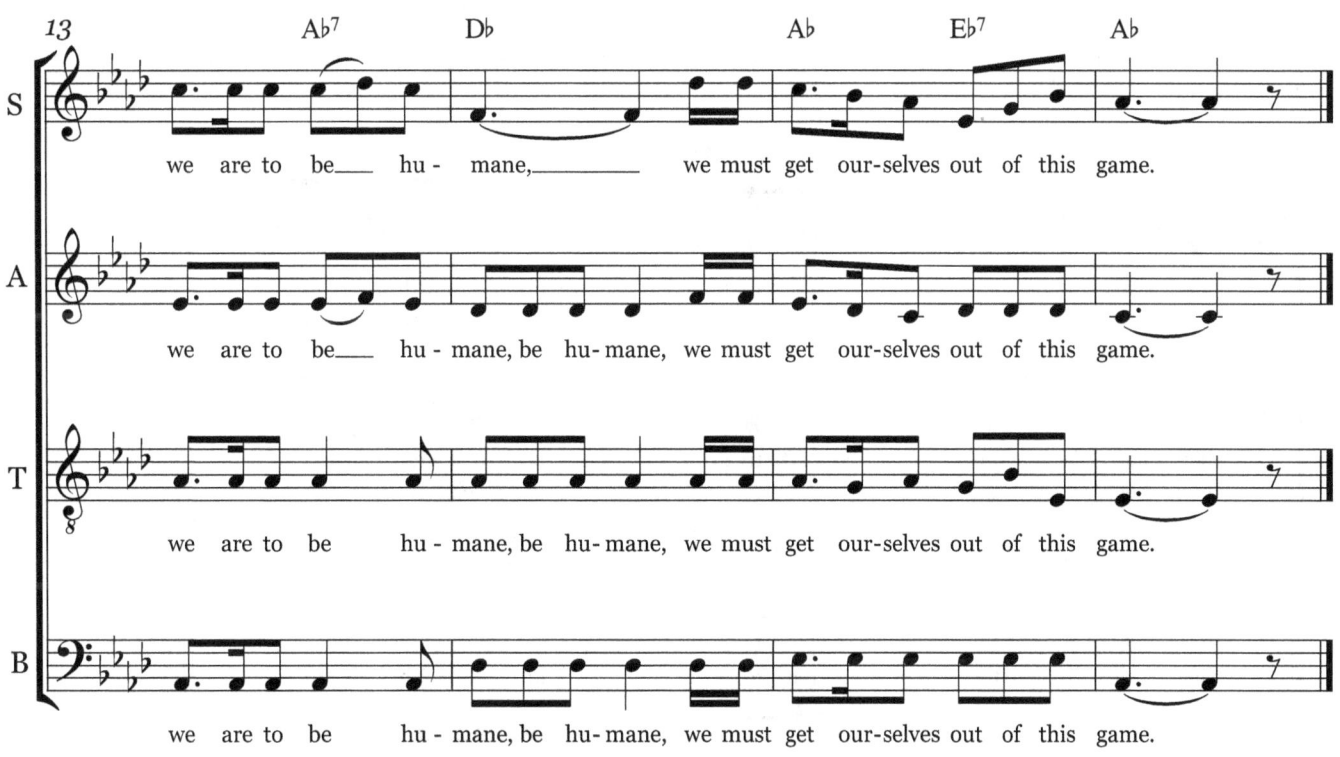

(Note: chord symbols support the soprano melody, not necessarily the SATB harmony)

(Helpful Hint: there are 5 dotted eighth notes - and they only occur with the word "better")

(Note: chord symbols support the soprano melody, not necessarily the SATB harmony)

108. There's a Road Between Our Lands

(From the Secular Hymnal)

Words: Secretary Michael

Music: "Royal Oak" (a 17th century English melody)
Arranged by Martin Shaw, 1915
(traditional hymn: "All Things Bright and Beautiful")

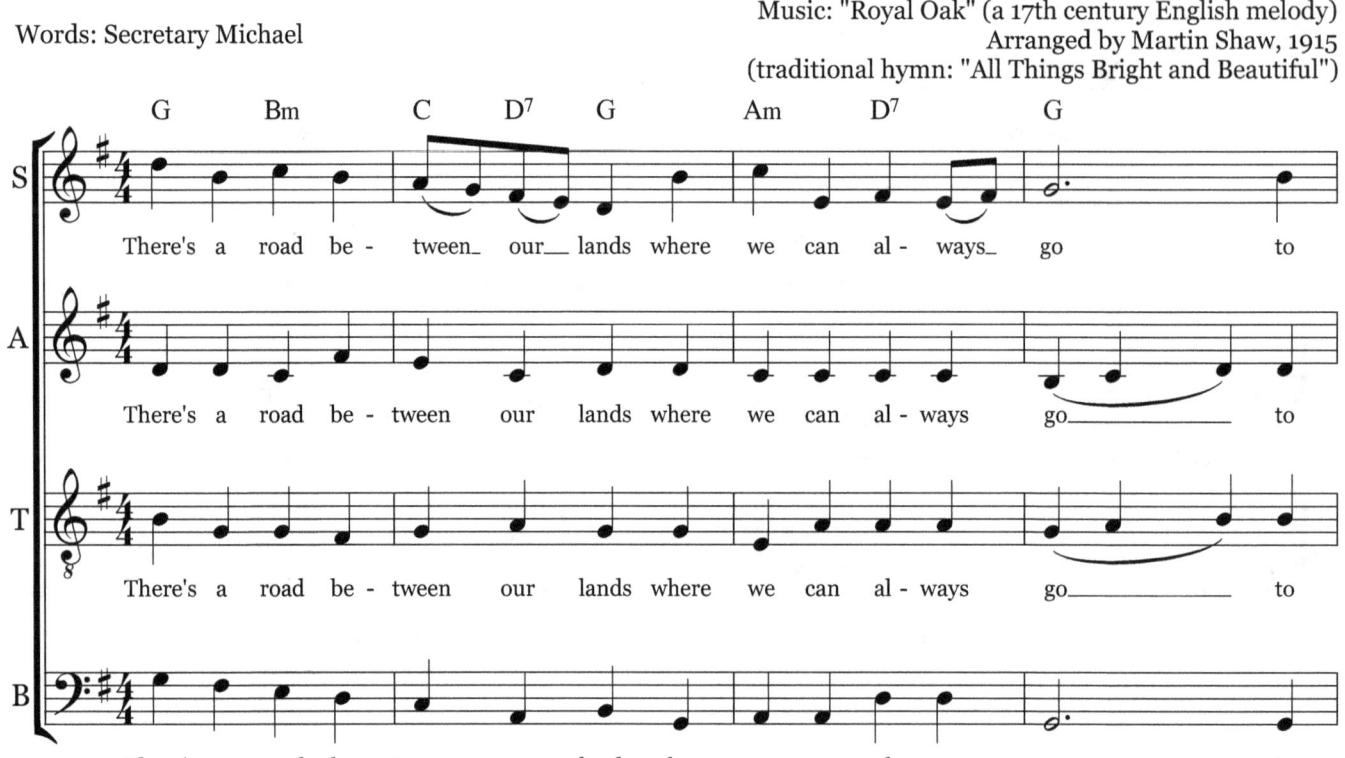

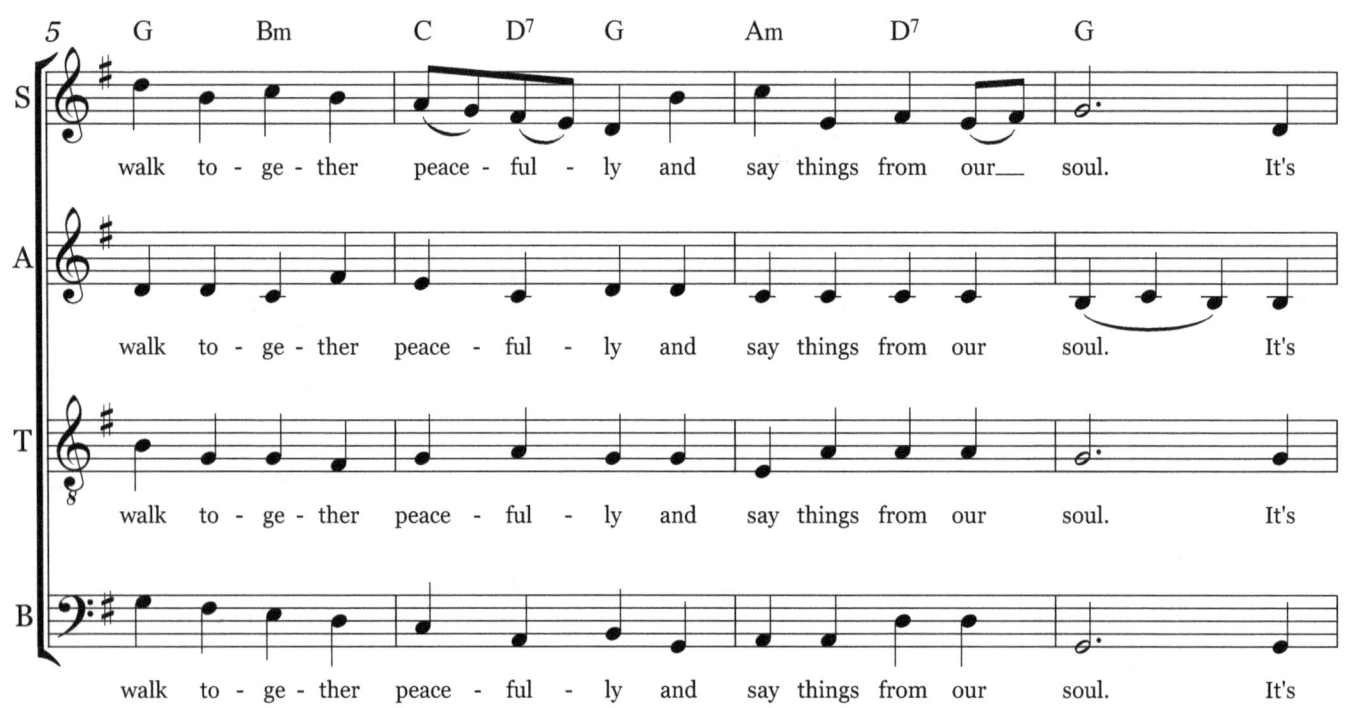

All works by Secretary Michael have been placed in the Public Domain. They may be freely copied and performed.

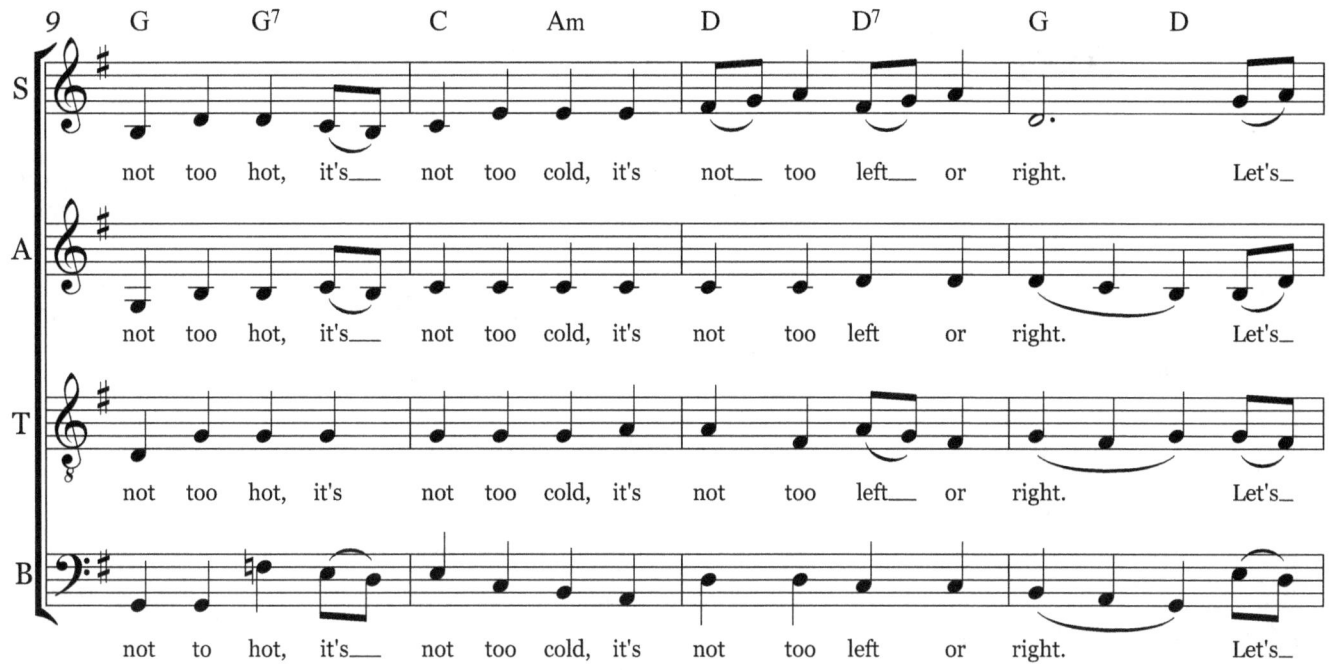

(Note: chord symbols support the soprano melody, not necessarily the SATB harmony)

109. There's Claim Number One

(From the Secular Hymnal)

Words: Secretary Michael

Music: "Revive Us Again" by John Jenkins Husband, c.1815
(traditional hymn: "Revive Us Again")

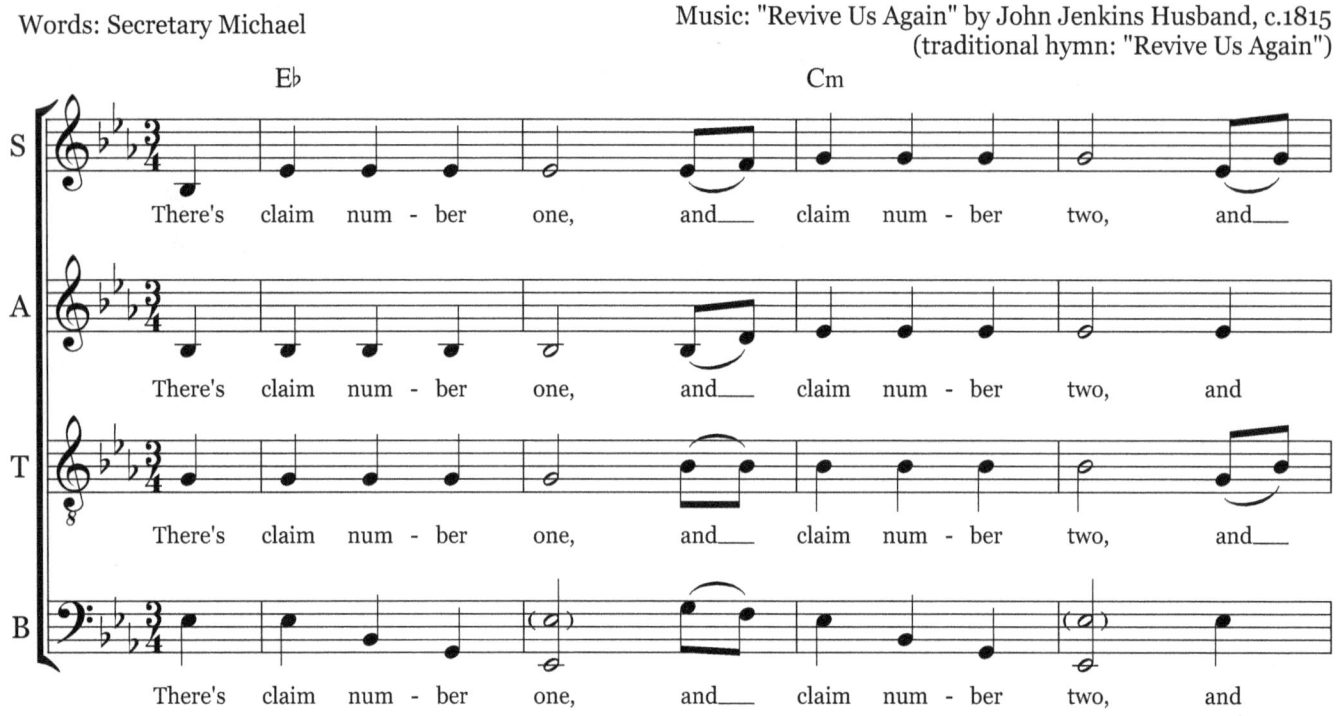

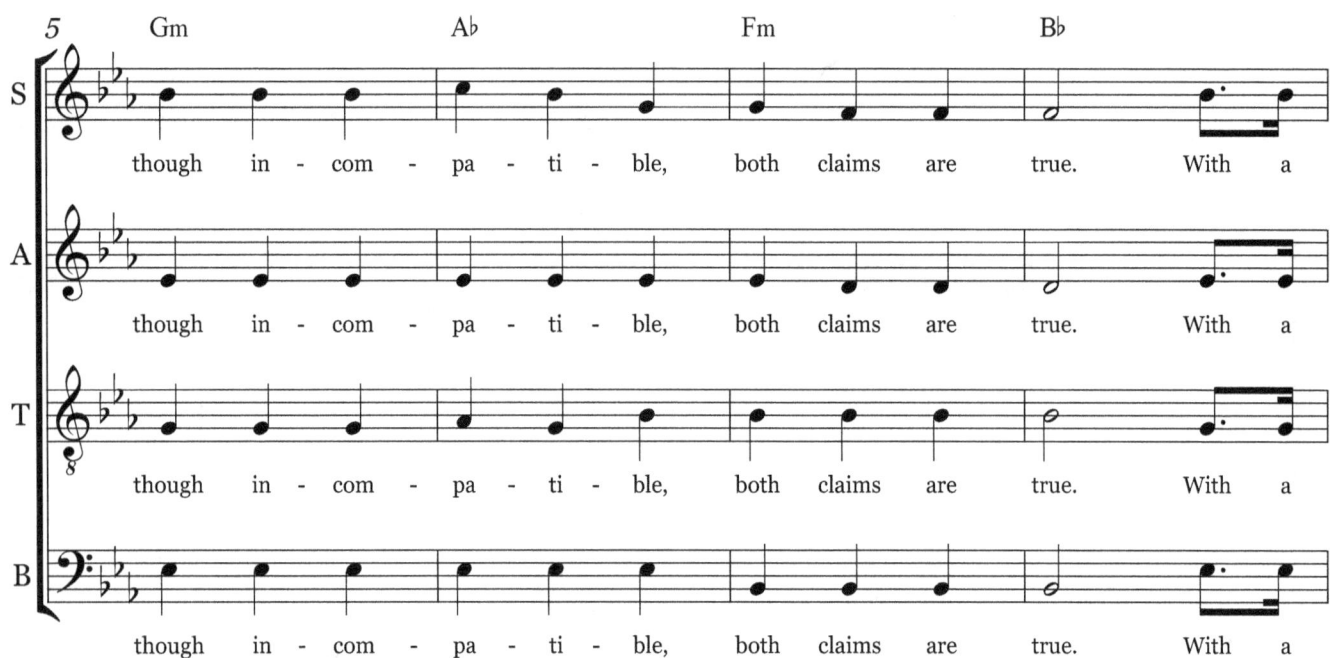

All works by Secretary Michael have been placed in the Public Domain. They may be freely copied and performed.

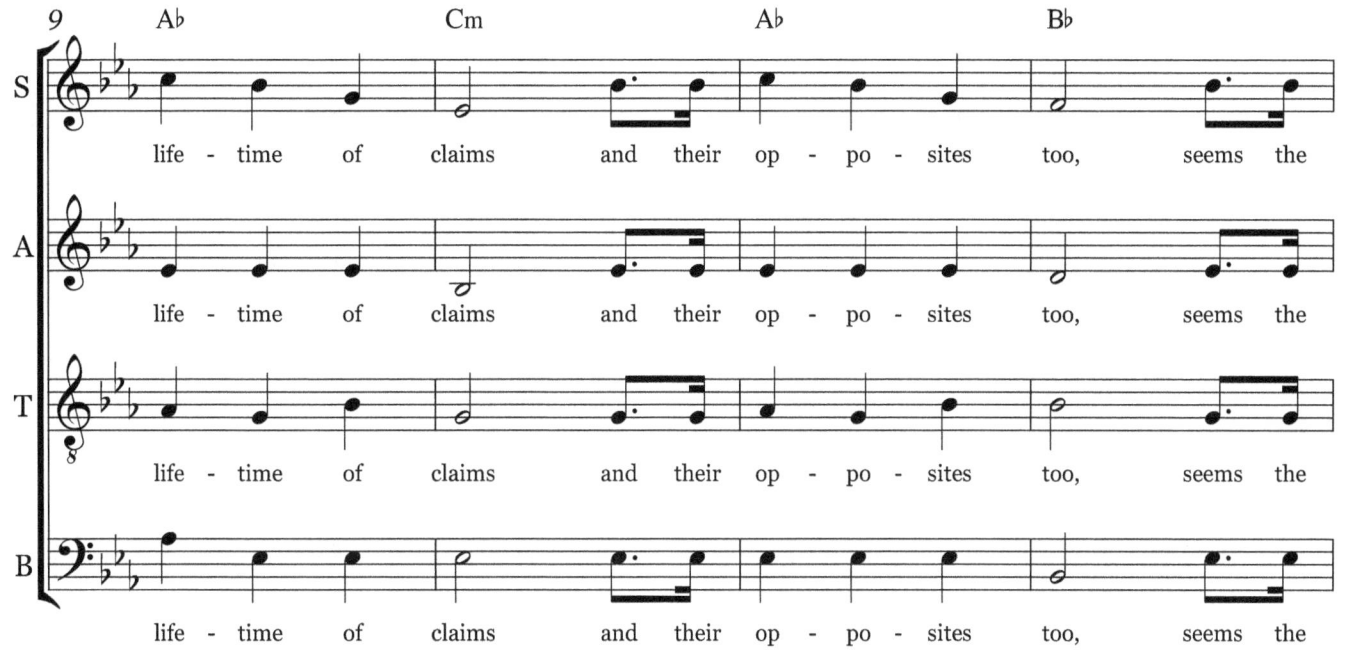
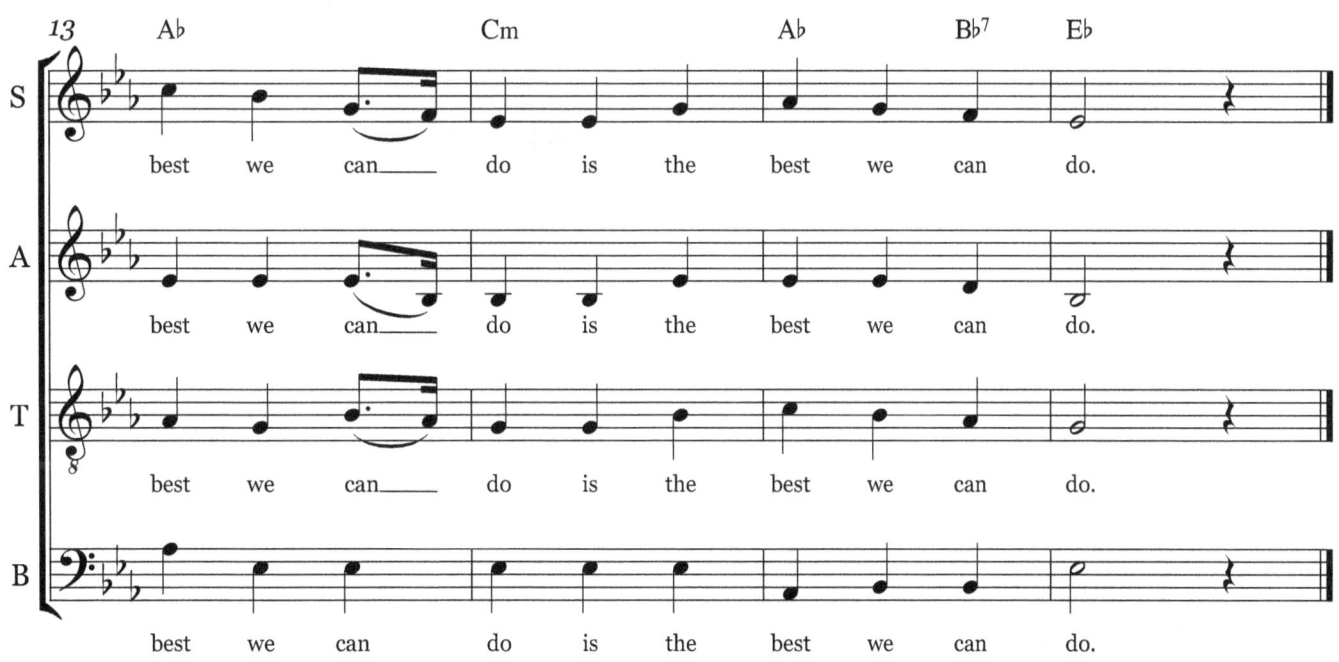

(Note: chord symbols support the soprano melody, not necessarily the SATB harmony)

110. There's More Than One Way

(From the Secular Hymnal)

Words: Secretary Michael

Music: "Hanover" by William Croft, 1708
(traditional hymn: "Ye Servants of God")

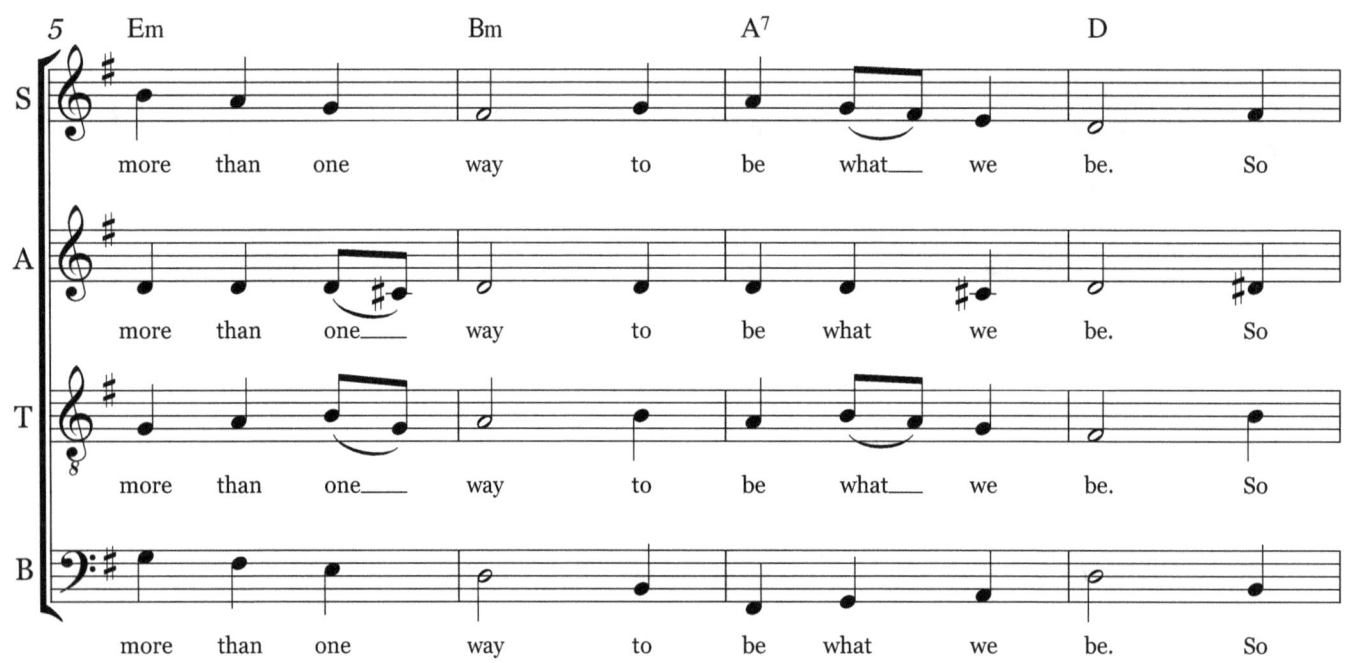

All works by Secretary Michael have been placed in the
Public Domain. They may be freely copied and performed.

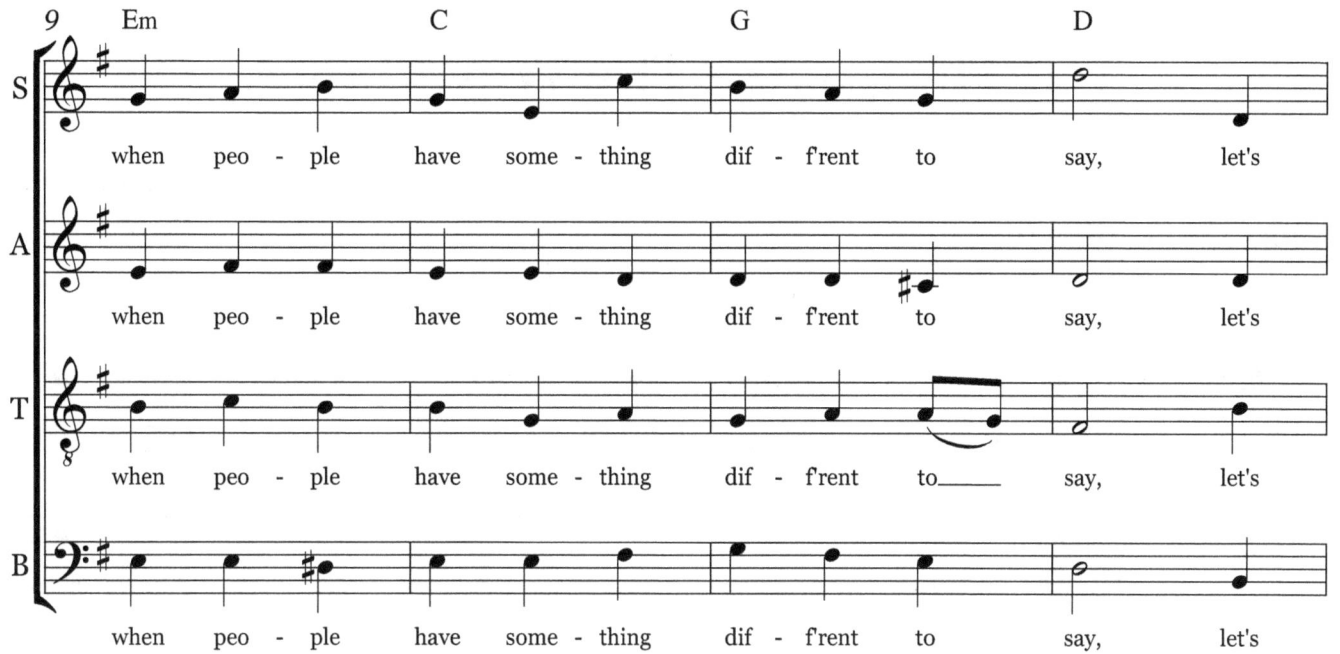
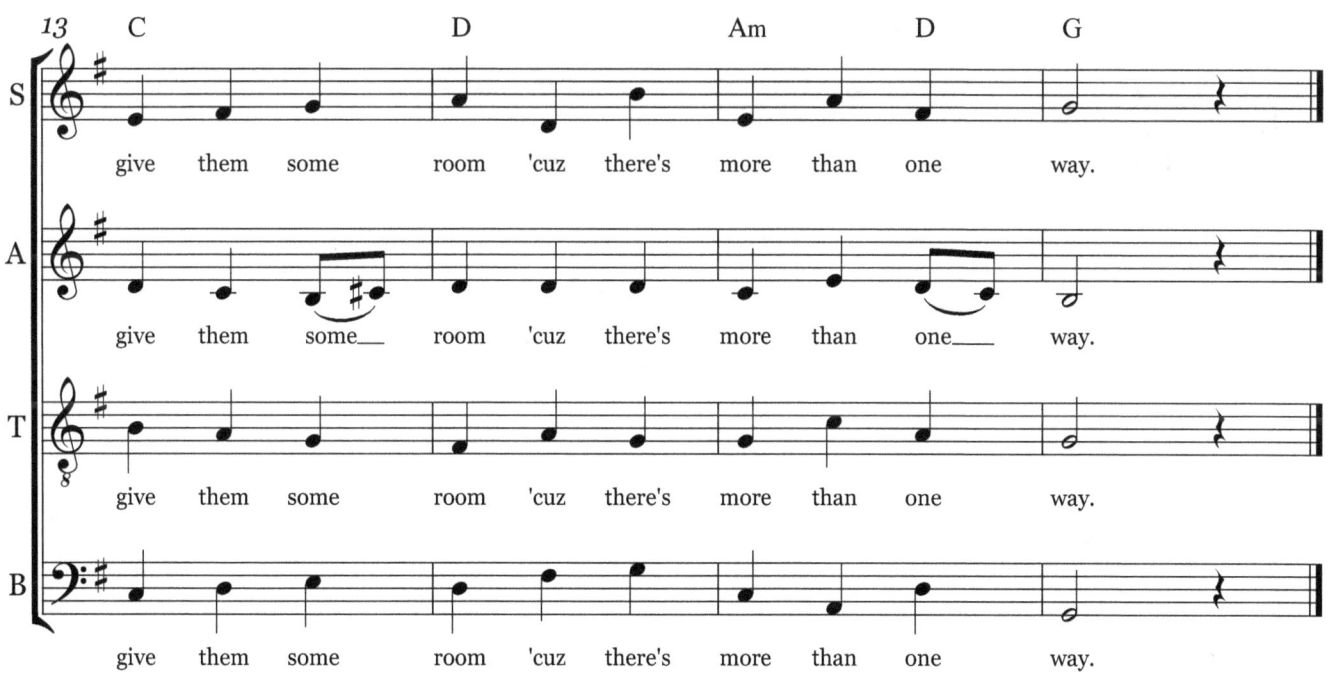

(Note: chord symbols support the soprano melody, not necessarily the SATB harmony)

111. Things Are The Way They Are

(From the Secular Hymnal)

Words: Secretary Michael

Tune: "Nun Danket" by Johann Crueger, 1647
SATB Arrangement by Secretary Michael
(traditional hymn: "Now Thank We All Our God")

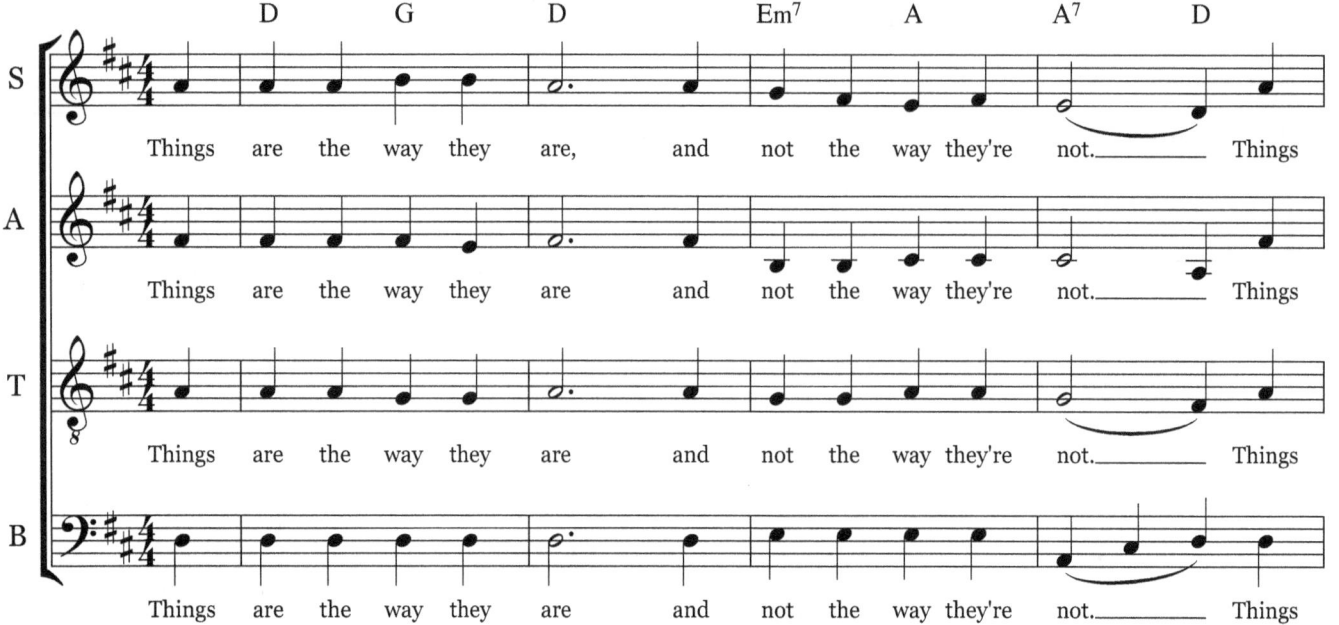

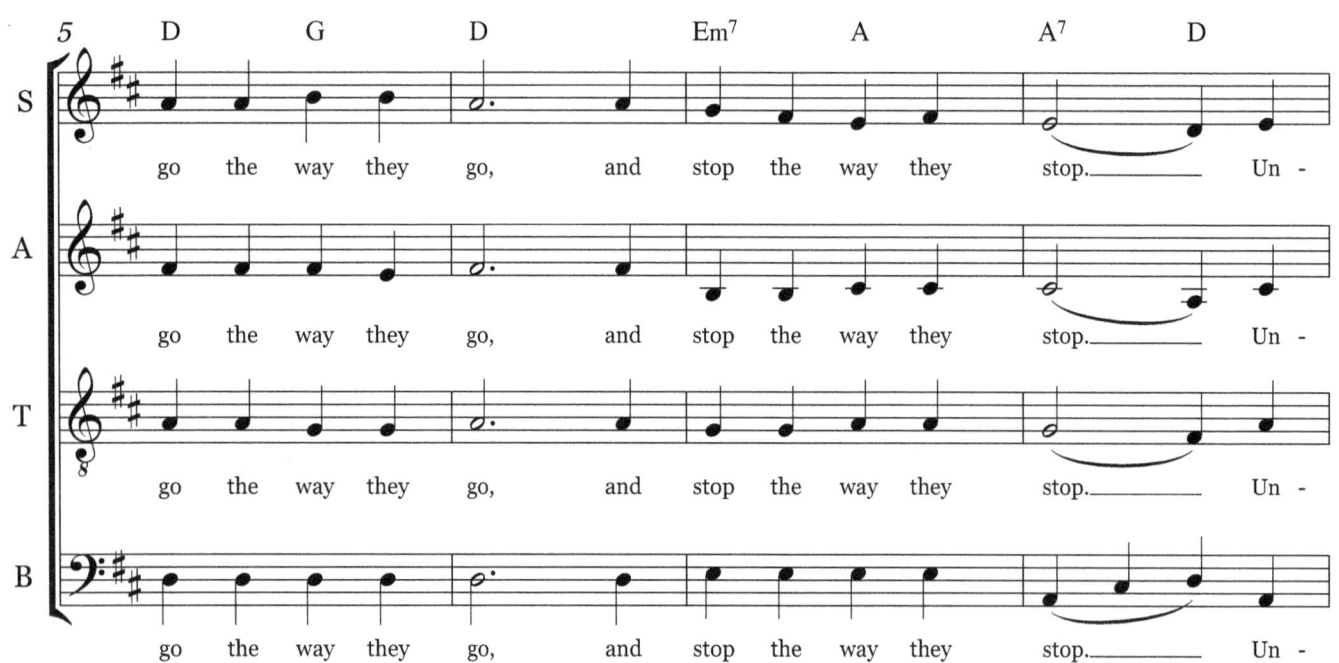

All works by Secretary Michael have been placed in the Public Domain. They may be freely copied and performed.

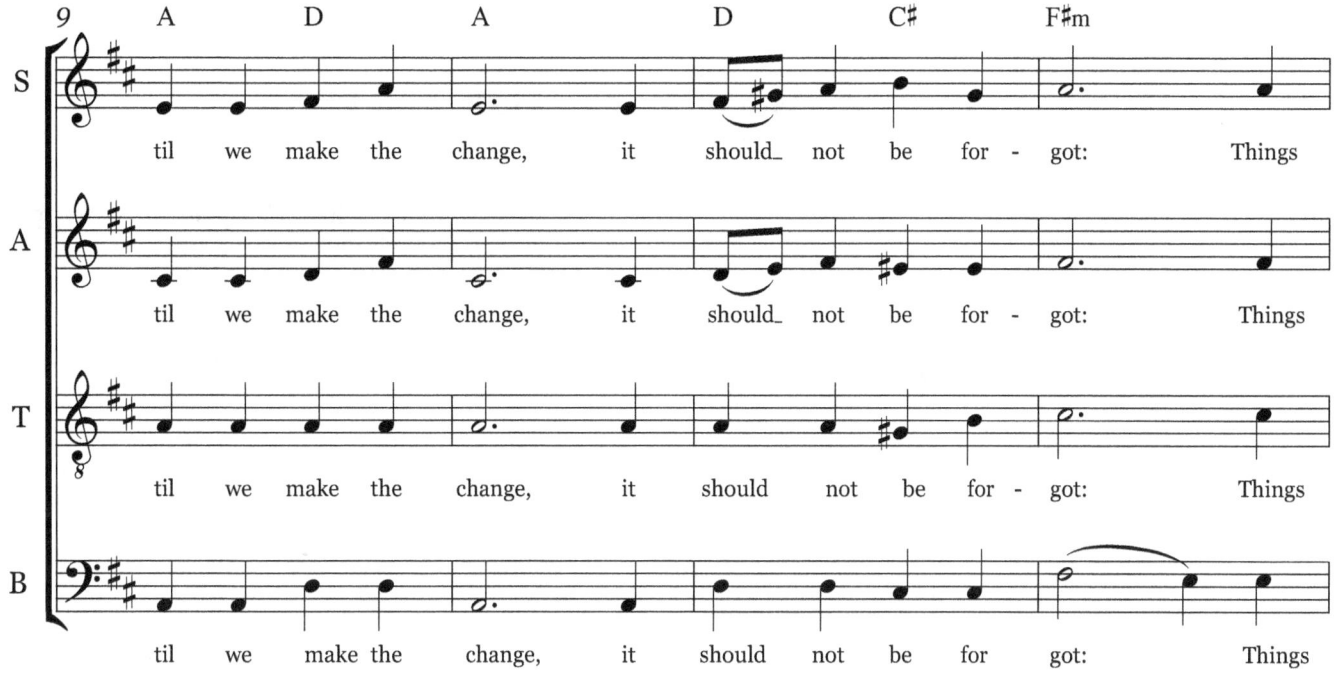
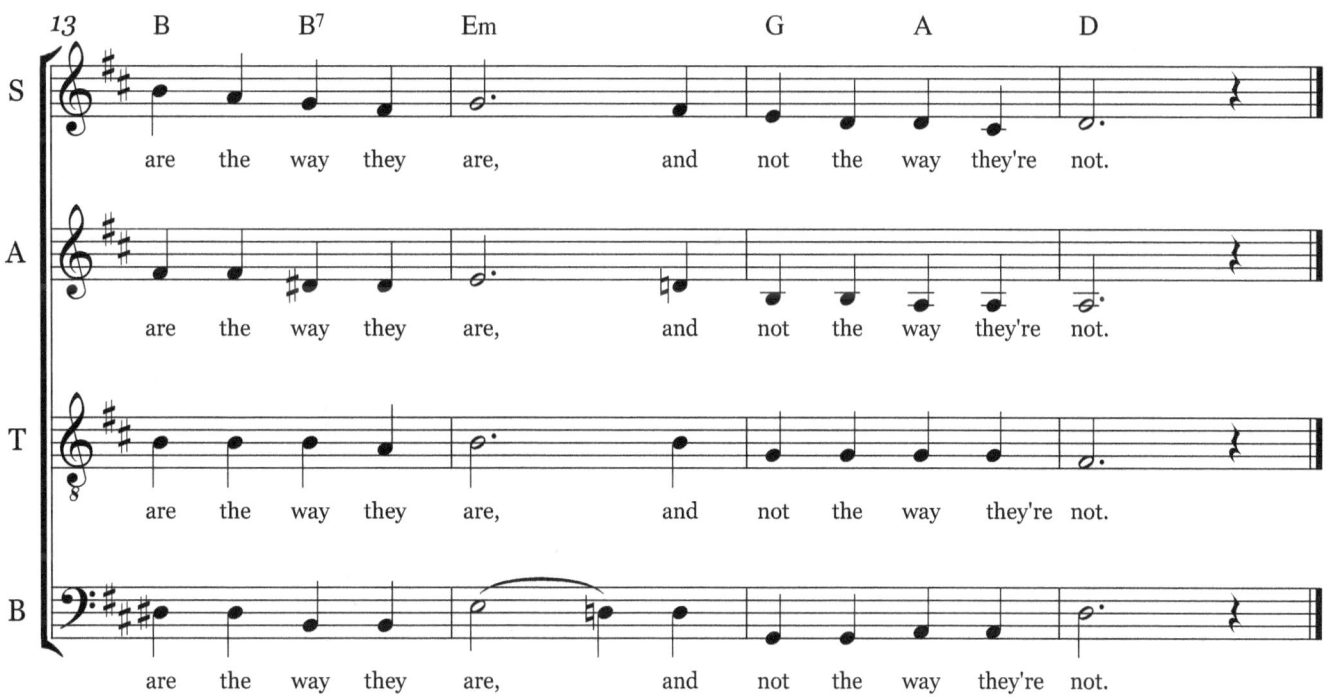

(Note: chord symbols support the soprano melody, not necessarily the SATB harmony)

112. This Day, This Day
(From the Secular Hymnal)

Words: Secretary Michael

Music: "Sine Nomine" by Ralph Vaughan Williams, 1906
(traditional hymn: "For All the Saints")

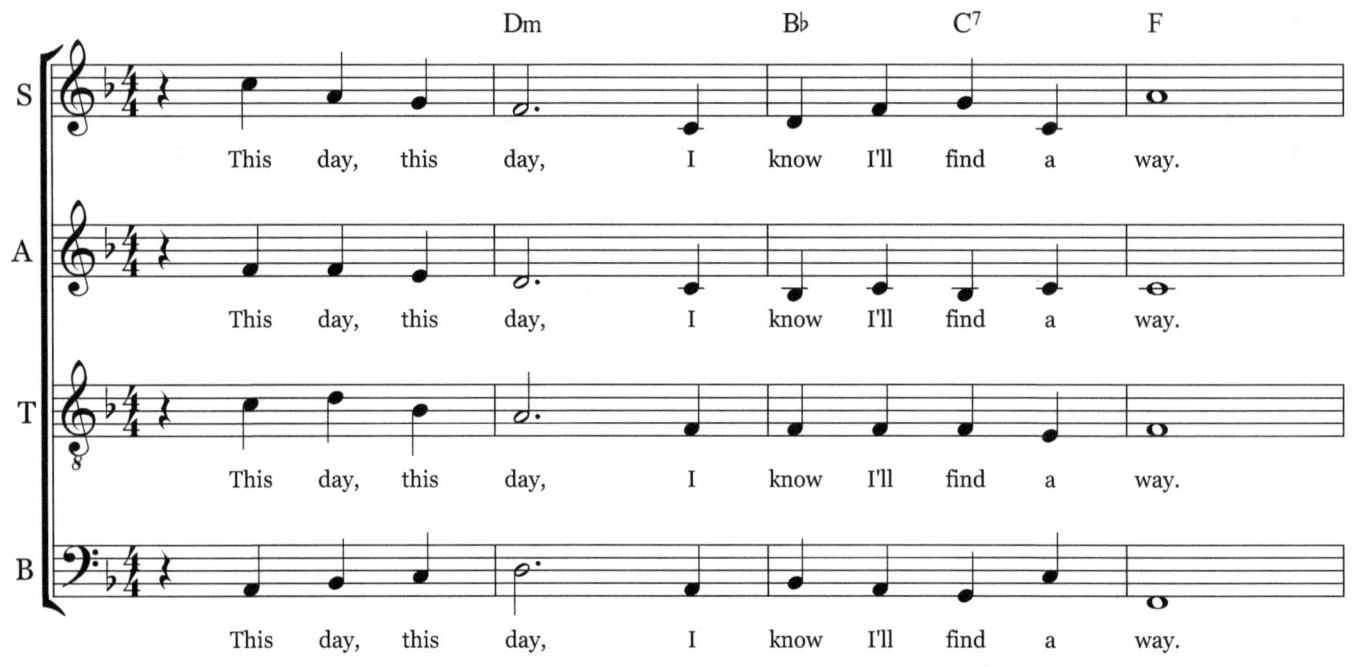

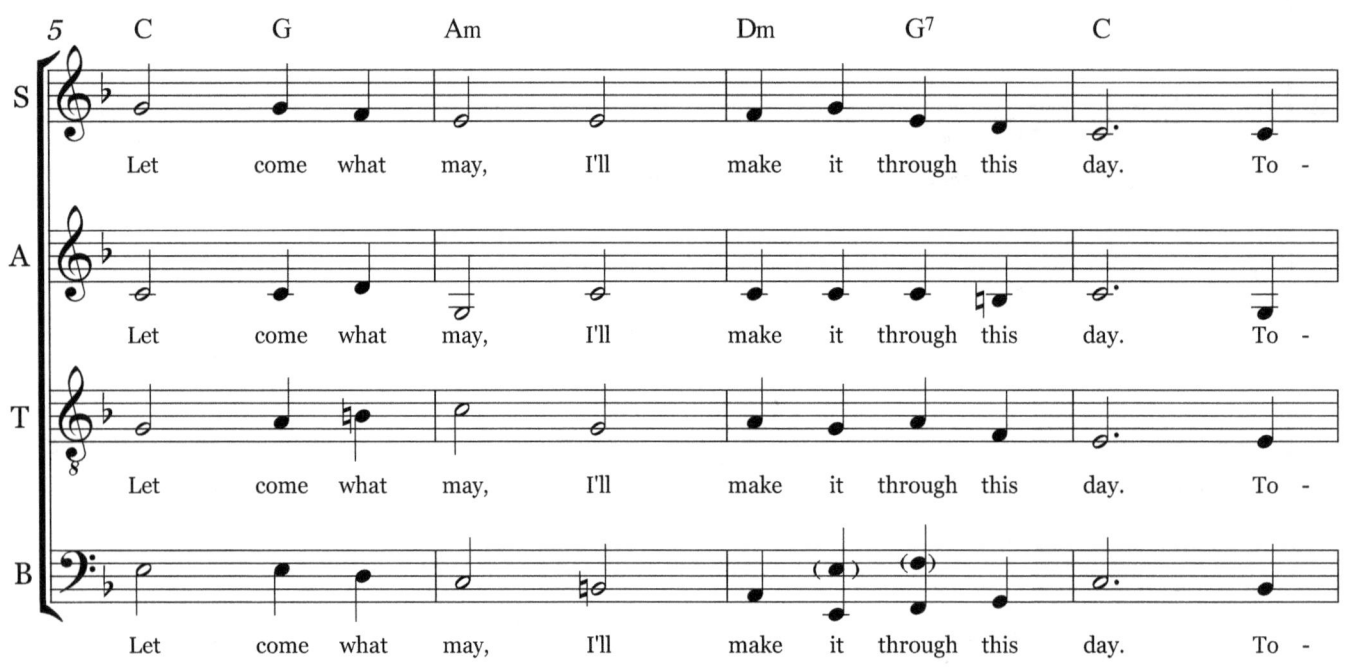

All works by Secretary Michael have been placed in the Public Domain. They may be freely copied and performed.

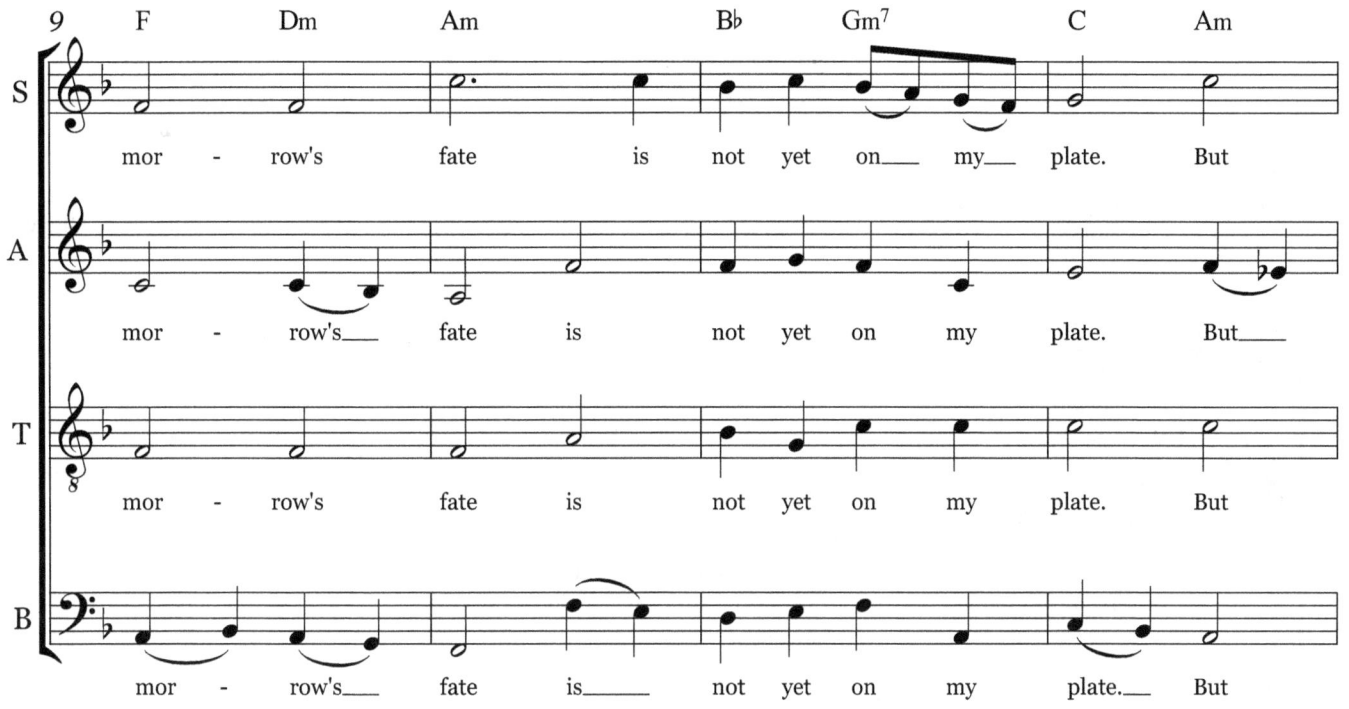
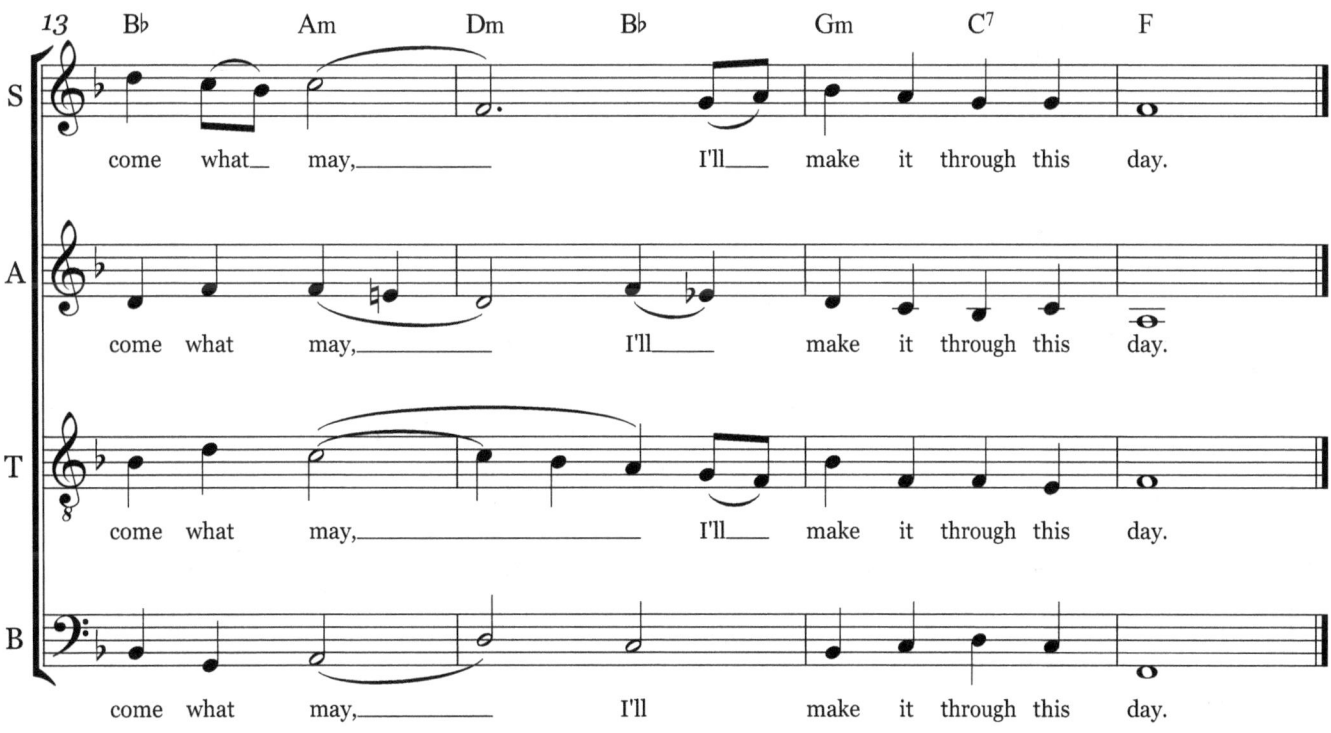

(Note: chord symbols support the soprano melody, not necessarily the SATB harmony)

113. Tick-Tock

(From the Secular Hymnal)

Words: Secretary Michael

Music: "Regent Square" by Henry Thomas Smart, 1867
(traditional hymn: "Angels From the Realms of Glory")

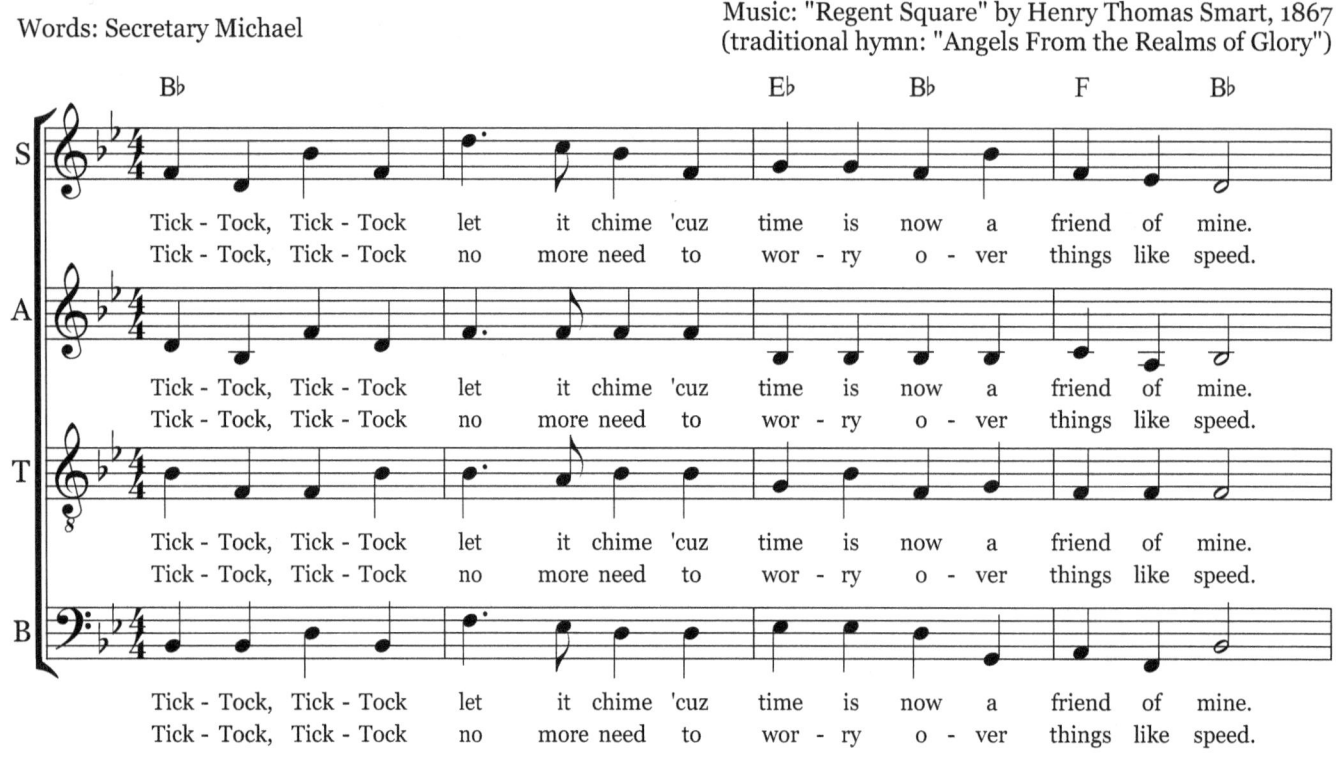

All works by Secretary Michael have been placed in the
Public Domain. They may be freely copied and performed.

(Note: chord symbols support the soprano melody, not necessarily the SATB harmony)

114. 'Tis a Gift

(From the Secular Hymnal)

Words: Joseph Bracket, 1848

Tune: "Simple Gifts" by Joseph Bracket, 1848
SATB Arrangement: Secretary Michael
(traditional hymn: "Simple Gifts")

All works by Secretary Michael have been placed in the Public Domain. They may be freely copied and performed.

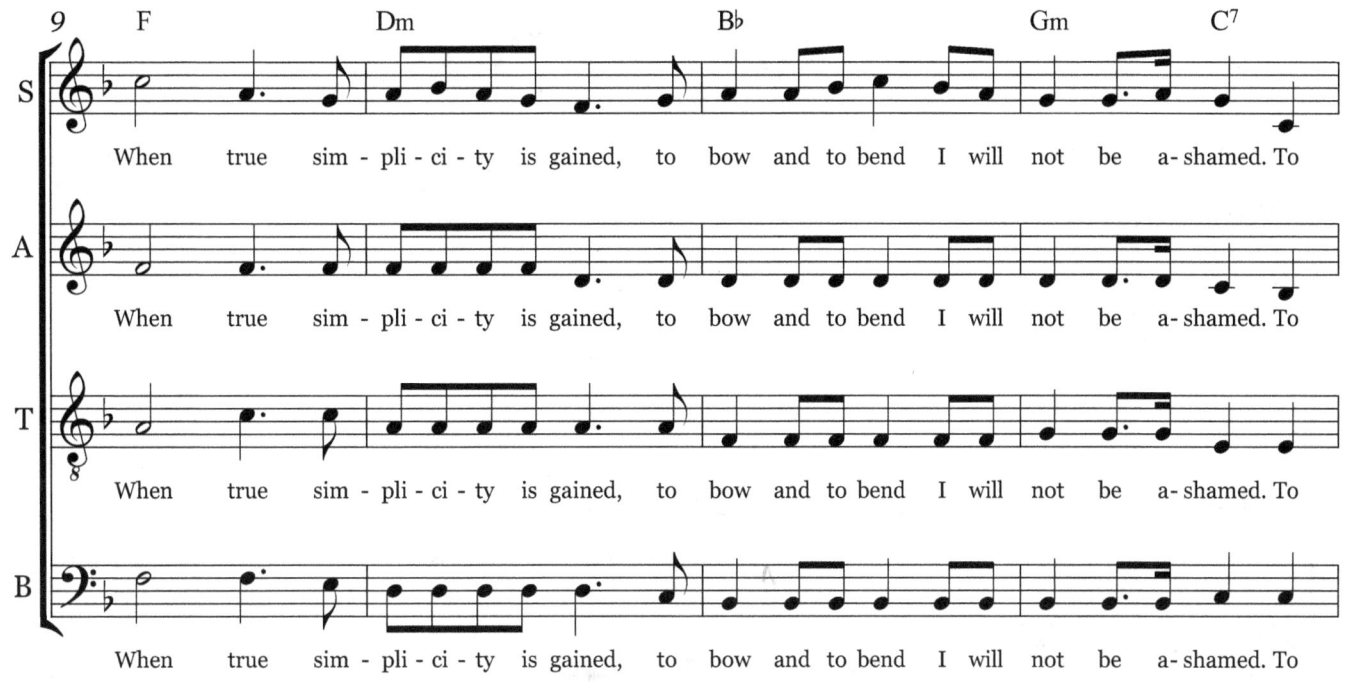

115. To Find a Place
(From the Secular Hymnal)

Words: Secretary Michael   Music: "Crucifer" by Sydney Hugo Nicholson, 1916
(traditional hymn: "Lift High the Cross")

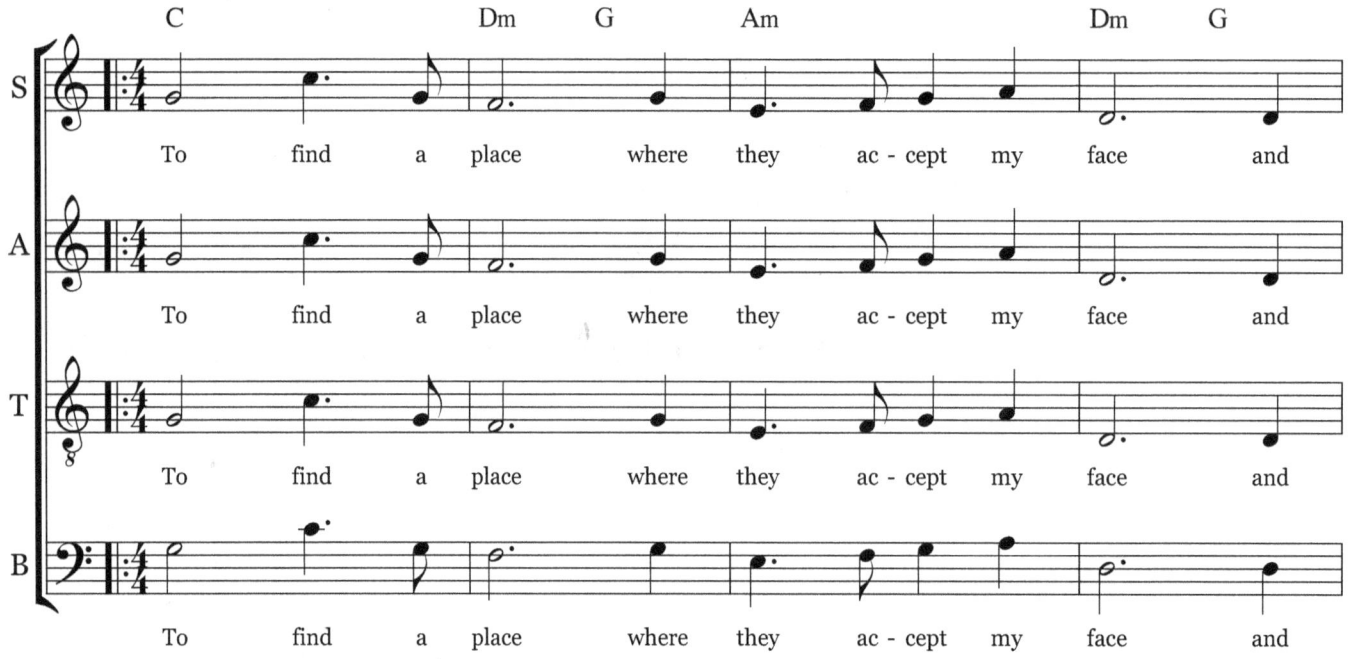

(PD) *All works by Secretary Michael have been placed in the Public Domain. They may be freely copied and performed.*

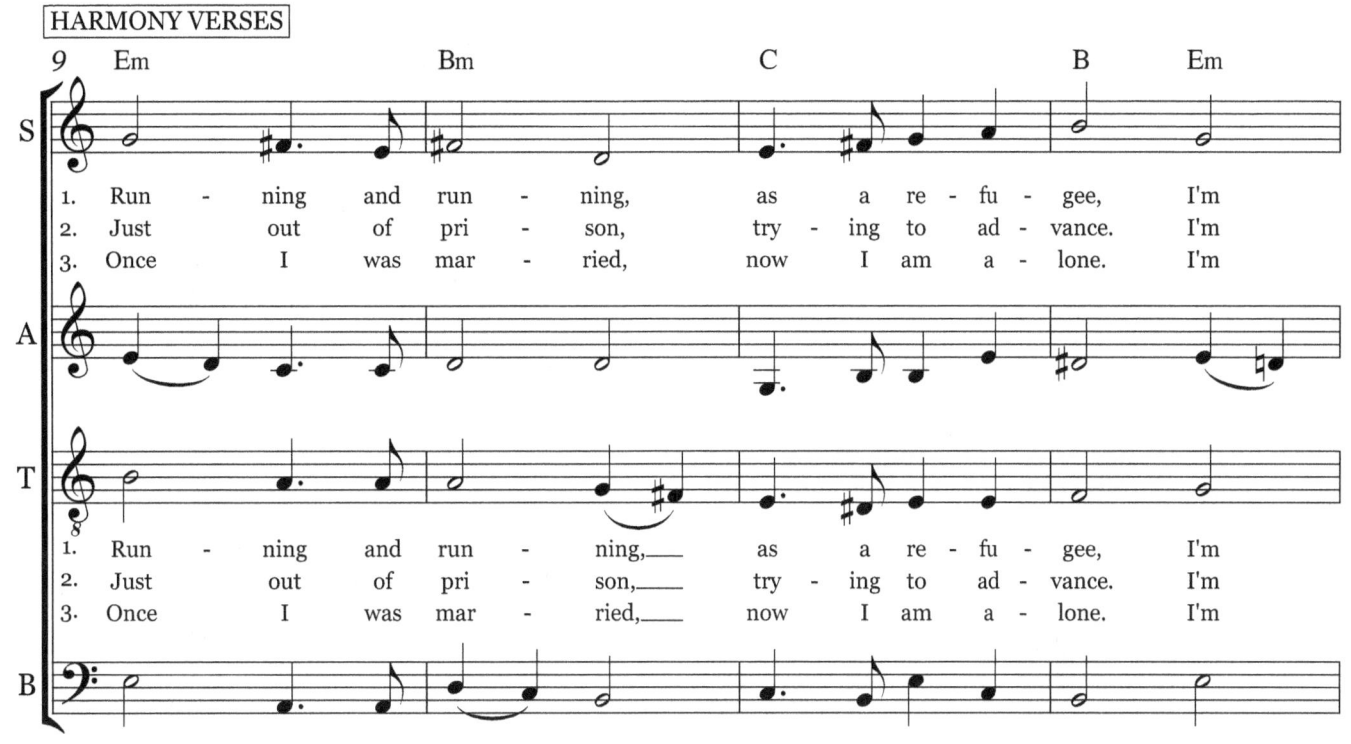
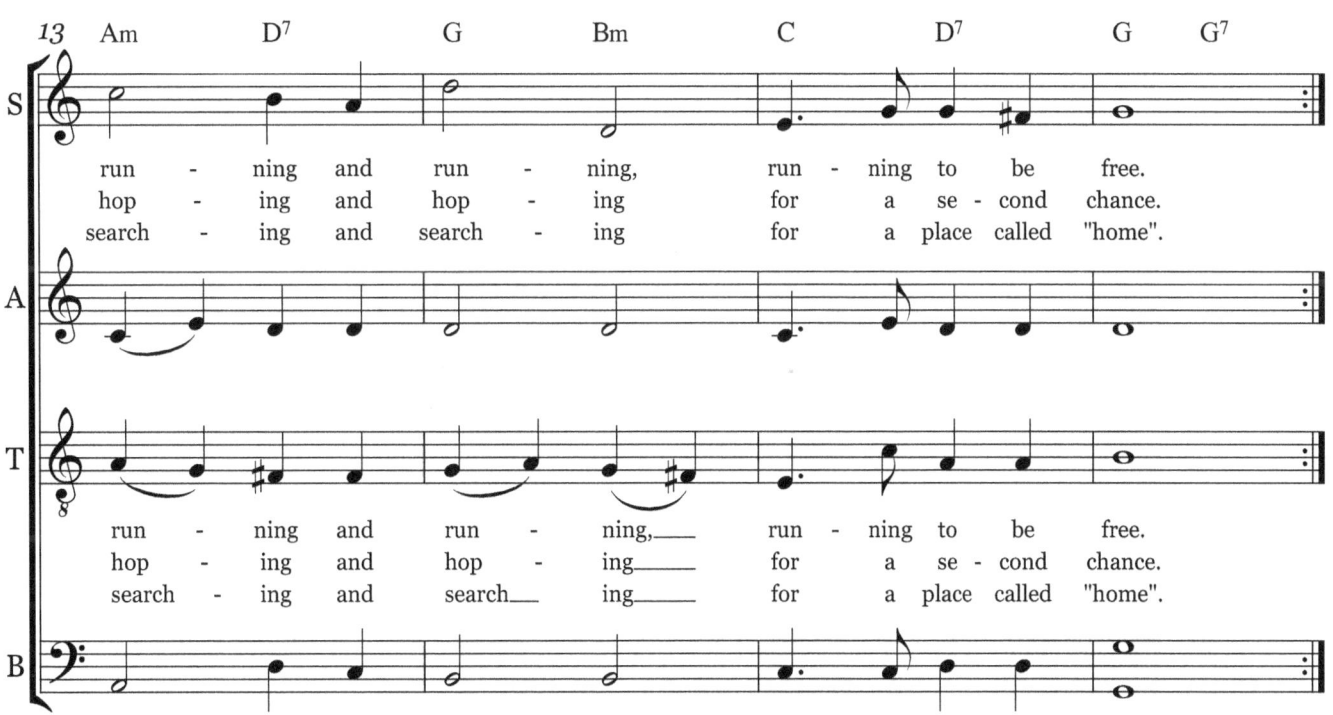

(Note: chord symbols support the soprano melody, not necessarily the SATB harmony)

116. To Live Our Lives Addiction-Free

(From the Secular Hymnal)

Words: Secretary Michael

Melody: "Deus Tuorum Militum", 1753
SATB Arrangement by Secretary Michael
(traditional hymn: "Bless Thou the Gifts")

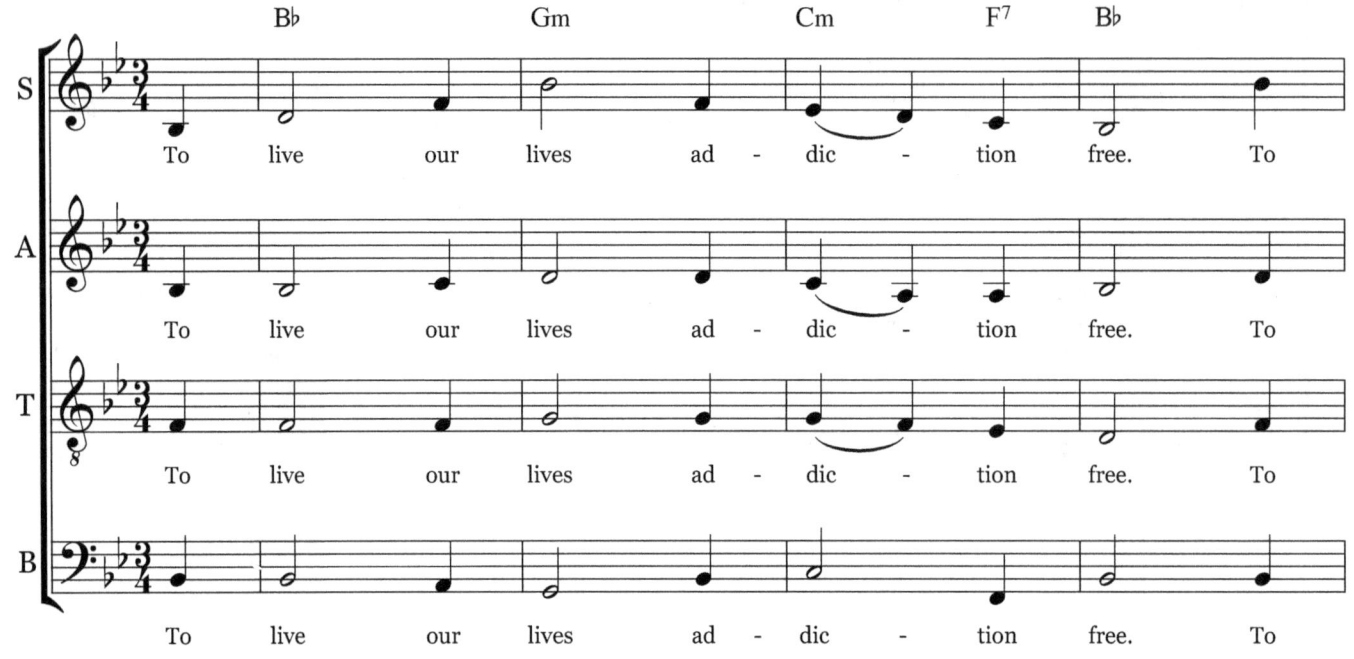

All works by Secretary Michael have been placed in the Public Domain. They may be freely copied and performed.

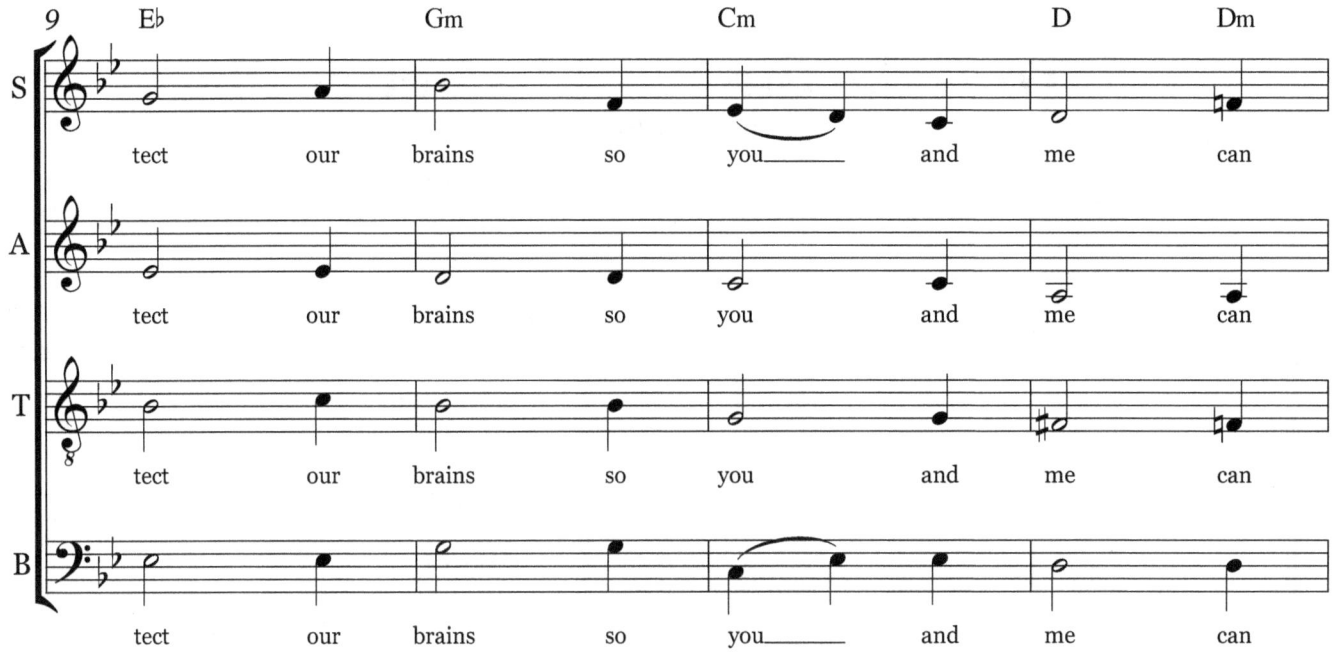
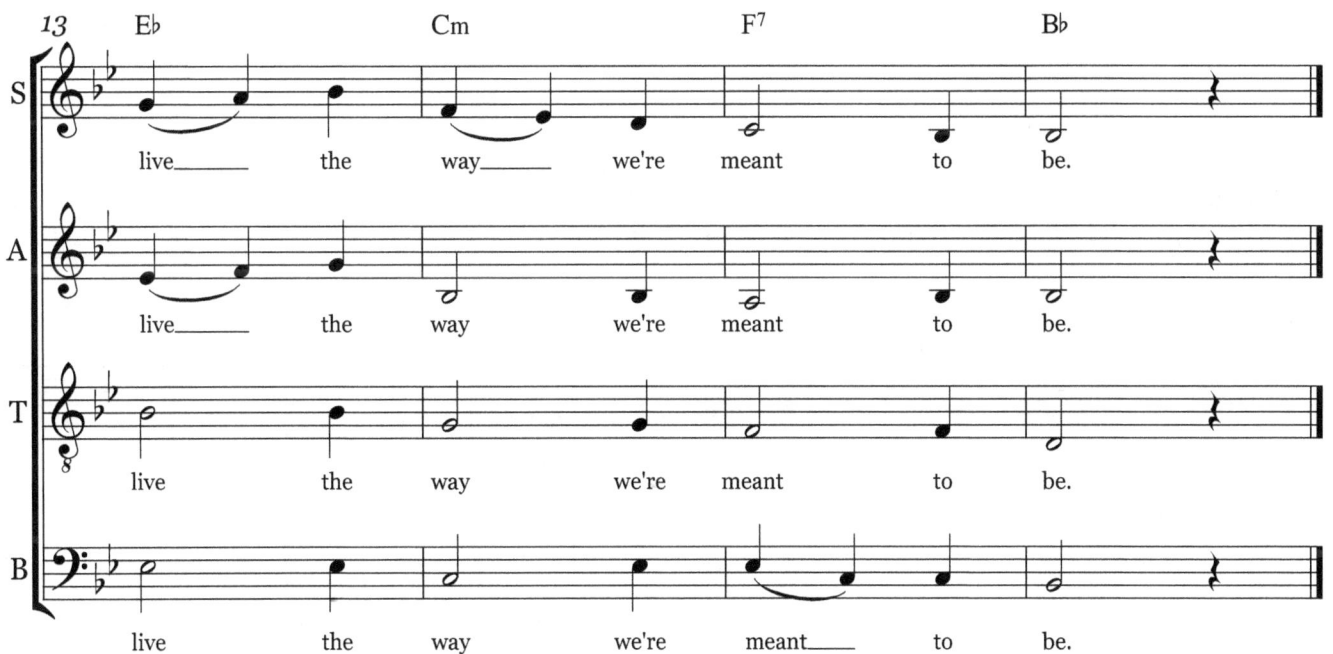

117. To Make the World a Better Place
(From the Secular Hymnal)

Words: Secretary Michael

Music: "Horsley" by William Horsley, 1830
(traditional hymn: "There Is a Green Hill Far Away")

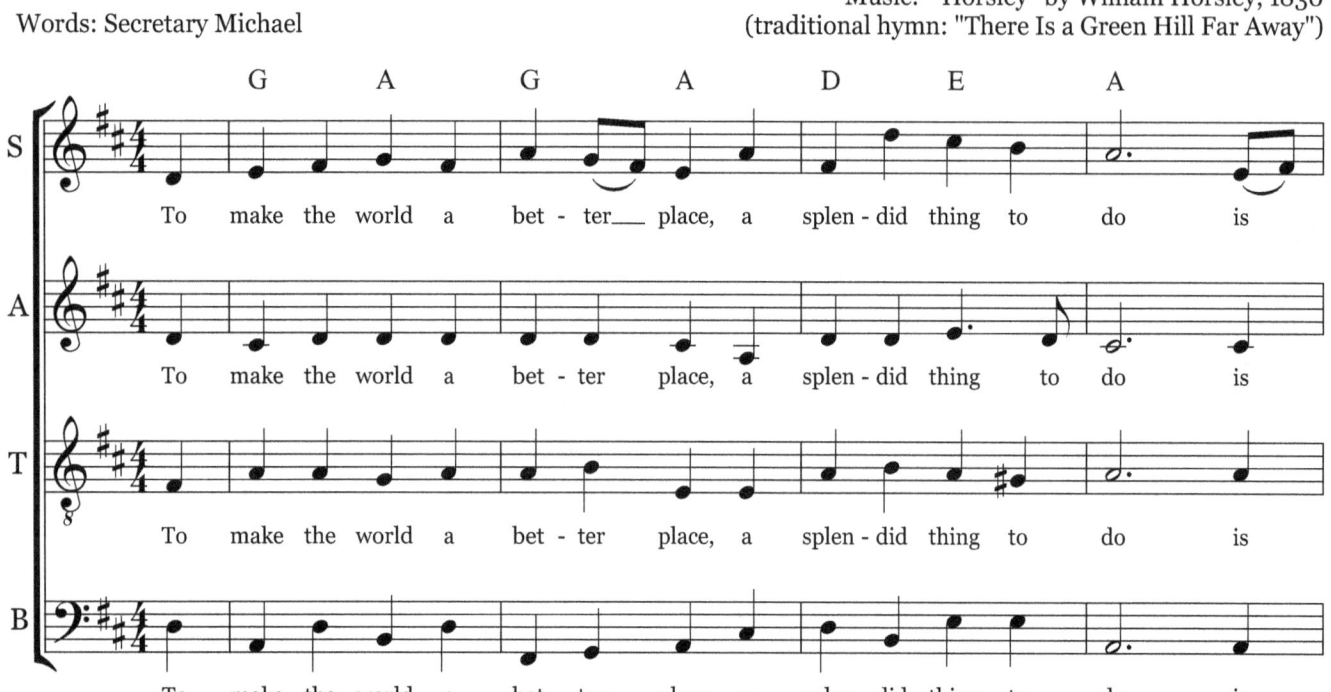
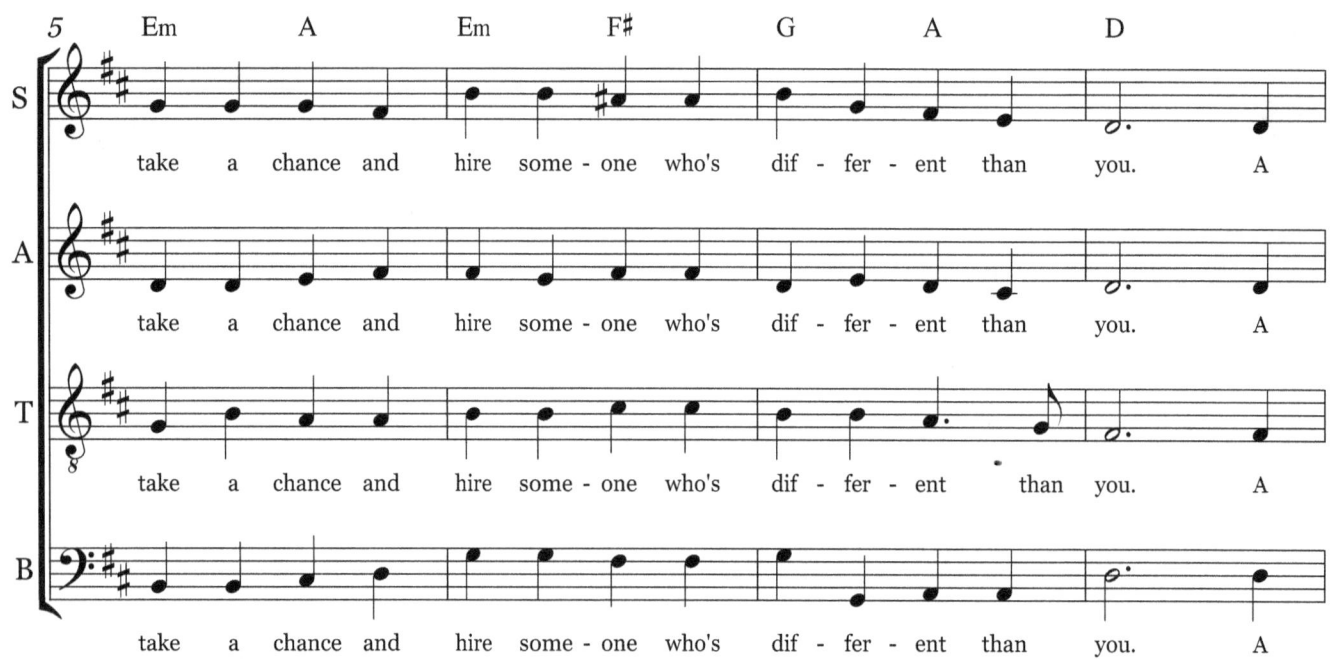

All works by Secretary Michael have been placed in the Public Domain. They may be freely copied and performed.

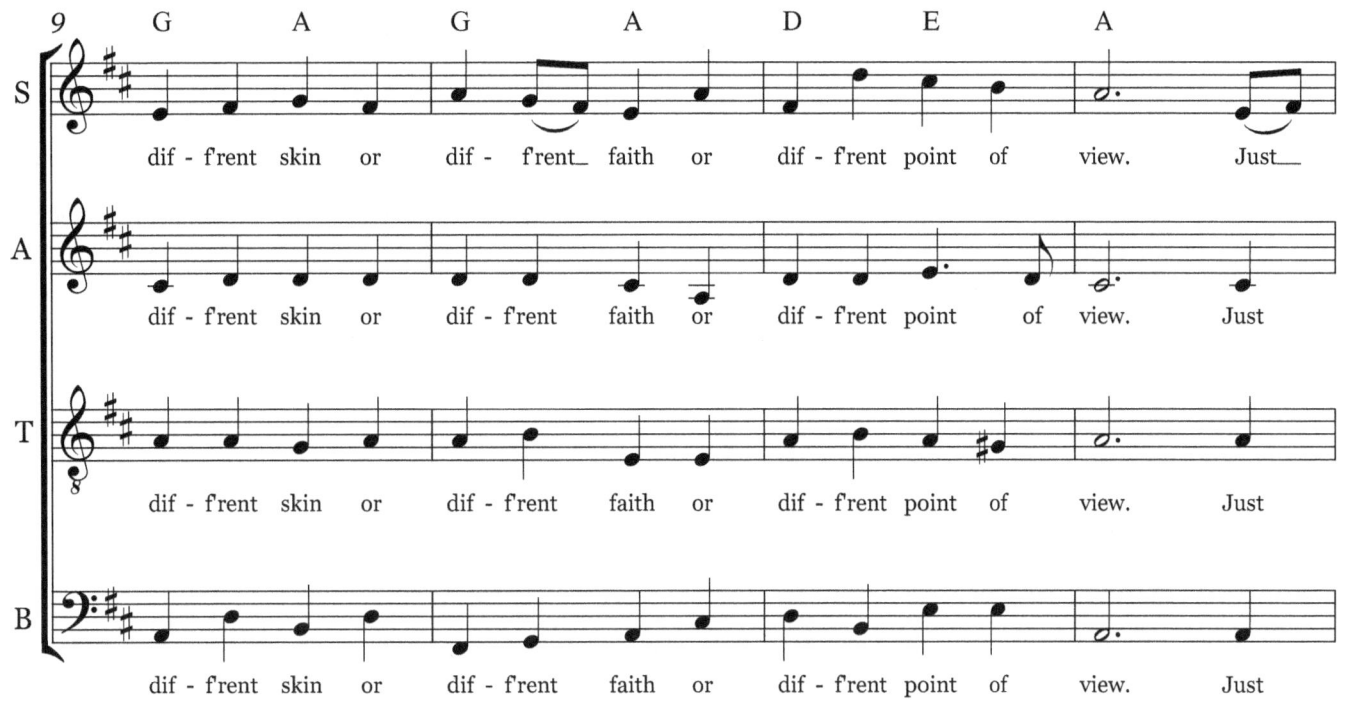
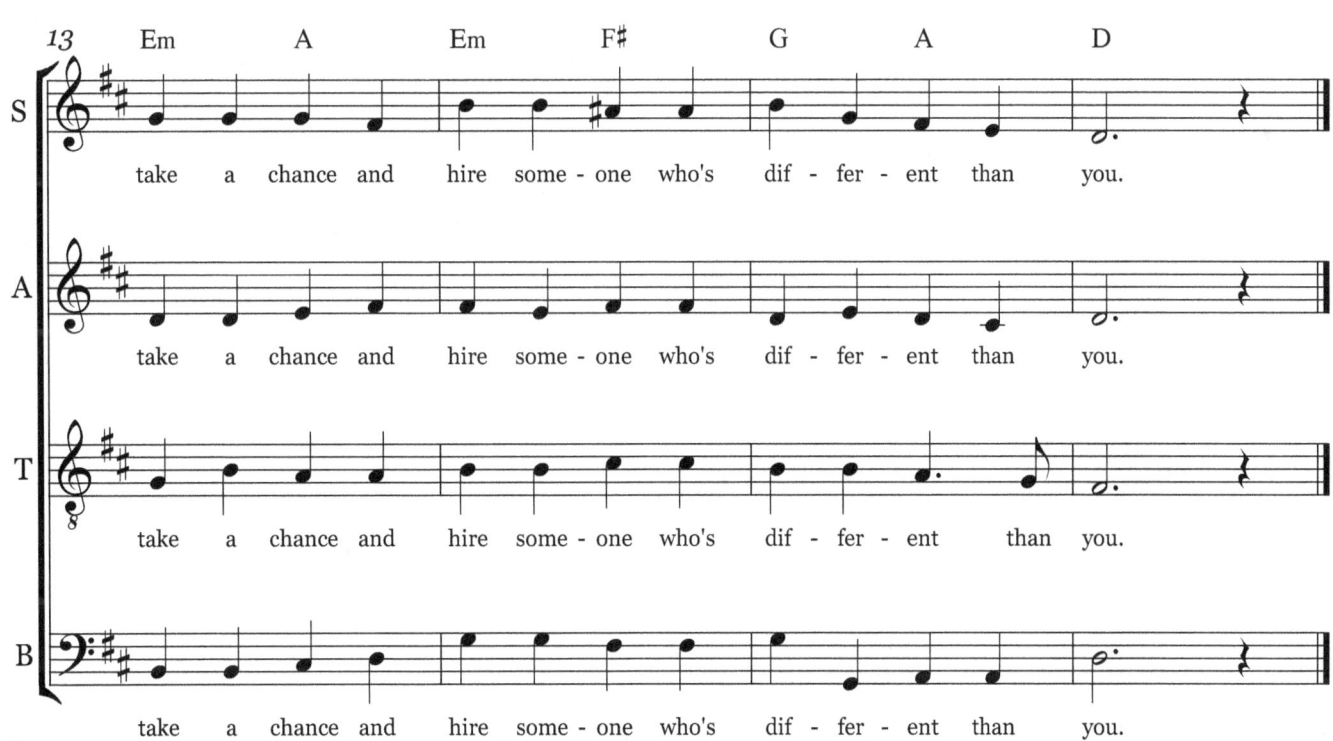

(Note: chord symbols support the soprano melody, not necessarily the SATB harmony)

118. To Soldiers Lost
(From the Secular Hymnal)

Words: Secretary Michael

Melody: "St. Patrick's Breastplate" (traditional Irish)
SATB Arrangement: Secretary Michael
(traditional hymn: "I Bind Unto Myself Today")

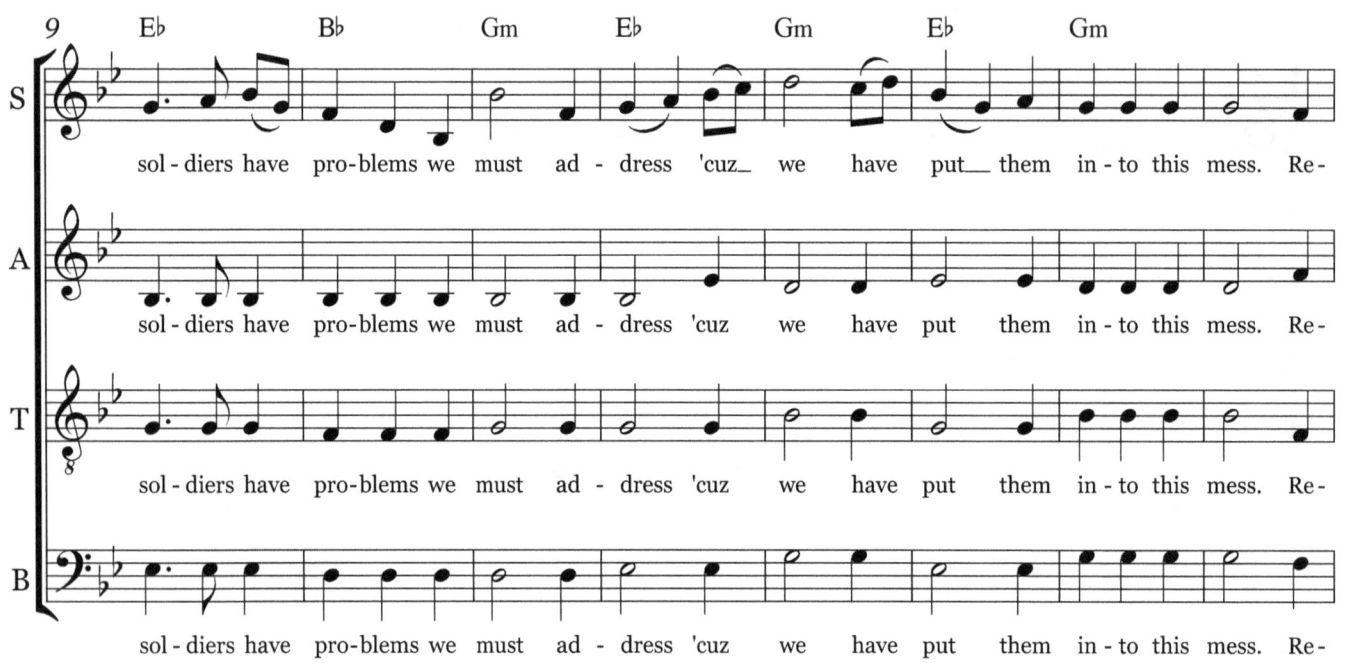

All works by Secretary Michael have been placed in the Public Domain. They may be freely copied and performed.

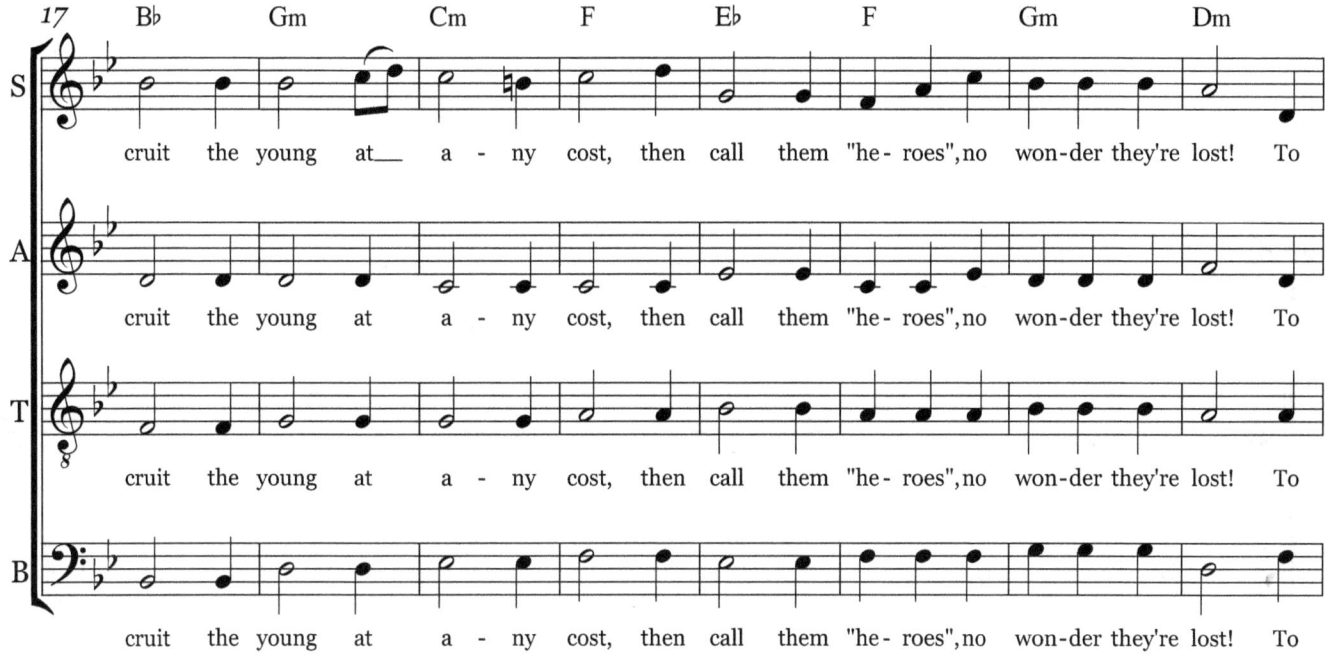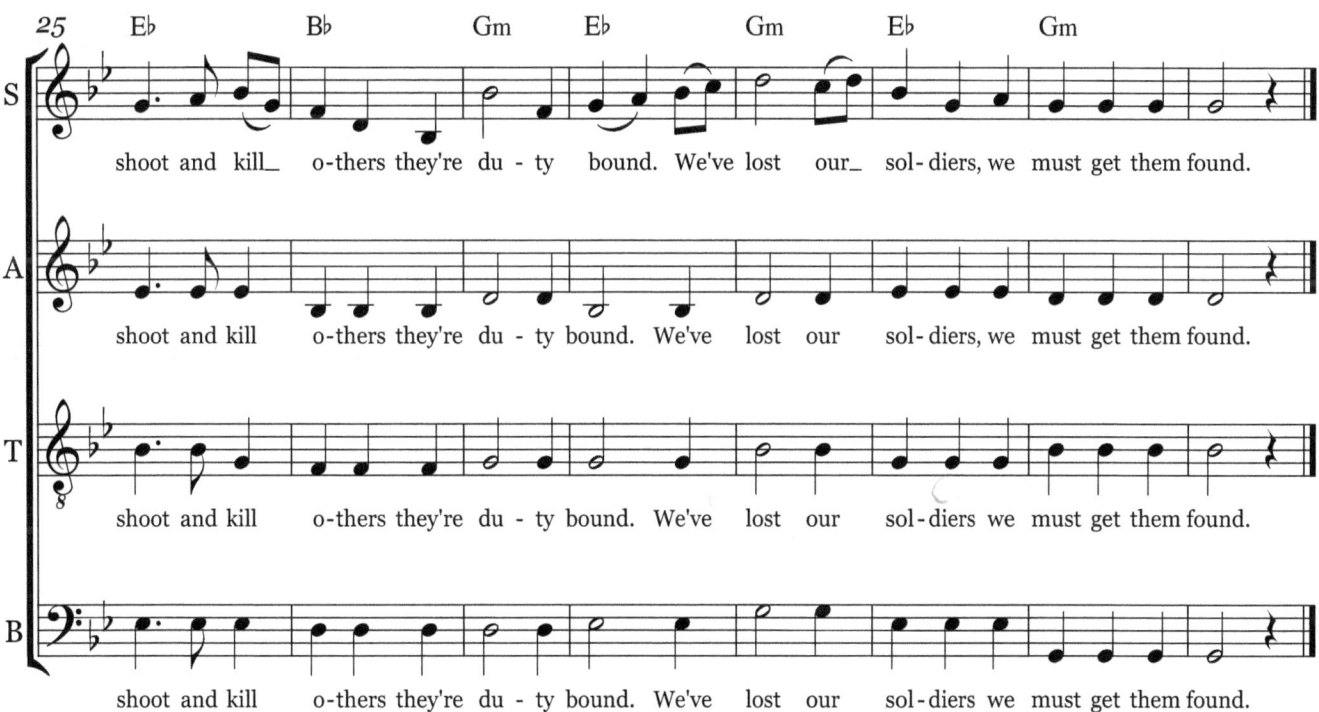

119. To Those Who Came Before

(From the Secular Hymnal)

Words: Secretary Michael

Music: "Down Ampney" by Ralph Vaughan Williams, 1906
(traditional hymn: "Come Down O Love Divine")

All works by Secretary Michael have been placed in the Public Domain. They may be freely copied and performed.

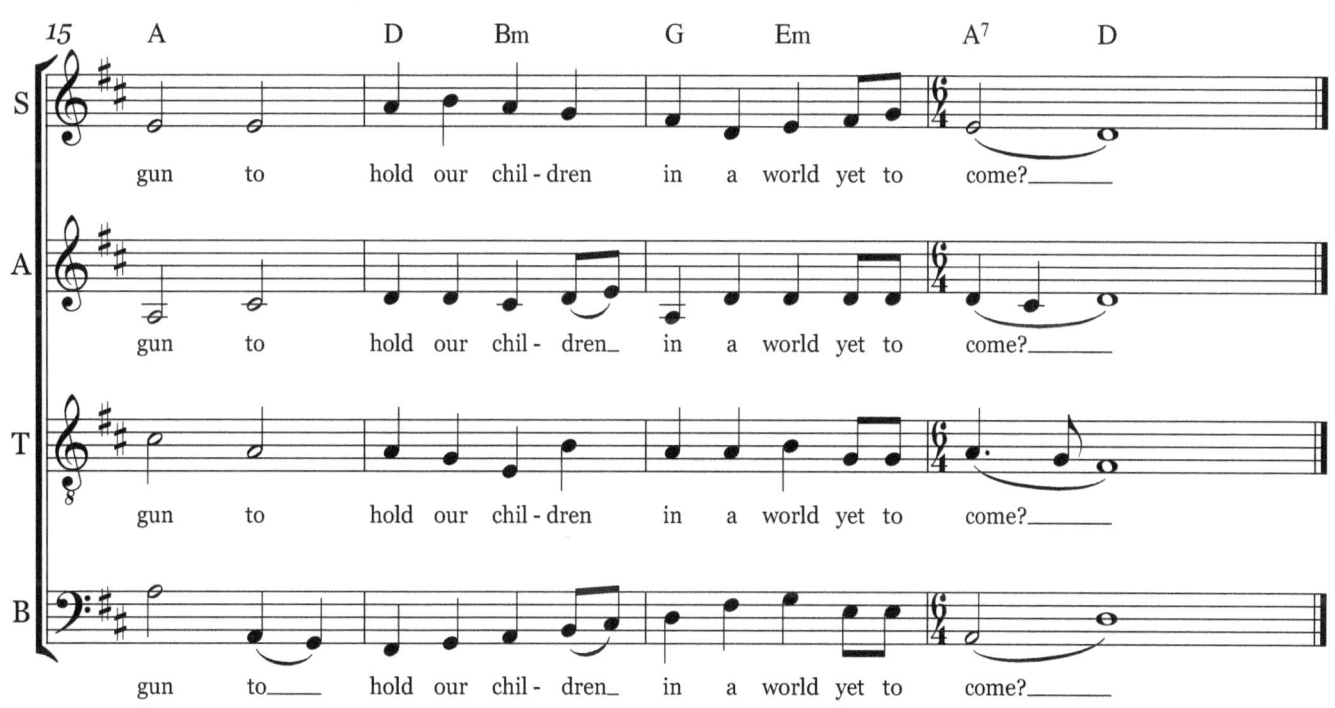

(Note: chord symbols support the soprano melody, not necessarily the SATB harmony)

120. Today is My Day
(From the Secular Hymnal)

Words: Secretary Michael

Music: "Trust and Obey" by Daniel Brink Towner, c.1887
Meter changes made by Secretary Michael
(traditional hymn: "Trust and Obey")

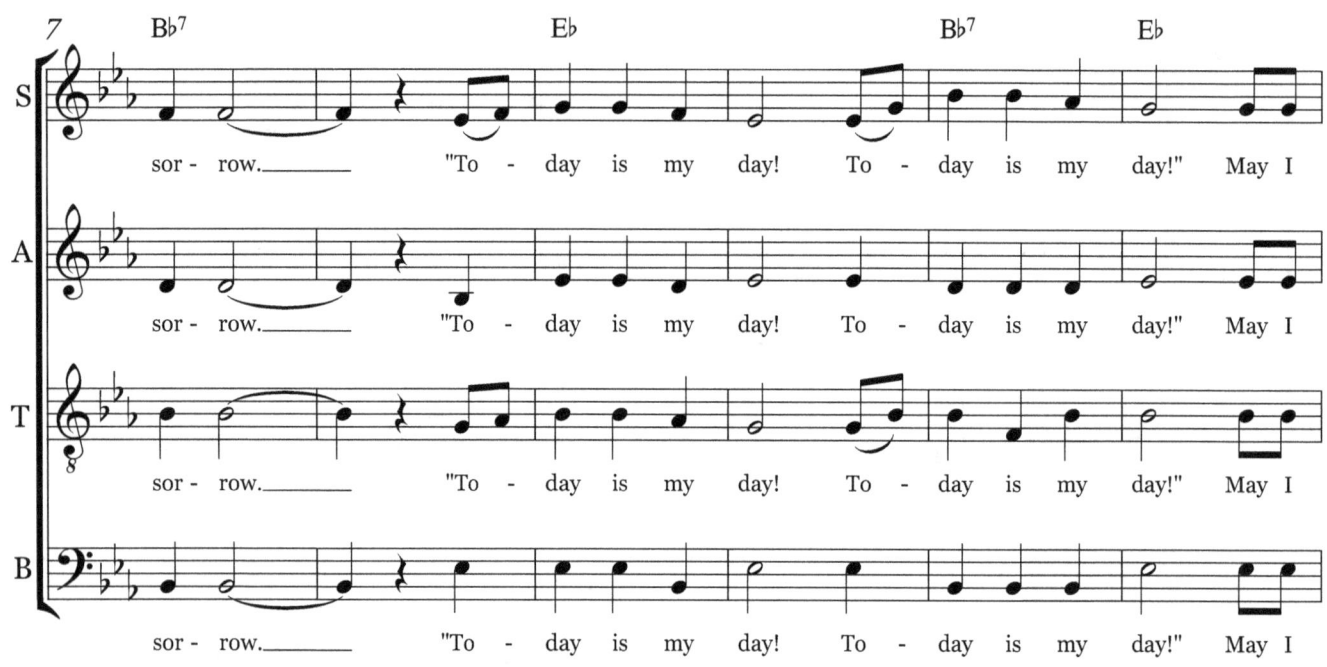

All works by Secretary Michael have been placed in the Public Domain. They may be freely copied and performed.

(Note: chord symbols support the soprano melody, not necessarily the SATB harmony)

121. Today's the Day
(From the Secular Hymnal)

Words: Secretary Michael

Music: "Darwall's 148th" by John Darwall, 1770
(traditional hymn: "Rejoice, the Lord Is King")

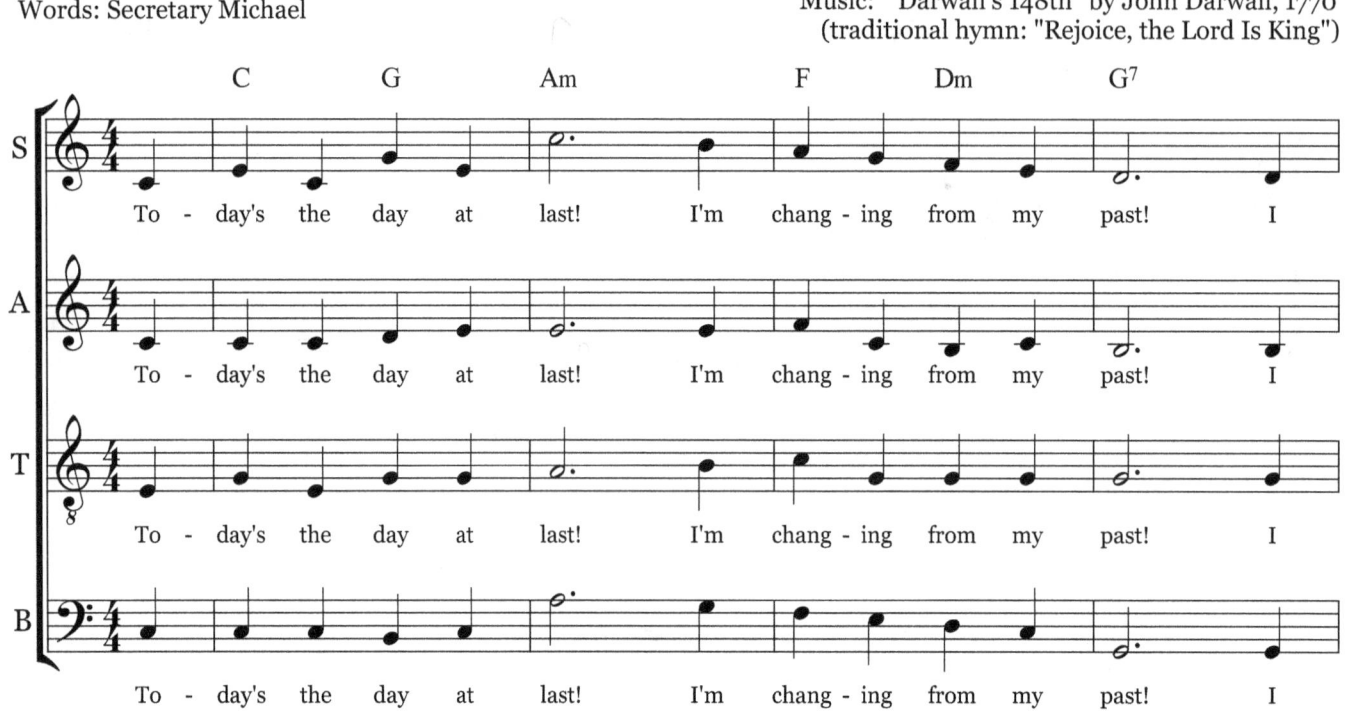

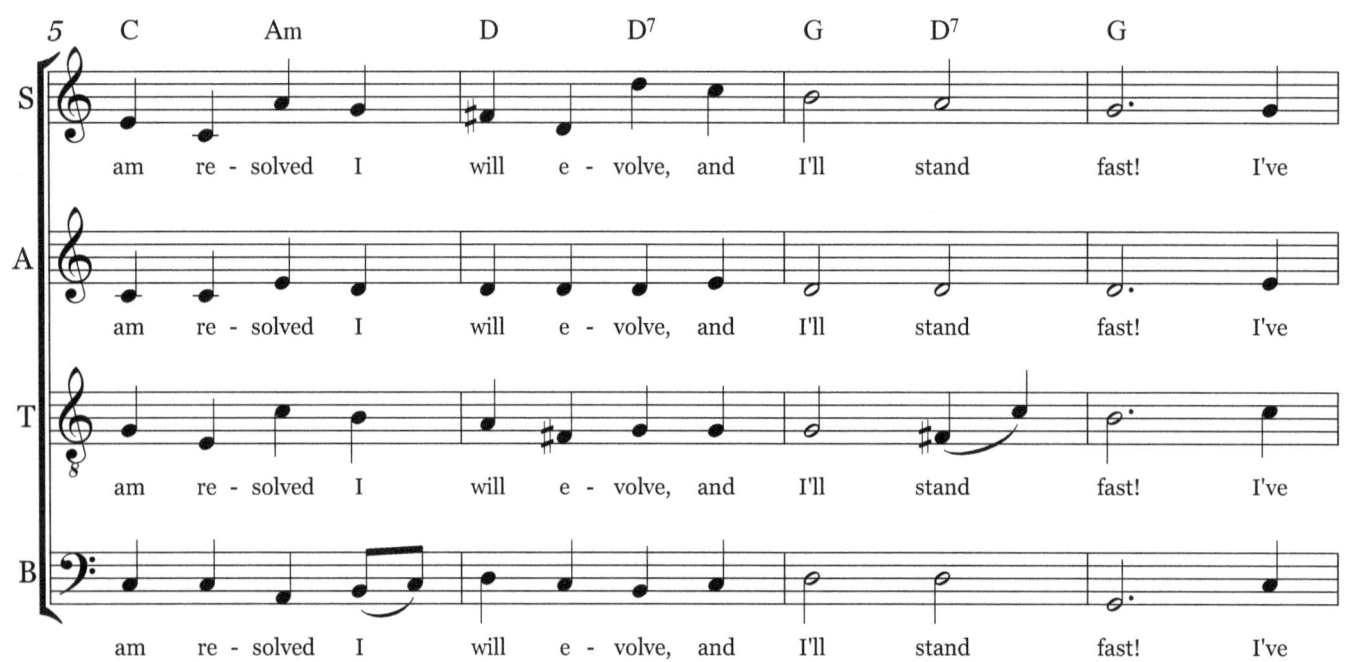

All works by Secretary Michael have been placed in the Public Domain. They may be freely copied and performed.

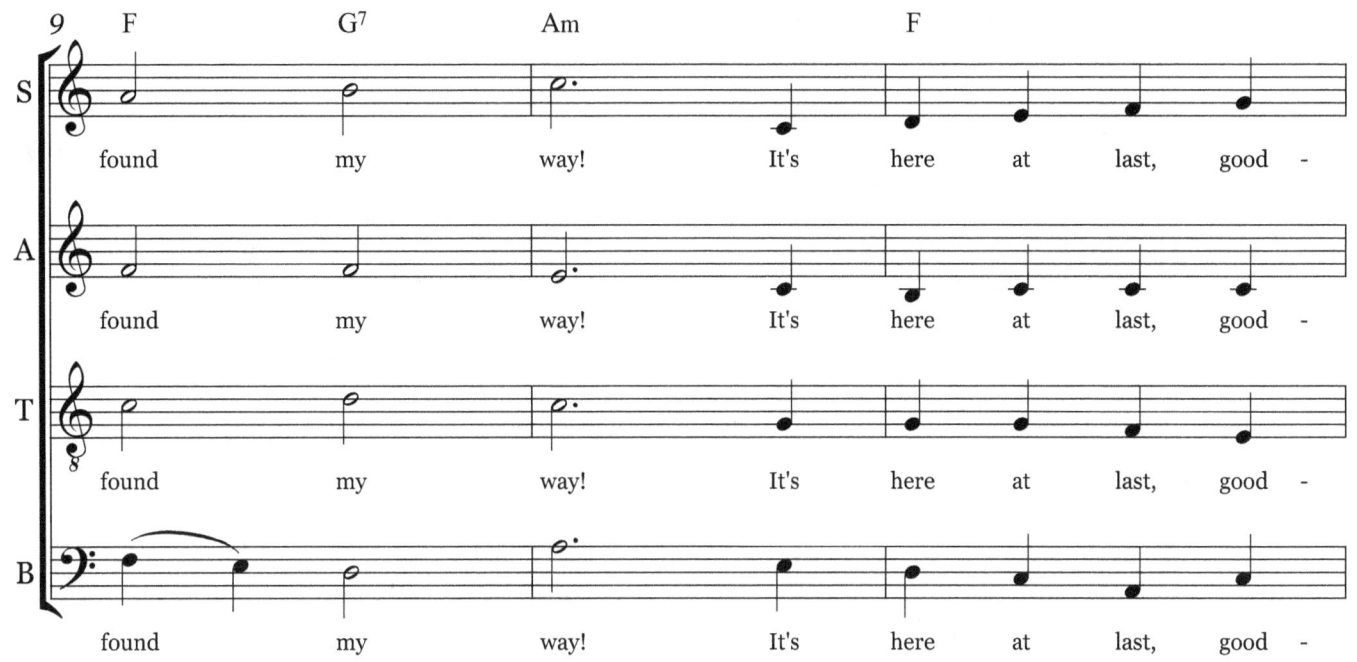
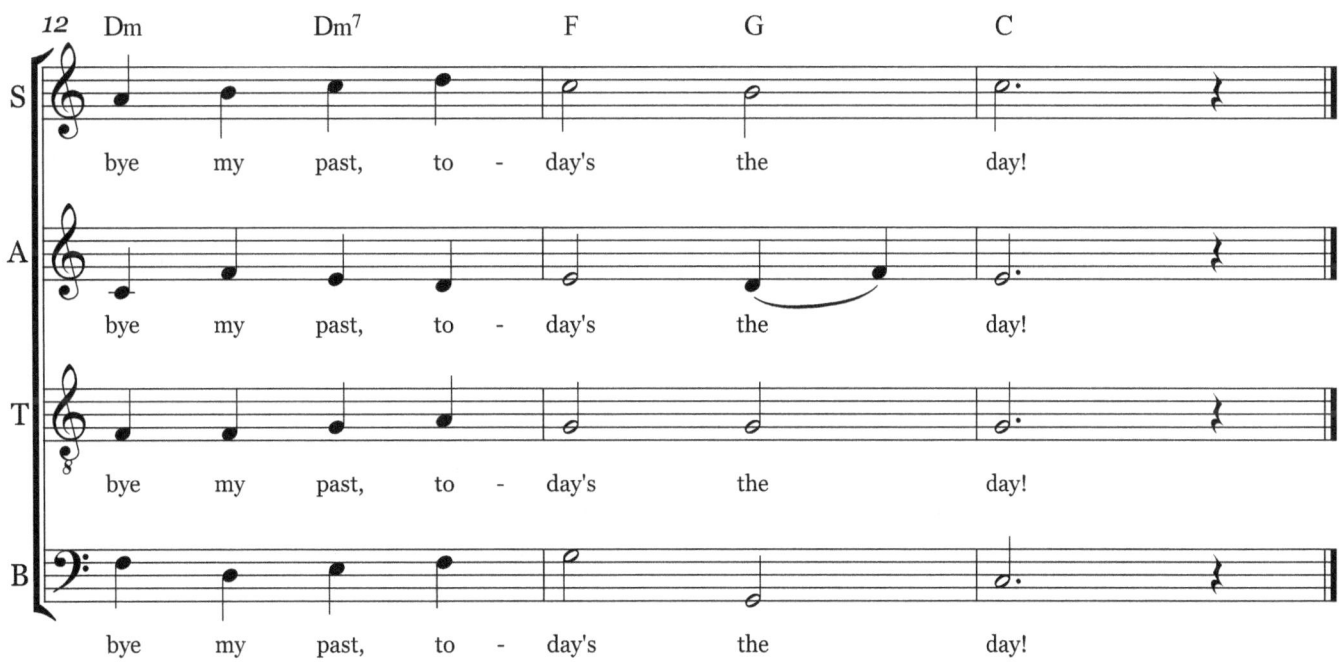

(Note: chord symbols support the soprano melody, not necessarily the SATB harmony)

122. Together For So Long

(From the Secular Hymnal)

Words: Secretary Michael

Music: "Lenox" by Lewis Edson, 1782
(traditional hymn: "Arise, My Soul, Arise!")

1. To-gether for so long, but seldom do we fight. The others want to know what we are doing right. We talk and listen, talk and listen, talk and listen day and night and
2. With family and friends, or strangers met to-day, at home or work or school, things always go o-kay. We talk and listen, talk and listen, talk and listen day and night and

All works by Secretary Michael have been placed in the Public Domain. They may be freely copied and performed.

(Note: chord symbols support the soprano melody, not necessarily the SATB harmony)

123. T'wards a World That Has No Guns
(From the Secular Hymnal)

Words: Secretary Michael

Music: from Ludwig van Beethoven's Ninth Symphony, 1824
Adapted: Edward Hodges, 1864
(traditional hymn: "Joyful, Joyful, We Adore Thee")

All works by Secretary Michael have been placed in the Public Domain. They may be freely copied and performed.

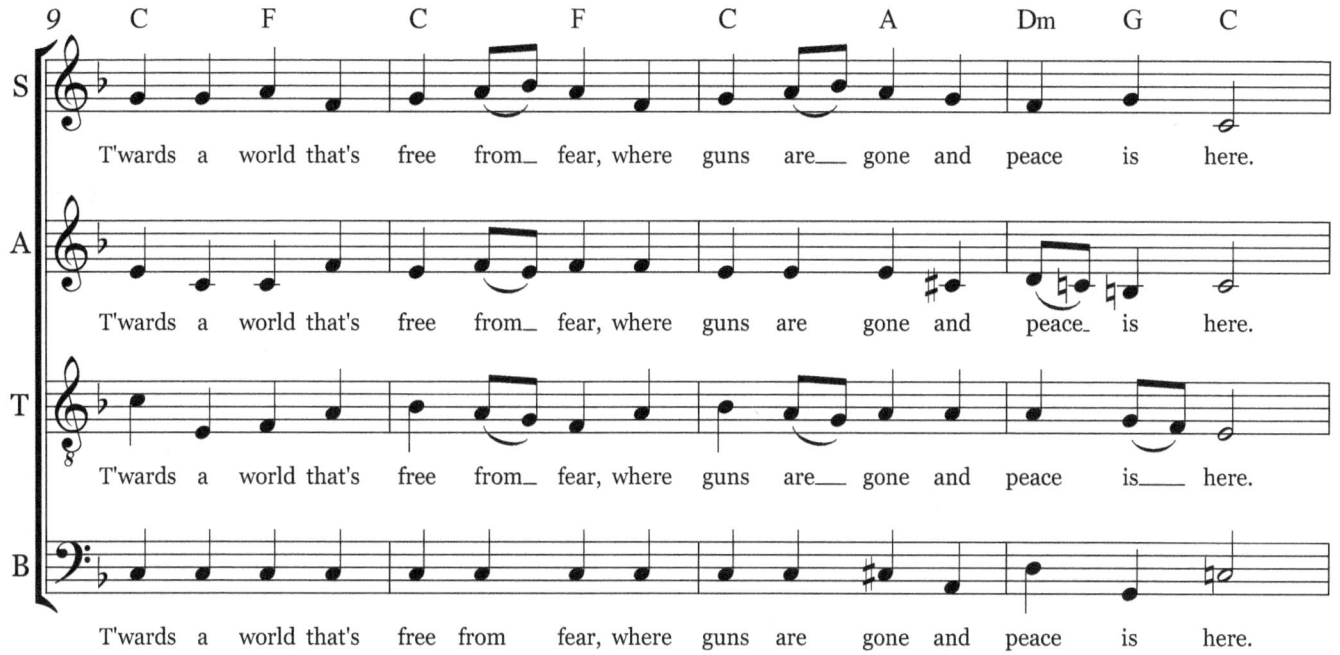

(Note: chord symbols support the soprano melody, not necessarily the SATB harmony)

124. Trusting You, Trusting Me

(From the Secular Hymnal)

Words: Secretary Michael

Music: Largo from the "New World Symphony" by Antonin Dvorak, 1893
SATB Arrangement by Secretary Michael
(popularly known as: "Going Home")

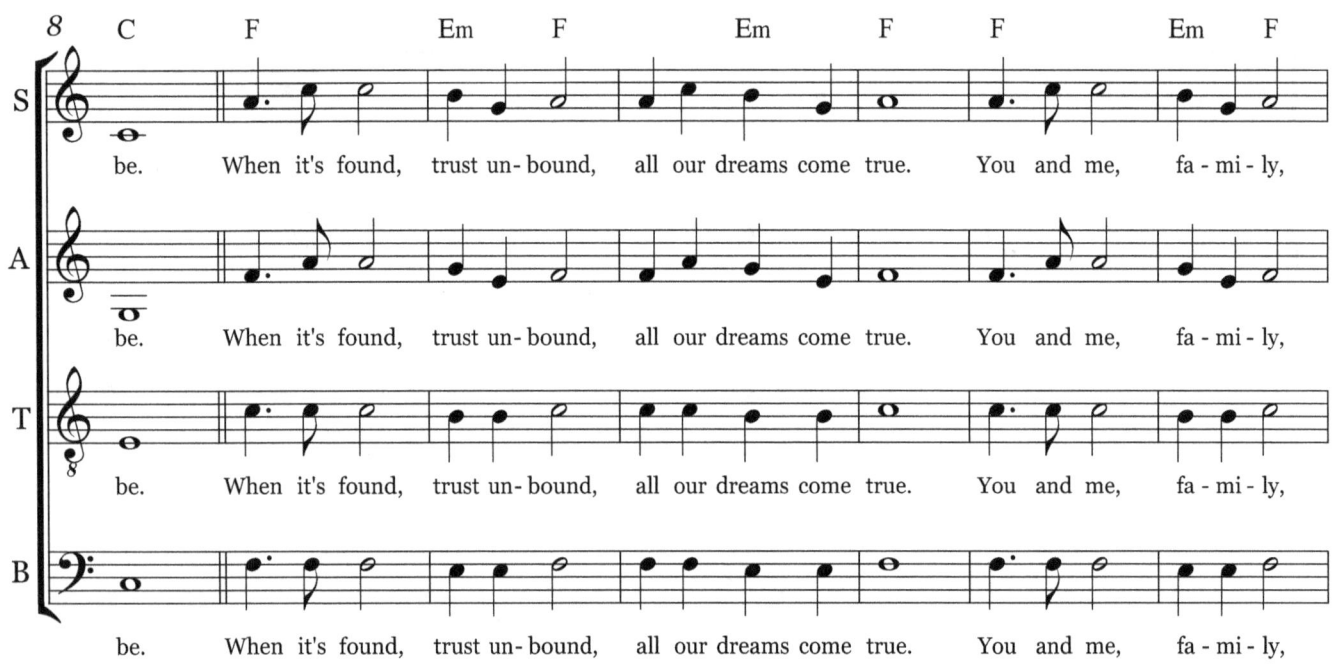

All works by Secretary Michael have been placed in the Public Domain. They may be freely copied and performed.

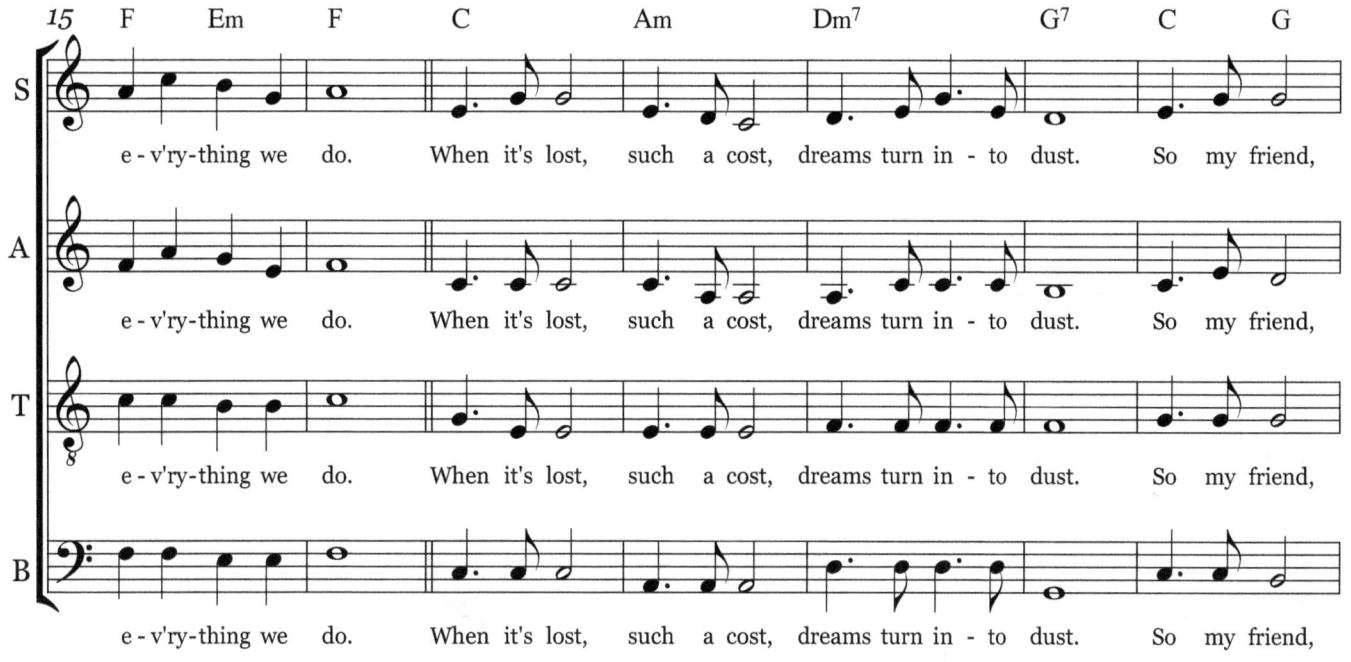
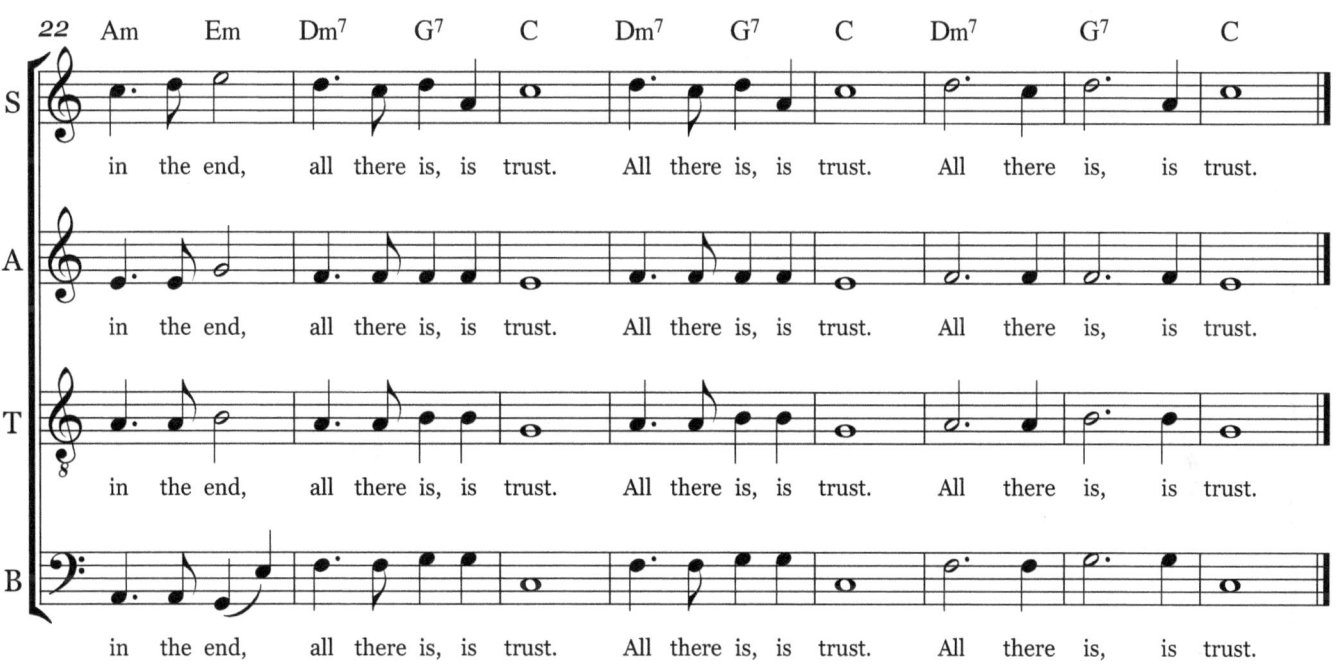

125. Ultimately We May Not Have Free Will

(From the Secular Hymnal)

Words: Secretary Michael

Music: "Noël Nouvelet" (an old French melody)
Harmonized and Arranged for SATB by Secretary Michael

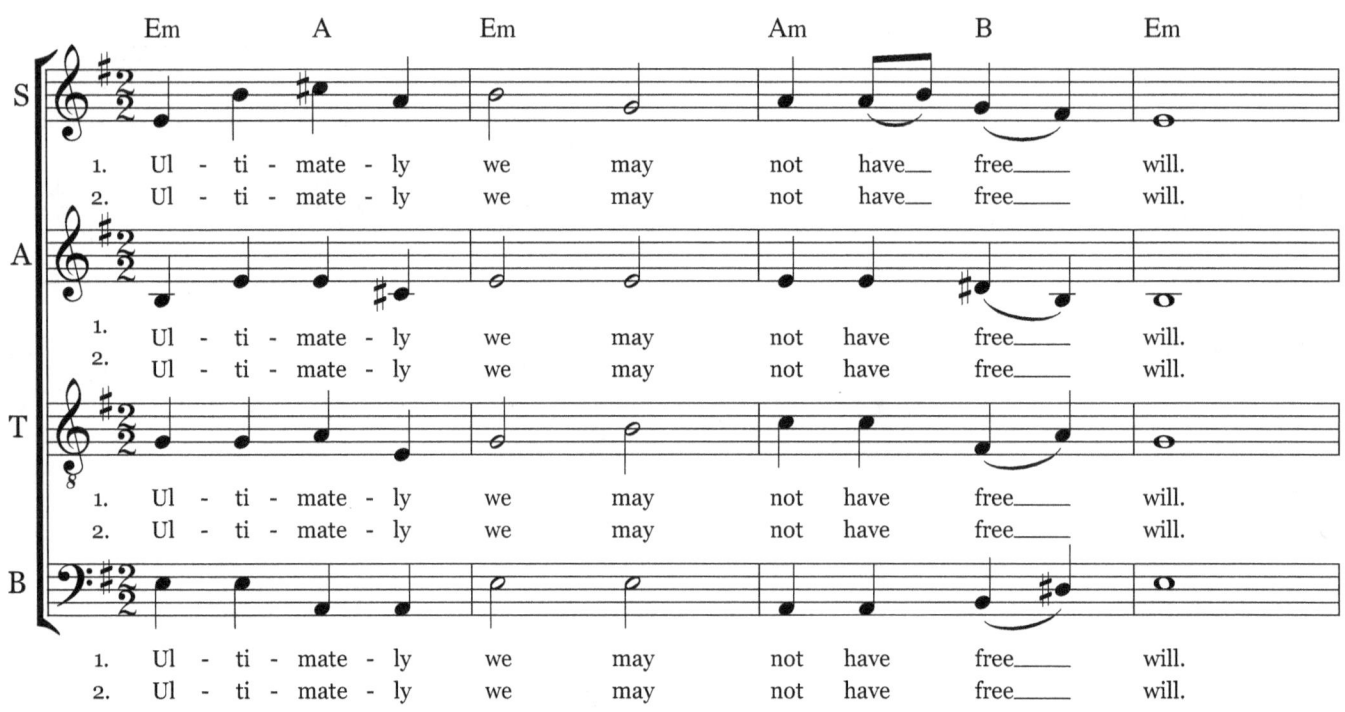

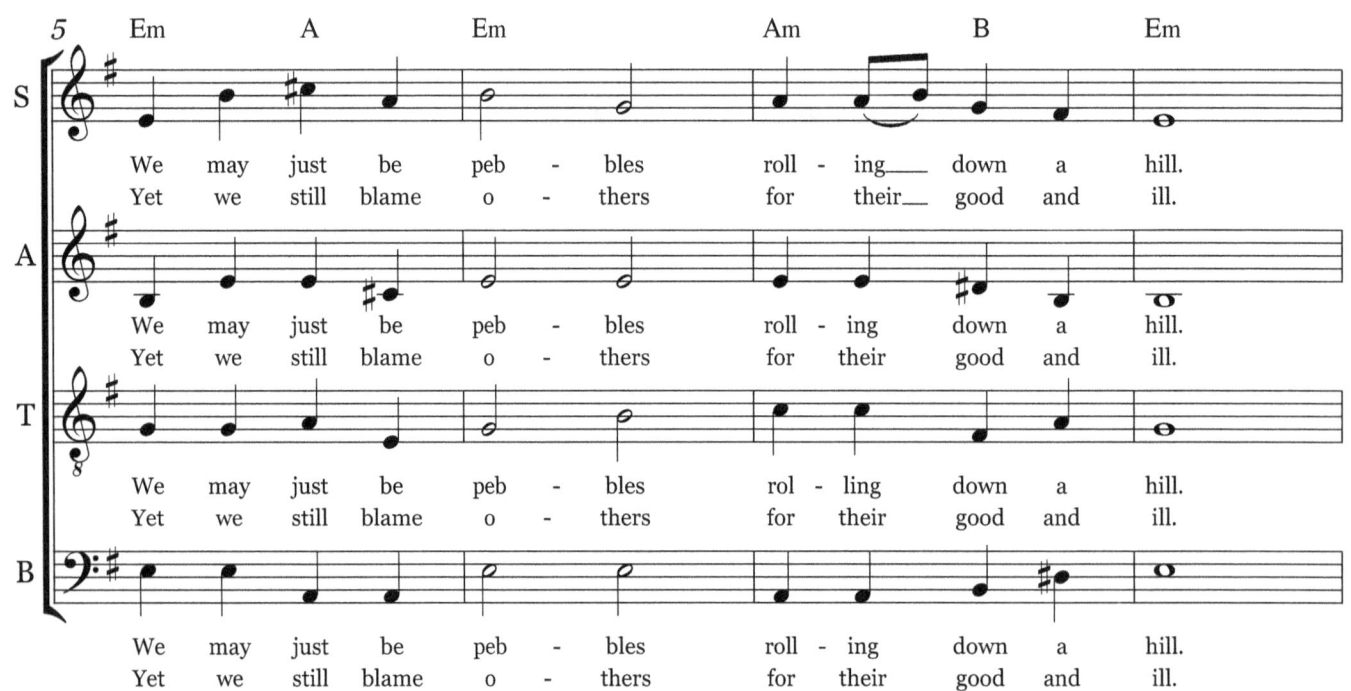

All works by Secretary Michael have been placed in the Public Domain. They may be freely copied and performed.

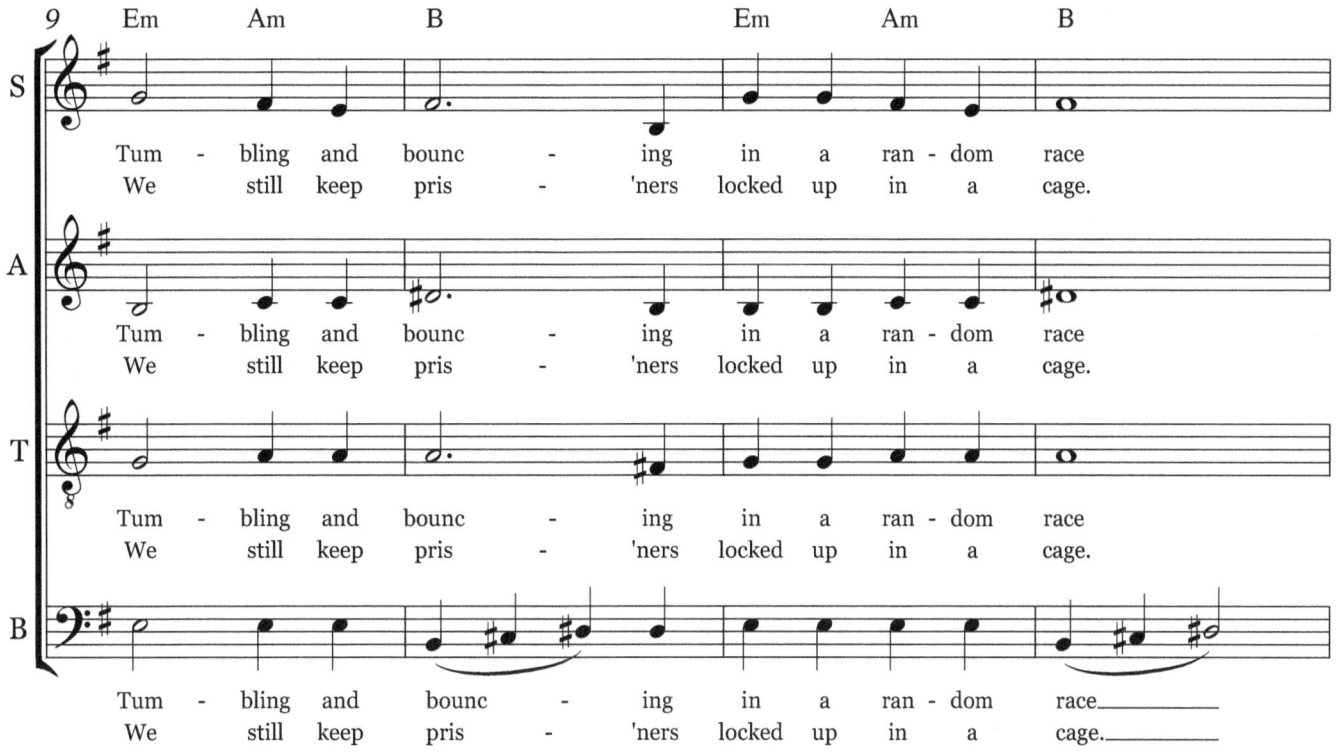
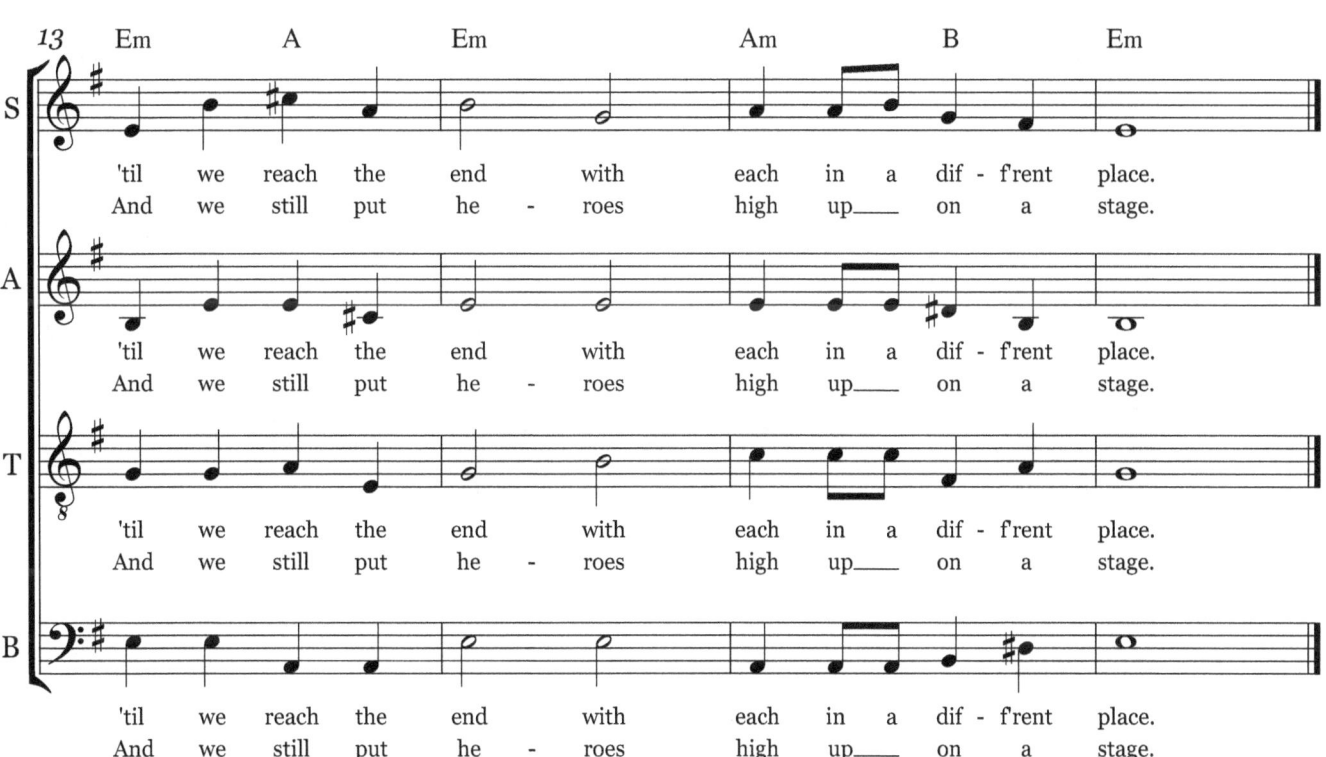

126. Unconscious Bias

(From the Secular Hymnal)

Words: Secretary Michael

Music: "Ebenezer" by Thomas John Williams, 1890
(traditional hymn: "Singing Songs of Expectation")

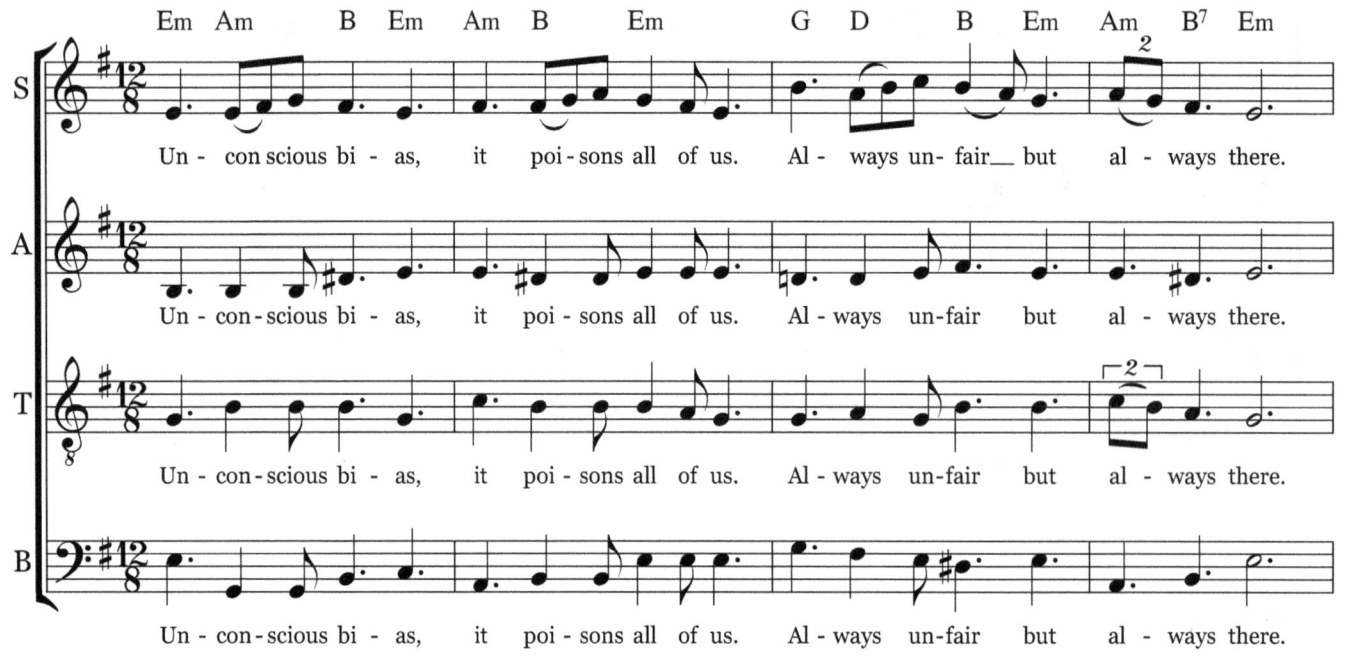

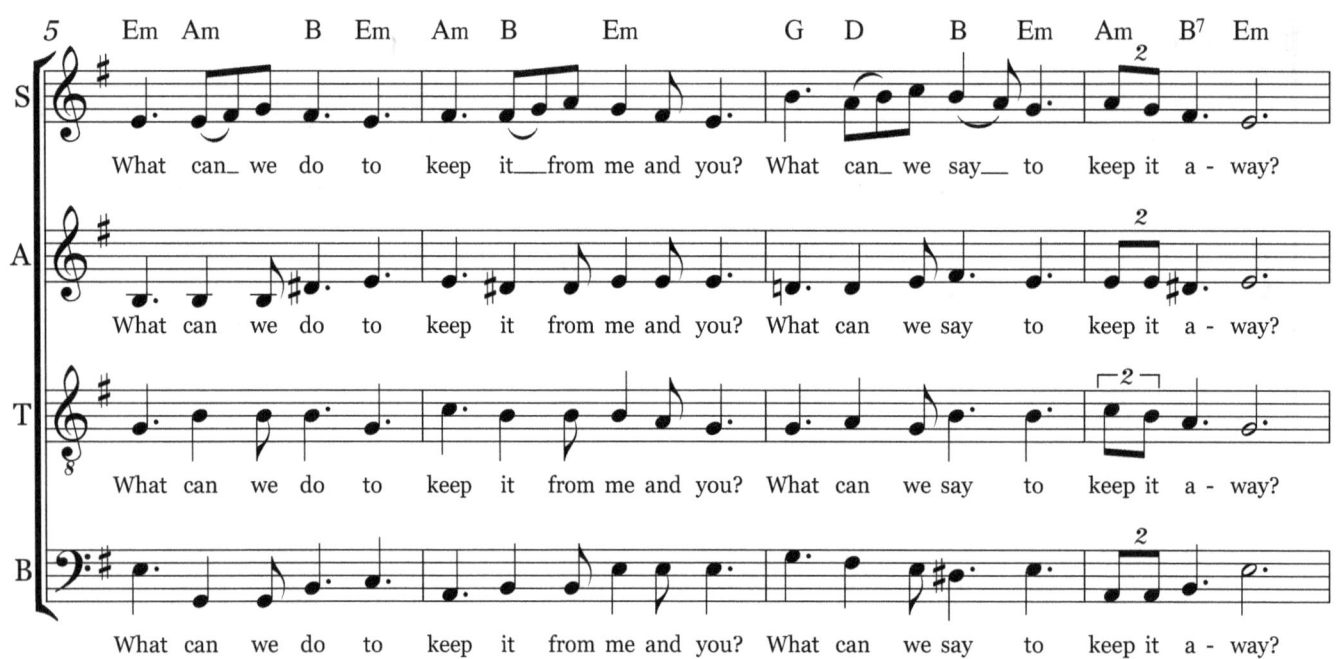

All works by Secretary Michael have been placed in the Public Domain. They may be freely copied and performed.

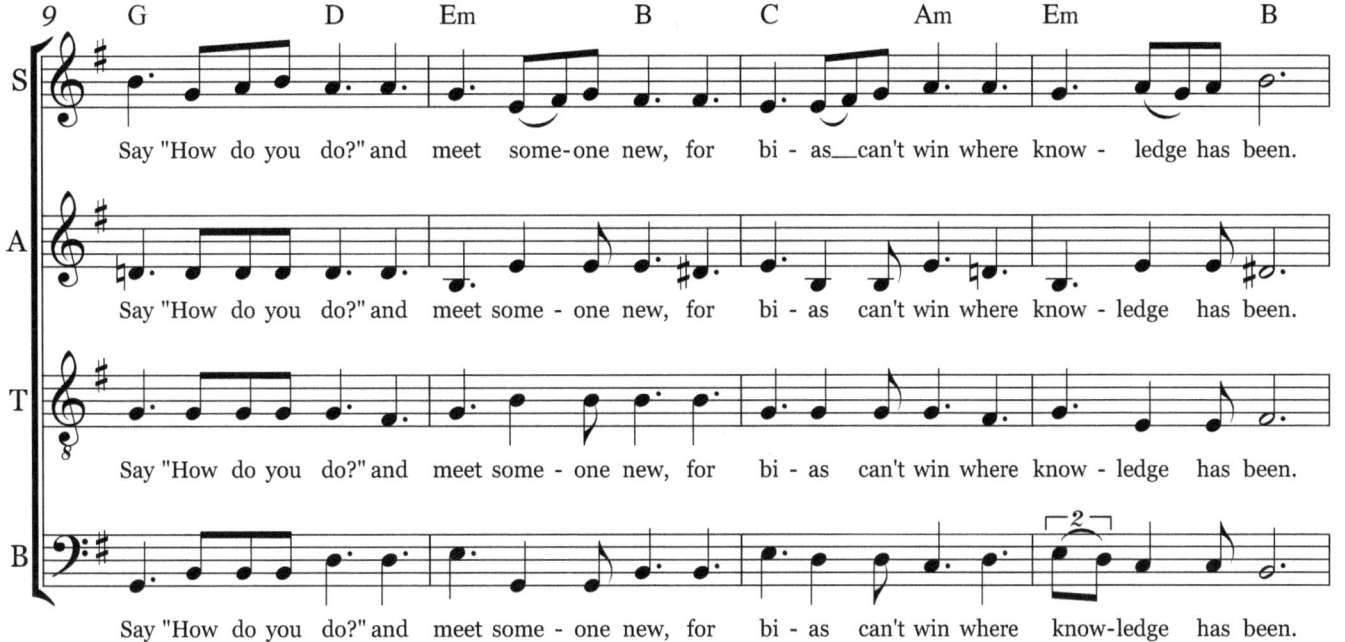
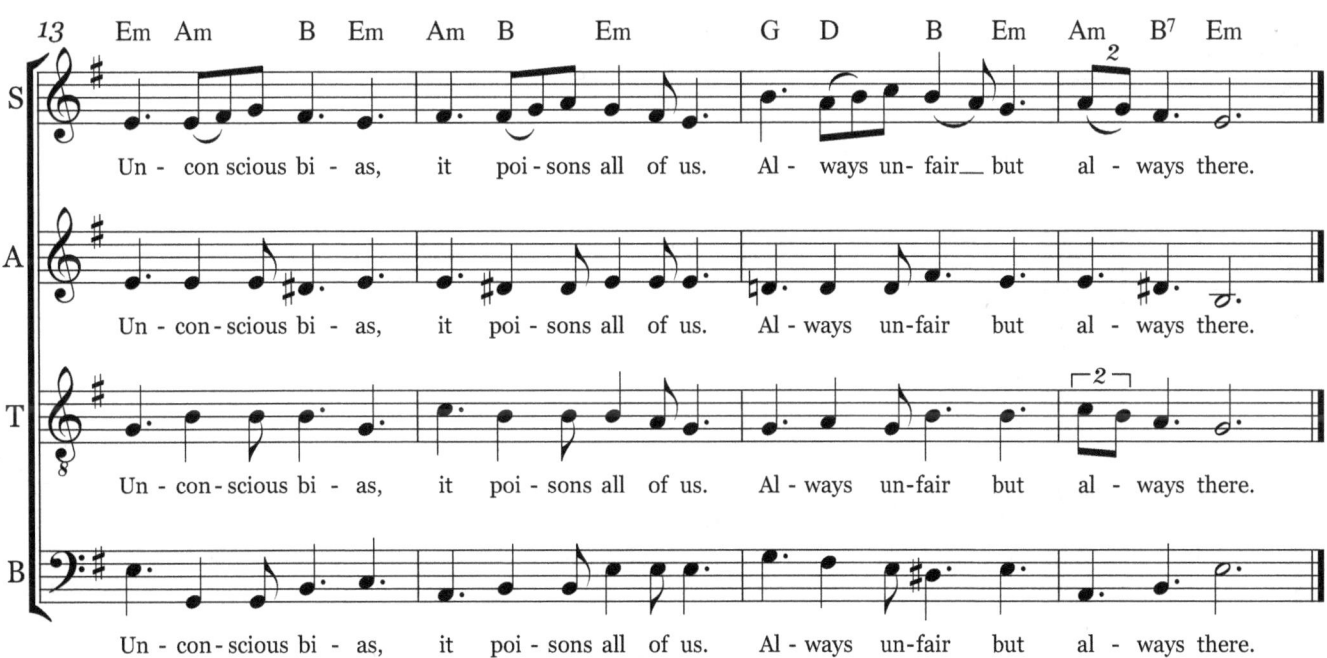

(Note: chord symbols support the soprano melody, not necessarily the SATB harmony)

127. Unless There's No-One Watching

(From the Secular Hymnal)

Words: Secretary Michael

Music: "Endless Song" by Robert Lowry, 1860
(traditional hymn: "How Can I Keep From Singing")

All works by Secretary Michael have been placed in the Public Domain. They may be freely copied and performed.

(Note: chord symbols support the soprano melody, not necessarily the SATB harmony)

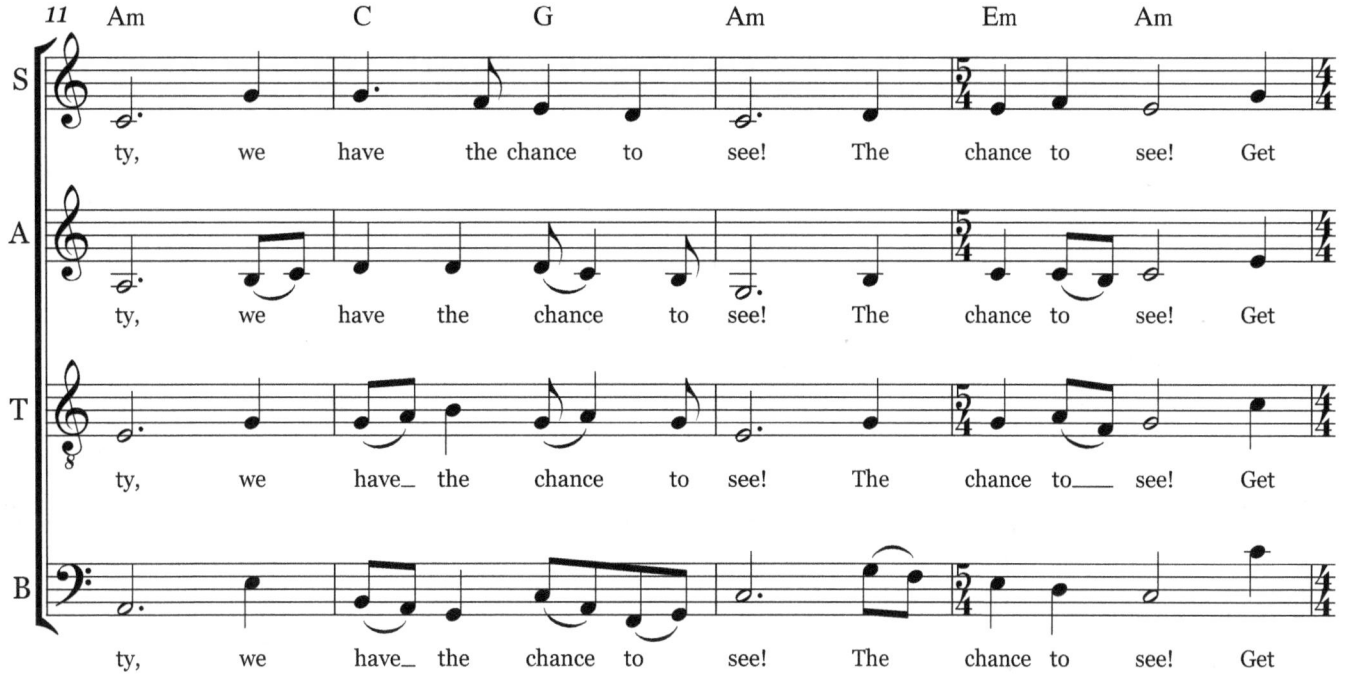

(Note: the time signature changes in measures 9 and 14 were added to avoid the fermatas of the traditional version)

(Note: chord symbols support the soprano melody, not necessarily the SATB harmony)

129. Walking in Someone's Shoes

(From the Secular Hymnal)

Words: Secretary Michael

Music: Silesian Melody
Arrangement: Joseph Roff, 1842
(traditional hymn: "O God Of Loveliness")

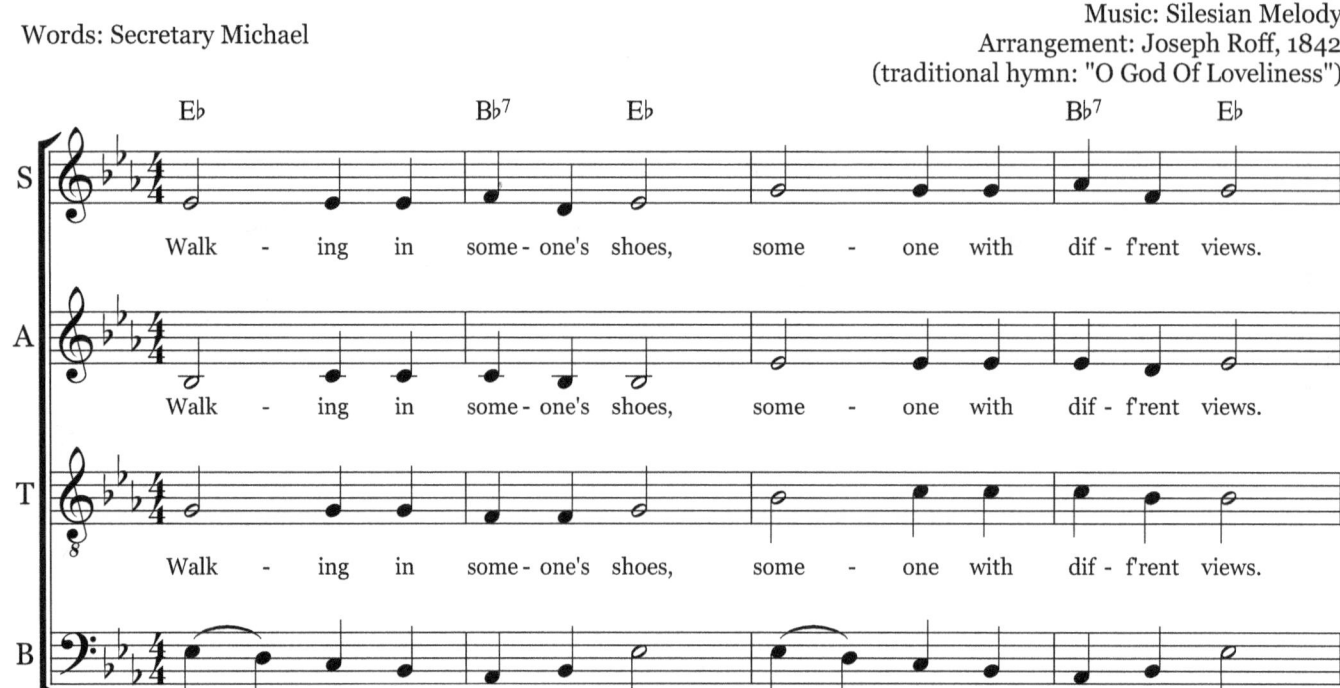

Walk-ing in some-one's shoes, some-one with dif-f'rent views.

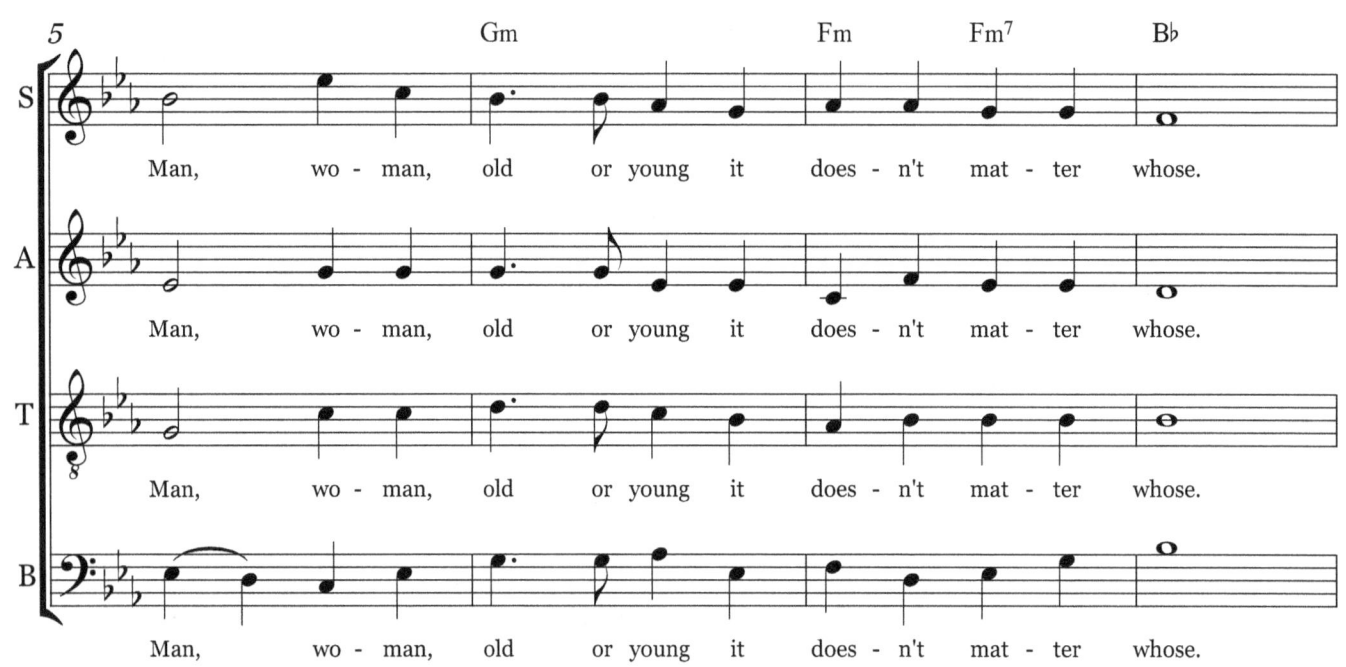

Man, wo-man, old or young it does-n't mat-ter whose.

All works by Secretary Michael have been placed in the Public Domain. They may be freely copied and performed.

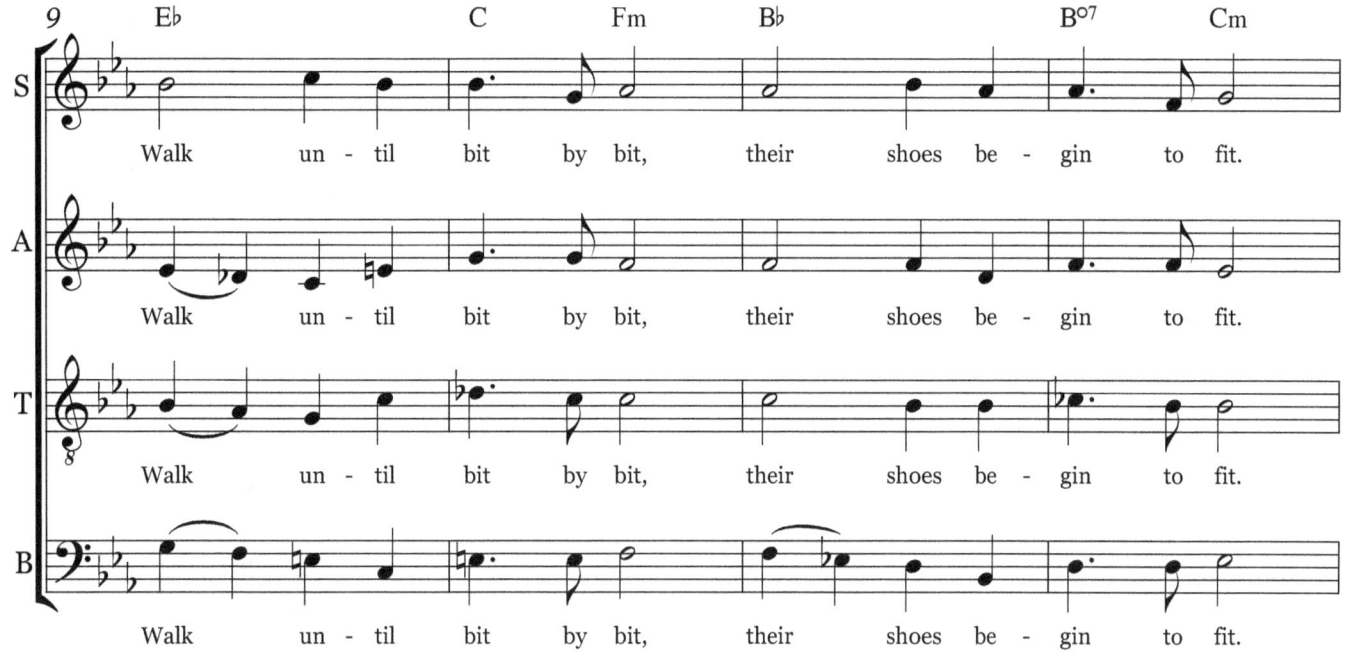

(Note: chord symbols support the soprano melody, not necessarily the SATB harmony)

130. We Are People, Plastic People
(From the Secular Hymnal)

All works by Secretary Michael have been placed in the Public Domain. They may be freely copied and performed.

(Note: chord symbols support the soprano melody, not necessarily the SATB harmony)

131. We Are Searching

(From the Secular Hymnal)

Words: Secretary Michael

Music: "Wondrous Story" by Peter Philip Bilhorn, 1886
(traditional hymn: "I Will Sing the Wondrous Story")

All works by Secretary Michael have been placed in the Public Domain. They may be freely copied and performed.

(Note: chord symbols support the soprano melody, not necessarily the SATB harmony)

132. We Can Be Tolerant
(From the Secular Hymnal)

Words: Secretary Michael

Melody: "Slane" (traditional Irish)
SATB arrangement by Secretary Michael
(traditional hymn: "Be Thou My Vision")

All works by Secretary Michael have been placed in the Public Domain. They may be freely copied and performed.

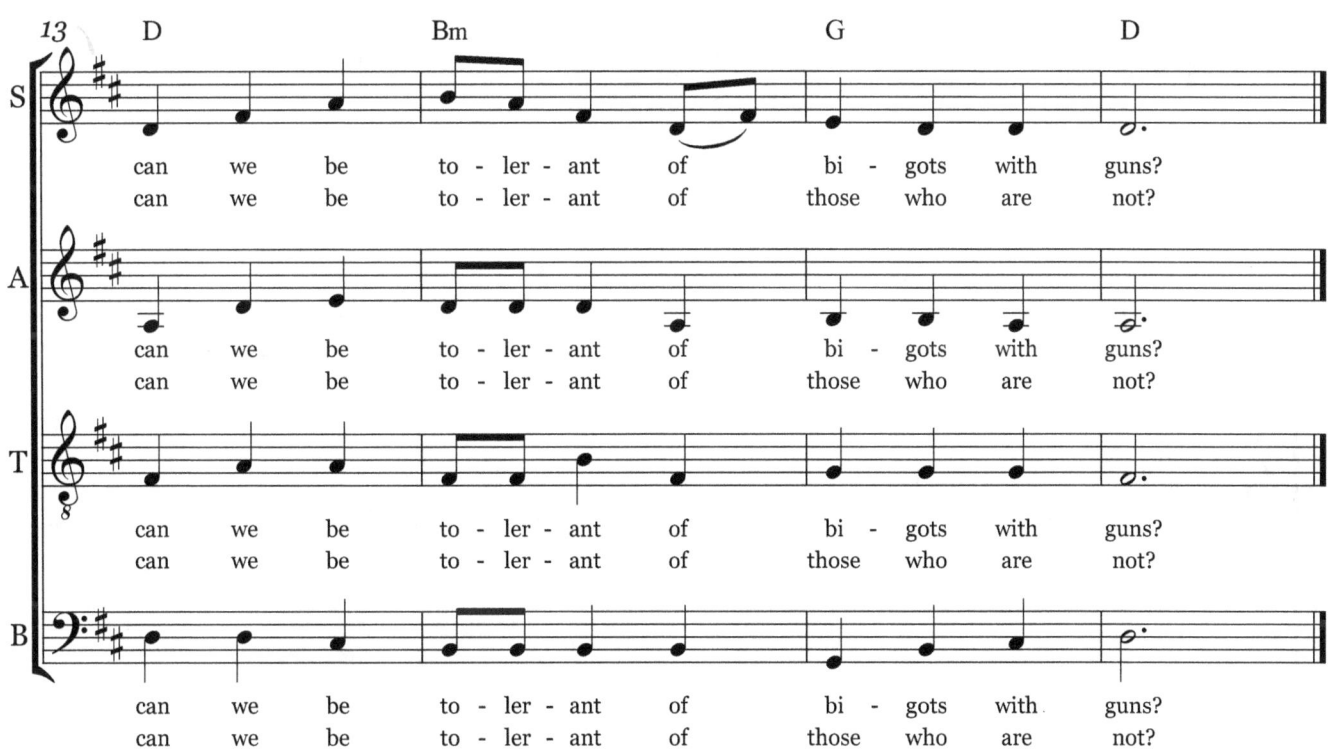

(Note: chord symbols support the soprano melody, not necessarily the SATB harmony)

133. We Can Get Things To Happen

(From the Secular Hymnal)

Words: Secretary Michael

Music: traditional African-American spiritual
SATB Arrangement: Secretary Michael
(traditional hymn: "Let Us Break Bread Together")

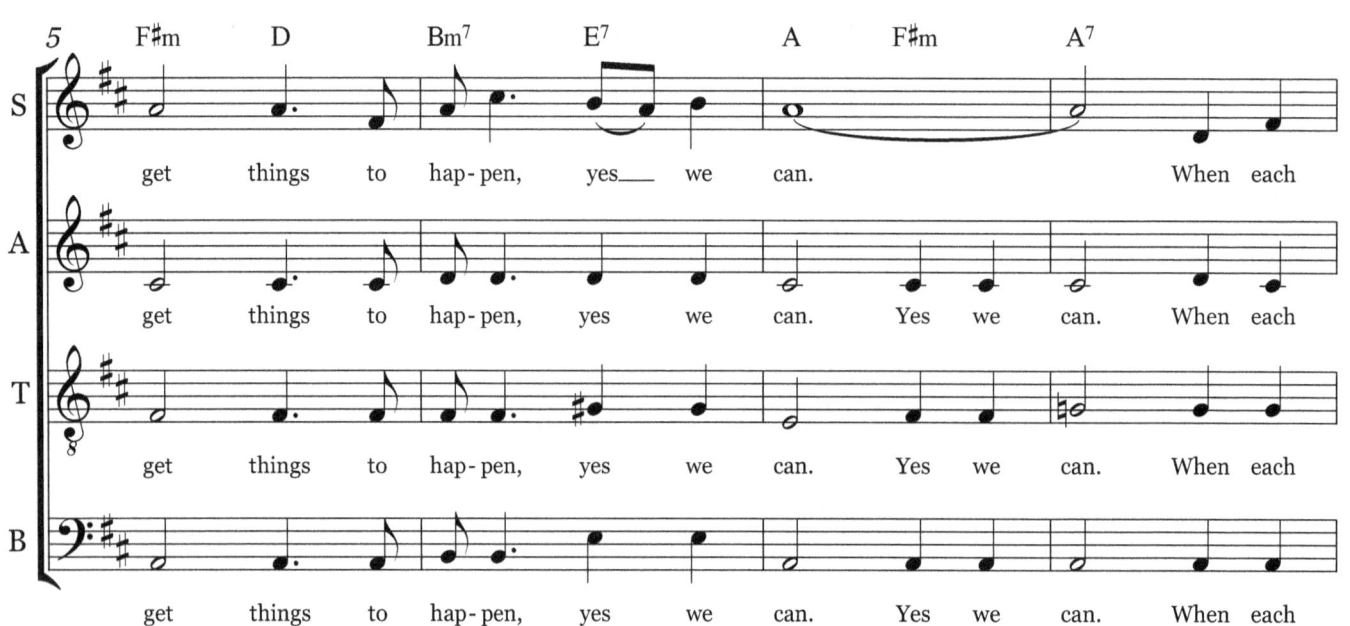

All works by Secretary Michael have been placed in the Public Domain. They may be freely copied and performed.

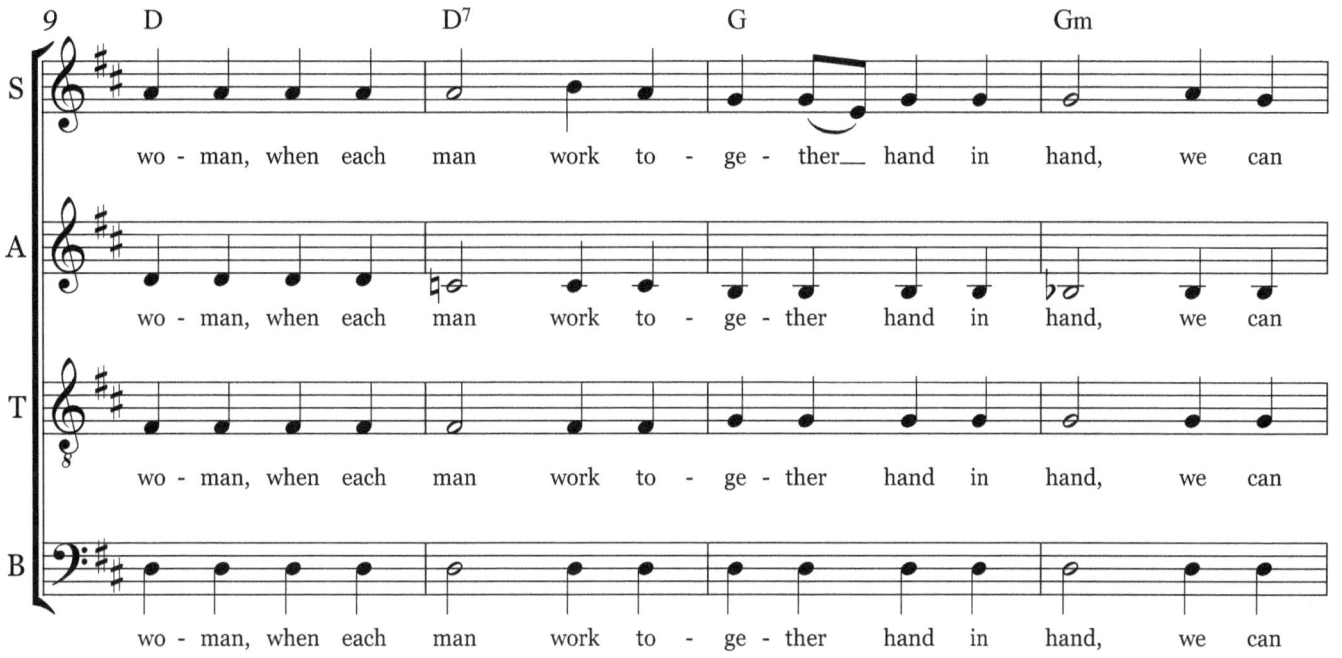
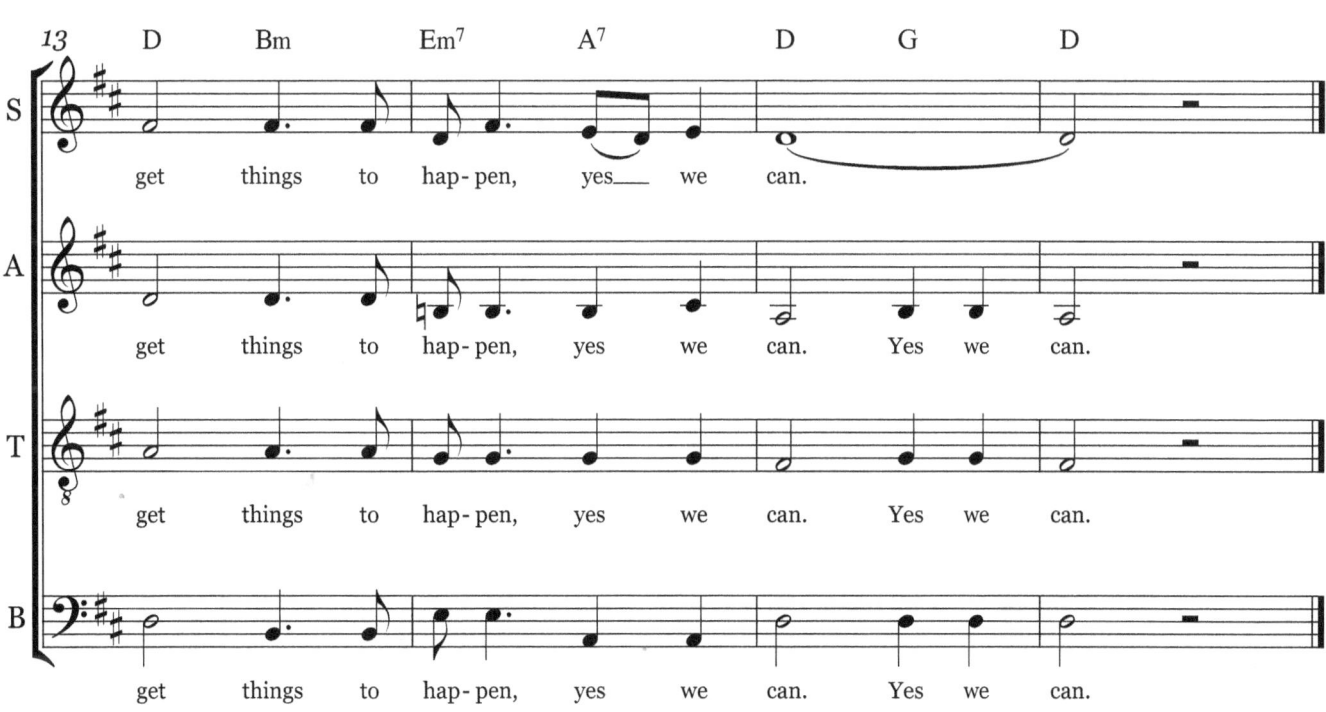

134. We Mean "Will You Love Me?"

(From the Secular Hymnal)

Words: Secretary Michael

Music: "Gordon" by Adoniram Judson Gordon, 1876
(traditional hymn: "My Jesus I Love Thee I Know Thou Art Mine")

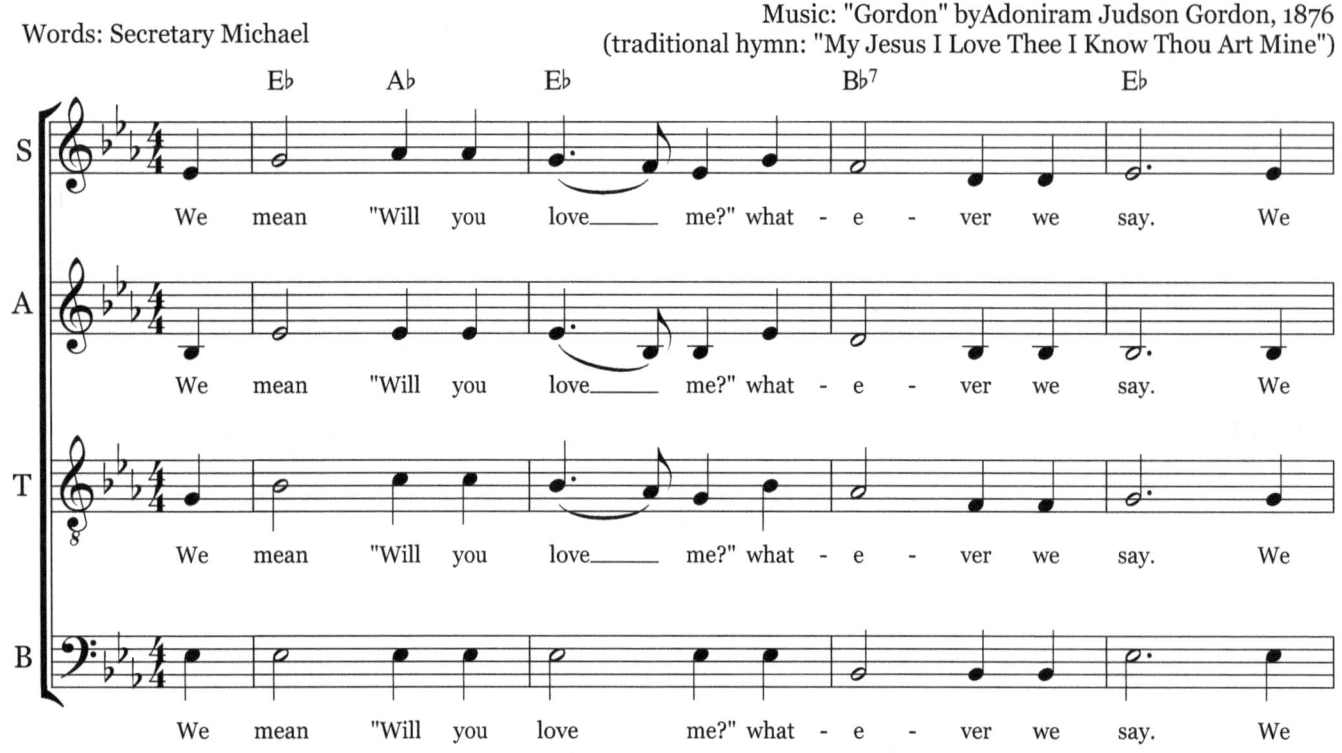

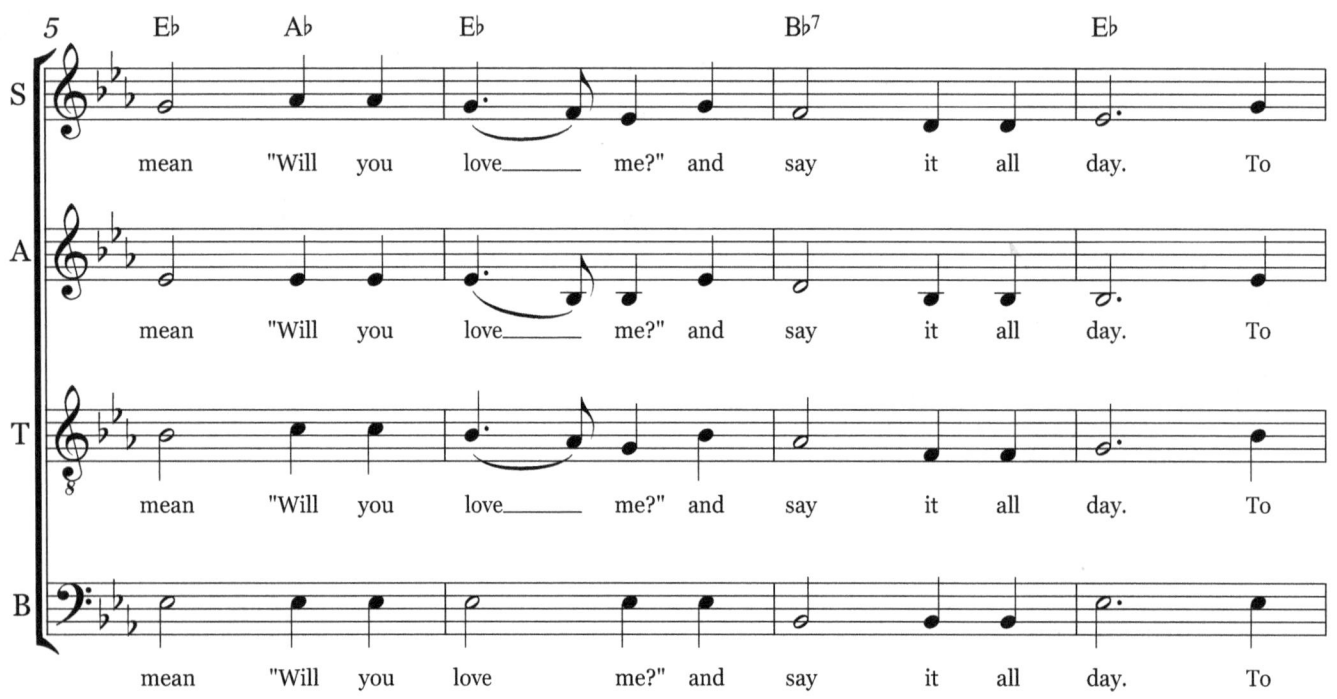

All works by Secretary Michael have been placed in the Public Domain. They may be freely copied and performed.

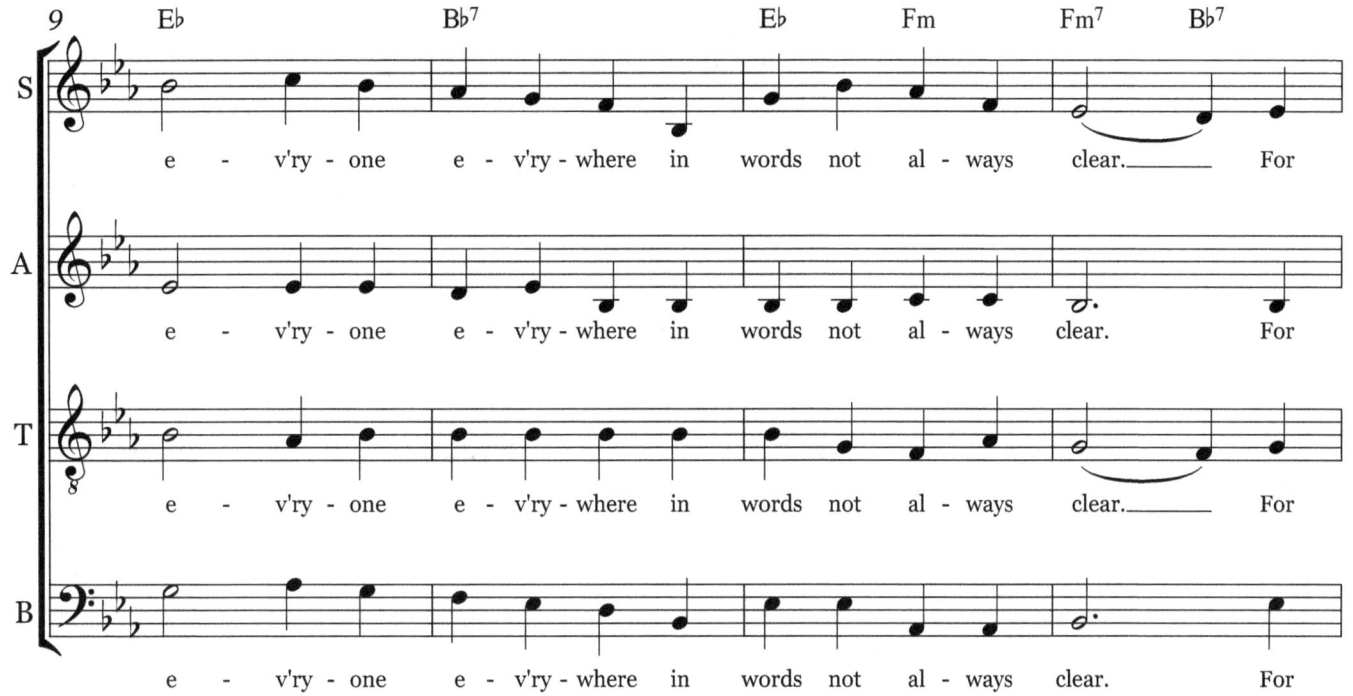

(Note: chord symbols support the soprano melody, not necessarily the SATB harmony)

135. We're Not Alone
(From the Secular Hymnal)

Words: Secretary Michael

Music: "Londonderry Air" (traditional Irish melody)
(traditional hymn: "I Cannot Tell")

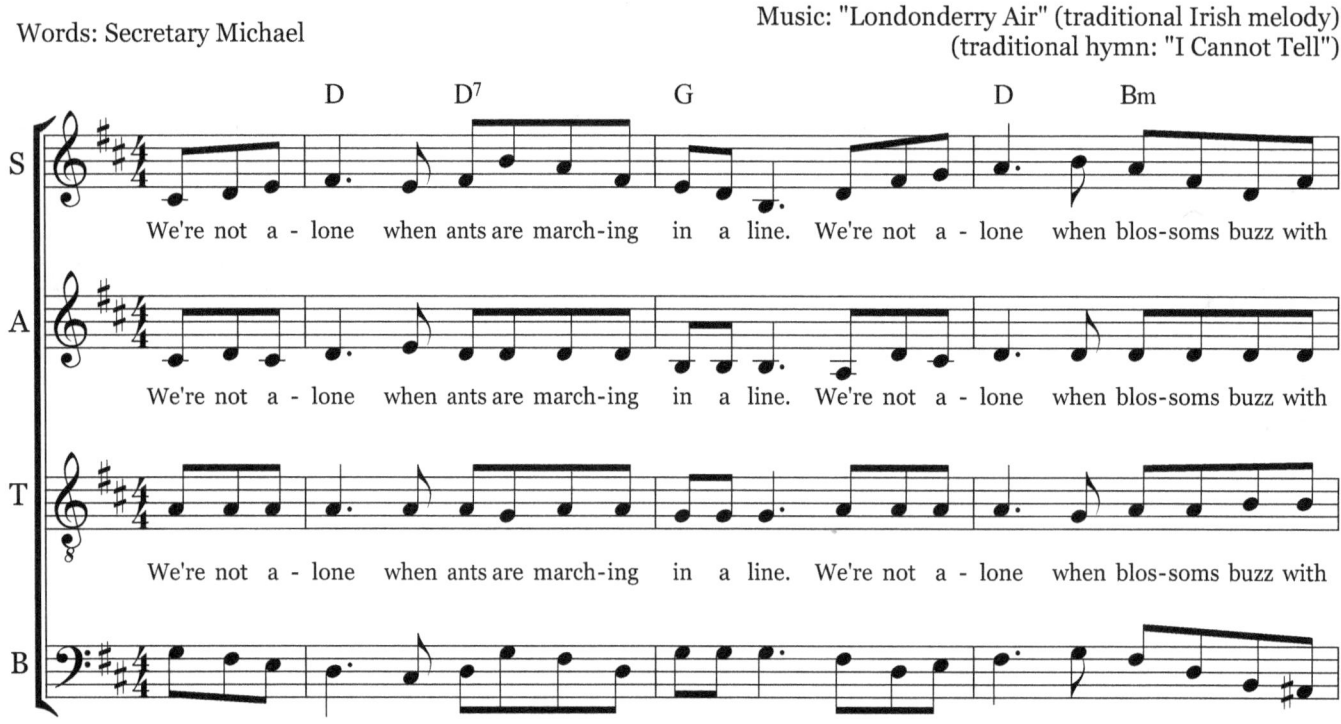

All works by Secretary Michael have been placed in the Public Domain. They may be freely copied and performed.

(Note: chord symbols support the soprano melody, not necessarily the SATB harmony)

136. We're Not At Our Best

(From the Secular Hymnal)

Words: Secretary Michael

Music: "St. Denio" (Welsh melody)
Adapted and Harmonized by John Roberts, 1839
(traditional hymn: "Immortal, Invisible, God Only Wise")

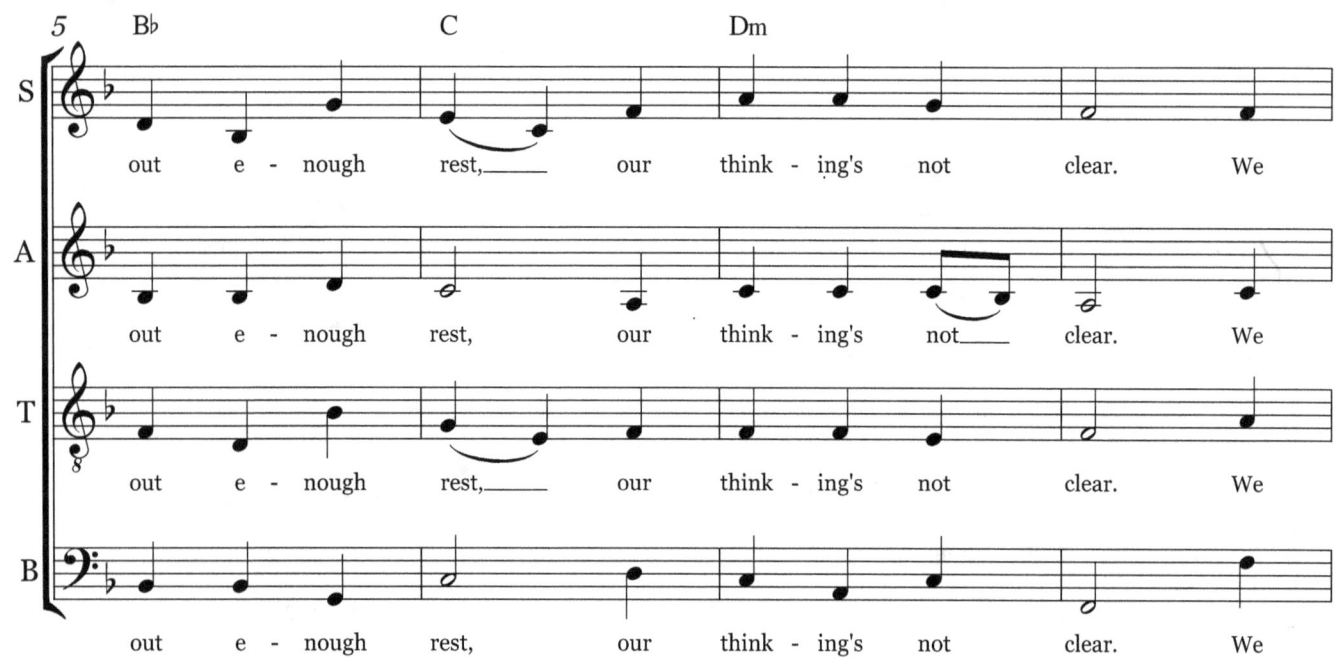

All works by Secretary Michael have been placed in the Public Domain. They may be freely copied and performed.

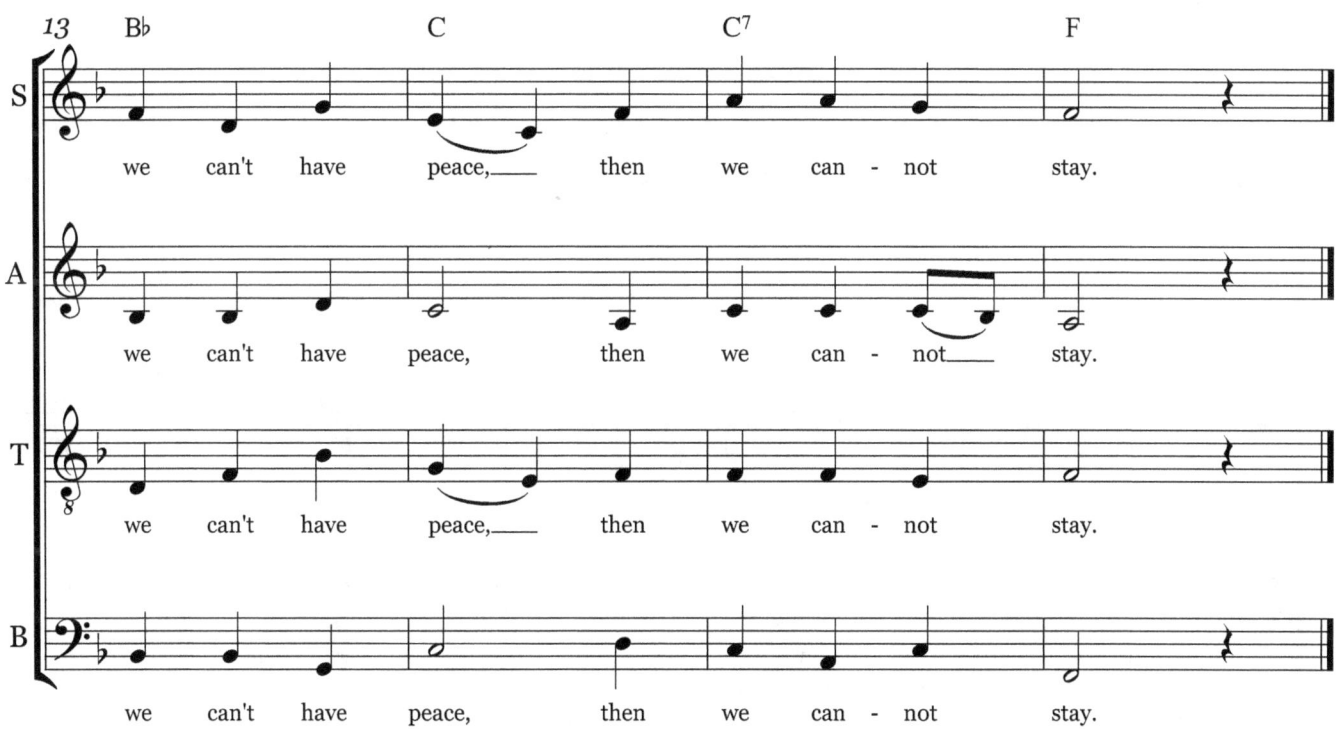

(Note: chord symbols support the soprano melody, not necessarily the SATB harmony)

137. We're Parents of a Soldier

(From the Secular Hymnal)

All works by Secretary Michael have been placed in the Public Domain. They may be freely copied and performed.

(Note: chord symbols support the soprano melody, not necessarily the SATB harmony)

138. What Are We Doing?

(From the Secular Hymnal)

Words: Secretary Michael

Music: "Macchabaeus" by George Frederick Handel, 1747
(traditional hymn: "Thine Be the Glory")

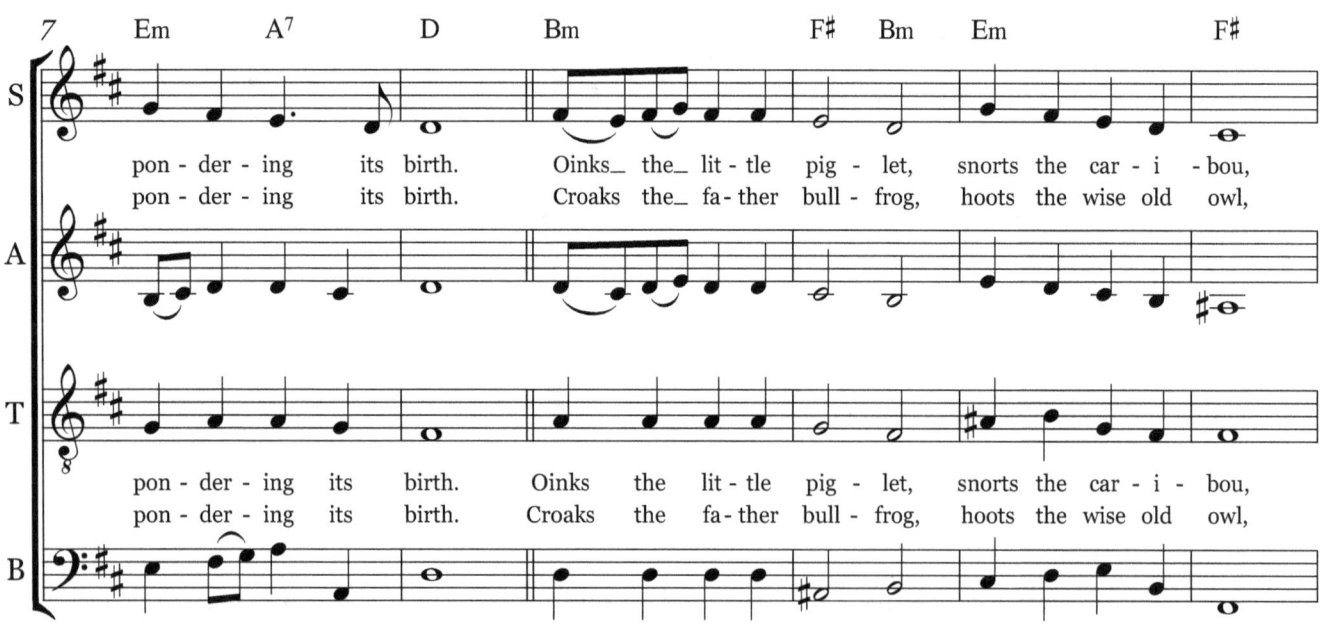

All works by Secretary Michael have been placed in the Public Domain. They may be freely copied and performed.

(Note: chord symbols support the soprano melody, not necessarily the SATB harmony)

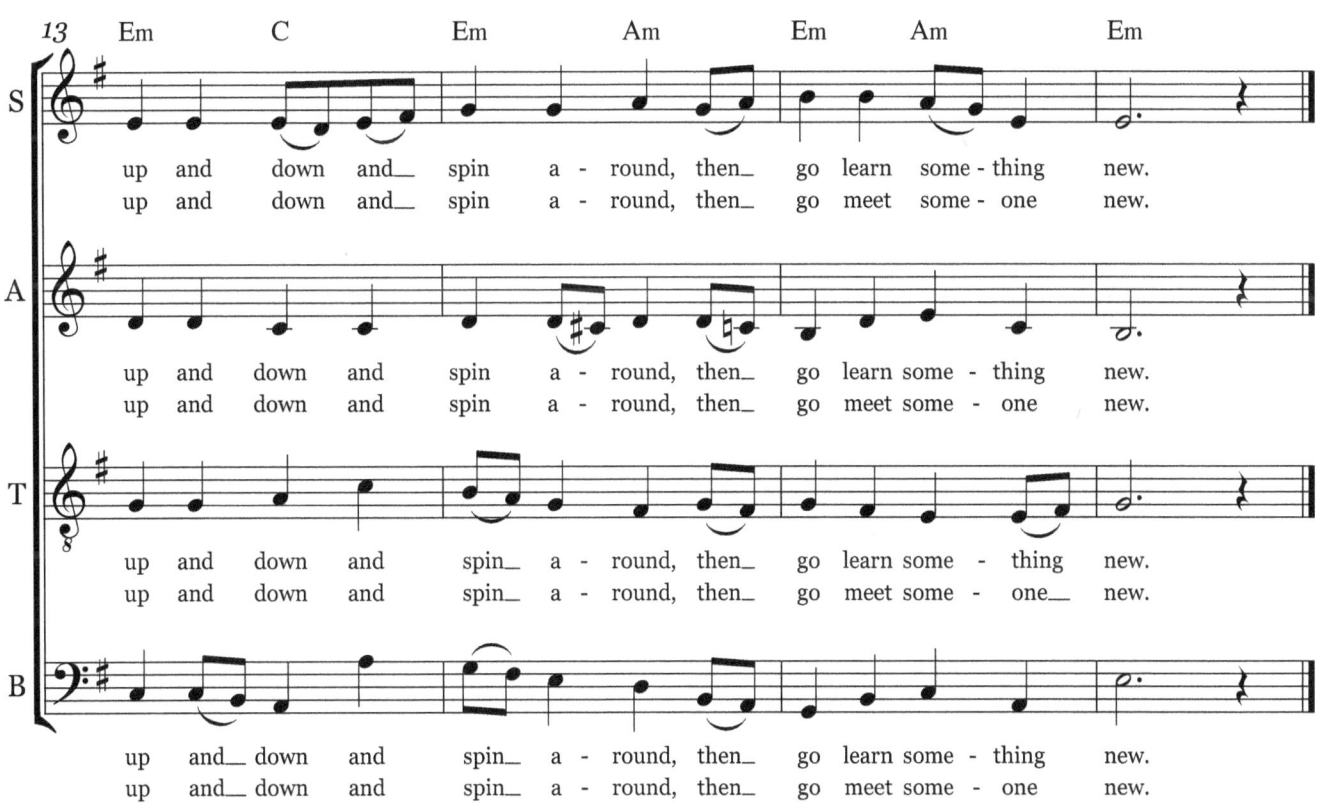

(Note: chord symbols support the soprano melody, not necessarily the SATB harmony)

140. When I Am Down

(From the Secular Hymnal)

Words: Secretary Michael

Tune: Traditional African-American spiritual
SATB Arrangement: Secretary Michael
(traditional hymn: "Down to the River to Pray")

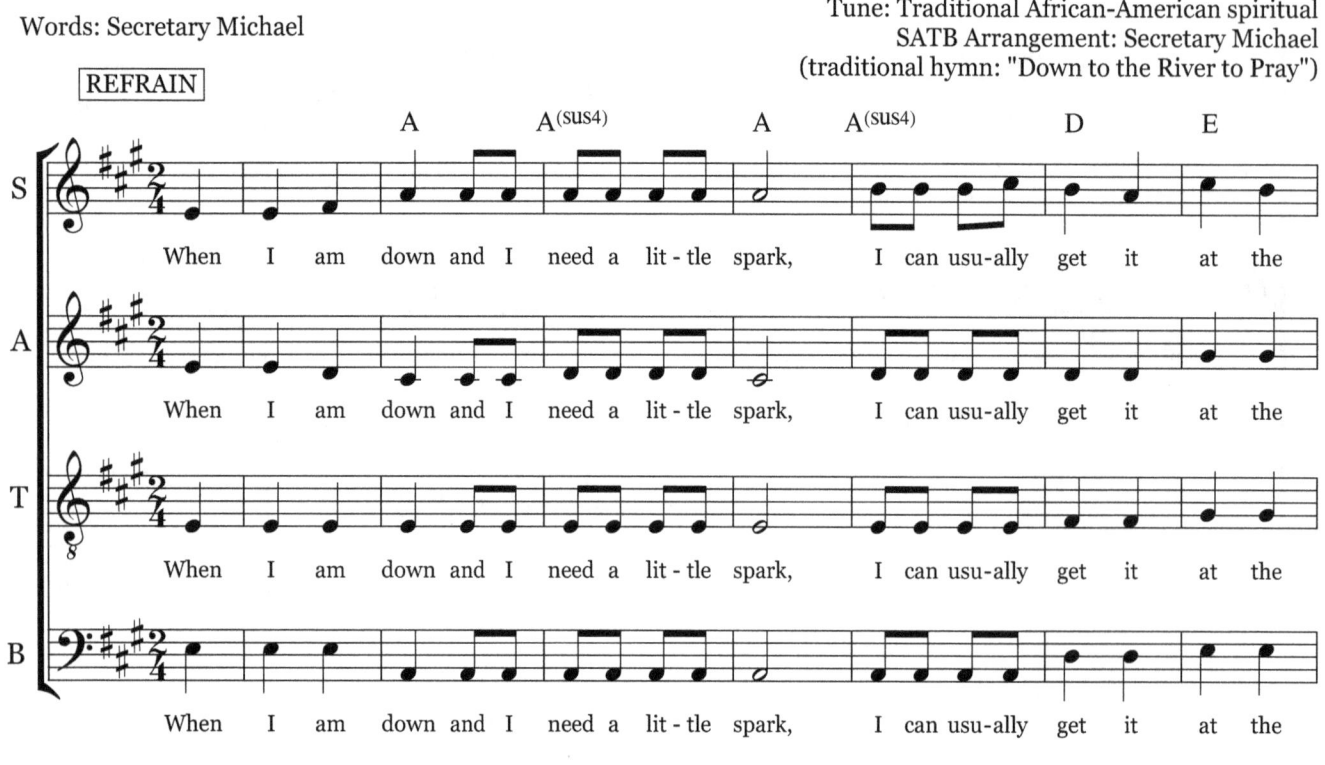

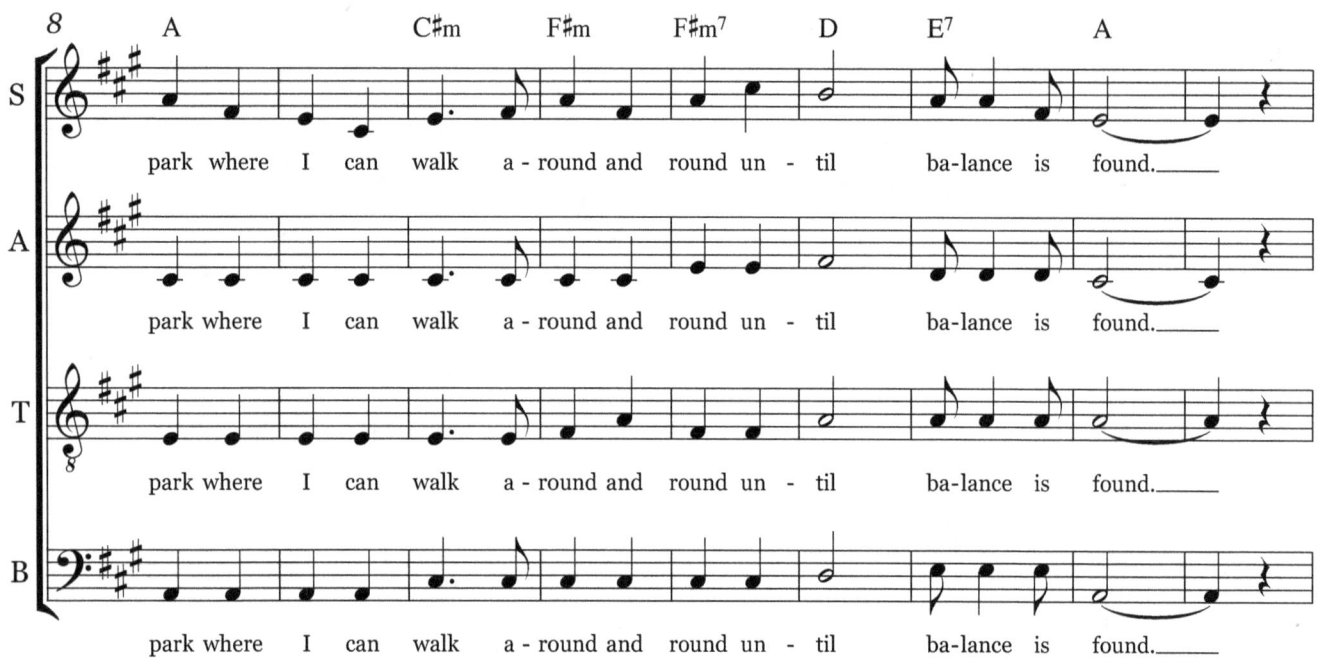

All works by Secretary Michael have been placed in the Public Domain. They may be freely copied and performed.

VERSES
17
E E7 A F♯m D A
S
1. Hey, who is that I see? It's my BOSS, come to walk with me.
2. Hey, who is that I see? It's my PAR - ENTS...
3. Hey, who is that I see? It's my FRIEND...
A
Hey, who is that I see? It's my BOSS, come to walk with me.
Hey, who is that I see? It's my PAR - ENTS...
Hey, who is that I see? It's my FRIEND...
T
Hey, who is that I see? It's my BOSS, come to walk with me.
Hey, who is that I see? It's my PAR - ENTS...
Hey, who is that I see? It's my FRIEND...
B
Hey, who is that I see? It's my BOSS, come to walk with me.
Hey, who is that I see? It's my PAR - ENTS...
Hey, who is that I see? It's my FRIEND...
25
E E7 A F♯m D E7 A
S
Let's walk and talk un - til we feel peace-ful and still.
A
Let's walk and talk un - til we feel peace-ful and still.
T
Let's walk and talk un - til we feel peace-ful and still.
B
Let's walk and talk un - til we feel peace-ful and still.

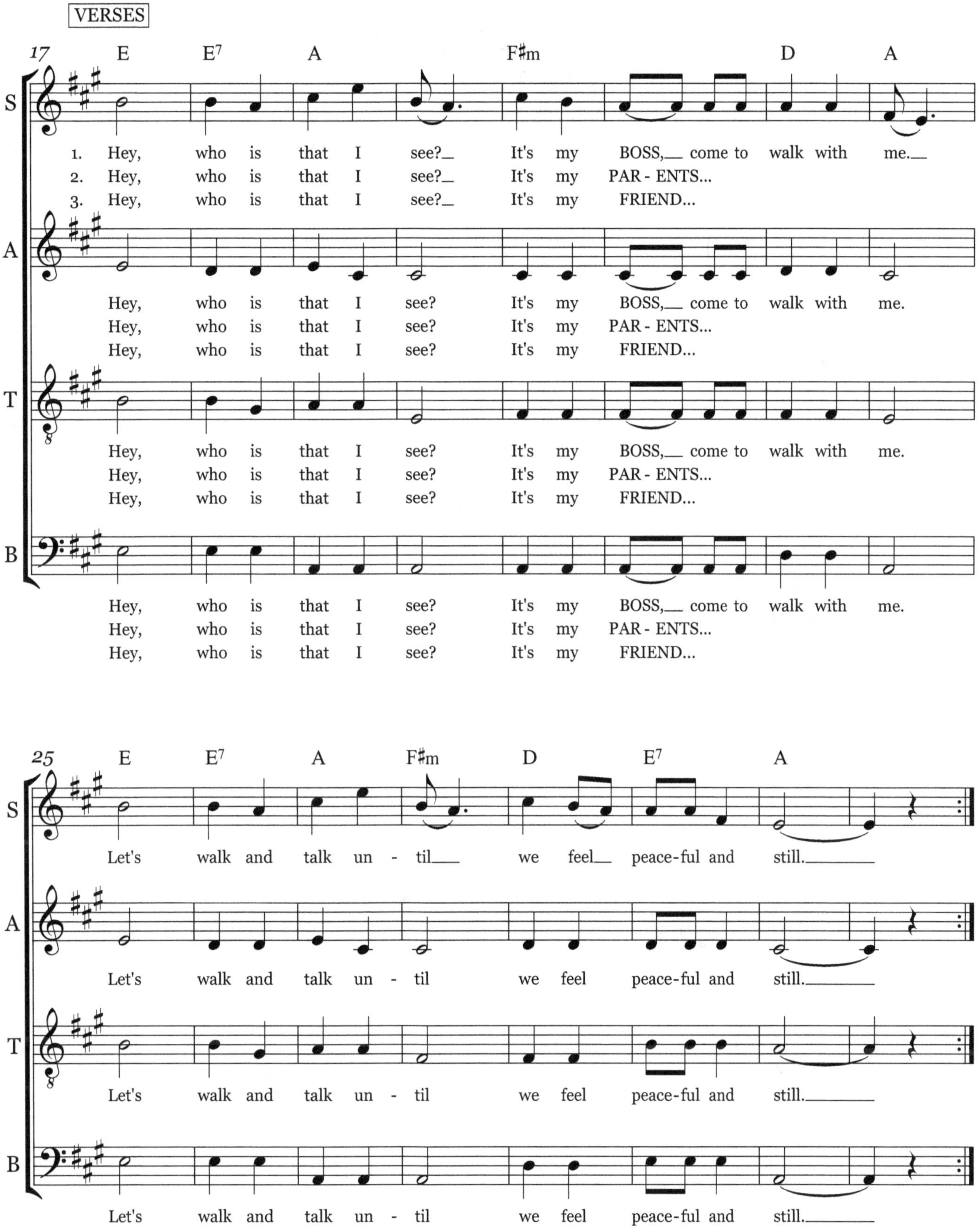

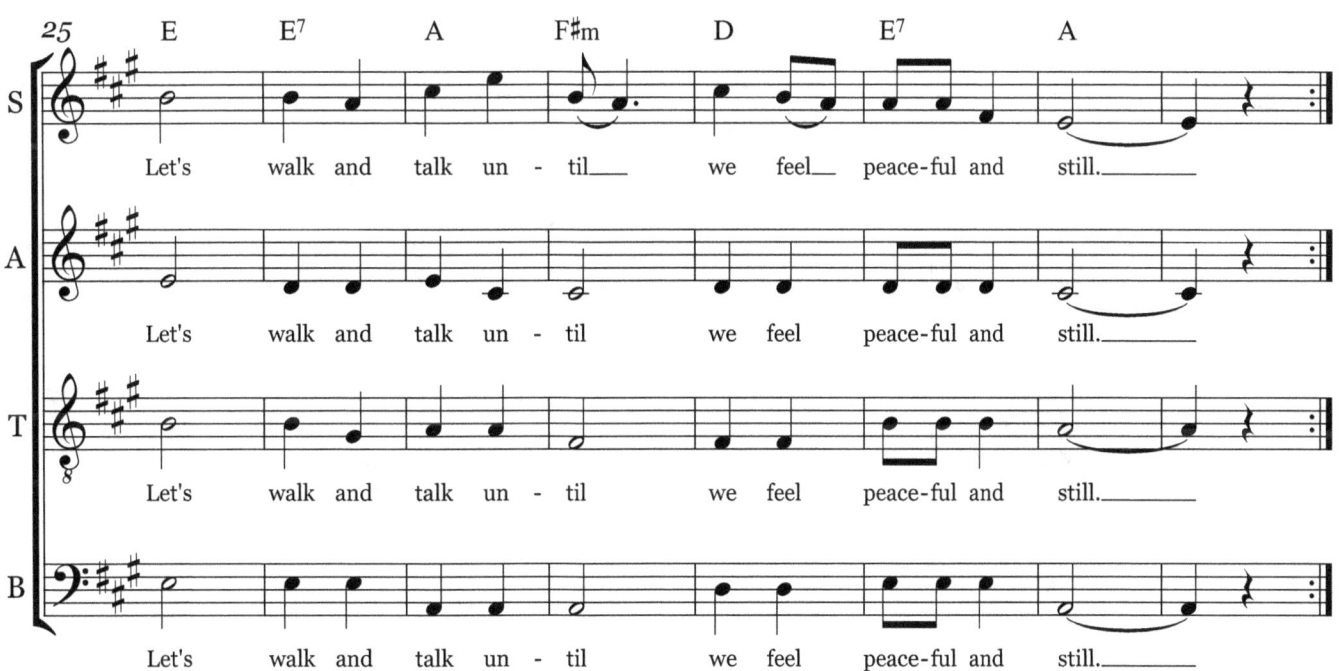

141. When Playing Cards
(From the Secular Hymnal)

Words: Secretary Michael

Melody: "*O Store Gud*" (a Swedish folk tune)
SATB Arrangement by Secretary Michael
(traditional hymn: "How Great Thou Art")

All works by Secretary Michael have been placed in the Public Domain. They may be freely copied and performed.

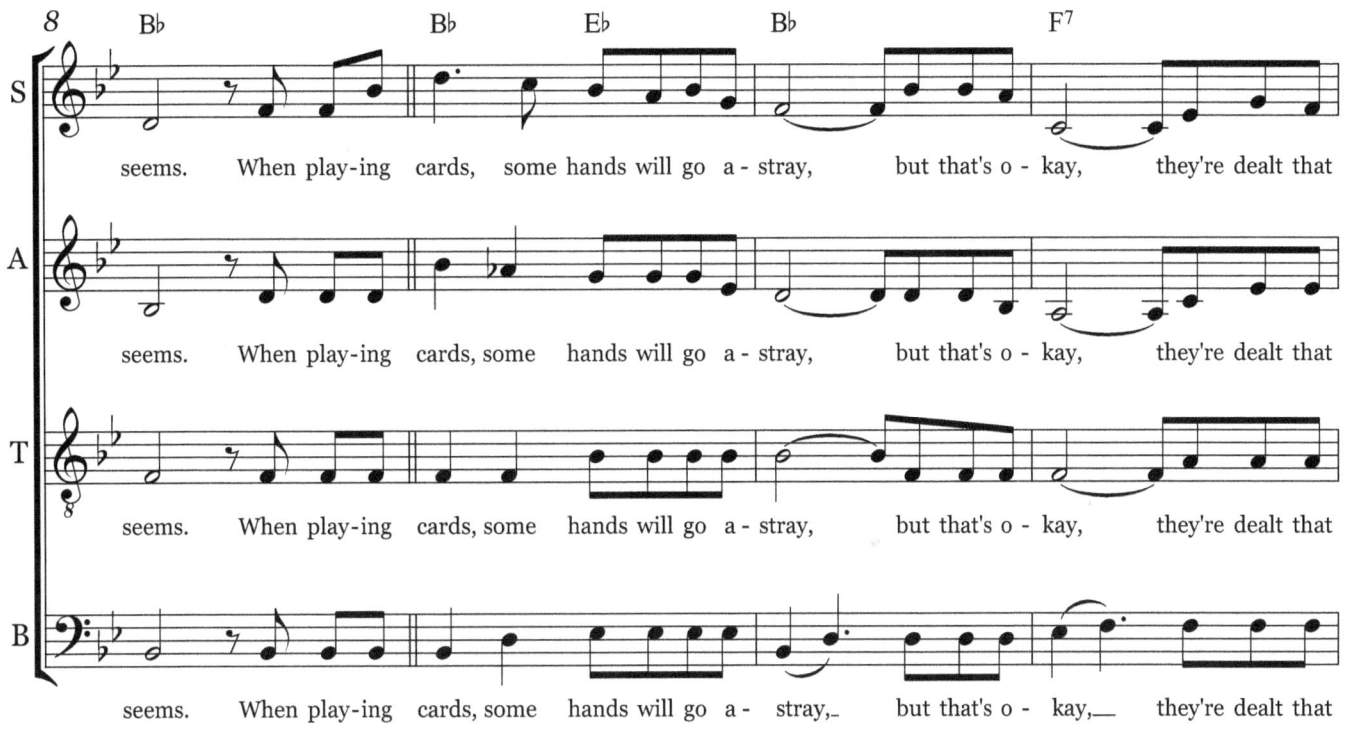

(Note: chord symbols support the soprano melody, not necessarily the SATB harmony)

142. Who's My Neighbor?

(From the Secular Hymnal)

Words: Secretary Michael

Music: "Victory" by Palestrina, 1588
Adapted by William Henry Monk, 1861
(traditional hymn: "The Strife Is O'er")

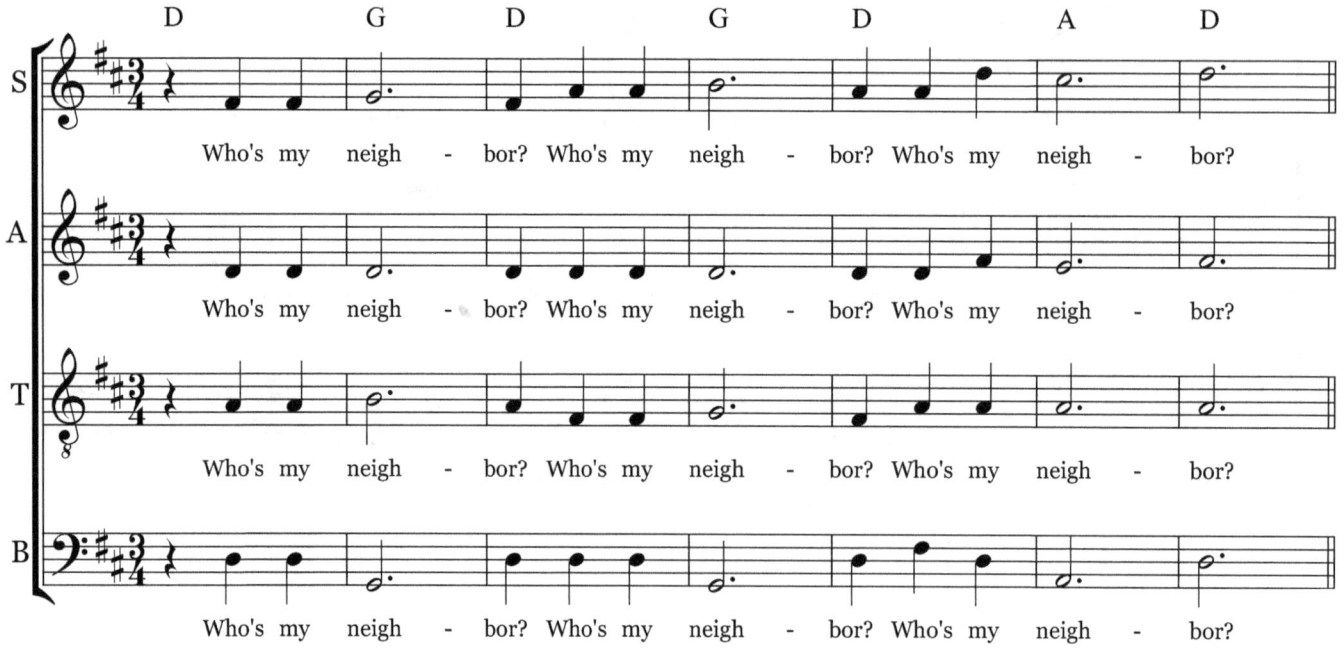

All works by Secretary Michael have been placed in the Public Domain. They may be freely copied and performed.

(Note: chord symbols support the soprano melody, not necessarily the SATB harmony)

143. Why Does This Phrase Have Five Measures?

(From the Secular Hymnal)

Words: Secretary Michael

Music: "Lauda Anima" by John Goss, 1869
(traditional hymn: "Praise My Soul the King of Heaven")

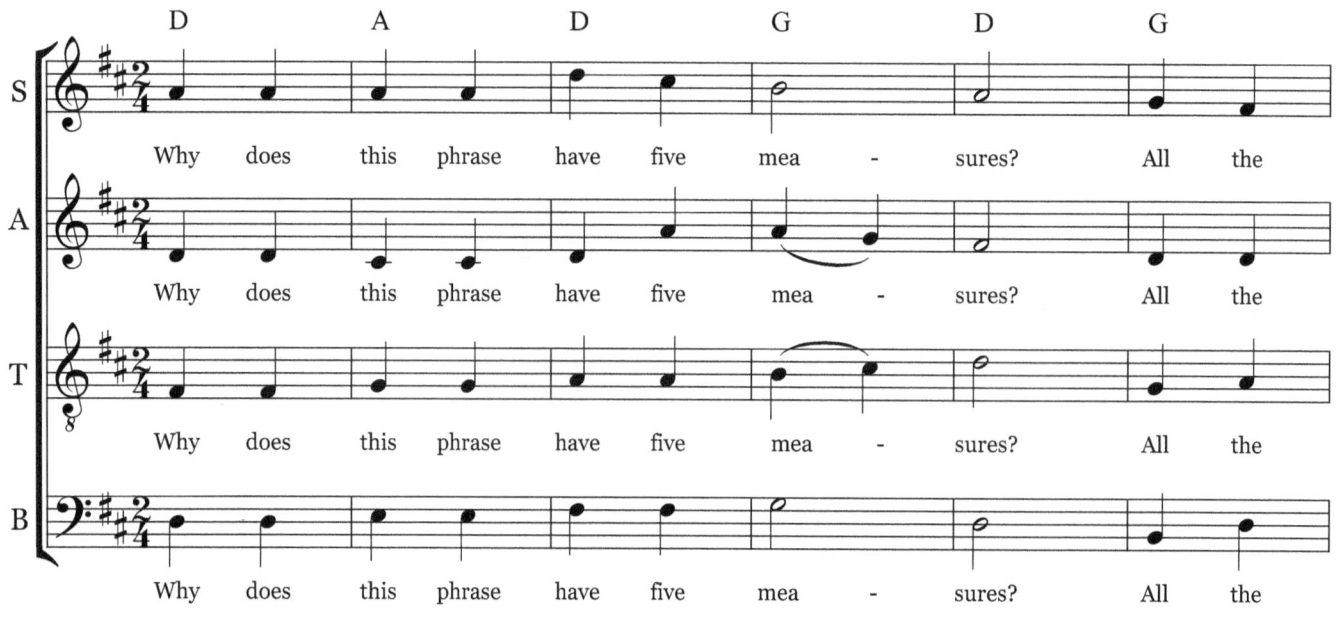

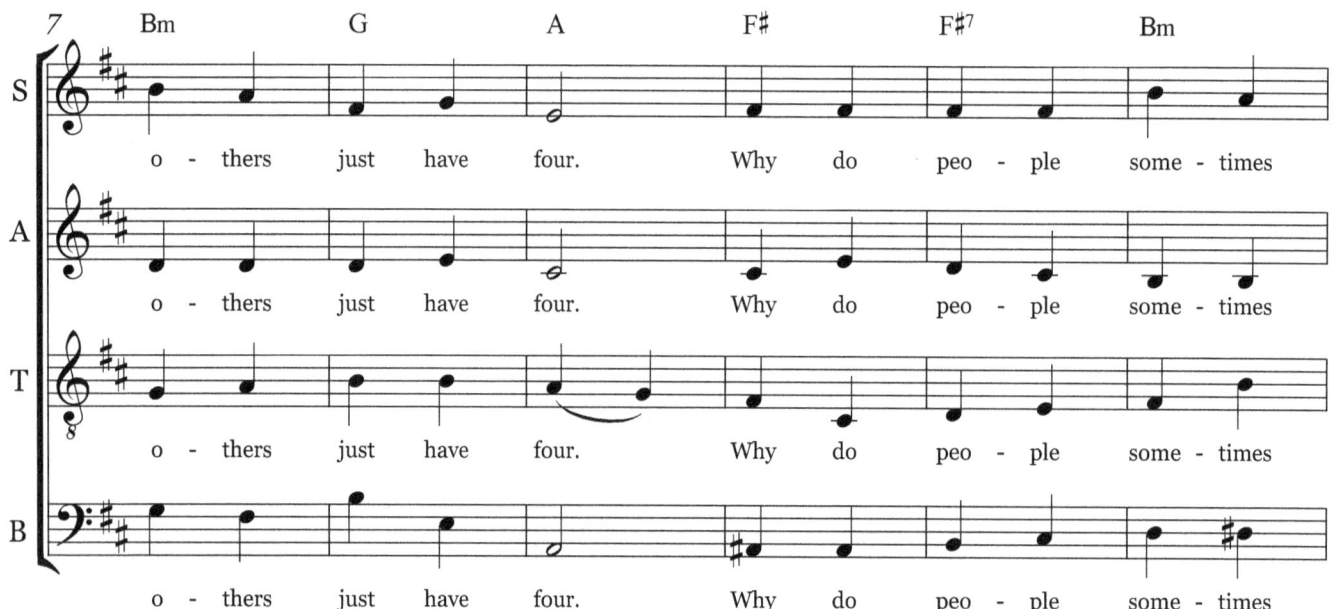

All works by Secretary Michael have been placed in the Public Domain. They may be freely copied and performed.

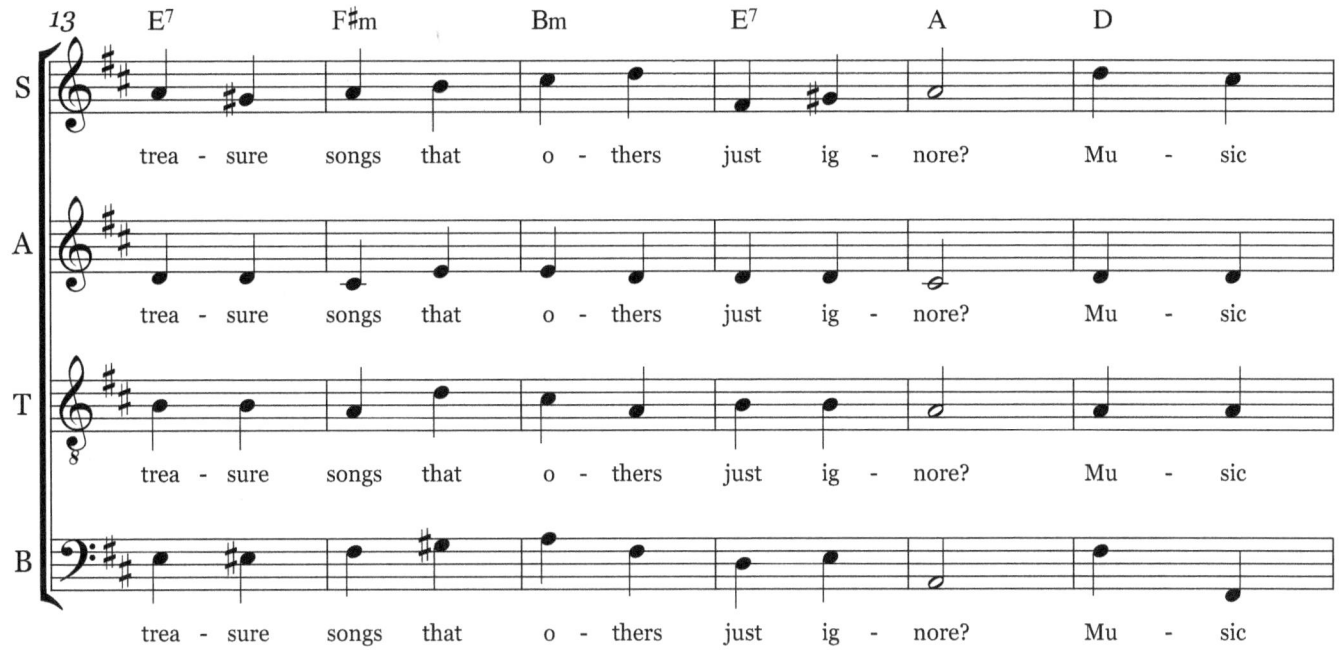

(Note: chord symbols support the soprano melody, not necessarily the SATB harmony)

144. You Took the One Road

(From the Secular Hymnal)

Words: Secretary Michael

Tune: "Loch Lomand" (traditional Scottish folk song)
SATB Arrangement by Secretary Michael

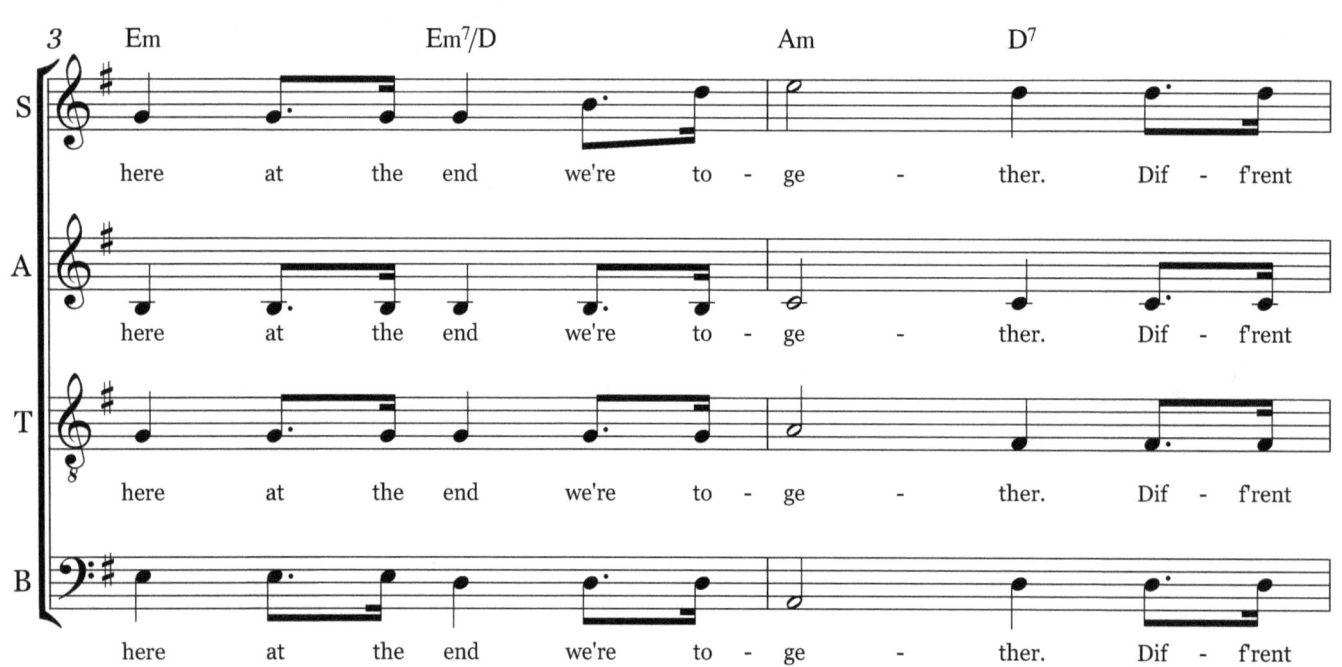

All works by Secretary Michael have been placed in the Public Domain. They may be freely copied and performed.

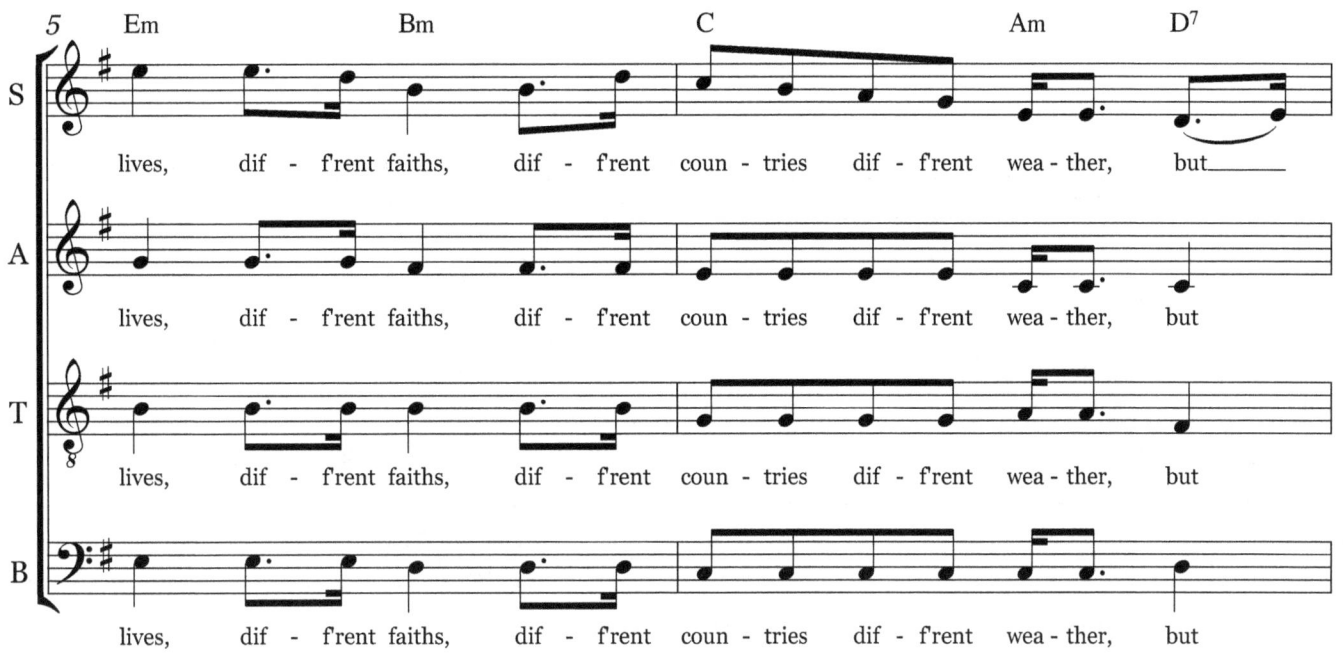
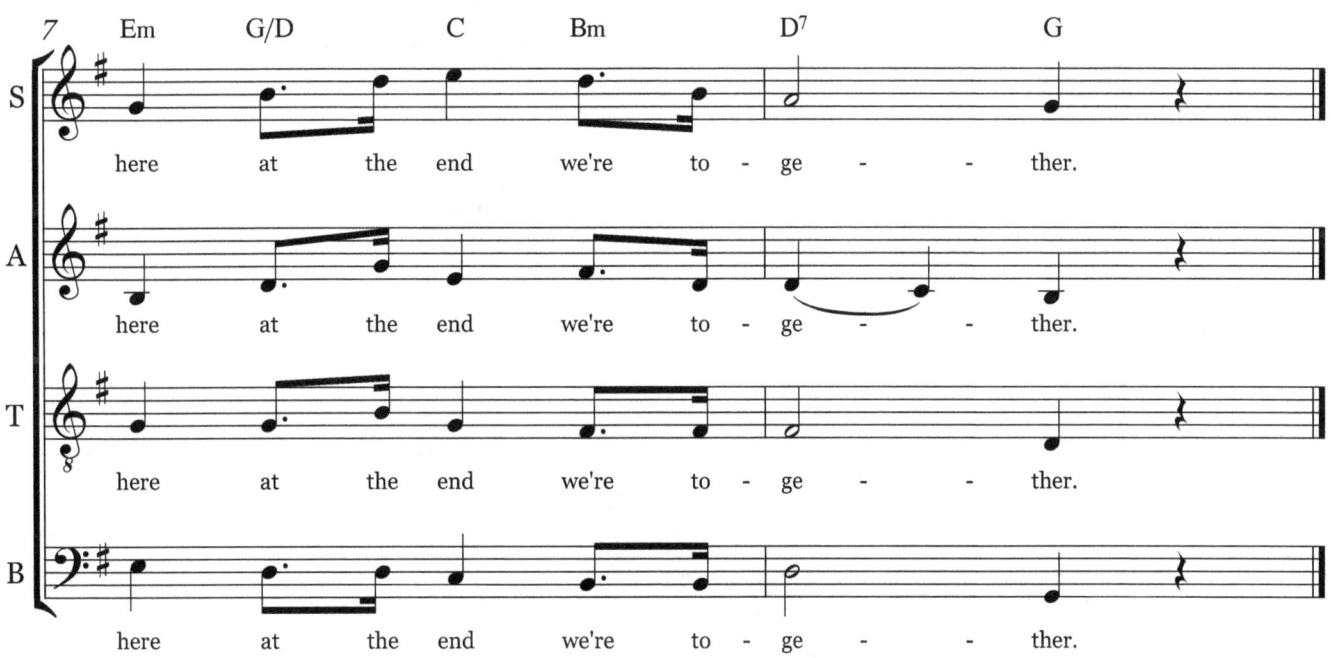

This table is useful for matching traditional hymns to their corresponding Secular Hymns.

TRADITIONAL TO SECULAR CORRELATION TABLE

Traditional Hymn	*Secular Hymn*
A Mighty Fortress Is Our God	1. A Beauty Hides In Everyone
Aberystwyth	80. People are More
Abide With Me	6. All Need To Feel Significant
Adelaide	75. Pain Can Cause
All Creatures Of Our God and King	101. Them Over There
All Hail the Power of Jesus' Name	17. Communication is the Answer
All in the April Evening	68. Nonviolence Must Be Taught
All My Hope On God is Founded	62. Long Road
All People That On Earth Do Dwell	47. I'm Marching, Marching
All Praise to Him who Reigns Above	107. There's a Better Way
All Things Bright and Beautiful	108. There's a Road Between Our Lands
All to Christ	102. There Are Times
Alleluia! Sing to Jesus	56. Land of Gray
Alleluia, Alleluia Hearts to Heaven	123. Towards a World That Has No Guns
And Can It Be	45. I Will Look and I Will See
And Did Those Feet in Ancient Time	98. The Greatest Walk
Angel Voices Ever Singing	130. We Are People, Plastic People
Angel's Story	5. Achieving Disagreement
Angels From the Realms of Glory	113. Tick-Tock
Arise, My Soul, Arise!	122. Together for So Long
Arizona	35. Harvesting Hunger
Assurance	48. In The End
At the Cross	3. A Peaceful Walk
At the Lamb's High Feast	25. Every Space for Every Face
At the Name of Jesus	15. Climbing Up the Mountain
Azmon	53. I've Never Known a Sinner
Battle Hymn of the Republic	137. We're Parents of a Soldier
Be Still My Soul	99. The Many Truths
Be Thou My Vision	132. We Can Be Tolerant
Beautiful Savior	81. People We Need to Meet
Bethany	85. Seen, Heard and Understood
Billing	87. So Many Ways
Bless Thou The Gifts	116. To Live Our Lives Addiction-Free
Blessed Assurance	48. In The End
Blessed Be the Name	107. There's a Better Way
Blessed Name	107. There's a Better Way
Blest Be the Tie That Binds	89. Someday When Guns Are Gone
Blow Ye Trumpet, Blow	122. Together for So Long
Bread of Heaven	90. Someone Should

Traditional Hymn	Secular Hymn
Breathe On Me	36. I Am a Terrorist
Brethren, We Have Met To Worship	84. Rise and Shine
Bring Them In	103. There is a Game
Christ for the World We Sing	57. Let's Make a Right
Christ is Made the Sure Foundation	86. Skating, Skating
Christ is Made the Sure Foundation	113. Tick-Tock
Christ the Lord is Risen Today	18. Crank and Sprocket
Come Down O Love Divine	119. To Those Who Came Before
Come Let Us All Go Down	140. When I Am Down
Come O Spirit, Dwell Among Us	126. Unconscious Bias
Come Thou Almighty King	57. Let's Make a Right
Come Thou Fount of Every Blessing	19. Disassemble Every Gun
Come Thou Fount of Every Blessing	24. Education is our Destination
Come Thou Long Expected Jesus	56. Land of Gray
Come To The Savior Make No Delay	44. I Think I'm Right
Come We That Love the Lord	70. Oh Child Do Not Despair
Come, Holy Ghost (*Lambillotte*)	30. For What I've Done
Consolation	28. Everything's Changing
Coronation	17. Communication is the Answer
Crown Him With Many Crowns	104. There is a Rule of Thumb
Crucifer	115. To Find a Place
Crusader's Hymn	81. People We Need to Meet
Cwm Rhondda	90. Someone Should
Danny Boy	135. We're Not Alone
Darwall's 148th	121. Today's the Day
Day of Judgment! Day of Wonders!	62. Long Road
Dear Lord and Father of Mankind	52. It's Great To Know Some Things By Heart
Deus Tuorum Militum	116. To Live Our Lives Addiction-Free
Diademata	104. There is a Rule of Thumb
Dix	96. Swapping Shoes
Down Ampney	119. To Those Who Came Before
Down To The River To Pray	140. When I Am Down
Dundee	31. Go Further Farther
Ebenezer	126. Unconscious Bias
Eine Feste Burg	1. A Beauty Hides In Everyone
Endless Song	127. Unless There's No-One Watching
Eternal Father Strong to Save	2. A Long Long Way We've Come Today
Eventide	6. All Need To Feel Significant
Fairest Lord Jesus	81. People We Need to Meet
Faith of Our Fathers	13. Building a Door
Fight the Good Fight	95. Striving To Be
Finlandia (Sibelius)	99. The Many Truths
For All the Saints	112. This Day, This Day
For the Beauty of the Earth	96. Swapping Shoes
Foundation	63. Make Just One Brand New Friend

Traditional Hymn	Secular Hymn
From All That Dwell Below The Skies	101. Them Over There
Garden	58. Let's Ride In Our Time Machines
Glorious Things of Thee are Spoken	73. Open, Open Up the Window
God Be With You Till We Meet Again	54. Journey Forward
God Moves in a Mysterious Way	31. Go Further Farther
Going Home	124. Trusting You, Trusting Me
Guide Me, O Thou Great Jehovah	90. Someone Should
Hail Holy Queen Enthroned Above	21. Don't Choose Sides
Hamburg	92. Standing At Bat
Hanover	110. There's More Than One Way
Hanson Place	46. If We're Not the Ones
Hark! Tis the Shepherd's Voice I Hear	103. There is a Game
Have Thine Own Way, Lord	75. Pain Can Cause
He Who Would Valiant Be	55. Just Because
Helmsley	49. Informed People
Hendon	69. Nothing's Heavy with Lots of Hands
Here is Love, Vast as the Ocean	38. I Declare a Brand-New Me
His Eye is on the Sparrow	60. Let's Stop Making Weapons
Holy God We Praise Thy Name	71. Ojalá
Holy Manna	84. Rise and Shine
Holy, Holy Holy	14. Climbing Up The Ladder
Horsley	117. To Make The World A Better Place
How Can I Keep From Singing?	127. Unless There's No-One Watching
How Firm a Foundation	63. Make Just One Brand New Friend
How Great Thou Art	141. When Playing Cards
How Sweet the Name of Jesus Sounds	40. I Have a Puzzle of the World
Hyfrydol	56. Land of Gray
I Bind Unto Myself Today	118. To Soldiers Lost
I Cannot Tell	135. We're Not Alone
I Come to the Garden Alone	58. Let's Ride In Our Time Machines
I Heard the Voice of Jesus Say	139. When Feeling Lost
I Love Thy Kingdom, Lord	70. Oh Child Do Not Despair
I Need Thee Ev'ry Hour	83. Relieving Suffering
I Surrender All	42. I Surrender
I to the Hills Will Lift My Eyes	31. Go Further Farther
I Vow to Thee My Country	59. Let's Start a Big Commotion
I Will Sing the Wondrous Story	131. We Are Searching
Immaculate Mary	41. I Once Was So Certain
Immortal, Invisible, God Only Wise	136. We're Not At Our Best
In Heavenly Love Abiding	4. Accommodating Others
In the Garden	58. Let's Ride In Our Time Machines
It Is Well With My Soul	22. Don't Know How I Got Here
Italian Hymn	57. Let's Make a Right
Jerusalem	98. The Greatest Walk
Jesus Christ is Risen Today	18. Crank and Sprocket

Traditional Hymn	Secular Hymn
Jesus Lover Of My Soul	80. People are More
Jesus Loves Me This I Know	93. Step by Step
Jesus Paid It All	102. There Are Times
Jesus Shall Reign Where'er The Sun	64. May We Make Moments of Peace
Jesus, Thou Divine Companion	27. Everyone Must Make a Living
Join All the Glorious Names	121. Today's the Day
Joyful, Joyful	123. Towards a World That Has No Guns
Just A Closer Walk With Thee	8. All the Seven Deadly Sins
Kingsfold	139. When Feeling Lost
Largo from Dvorak's "New World Symphony"	124. Trusting You, Trusting Me
Lasst Uns Erfreuen	101. Them Over There
Lauda Anima	143. Why Does This Phrase Have Five Measures?
Lead Us Heavenly Father Lead Us	77. Past Performance is No Guarantee
Lenox	122. Together for So Long
Let All Mortal Flesh Keep Silence	10. Bad is Not a Name
Let Us Break Bread Together	133. We Can Get Things To Happen
Lift High The Cross	115. To Find a Place
Lo He Comes With Clouds Descending	49. Informed People
Lo He Comes With Clouds Descending	113. Tick-Tock
Lobe Den Herren	82. People Will Change
Loch Lomond	144. You Took the One Road
Londonderry Air	135. We're Not Alone
Lord Of All Being	35. Harvesting Hunger
Lord of the Dance	114. 'Tis a Gift
Lord, Enthroned in Heavenly Splendor	94. Storms Will Come
Lourdes Hymn	41. I Once Was So Certain
Love Divine, All Loves Excelling	56. Land of Gray
Love Unknown	20. Diversity in Thought
Lyons	9. Assuming There's Peace
Macchabaeus	138. What Are We Doing?
Majestic Sweetness Sits Enthroned	117. To Make The World A Better Place
Make Me a Captive, Lord	104. There is a Rule of Thumb
Marines Hymn	11. Because Violence Can't End Violence
Meine Hoffnung Stehet Feste	62. Long Road
Melita	2. A Long Long Way We've Come Today
Mine Eyes Have Seen The Glory	137. We're Parents of a Soldier
My Hope Is Built On Nothing Less	39. I Have a Garden in the Park
My Jesus I Love Thee I Know Thou Art Mine	134. We Mean "Will You Love Me?"
My Song Is Love Unknown	20. Diversity in Thought
Nearer My God To Thee	85. Seen, Heard and Understood
Need	83. Relieving Suffering
Nettleton	19. Disassemble Every Gun
Nicaea	14. Climbing Up The Ladder
Noël Nouvelet	125. Ultimately We May Not Have Free Will
Now Thank We All Our God	111. Things Are The Way They Are

Traditional Hymn	Secular Hymn
Nun Danket	111. Things Are The Way They Are
O Bless the Lord, My Soul!	70. Oh Child Do Not Despair
O For A Thousand Tongues	53. I've Never Known a Sinner
O God Of Bethel By Whose Hand	31. Go Further Farther
O God of Loveliness	129. Walking in Someone's Shoes
O Jesus I Have Promised	5. Achieving Disagreement
O Love That Wilt Not Let Me Go	51. Intelligence is a Bouquet
O Love, How Deep	116. To Live Our Lives Addiction-Free
O Perfect Love	65. No Cheers For David
O Sacred Head, Sore Wounded	74. Our Garden Full of Flowers
O Sing a Song of Bethlehem	139. When Feeling Lost
O Store Gud	141. When Playing Cards
O the Deep Deep Love of Jesus	126. Unconscious Bias
Ode to Joy (Beethoven)	123. Towards a World That Has No Guns
Oh Worship The King	9. Assuming There's Peace
Old Hundredth	47. I'm Marching, Marching
Once to Every Man and Nation	126. Unconscious Bias
Onward Christian Soldiers	72. Onward, Upward
Our God Our Help In Ages Past	100. The Only Path to Peace is Peace
Our Great Savior	56. Land of Gray
Peace Like a River	79. Peace Like a River
Penlan	4. Accommodating Others
Picardy	10. Bad is Not a Name
Pleading Savior	27. Everyone Must Make a Living
Poor Wayfaring Man of Grief	37. I Am the Captain of My Boat
Praise God from Whom all Blessings Flow	47. I'm Marching, Marching
Praise My Soul The King Of Heaven	143. Why Does This Phrase Have Five Measures?
Praise the Lord, Ye Heavens	56. Land of Gray
Praise to God, Immortal Praise	96. Swapping Shoes
Praise to the Holiest in the Height	87. So Many Ways
Praise To The Lord	82. People Will Change
Redeemed	67. Nonviolence May Take a Long Time
Regent Square	113. Tick-Tock
Rejoice, The Lord Is King	121. Today's the Day
Repton	52. It's Great To Know Some Things By Heart
Revive Us Again	109. There's Claim Number One
Rhosymedre	20. Diversity in Thought
Ring Out The Old, Ring In The New	116. To Live Our Lives Addiction-Free
Rise Up, O Men of God!	70. Oh Child Do Not Despair
Rock Of Ages	33. Grief Has Got To Take Its Time
Royal Oak	108. There's a Road Between Our Lands
Salve Regina	21. Don't Choose Sides
Salzburg	25. Every Space for Every Face
Shall We Gather At The River	46. If We're Not the Ones
Simple Gifts	114. 'Tis a Gift

Traditional Hymn	Secular Hymn
Since Jesus Came Into My Heart	32. Going Up, Going Up
Sine Nomine	112. This Day, This Day
Sing of Mary	27. Everyone Must Make a Living
Singing Songs of Expectation	126. Unconscious Bias
Slane	132. We Can Be Tolerant
Soldiers of Christ, Arise	104. There is a Rule of Thumb
Sparrow	60. Let's Stop Making Weapons
St. Gertrude	72. Onward, Upward
St. Helen	94. Storms Will Come
St. Patrick's Breastplate	118. To Soldiers Lost
St. Thomas	70. Oh Child Do Not Despair
Still, Still With Thee	28. Everything's Changing
Surrender	42. I Surrender
Sutra Hymn	23. Each Little Raindrop
Take My Life and Let It Be	69. Nothing's Heavy with Lots of Hands
Tell Me The Old Old Story	61. Let's Try Something Different
The Church's One Foundation	105. There is an Empty Box
The Day Thou Gavest Lord Is Ended	50. Injustice to You is Injustice to Me
The Jubilee	122. Together for So Long
The King Of Love My Shepherd Is	97. Tall Oaks From Little Acorns Grow
The Lord Is King, Lift Up Thy Voice	116. To Live Our Lives Addiction-Free
The Old Rugged Cross	106. There is Something Wrong
The Solid Rock	2. A Long Long Way We've Come Today
The Solid Rock	39. I Have a Garden in the Park
The Strife is O'er	142. Who's My Neighbor?
There is a Balm in Gilead	26. Everybody Has Their Issues
There Is A Green Hill Far Away	117. To Make The World A Better Place
Thine Be The Glory (Handel)	138. What Are We Doing?
Thy Strong Word Did Cleave the Darkness	126. Unconscious Bias
Tis a Gift	114. 'Tis a Gift
Tis So Sweet to Trust in Jesus	34. Happy Be
To God Be The Glory	7. All Praise to the Troubled
Ton-y-Botel	126. Unconscious Bias
Toplady	33. Grief Has Got To Take Its Time
Trentham	36. I Am a Terrorist
Trust And Obey	120. Today Is My Day
Trust in Jesus	34. Happy Be
Turn Your Eyes Upon Jesus	43. I Think I Could Work in a Castle
Twimfina	12. Borders, Boundaries, Walls and Fences
Twimfina	16. Come Live With Us
Victory	142. Who's My Neighbor?
Ville Du Havre	22. Don't Know How I Got Here
Wachet Auf	128. Wake, Awake
Wake, Awake, for Night is Flying	128. Wake, Awake
Warrenton	24. Education is our Destination

Traditional Hymn	Secular Hymn
We Cannot Measure How You Heal	29. For Those Who Have Beliefs Bizarre
We Have and Anchor	88. Some Are Young, Some Old
We Plough The Fields And Scatter	66. No Need To Sing The Same Notes
We Rest on Thee	99. The Many Truths
Were You There?	91. Spent Our Treasure
Westminster Abbey	86. Skating, Skating
What a Friend We Have in Jesus	78. Peace Is Not What I Looked For
What Thanks and Praise To Thee We Owe	116. To Live Our Lives Addiction-Free
What Wondrous Love is This	76. Parents Gone
When I Survey the Wondrous Cross	92. Standing At Bat
When Peace Like a River	22. Don't Know How I Got Here
Will Your Anchor Hold	88. Some Are Young, Some Old
Wondrous Love	76. Parents Gone
Wye Valley	15. Climbing Up The Mountain
Ye Banks and Braes	29. For Those Who Have Beliefs Bizarre
Ye Servants of God	110. There's More Than One Way

Your *SATB Edition* of the Secular Hymnal is a complete compilation of all 12 of the "Roadway" booklets shown on the facing page. The SATB Edition is best for choirs, quartets, friends and families who like to sing in harmony. It's also great for students of music theory and counterpoint.

The *Solo Edition* of the Secular Hymnal (pictured above) is best for individual singers and groups that sing in unison. It contains the soprano (melody) lines and nice large chord symbols to all 144 Secular Hymns. Since there's no more worry about squashing the alto, tenor and bass voices, the Solo Edition contains melody lines that are in a lower, more comfortable range for us everyday singers.

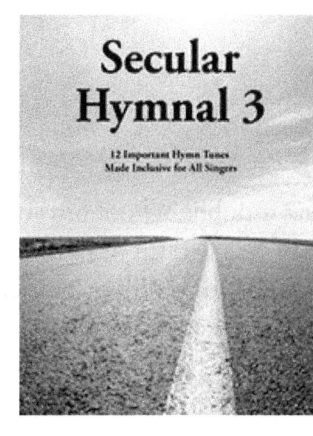

PERSONAL NOTES AND EXPLANATIONS

LYRICS

When I was a public school music teacher, I was made *very* aware that church hymns were inappropriate for the classroom. I was careful to never cross that line. At the same time, I knew from personal experience how useful hymn singing is for building musicianship, for tightening-up a choir, and for learning to sight-read. There is something special about hymns - they're like musical vitamins. This is the reason why I wrote the Secular Hymnal. By substituting all religious content with lyrics that everybody would feel comfortable with, we classroom teachers could have our cake and eat it too. We could make use of our heritage of chorale music without violating the religious sensitivities of others.

Lyrics are always "about" something. What should I write about that would be appropriate to this revered music? I certainly couldn't write 144 sets of lyrics about "oatmeal". And I have zero appetite for sugary, meaningless lyrics with contrived rhymes. As I hope you will discover, all the lyrics turned-out to be *about* something, with "Peace" and "Equality" being among the predominant themes. I hope that you find these new verses to be worthy substitutes for the much loved verses that they replace.

WORD DIVISION

As for dividing words into syllables, I used to be a purest about dividing words so that each syllable began with a consonant. It made sense because that's how the tongue, teeth and lips work in the mouth to actually form the syllables. And so I was strict about it and paid no regard to how words are conventionally divided in the dictionary. But even though my syllabification may have been "anatomically" correct, I began to realize that it might not always result in good communication. Maybe singers can't as readily grasp the meaning of a word when it is divided unconventionally. So now I'm no longer a purist - not even always consistent. I still prefer to begin syllables with a consonant, but I'll happily start with a vowel if I think it might make communication more clear. For example, words ending with the suffix "-ing" will probably be written that way (without a consonant) simply because they seem easier to read.

SOL-FA SONGS

There are 44 hymns that contain only diatonic notes - only the 7 notes that belong to the hymn's key. There are no outsiders from other keys present to complicate things. That makes these 44 hymns extra easy and fun to sing in solfege (the "Do, Re, Mi, Fa, So, La, Ti, Do" syllables).

In early editions of the Secular Hymnal, the solfege syllables were actually printed above the notes for these songs. But no more. It made the scores look too busy and confusing. So now you'll have to provide your own solfege syllables (which is probably a better way to learn anyhow).

The 44 songs that will make the best candidates for solfege singing are all in major keys and are purely diatonic in all voices. They are identified in the index at the front of the book. Each has a "SOL-FA" label after its name.

CHORD SYMBOLS

The chord symbols (written above the soprano voice only) are included so that a guitar or piano can be used to support the singing of the melody line. These chords are *not* meant to support the SATB parts - in fact they often clash with them! The chosen chord symbols seem to me to create the most clean, logical, functional harmony for unison or solo singing of the soprano line.

CHANGES TO THE TRADITIONAL MUSIC

<u>Hymn Tunes</u>: I feel an obligation to not change a hymn's melody line. And so the hymn tunes in the Secular Hymnals usually sound exactly the same as the hymn tunes in any other hymnal. The whole purpose of the Secular Hymnal project is to shape new lyrics to the original tunes, not the other way around. Occasionally I may need to make insignificant changes (for example, changing a quarter note to two eighths to accommodate an extra syllable - or vice versa). On rare occasions I might repeat a section. But these minor changes seldom effect the integrity of the original hymn tune.

<u>Alto, Tenor, Bass Parts</u>: I only change the harmony parts when necessary. Even if the parts are choppy and violate every part-writing rule, I usually leave them the way they are. In fact wild harmony parts can be fun to sing (as Sacred Harp singers can attest to). However sometimes it is necessary to rewrite the parts in order to avoid copyright infringement (rather common) or when the vocal range is too wide to be humanly singable (rare).

<u>Key</u>: I don't feel much allegiance to the original key. Being a choir singer myself, I always try to make the singers as comfortable as possible. Who in the world wants to sing outside his or her range? My duty is to find the most comfortable key regardless of how it was originally written.

SOURCES

Although I researched all of the hymns, none of the research was "primary" research. Instead I've relied entirely on established sources for my information. The internet is rich with hymn source material and information (such as "www.hymnary.org") for which I am very grateful. For note-by-note transcription of the old hymns into secular hymns, I more often than not relied on my own copy of "The Christian Life Hymnal" [2012 Printing]. I appreciate its crisp scores and its clear references.

<u>Choice of Hymns</u>: In choosing which traditional hymns to transform into secular hymns, my objective was to find tunes that people considered "favorites". It's largely from the many published lists of "favorite hymns" that the tunes for the Secular Hymnal were chosen. They were chosen for their diversity, importance, and above all beauty.

<u>Errors</u>: Having checked and double-checked countless times, I'm tempted to claim that there aren't any mistakes left anywhere in the book. But I know better than to say something so stupid. So if you find any errors, please let me know so that I may correct them.

COPYRIGHT

To my knowledge I have violated no copyright claims. Whenever there was even a hint of doubt about the copyright status of an arrangement, I would reharmonize it and then arrange it myself. If you find that I have inadvertently violated someone's copyright, please let me know and I will make the necessary changes immediately. (Personally I find that our current copyright law lasts way too long and is unreasonably restrictive. I suggest that composers choose a "Creative Commons" category or just put their material into the public domain as I do).

TYPESETTING

The Secular Hymnal's **notation** was created using Sibelius 6 (font: Keyboard Helsinki with Georgia text).
The Secular Hymnal's **text** was created using Adobe InDesign CS6 (font: Adobe Garamond Pro).

NOTES ON THE INDIVIDUAL HYMNS

1. <u>A Beauty Hides in Everyone</u>:
This Secular Hymn is built on the 1529 song "Ein Feste Burg" written by none other than Martin Luther himself. Nowadays the tune is best known as the hymn "A Mighty Fortress Is Our God" [#22 in the Christian Life Hymnal], which is the source that I used.
Topic of Song: finding beauty in everyone;

2. <u>A Long Long Way We've Come Today</u>:
This Secular Hymn is built on the tune "Melita" by John Bacchus Dykes in 1861. Today the tune is best known by the hymns "The Solid Rock" [#411 in the Christian Life Hymnal], and "Eternal Father, Strong to Save" [#600 in the Christian Life Hymnal] which is the source that I used.
Topic of Song: creating peace is an accomplishment worth celebrating;

3. <u>A Peaceful Walk</u>:
This Secular Hymn is based on a tune composed by Ralph E Hudson. Later the hymn "At the Cross" [#525 in the Christian Life Hymnal] was created from the tune, which is the source that I used.
Topic of Song: peace / nonviolence;

4. <u>Accommodating Others</u>:
This Secular Hymn is based on the tune "Penlan" written by David Jenkins in 1898. It is more commonly known today as the hymn "In Heavenly Love Abiding" [found on the website "hymnary.org], which is the source that I used.
Topic of Song: strong people are those who accommodate others;

5. <u>Achieving Disagreement</u>:
This Secular Hymn is built on the tune "Angel's Story", written by Arthur Henry Mann in 1881. Today it is more commonly known as the hymn "O Jesus I Have Promised" [#446 in the Christian Life Hymnal], which is the source that I used.
Topic of Song: respectful disagreement can be something positive;

6. <u>All Need To Feel Significant</u>:
This Secular Hymn is based on the 1861 tune "Eventide" composed by William Henry Monk, which was subsequently used for the hymn "Abide With Me" [#575 in the Christian Life Hymnal] which is the source that I used.
Topic of Song: seeing others as ourselves;

7. <u>All Praise to the Troubled</u>:
This Secular Hymn is based on the 1875 Hymn "To God Be the Glory [#31 in the Christian Life Hymnal] written by William Howard Doane, which is the source that I used.
Topic of Song: accepting others, seeing personality differences as a positive;

8. <u>All the Seven Deadly Sins</u>:
This Secular Hymn is based on a traditional folksong which is now popularly known as the hymn "Just a Closer Walk With Thee" [#461 in the Christian Life Hymnal] which is the source that I used.
Topic of Song: humorous hymn about "wrath, gluttony, envy, pride, greed, sloth, and lust";

9. <u>Assuming There's Peace</u>:
This Secular Hymn is built on the tune "Lyons", written by Johann Michael Haydn (the younger brother of Joseph Haydn) in 1770. It was later arranged by William Gardiner in 1815. It is popularly known today as the hymn "O Worship the King" [#10 in the Christian Life Hymnal], which is the source that I used.
Topic of Song: acting as if there were peace is a good strategy for creating peace;

10. <u>"Bad" is Not a Name</u>:
This Secular Hymn is built on a traditional French tune titled "Picardy". It is popular today as the hymn "Let All Mortal Flesh Keep Silence". It can be found as Hymn #82 in the Christian Life Hymnal and as Hymn #46 in the Book of Catholic Worship (1966 Edition). However in these and in other hymnals, the song curiously only occurs as a unison melody. So to be consistent with the other hymns, I decided to harmonize it and arrange it as a 4-part chorale.
Topic of Song: avoid labeling people;

11. <u>Because Violence Can't End Violence</u>:
This Secular Hymn is built on a melody that seems to have started in the 1867 Jacques Offenbach opera buffa titled: "Geneviève de Brabant" (Genevieve of Brabant). The song (Gendarmes' Duet) was a duet between two police officers. But it is much more popularly known today as the Marines' Hymn ("From the Halls of Montezuma"). I arranged it as an SATB chorale.
Topic of Song: there are better ways to resolve disputes;

12. <u>Borders, Boundaries, Walls and Fences</u>:
This Secular Hymn is taken from my musical "Twimfina". It's not structured like a hymn, but I included it simply because I like it so much. In fact the refrain "The World Is My Family, I'm Not Afraid" makes the acronym "TWIMFINA", the name of the play.
Topic of Song: the world is my family, I'm not afraid;

13. <u>Building a Door</u>:
This Secular Hymn is built on the tune "St. Catherine" written by Henri F. Henry in 1864 (and arranged by James George Walton in the same year). It is popularly known today as the hymn "Faith Of Our Fathers" [#322 in the Christian Life Hymnal], which is the source that I used.
Topic of Song: mixing with others is healthful;

14. <u>Climbing Up The Ladder</u>:
This Secular Hymn is based on the tune "Nicaea" written by John Bacchus Dykes in 1861. It is known everywhere as the famous hymn "Holy, Holy, Holy" [#1 in the Christian Life Hymnal], which is the source that I used.
Topic of Song: seeing others as ourselves;

15. <u>Climbing Up The Mountain</u>:
This Secular Hymn is built on the song "Wye Valley", written by James Mountain in 1876. It is popularly known today as the hymn "At the Name of Jesus" [#207 in the Christian Life Hymnal], which is the source that I used.
Topic of Song: no pain, no gain;

16. <u>Come Live With Us</u>:
This Secular Hymn is the Afterword in my musical "Twimfina".
Topic of Song: living in a "Love Thy Neighbor" world;

NOTES ON THE INDIVIDUAL HYMNS (continued)

17. Communication is the Answer:
This Secular Hymn is based on the tune "Coronation", written by Oliver Holden in 1793. Among the hymns that were subsequently built on the "Coronation" tune is the hymn "All Hail the Power of Jesus' Name" [#57 in the Christian Life Hymnal], which is the source that I used.
Topic of Song: communication;

18. Crank and Sprocket:
This Secular Hymn is based on the tune "Easter Hymn" which can be found in the Lyra Davidson collection of 1708. It is popularly known today as the hymn "Jesus Christ is Risen Today" [#45 in the Book of Catholic Worship - 1966 Edition], which is the source that I used.
Topic of Song: people act the way they are "built", and so we must be kind to everybody;

19. Disassemble Every Gun:
This Secular Hymn is built on the 1813 tune "Nettleton". It is better known today as the hymn "Come Thou Fount of Every Blessing" [#13 in the Christian Life Hymnal] which is the source that I used.
Topic of Song: take apart a gun with a screwdriver and then scatter the parts;

20. Diversity in Thought:
This Secular Hymn is built on the tune "Rhosymedre", written by John Edwards in 1840. It is more commonly known today as the hymn "My Song Is Love Unknown" [#164 in the Christian Life Hymnal], which is the source that I used.
Topic of Song: it's healthful to shake-up our fixed ways from time to time;

21. Don't Choose Sides:
This Secular Hymn is built on the old song "Salve Regina" written in Latin a millennium ago (c.1050). A very popular English setting of the tune is the hymn "Hail Holy Queen Enthroned Above" [#35 in the Book of Catholic Worship - 1966 Edition], which is the source that I used.
Topic of Song: peace / conflict resolution;

22. Don't Know How I Got Here:
This Secular Hymn is built on the 1876 tune "Ville Du Havre" by Philip Paul Bliss. Nowadays the tune is best known as the hymn "It Is Well With My Soul" also known by the beginning words "When Peace Like a River" [#363 in the Christian Life Hymnal], which is the source that I used.
Topic of Song: accepting life;

23. Each Little Raindrop:
This Secular Hymn isn't based on a traditional hymn. Hoping to have a diversity of hymns in my collection, I composed this with a "Buddhist" flavor and titled it "Sutra Hymn". The pentatonic scale gives it that Asian sound. Later when I was writing new lyrics to all the hymns, this hymn was among them.
Topic of Song: "What if everybody did that?" (Immanuel Kant's "Categorial Imperative")

24. Education Is Our Destination:
This Secular Hymn is based on the old song "Warrenton", which is found in the 1844 Sacred Harp book. Among the modern hymns built on the "Warrenton" tune is "Come Thou Fount of Every Blessing" [#14 in the Christian Life Hymnal]. I could find no arrangements free of copyright protection, so I arranged it myself to sound like a train.
Topic of Song: right to an education;

25. Every Space for Every Face:
This Secular Hymn is built on the tune "Salzburg", written by Jacob Hintze in 1678. It was later harmonized by none other than J.S. Bach. Today it is popularly known as the hymn "At the Lamb's High Feast We Sing [#326 in the Christian Life Hymnal], which is the source that I used.
Topic of Song: certain parts of life should not be sectored off for certain "types" of people;

26. Everybody Has Their Issues:
This Secular Hymn is based on the popular African-American spiritual "There is a Balm in Gilead". I was unable to find any copyright-free arrangements, so I made the SATB arrangement myself and put it in the public domain.
Topic of Song: although some people are good at hiding it, everybody goes through periods of mental instability;

27. Everyone Must Make a Living:
This Secular Hymn is based on the tune "Pleading Savior" by Joshua Leavitt (c.1830). It can also be found as the hymn "Jesus, Thou Divine Companion" [#148 in the Christian Life Hymnal]. However our source is the hymn "Sing of Mary" [#76 in the Book of Catholic Worship - 1966 Edition].
Topic of Song: seeing others as ourselves;

28. Everything's Changing:
This Secular Hymn is built on the 1834 piano composition "Consolation" by Felix Mendelssohn. Today it is popularly known as the hymn "Still, Still With Thee" [#574 in the Christian Life Hymnal] which is the source that I used.
Topic of Song: everything is changing; we can be a part of the change;

29. For Those Who Have Beliefs Bizarre:
This Secular Hymn is based on the traditional Scottish folk tune "Ye Banks and Braes". It is more commonly known as the hymn "We Cannot Measure How You Heal" [which can be found at hymnary.org]. The arrangements are still under copyright protection so I made the SATB arrangement myself and placed it in the public domain.
Topic of Song: accepting people regardless of their strange ideas;

30. For What I've Done:
This Secular Hymn is based on the 1840 hymn "Come Holy Ghost" by Louis Lambillotte. It can be found as Hymn #14 in the Book of Catholic Worship [1966 Edition], which is the source that I used.
Topic of Song: asking for forgiveness;

31. Go Further Farther:
This Secular Hymn is based on a tune from the 1615 Scottish Psalter titled "Dundee". It was harmonized by Thomas Ravenscroft (who lived from 1592 to 1635). It is more commonly known as the hymns: "O God of Bethel By Whose Hand", and "I To the Hills Will Lift My Eyes", and "God Moves in a Mysterious Way". My source for the Dundee arrangement was the online website "hymnary.org".
Topic of Song: keep progressing further and farther;

NOTES ON THE INDIVIDUAL HYMNS (continued)

32. Going Up, Going Up:
This Secular Hymn is built on the tune "McDaniel", written by Charles Hutchinson Gabriel in 1914. Today it is more commonly known as the hymn "Since Jesus Came Into My Heart" [#514 in the Christian Life Hymnal], which is the source that I used.
Topic of Song: motivational;

33. Grief Has Got To Take Its Time:
This Secular Hymn is built on the tune "Toplady" written by Thomas Hastings in 1830. Today it is popularly known as the hymn "Rock of Ages" [#284 in the Christian Life Hymnal], which is the source that I used.
Topic of Song: grief is slow but plays a role;

34. Happy Be:
This Secular Hymn is based on an 1882 song by William James Kirkpatrick titled "Trust in Jesus". It is more popularly known today as the hymn "Tis So Sweet to Trust in Jesus" [#414 in the Christian Life Hymnal], which is the source that I used.
Topic of Song: 12 contemporary beatitudes;

35. Harvesting Hunger:
This Secular Hymn is based on the tune "Arizona", written by Robert Henry Earnshaw (who lived from 1856-1929). Today the tune is more commonly known by the hymn "Lord of All Being" [found online at "hymnary.org"] which is the source that I used.
Topic of Song: the importance of education;

36. I am a Terrorist:
This Secular Hymn is built on the 1888 tune "Trentham" by Robert Jackson. Today the tune is more commonly known by the hymn "Breathe On Me" [#225 in the Christian Life Hymnal], which is the source that I used.
Topic of Song: capital punishment / human condition;

37. I am the Captain of My Boat:
This Secular Hymn is built on the song "A Poor Wayfaring Man of Grief" written by George Coles back around 1880. The Latter Day Saints have a version of it [#29 in their 1985 English Language Hymnal]. I like the jaunty melody, but since the copyright status of the LDS arrangement was not clear, I had to do my own SATB arrangement.
Topic of Song: acceptance of life / anti-pride;

38. I Declare a Brand-New Me:
This Secular Hymn is built on the tune "Cymraeg", written by Robert Lowry in 1876. It is more commonly known today as the hymn "Here is Love Vast as the Ocean" [#254 in the Christian Life Hymnal], which is the source that I used.
Topic of Song: it is healthy to give ourselves a second chance;

39. I Have a Garden in the Park:
This Secular Hymn is built on the tune "Solid Rock" by William Batchelder Bradbury, written in 1863. It is more commonly known today as the hymn "My Hope Is Built On Nothing Less" [#410 in the Christian Life Hymnal], which is the source that I used.
Topic of Song: parks are important, even for homeless people;

40. I Have a Puzzle of the World:
This Secular Hymn is built on the tune "St. Peter" written by Alexander Robert Reinagle in 1836. It is more popularly known today as the hymn "How Sweet the Name of Jesus Sounds" [#399 in the Christian Life Hymnal], which is the source that I used.
Topic of Song: solving the world's problems requires cooperation;

41. I Once Was So Certain:
This Secular Hymn is based on a traditional French tune known as the "Lourdes Hymn". However my source is the hymn "Immaculate Mary" [#43 in the Book of Catholic Worship - 1966 Edition].
Topic of Song: importance of being open and accepting mistakes;

42. I Surrender:
This Secular Hymn is built on the 1896 tune "Surrender" by Winfield Scott Weeden. Nowadays the tune is best known as the hymn "I Surrender All" [#305 in the Christian Life Hymnal], which is the source that I used.
Topic of Song: rejecting shiny things;

43. I Think I Could Work in a Castle:
This Secular Hymn is built on a 1922 tune by Helen Howarth Lemmel. It is more popularly known today as the hymn "Turn Your Eyes Upon Jesus" [#297 in the Christian Life Hymnal], which is the source that I used.
Topic of Song: contentment;

44. I Think I'm Right:
This Secular Hymn is based on a tune written by George Frederick Root in 1870. Today it is known by the hymn "Come to the Savior, Make No Delay" [found at the "cyberhymnal.org" website], which is the source that I used.
Topic of Song: it is very important that we be open to the possibility of being wrong;

45. I Will Look and I Will See:
This Secular Hymn is based on the tune "Sagina", written by Thomas Campbell in 1825. It is popularly known today as the hymn "And Can It Be?" [#247 in the Christian Life Hymnal], which is the source that I used.
Topic of Song: "looking for beauty" is a prerequisite for "finding beauty";

46. If We're Not the Ones:
This Secular Hymn is built on the tune "Hanson Place" written by Robert Lowry in 1864. It is popularly known today as the hymn "Shall We Gather at the River" [#559 in the Christian Life Hymnal], which is the source that I used.
Topic of Song: if we don't do it, it won't get done;

47. I'm Marching, Marching:
This secular hymn is built on the ancient song "Old Hundredth", which is popular today as the hymn "Praise God from Whom all Blessings Flow". More than one version is found in the Christian Life Hymnal. I mixed and matched, using the harmony and arrangement from Hymn #21 but the meter and rhythm from Hymn 621 (to avoid the imprecision of fermatas).
Topic of Song: stepping out of your group;

48. In The End:
This Secular Hymn is built on the 1873 tune "Assurance" by Phoebe Palmer Knapp. Nowadays the tune is best known as the hymn "Blessed Assurance" [#362 in the Christian Life Hymnal], which is the source that I used.
Topic of Song: accepting life, being realistic;

NOTES ON THE INDIVIDUAL HYMNS (continued)

49. <u>Informed People</u>:
This Secular Hymn is built on the traditional English melody "Helmsley". Today the tune is more commonly known as the hymn "Lo He Comes With Clouds Descending" [#211 in the Christian Life Hymnal], which is the source that I used.
Topic of Song: informed people tend to behave more responsibly;

50. <u>Injustice to You is Injustice to Me</u>:
This Secular Hymn is based on the song "St. Clement", written by Clement Cotterill Scholefield in 1874. It is popular today as the hymn "The Day Thou Gavest Lord Is Ended" [#578 in the Christian Life Hymnal], which is the source that I used.
Topic of Song: injustice to one is injustice to all;

51. <u>Intelligence is a Bouquet</u>:
This Secular Hymn is built on the tune "St. Margaret", written by Albert Lister Peace. It is more commonly known today as the hymn "O Love That Will Not Let Me Go" [#389 in the Christian Life Hymnal], which is the source that I used.
Topic of Song: there are many kinds of intelligence;

52. <u>It's Great To Know Some Things By Heart</u>:
This Secular Hymn is built on the tune "Repton" by Charles Hubert Hastings Parry in 1888. It is popularly known today as the unison hymn "Dear Lord and Father of Mankind" [#475 in the Christian Life Hymnal]. Since the Secular Hymns are all in chorale style, I used the melody to create an SATB arrangement.
Topic of Song: the joy of memorizing;

53. <u>I've Never Known a Sinner</u>:
This Secular Hymn is built on the 1828 tune "Azmon" by Carl Gotthelf Glaser. It was arranged in 1839 by Lowell Mason. Nowadays the tune is best known as the hymn "O for a Thousand Tongues to Sing" [#49 in the Christian Life Hymnal], which is the source that I used.
Topic of Song: accepting others, compassion;

54. <u>Journey Forward</u>:
This Secular Hymn is based on the 1880 hymn "God Be With You Till We Meet Again" written by William Tomer [#586 in the Christian Life Hymnal], which is the source that I used.
Topic of Song: importance of education;

55. <u>Just Because</u>:
This Secular Hymn is based on a traditional English tune "Monks Gate". In 1904 Ralph Vaughan Williams arranged it. It is popularly known today as the hymn "He Who Would Valiant Be" (which I was able to find at "openhymnal.org"). The hymn appeared in the movie "Chariots of Fire" and was sung at Margaret Thatcher's funeral. The hymn is very irregular and difficult to learn (and difficult to write new lyrics for). And so I (rightly or wrongly) made some simplifying changes so that it could be squeezed into a regular 4/4 meter, 16-bar chorale format. Sorry Ralph.
Topic of Song: things aren't always they way they're presented - critical thinking is necessary;

56. Land of Gray:
This Secular Hymn is built on the old tune "Hyfrydol" written by Rowland Hugh Prichard around 1830. It is a popular tune for hymns, in fact in the Christian Life Hymnal alone there are 5 hymns that use Hyfrydol as their tune, including "Love Divine, All Loves Excelling" [#42 in the Christian Life Hymnal], which is the source that I used.
Topic of Song: living with diversity;

57. Let's Make a Right:
This Secular Hymn is based on "Italian Hymn", written by Felice de Giardini in 1769. It is popular today as the hymn "Come Thou Almighty King" [#4 in the Christian Life Hymnal], which is the source that I used. The list of "world needs" itemized in this Secular Hymn was gleaned from the film "One Peace at a Time".
Topic of Song: a life of service to others;

58. Let's Ride in our Time Machines:
This Secular Hymn is based on the 1912 tune "Garden" composed by Charles Austin Miles, which became the hymn "In the Garden" [#456 in the Christian Life Hymnal] which is the source that I used.
Topic of Song: accepting life, accepting others, positive attitude;

59. Let's Start a Big Commotion:
This Secular Hymn is built on the music "Thaxted", written by Gustaf Holst in 1921. It is popularly known today as the stirring hymn "I Vow to Thee, My Country" [found at the website "newchurchmusic.org"], which is the source that I used.
Topic of Song: sometimes attention to injustice can only be achieved by making lots of noise;

60. Let's Stop Making Weapons:
This Secular Hymn is built on the 1905 song "Sparrow" by Charles Hutchinson Gabriel. It is popularly known today as the hymn "His Eye is on the Sparrow" [#378 in the Christian Life Hymnal] which is the source that I used.
Topic of Song: against the manufacture of weapons;

61. Let's Try Something Different:
This Secular Hymn is built on the tune "Evangel" written by William Howard Doane in 1867. It is popularly known today as the hymn "Tell Me the Old, Old Story" [#532 in the Christian Life Hymnal], which is the source that I used.
Topic of Song: it is a good lifestyle to constantly learn new things;

62. Long Road:
This Secular Hymn is built on a tune written by Joachim Neander in 1680 (the year the young man died). The tune began with the lyrics: "Meine Hoffnung Stehet Feste" (My Hope Stands Firm). In 1723 it was adapted and harmonized by J.S. Bach for his Cantata 40. Other hymns that use this tune include: "All My Hope On God is Founded" and "Day of Judgment! Day of Wonders!" My source was the website "hymnary.org".
I admit to changing one melody note (the last note of measure 4 and its chord) to give the cadence a more interrogative character.
Topic of Song: perseverance; committing to the long haul;

63. Make Just One Brand-New Friend:
This Secular Hymn is based on the 1832 song "Foundation" by Joseph Funk. It is more commonly known today as the hymn "How Firm a Foundation" [#392 in the Christian Life Hymnal] which is the source that I used.
Topic of Song: the importance of having a diversity of friends;

NOTES ON THE INDIVIDUAL HYMNS (continued)

64. May We Make Moments of Peace:
This Secular Hymn is built on the tune "Duke Street", written by John Hatton in 1793. It is more commonly known today as the hymn "Jesus Shall Reign, Where'er the Sun" [#39 in the Christian Life Hymnal], which is the source that I used.
Topic of Song: little moments accumulate, so create them wisely;

65. No Cheers For David:
This Secular Hymn is built on a the popular hymn "O Perfect Love", written by Joseph Barnby in 1889. It was later arranged by John Stainer in 1898. It can be found as Hymn #546 in the Christian Life Hymnal (which is the source that I used).
Topic of Song: supporting peace is better than supporting war;

66. No Need To Sing The Same Notes:
This Secular Hymn is built on the German song "Wir Pflugen" (We Plow), written by Johann A.P. Schutz in 1800. The English hymn is titled "We Plow The Fields And Scatter", which is the source that I used, having found it at the website "hymnary.org". I only used the first 16 bars.
Topic of Song: diversity is richer;

67. Nonviolence May Take a Long Time:
This Secular Hymn is built on the song "Redeemed", written by William James Kirkpatrick in 1882. The hymn "Redeemed" [#268 in the Christian Life Hymnal] is the source that I used.
Topic of Song: nonviolence;

68. Nonviolence Must Be Taught:
This Secular Hymn is built on the 1911 tune "All in the April Evening" by Scottish composer Hugh S. Roberton. I harmonized the tune and arranged it for SATB to avoid possible copyright infringement. (However I put my arrangement in the public domain so you may copy and perform it without worry.)
Topic of Song: nonviolence, like other important skills, needs to be taught;

69. Nothing's Heavy with Lots of Hands:
This Secular Hymn is built on the 1827 tune "Hendon" by Cesar Malan. Nowadays the tune is better known as the hymn "Take My Life and Let It Be" [#302 in the Christian Life Hymnal], which is the source that I used.
Topic of Song: working together;

70. Oh Child, Do Not Despair:
The original tune (St. Thomas) was written back in the 1760's by Aaron Williams. A number of hymns were written on the St. Thomas tune, including "O Bless the Lord, My Soul" [#35 in the Christian Life Hymnal] and "I Love Thy Kingdom, Lord" [#320 in the Christian Life Hymnal]. However I originally got the melody from the Sacred Harp book - the book of shape-note songs in which the melodies are in the tenor voice instead of the soprano voice. This is why I ended-up writing the arrangement - to get that melody back up into the soprano voice.
Topic of Song: welfare of children;

71. <u>Ojalá</u>:
Pronounced "Oh-ha-LA", this Secular Hymn is based on the traditional hymn "Holy God, We Praise Thy Name" which can be found in a 1686 Catholic songbook and currently as Hymn #39 in the Book of Catholic Worship - 1966 edition (which I used as my source).
Topic of Song: accepting life;

72. <u>Onward, Upward</u>:
This Secular Hymn is built on the song "St. Gertrude", written by Arthur Seymour Sullivan in 1871. It is popularly known today as the hymn "Onward Christian Soldiers" [#438 in the Christian Life Hymnal], which is the source that I used.
Topic of Song: a life of service to others;

73. <u>Open Open Up The Window</u>:
This Secular Hymn is built on the "Austrian Hymn" written by non other than Franz Joseph Hayden in 1797. It is popularly known today by the hymn "Glorious Things of Thee Are Spoken" [#319 in the Christian Life Hymnal] which is the source that I used.
Topic of Song: face the world and learn from it;

74. <u>Our Garden Full of Flowers</u>:
This Secular Hymn is based on the "Passion Chorale" written in 1601 by Leo Hans Hassler. More than a century later, in 1729, it was harmonized by non other than J.S. Bach. Today the tune is sung in the familiar hymn "O Sacred Head, Now Wounded" [#169 in the Christian Life Hymnal], which is the source that I used.
Topic of Song: growing peace;

75. <u>Pain Can Cause</u>:
This Secular Hymn is built on the 1907 song "Adelaide" by George Coles Stebbins. Nowadays the tune is best known as the hymn "Have Thine Own Way, Lord" [#298 in the Christian Life Hymnal], which is the source that I used.
Topic of Song: be slow to judge people;

76. <u>Parents Gone</u>:
This Secular Hymn is built on the old song "Wondrous Love". The haunting melody (in dorian mode) is thought to be hundreds of years old. Our arrangement is from the hymn "What Wondrous Love Is This" [#174 in the Christian Life Hymnal].
Topic of Song: allegiance to parents;

77. <u>Past Performance is No Guarantee</u>:
This Secular Hymn is based on the tune "Mannheim", written by Friedrich Filitz in 1847. It is popularly known today as the Episcopalian hymn "Lead Us Heavenly Father Lead Us" [found at the "hymnary.org" website], which is the source that I used. (I rightly or wrongly repeated the first 4 measures to give the hymn a more user-friendly AABA structure.)
Topic of Song: plan for the future, because that which got us through youth may not work when we are older;

78. <u>Peace Is Not What I Looked For</u>:
This Secular Hymn is based on music written by Charles Crozat Converse in 1868. Today it is popularly known as the hymn "What a Friend We Have in Jesus" [#460 in the Christian Life Hymnal], which is the source that I used.
Topic of Song: peace comes to those who look for it;

NOTES ON THE INDIVIDUAL HYMNS (continued)

79. <u>Peace Like a River</u>:
This hymn was already secular so no changes were made to the words. There are many arrangements of this famous African-American song on the internet. The source I used was Hymn #408 in my Christian Life Hymnal. My only contributions are the chord symbols for the soprano melody and the fun 4th verse (which I had heard before, probably at camp).
Topic of Song: I've got peace, love and joy like a river;

80. <u>People are More</u>:
This secular hymn is built on the hard-to-spell tune "Aberystwyth", written by Joseph Parry in 1879. It is more commonly known today as the hymn "Jesus Lover of My Soul [#395 in the Christian Life Hymnal], which is the source that I used.
Topic of Song: we tend to imprison people with labels;

81. <u>People We Need to Meet</u>:
This Secular Hymn is based on a Silesian folksong. It is popularly known today as the hymn "Fairest Lord Jesus" [#53 in the Christian Life Hymnal], which is the source that I used.
Topic of Song: accepting those we once rejected;

82. <u>People Will Change</u>:
This Secular Hymn is based on the 1685 German chorale "Lobe Den Herren" by Joachim Neander. It is popularly known today as the hymn "Praise to the Lord" [#11 in the Christian Life Hymnal], which is the source that I used.
Topic of Song: people change whether they know it or not; we must hold on to them;

83. <u>Relieving Suffering</u>:
This Secular Hymn is built on the song "Need", written by Robert Lowry in 1872. The tune is commonly known today as "I Need Thee Every Hour" [#459 in the Christian Life Hymnal], which is the source that I used.
Topic of Song: relieving suffering in others;

84. <u>Rise and Shine</u>:
This Secular Hymn comes from an old 1825 pentatonic tune called "Holy Manna". (Pentatonic songs are built on 5-note scales. They can be played using only the black keys of the piano. To my ear these tunes are special and have a Chinese flavor to them.) The hymn "Brethren, We Have Met to Worship" [#581 in the Christian Life Hymnal] is built on this tune and is the source that I used.
Topic of Song: motivational;

85. <u>Seen, Heard and Understood</u>:
This Secular Hymn is based on the tune "Bethany", written by Lowell Mason in 1856. It is known today as the hymn "Nearer, My God, to Thee" [#426 in the Christian Life Hymnal], which is the source that I used.
Topic of Song: needs of others;

86. <u>Skating, Skating</u>:
This Secular Hymn is built on "Westminster Abbey", written by Henry Purcell around 1680. It is more commonly known today as the hymn "Christ is Made the Sure Foundation" [#318 in the Christian Life Hymnal], which is the source that I used.
Topic of Song: making mistakes is healthy;

87. So Many Ways:
This Secular Hymn is built on the 1912 tune "Billing" by Sir Richard Runciman Terry. It is more commonly known today as the hymn "Praise to the Holiest in the Height". The score can be found online at hymnary.org (which is the source that I used).
Topic of Song: choosing to live our lives to reduce suffering;

88. Some Are Young, Some Old:
This Secular Hymn is based on the hymn "Will Your Anchor Hold" or "We Have An Anchor", written by William James Kirkpatrick in 1882 [#423 in the Christian Life Hymnal], which is the source that I used.
Topic of Song: we have to accept that a natural community has a wide assortment of people;

89. Someday When Guns Are Gone:
This Secular Hymn is built on the tune "Dennis" by Johann Georg Nageli. It was arranged by Lowell Mason in 1845. It is popularly known today as the hymn "Blest Be The Tie That Binds" [#334 in the Christian Life Hymnal], which I used as my source. (I added an extra bar at measures 3 and 6 to prolong the held pitches. This regularizes the structure and reflects how the hymn is actually sung in practice.)
Topic of Song: future generations will look back in horror at our use of guns;

90. Someone Should:
This Secular Hymn is built on the strangely spelled Welsh tune "Cwm Rhondda", composed in 1905 by John Hughes. However our source is a later hymn titled "Guide Me, O Thou Great Jehovah" [#413 in the Christian Life Hymnal].
Topic of Song: supporting community;

91. Spent Our Treasure:
This secular hymn is based on the traditional African-American spiritual "Were You There". It can be found as Hymn #161 in the Christian Life Hymnal and can also be found online at hymnary.org (which is the source that I used).
Topic of Song: the money we spend on weapons could allow our schools and health care services to flourish;

92. Standing At Bat:
This Secular Hymn is built on the 1824 song "Hamburg" by Lowell Mason. This is a very simple tune, using only 5 pitches. It is popularly known today as the hymn "When I Survey the Wondrous Cross" [#171 in the Christian Life Hymnal] which is the source that I used.
Topic of Song: stepping out of your group;

93. Step by Step:
This Secular Hymn is built on the tune "China", written by William Batchelder Bradbury in 1862. It is quite popularly known today as the hymn "Jesus Loves Me, This I Know" [#274 in the Christian Life Hymnal], which is the source that I used.
Topic of Song: unrelenting pursuit of goals should be balanced with other things;

94. Storms Will Come:
This Secular Hymn is based on the hymn tune "St. Helen", written by Sir George C Martin in 1889. It is more commonly known today as the hymn "Lord Enthroned in Heavenly Splendor". The hymn score can be found online at musescore.com and at other sites.
Topic of Song: storms are sure to come - but storms are also sure to go;

NOTES ON THE INDIVIDUAL HYMNS (continued)

95. <u>Striving To Be</u>:
This Secular Hymn is based on the tune "Pentecost", written by William Boyd in 1868. It is popularly known today as the hymn "Fight the Good Fight" (which was used in the film "Chariots of Fire"). The source I used was found online at cyberhymnal.org.
Topic of Song: striving to be poor instead of wealthy;

96. <u>Swapping Shoes</u>:
This Secular Hymn is built on the curiously-named tune "Dix" written by Conrad Kocher in 1838 (and arranged by William Henry Monk in 1865). It is more commonly known today as the hymns "Praise to God, Immortal Praise" [#595 in the Christian Life Hymnal] and "For the Beauty of the Earth" [#171 in the Christian Life Hymnal] which is the source I used.
Topic of Song: by putting ourselves into someone else's predicament, we learn that we would act the same;

97. <u>Tall Oaks From Little Acorns Grow</u>:
This Secular Hymn is built on the traditional Irish melody "St. Columba". It was harmonized by Charles Villiers Stanford in 1906. It is popularly known today as the hymn "The King of Love My Shepherd Is" [#370 in the Christian Life Hymnal] which is the source that I used.
Topic of Song: friendships often begin with the word "Hello";

98. <u>The Greatest Walk</u>:
This Secular Hymn is based on the tune "Jerusalem", a 1916 anthem written by Sir Hubert Parry. It was written to a poem by William Blake which began: "And did those feet in ancient time walk upon England's mountains green?" That subject matter is undoubtedly why it was sung by a choir at the end of "Chariots of Fire" (a 1981 movie about runners in the 1924 Olympics). It's also why our Secular Hymn is about "walking". Parry wrote it as a unison song, not as an SATB arrangement. It is a favorite song in England and is sung in Anglican and some Episcopalian churches. However I was unable to find any SATB arrangement that was not under copyright protection, so I created my own arrangement (and put it in the public domain).
Topic of Song: accepting others;

99. <u>The Many Truths</u>:
This Secular Hymn is built on a tune used in "Finlandia" by Sibelius. It was subsequently used in the hymn "Be Still My Soul" [#364 in the Christian Life Hymnal]. However that arrangement is still under copyright protection, so I created my own arrangement (and put it in the public domain).
Topic of Song: accepting others;

100. <u>The Only Path to Peace is Peace</u>:
This Secular Hymn is based on the tune "St. Anne", written by William Croft in 1708. It is more commonly known today as the hymn "Our God Our Help in Ages Past" [which can be found at the online site "openhymnal.org"], which is the source that I used.
Topic of Song: "fighting" for peace has a history of failure; "peace-ing" for peace must be our strategy;

101. <u>Them Over There</u>:
The source of this Secular Hymn is "Lasst Uns Erfreuen" (pre-1623). It was harmonized by Ralph Vaughan Williams in 1906. It is most popular today as the hymn "All Creatures Of Our God and King". However the hymn "From All That Dwell Below the Skies" [#19 in the Christian Life Hymnal] is the source that I used.
Topic of Song: seeing others as ourselves;

102. There Are Times:
This Secular Hymn is built on the 1868 song "All to Christ" by John Thomas Grape. It is known today as the hymn "Jesus Paid It All" [#265 in the Christian Life Hymnal] which is the source that I used.
Topic of Song: loss of identity through medication, drugs etc.

103. There is a Game:
This Secular Hymn is built on a hymn written by William Augustine Ogden in 1885, titled "Bring Them In", [#361 in the Christian Life Hymnal], which is the source that I used.
Topic of Song: behavior beyond control;

104. There is a Rule of Thumb:
This Secular Hymn is built on the song "Diademata" written by George Elvey back in the 1860's. The name "Diademata" comes from the Greek word for "crown". So it's not surprising that the most popular hymn written on this tune is titled: "Crown Him With Many Crowns" [#46 in the Christian Life Hymnal], which is the source that I used.
Topic of Song: acceptance of life;

105. There is an Empty Box:
This Secular Hymn is built on the tune "Aurelia", written by Samuel Sebastian Wesley is 1864. It is more commonly known today as the hymn "The Church's One Foundation" [#316 in the Christian Life Hymnal], which is the source that I used.
Topic of Song: we must preserve that which others consider meaningful and beautiful;

106. There is Something Wrong:
This Secular Hymn is built from the hymn "The Old Rugged Cross" written by George Bennard in 1913. The source I used was the Christian Life Hymnal (Hymn #167).
Topic of Song: "Killing the Bad Guy" is an ugly game;

107. There's a Better Way:
This Secular Hymn is built on the tune "Blessed Name", a 19th century American camp meeting melody. It was arranged by Ralph Erskine Hudson in 1887. The source I used is the hymn "Blessed Be The Name" [#37 in the Christian Life Hymnal].
Topic of Song: peace, anti-gun;

108. There's a Road Between Our Lands:
This Secular Hymn is built on a 17th century English melody titled "Royal Oak", which is recognized today as the popular hymn "All Things Bright and Beautiful" [#243 in the Christian Life Hymnal], which is the source that I used. It was arranged for choir in 1915 by Martin Shaw.
Topic of Song: even very different people have common interests that they can share;

109. There's Claim Number One:
This Secular Hymn is based on the hymn "Revive Us Again", written by John Jenkins Husband around 1815. I found it as Hymn #338 in my Christian Life Hymnal, which is the source that I used.
Topic of Song: sometimes we have to decide between two claims that are both true;

110. There's More Than One Way:
This Secular Hymn is built on the tune "Hanover", written by William Croft in 1708. Today it is more commonly known as the hymn "Ye Servants of God" [#209 in the Christian Life Hymnal] which is the source that I used.
Topic of Song: since there are many ways to live our lives, we should give the deviants some room;

NOTES ON THE INDIVIDUAL HYMNS (continued)

111. Things Are The Way They Are:
This Secular Hymn is based on the tune "Nun Danket", written by Johann Crueger in 1647. It is popularly known today as the hymn "Now Thank We All Our God". The available E-flat arrangement (by Felix Mendelssohn, I believe) had a rather high tessitura for the sopranos and some really low bass notes (E-flat). I try to avoid such low notes because few can sing them with any power. So I lowered the key to "D" and made a simpler, more user-friendly arrangement and put it in the public domain.
Topic of Song: things will remain as they are unless we make changes;

112. This Day, This Day:
This Secular Hymn is built on the music "Sine Nomine", composed by Ralph Vaughan Williams in 1906. It is popularly known today as the hymn "For All The Saints" [#547 in the Christian Life Hymnal], which is the source that I used.
Topic of Song: living one day at a time;

113. Tick-Tock:
This Secular Hymn is built on the tune "Regent Square", written by Henry Thomas Smart in 1867. The tune is more commonly known today by several hymns: "Angels From the Realms of Glory" [#98 in the Christian Life Hymnal], "Christ is Made the Sure Foundation" [#317 in the Christian Life Hymnal], and finally the source that I used: "Lo He Comes With Clouds Descending" [#210 in the Christian Life Hymnal].
Topic of Song: accepting "time";

114. 'Tis a Gift:
This Secular Hymn is built on the very familiar Shaker song "Simple Gifts", written by Joseph Bracket in 1848. The melody was popularized even more when Aaron Copland used it in his 1944 ballet "Appalachian Spring". I created the SATB arrangement and put it in the public domain.
Topic of Song: 'tis a gift to be simple;

115. To Find a Place:
This Secular Hymn is built on the tune "Crucifer" written by Sydney Hugo Nicholson in 1916. Today it is more commonly known by the hymn "Lift High the Cross" [#203 in the Christian Life Hymnal], which is the source that I used.
Topic of Song: the importance of having a home and community;

116. To Live Our Lives Addiction-Free:
This Secular Hymn is based on the 1753 tune "Deus Tuorum Militum" (the God of your soldiers). The tune is better known today by hymns such as: "O Love How Deep", "The Lord is King, Lift Up Thy Voice", "Ring Out the Old, Ring In the New", "What Thanks and Praise to Thee We Owe", and the source that I used from the website hymnary.org: "Bless Thou the Gifts".
Topic of Song: protecting ourselves from addictive substances will give us a kind of freedom;

117. To Make the World a Better Place:
This Secular Hymn is built on a tune by William Horsley in 1830. Today it is popularly known by the hymns "Majestic Sweetness Sits Enthroned" [#200 in the Christian Life Hymnal] and "There is a Green Hill Far Away" [#160 in the Christian Life Hymnal] which is the source I used.
Topic of Song: hiring someone different than you is very important;

118. <u>To Soldiers Lost</u>:
This Secular Hymn is based on the traditional Irish melody "St. Patrick's Breastplate". The melody is more commonly known today as the hymn "I Bind Unto Myself Today" [#6 in the Christian Life Hymnal], which is the source that I used. The source is a unison work, so I made the SATB arrangement myself and put it in the public domain.
Topic of Song: any social problems that veterans have is of our own making and is therefore our responsibility to solve;

119. <u>To Those Who Came Before</u>:
This Secular Hymn is based on the 1906 tune "Down Ampney" by Ralph Vaughan Williams. "Down Ampney" is the town in which Ralph Vaughan Williams was born (on October 12, 1872). It is more commonly known today as the hymn "Come Down O Love Divine" [#216 in the Christian Life Hymnal], which is the source that I used.
Topic of Song: we stand on foundations built by others;

120. <u>Today Is My Day</u>:
This Secular Hymn is based on the 1887 hymn "Trust and Obey" by Daniel Brink Towner [#504 in the Christian Life Hymnal] which is the source that I used. I added an extra bar after measures 7 and 15 to extend the held pitch. This regularizes the structure and notates the hymn the way it is actually sung in practice.
Topic of Song: working towards goals can help stave-off despair ;

121. <u>Today's the Day</u>:
This Secular Hymn is built on the tune "Darwall's 148th" written by John Darwall in 1770. It is more popularly known today as the hymns: "Rejoice, The Lord Is King" [#206 in the Christian Life Hymnal] and "Join All The Glorious Names" [#43 in the Christian Life Hymnal], both of which I used as sources.
Topic of Song: making a resolution to change;

122. <u>Together For So Long</u>:
This Secular Hymn is built on the old tune "Lenox" written by Lewis Edson in 1748. The familiar hymn "Arise, My Soul, Arise!" is also built on the "Lenox" tune and is the source that I used.
Topic of Song: communication;

123. <u>T'wards a World That Has No Guns</u>:
This Secular Hymn is built on Beethoven's 1824 song "Hymn to Joy" from his Ninth Symphony. It was adapted in 1864 by Edward Hodges. Today it appears in hymns such as "Joyful, Joyful, We Adore Thee" [#235 in the Christian Life Hymnal] or "Alleluia, Alleluia! Hearts to Heaven [#190 in the Christian Life Hymnal], which is the source that I used.
Topic of Song: peace, anti-gun;

124. <u>Trusting You, Trusting Me</u>:
This Secular Hymn is built on the famous "Largo" theme from Antonin Dvorak's 1893 "New World" symphony. It is popularly known today as the song "Going Home". I could find no copyright-free SATB arrangements of this song so I arranged it myself and put it into the public domain.
Topic of Song: so much of life depends on "trust";

NOTES ON THE INDIVIDUAL HYMNS (continued)

125. <u>Ultimately We May Not Have Free Will</u>:
This Secular Hymn is based on the old French melody "Noël Nouvelet", which can be found online at the website "chanted.com". It is only found as a unison song, so I harmonized it and arranged it for SATB choir.
Topic of Song: many of us understand that we don't have a "free will" and feel that our punitive prisons and our hero-worship is unfair. (Sales Pitch: I wrote a fictional book about a community of determinists with the title "Aren't We The Lucky Ones" which is still available);

126. <u>Unconscious Bias</u>:
This Secular Hymn is based on the tune "Ebenezer", written by Thomas John Williams in 1890. The tune is better known today by many hymns, including "Come O Spirit, Dwell Among Us", Thy Strong Word Did Cleave the Darkness", "Ton-y-Botel", "O the Deep, Deep Love of Jesus", "Once to Every Man and Nation", and "Singing Songs of Expectation" [#321 in the Christian Life Hymnal], which is the source that I used.
Topic of Song: we should be mindful of our unconscious biases;

127. <u>Unless There's No-One Watching</u>:
This Secular Hymn is built on the song "Endless Song" by Robert Lowry in 1860. It is popularly known today as "How Can I Keep From Singing" [#509 in the Christian Life Hymnal], which is the source that I used.
Topic of Song: relieving suffering in others;

128. <u>Wake, Awake</u>:
This Secular Hymn is built on the 1599 German tune "Wachet Auf" by Philipp Nicolai. J. S. Bach subsequently harmonized it and used it in a cantata, which is the source that I used.
Topic of Song: motivational;

129. <u>Walking in Someone's Shoes</u>:
This Secular Hymn is built on a Silesian melody and was arranged by Joseph Roff in 1842. Today the tune is best known by the hymn "O God of Loveliness" [#59 in the Book of Catholic Worship - 1966 Edition], which is the source that I used.
Topic of Song: understanding and accepting others;

130. <u>We Are People, Plastic People</u>:
This Secular Hymn is built on the hymn "Angel Voices Ever Singing", written by Edwin G. Monk in 1861. It can be found online at the website "openhymnal.org", which is the source that I used.
Topic of Song: it's not the people, it's the *situations* that they are put into that shape them into the characters that they are;

131. <u>We Are Searching</u>:
This Secular Hymn is based on the 1886 hymn written by Peter Philip Bilhorn titled "I Will Sing the Wondrous Story" [#507 in the Christian Life Hymnal], which is the source that I used.
Topic of Song: "searching" for answers is often more rewarding than "finding" the answers;

132. <u>We Can Be Tolerant</u>:
This Secular Hymn is built on a traditional Irish melody titled "Slane". It is popularly known today as the hymn "Be Thou My Vision" [#386 in the Christian Life Hymnal]. However that arrangement is still under copyright protection, so I reharmonized the melody, created a new arrangement, and put it in the public domain.
Topic of Song: a test of true tolerance;

133. We Can Get Things To Happen:
This Secular Hymn is built on the popular African-American spiritual "Let Us Break Bread Together". Since I could find no arrangements of this song that were copyright-free, I made the SATB arrangement myself and put it in the public domain.
Topic of Song: people working together can get things done;

134. We Mean "Will You Love Me?":
This Secular Hymn is built on the hymn "My Jesus I Love Thee I Know Thou Art Mine", written by Adoniram Judson Gordon in 1876. It is Hymn #61 in the Christian Life Hymnal, which is the source that I used.
Topic of Song: everything we say can be translated into "Will You Love Me?"

135. We're Not Alone:
This Secular Hymn is based on a very famous Irish melody. Although it may be familiar to some as the hymn "I Cannot Tell", it is known throughout the world as the folksong "Londonderry Air" or "Danny Boy". The tune can be found online at the "cyberhymnal" website (which is the source that I used). Since an SATB arrangement was not available, I arranged it myself and put it into the public domain.
Topic of Song: we're not alone as long as our nonhuman companions are alive and well;

136. We're Not At Our Best:
This Secular Hymn is built on the Welsh melody "St. Denio" which was adapted and harmonized by John Roberts in 1839. It is more commonly known today as the hymn "Immortal, Invisible, God Only Wise" [#18 in the Christian Life Hymnal], which is the source that I used;
Topic of Song: "fear" is a crippling emotion from which we must escape;

137. We're Parents of a Soldier:
This Secular Hymn is built on an old American camp-meeting tune, but it is very popularly known today as the "Battle Hymn of the Republic" [#603 in the Christian Life Hymnal], which is the source that I used.
Topic of Song: we are all parents of soldiers - but probably not good parents;

138. What Are We Doing?
This Secular Hymn is based on a melody from George Frederick Handel's 1747 oratorio "Macchabaeus". Among the hymns based on this tune is "Thine Be the Glory" [#188 in the Christian Life Hymnal], which was the source I used.
Topic of Song: acceptance of life / human condition;

139. When Feeling Lost:
This Secular Hymn is built on the traditional English melody "Kingsfold". It was arranged and harmonized by Ralph Vaughan Williams in 1906. It is more commonly heard today in the hymns "I Heard the Voice of Jesus Say" [#530 in the Christian Life Hymnal] and "O Sing a Song of Bethlehem" [#146 in the Christian Life Hymnal].
Topic of Song: it is healthful to learn new things and meet new people;

140. When I Am Down:
This Secular Hymn is built on the traditional African-American spiritual "Down To The River To Pray". Even though it has the conventional number of measures (16, or in this case 32) it feels to me curiously off-balance - enticingly off-balance - as if there are the right number of boxes but they are filled unevenly. I could find no SATB arrangements and so arranged it myself. This tune was used in the film "O Brother, Where Art Thou?"
Topic of Song: walking and talking can be a healing combination;

NOTES ON THE INDIVIDUAL HYMNS (continued)

141. <u>When Playing Cards</u>:
This Secular Hymn is built on the old song *O Store Gud* which I obtained from a 1903 Swedish songbook. The tune is popularly known today as "How Great Thou Art". The 1903 arrangement was not pleasing to me and the newer "How Great Thou Art" arrangement was still under copyright protection, so I wrote a new SATB arrangement and put it into the public domain.
Topic of Song: tolerance, accepting others;

142. <u>Who's My Neighbor?</u>
This Secular Hymn is built on the tune "Victory" by none other than Palestrina in 1588. It was arranged in 1861 by William Henry Monk. It is popularly known today as the hymn "The Strife is O'er" [#191 in the Christian Life Hymnal] which is the source that I used.
Topic of Song: our neighbors are those in need, whether near or far;

143. <u>Why Does This Phrase Have Five Measures?</u>
This Secular Hymn is built on the tune "Lauda Anima", written by John Goss in 1869. It is popularly known today as the hymn "Praise My Soul the King of Heaven" [#12 in the Christian Life Hymnal], which is the source that I used.
Topic of Song: all music has unexplored depths;

144. <u>You Took the One Road</u>:
This Secular Hymn is built on the traditional Scottish folk song "Loch Lomand", which the world knows by lyrics that go something like: "Oh, you take the high road and I'll take the low road and I'll be in Scotland before you". I arranged it for SATB choir and put it into the public domain.
Topic of Song: different people taking very different roads just might turn out the same at the end;

Recent Works by Secretary Michael

Jo Puma - Wild Choir Music
Collection of 36 traditional "Sacred Harp" arrangements with new secular lyrics for our diverse society. This collection has removed the 3 barriers that have kept this music out of our schools: inappropriate lyrics, poor shape-note legibility, and nonstandard use of standard solfege names. Now we all have a chance to experience this exciting early American music. (Book available; free download not yet available)

Secular Hymnal
Collection of 144 favorite hymn tunes from around the world. The hymn tunes have been re-notated and given thoughtful egalitarian lyrics that promote peace. Many public schools use them for choral sight-reading practice. Available in both unison/guitar and SATB choir editions. Now we all have a chance to share in these musical treasures. (Books available; free downloads available;)

Twimfina
A peace-themed musical play for singing groups of all ages. The story is about a young woman named "Twimfina" (an acronym for "The World Is My Family, I'm Not Afraid") who runs off to a hostile country. It is scored for voice and piano. The play is divided into 21 segments, many of which can stand alone. This allows an acting group to perform individual segments instead of the entire 2.5 hour play. (Book available; free download available;)

Lifesongs
A "lifesong" is a 4-movement choral work (with or without instruments) in which a rational argument is battled-out musically. There's only one rule: every lifesong must use the following four titles for its four movements: "Credo" - "One Hand" - "Other Hand" - "Go and Do"
Secretary Michael has begun working on a series of 6 lifesongs, some of which are available now; the rest will become available as they are completed in future years.

Aren't We the Lucky Ones
A book-length story about a group of college science students who share an understanding that people don't truly have a free will. There are no "good people" or "bad people", just lucky and unlucky ones. This insight carries with it the responsibility to protect the "unlucky" from the wrath of the "lucky". The students form a community in order to live out their ideals. (Book available - both paperback and digital).

Joy of Piggyback Songs
Dozens of fun, short choral works in which more than one melody is sung at the same time. Book (and free internet download) will become available after it is completed.

> *"Artists can change the world by correcting the misconceptions that divide people. Artists can also cause the misconceptions. We're all artists. We all must choose."*
> -Secretary Michael

www.ingramcontent.com/pod-product-compliance
Lightning Source LLC
Chambersburg PA
CBHW081505040426
42446CB00017B/3410